MORNING GLORY

MORNING GLORY

Memoirs from the Edge of History

SOMERSET DE CHAIR

CASSELL

First published privately
by Merlin Books, 1988

First published in this edition 1994
Cassell Publishers Ltd
Villiers House
41/47 Strand
London
WC2N 5JE

British Library Cataloguing-in-Publication Data
A catalogue record for this book is available from the British Library

ISBN 0–304–34499–0

Printed and bound in Great Britain by
Mackays of Chatham PLC, Chatham, Kent

CONTENTS

PART I

MORNING GLORY

YES

Yes, in my young and agile days,
Not in my old and fragile days,
I used to dance the whole night through
And think the world was made for two.

Yes, in my young and fruitful days,
Not in my old and bruteful days,
I loved, to make the world go round,
And not to populate the ground.

Yes, in my young unhurried days,
Not in my old and worried days,
I used to think things to the end,
Regardless of their dreadful trend.

Yes, in my young and eager days,
Not in my old and meagre days,
I lived in castles in the air,
Not knowing that the rent was dear.

Yes, in my young and fearless days,
Not in my old and cheerless days,
I made the world my oyster shell;
I did not want the pearl as well.

Yes, in my young inventive days,
Not in my old preventive days,
I used to plan far-reaching schemes,
Not knowing they were hopeless dreams.

Yes, in my young and guileless days
Not in my old and smileless days,
I thought that men were good or bad,
I did not know the good were mad.

INTRODUCTION

No amount of past glory will buy you a ticket on the lunch wagon. And it has taken me some time to come to terms with my own unimportance. I really thought, when I entered Parliament at 24, that if I served in it for 30 or 35 years, I should be Foreign Secretary, if not Prime Minister. In 1970 I would have been 59, after 36 years in politics, and I do not see how I could have done worse than Mr. Heath, who reduced the F.T. Index (now around 3000) to 150, and the working week of industry to three days, besides being humiliated by the Miners' Union and losing the election.

However, in 1950 I was divorced and was asked to resign my seat. This was before the days of various conservative MPs, who received the support of their constituency executives, in circumstances which make my divorce to marry my second wife seem like attar of roses. All I have to offer, therefore, is the account of someone who lived near the centre of affairs, during a critical period in our history — the Abdication in 1936, the Second World War, and the leadership of Winston Churchill. It will have to suffice.

And it seemed absurd in an autobiography to leave out the two most important episodes in my life — the capture of Baghdad, and of the Desert Fortress of Palmyra; although these had been covered earlier in *The Golden Carpet* and *The Silver Crescent*. As these books have been out of print for forty years, the episodes will come fresh to readers of my grandchildren's generation.

This book is an essay in self-portraiture. In painting it is only possible to depict the sitter at a given moment in time, although a series like the portraits of Philip IV of Spain by Velasquez or the series of self-portraits by Rembrandt show us the sitter as he changed and developed over the years. In literature it is possible to add the dimension of time to a portrait, but this is no doubt assisted by the addition of illustrations which show the change, and sometimes decay, of the subject, as in the portrait of Dorian Gray by Oscar Wilde. Every man is a Greek god at twenty, and a Greek sod at forty, as the progressive portraits of the author in this book will no doubt make clear. That is the only reason for including so many, when the reader might well say one is enough.

A word should perhaps be said about the origin of the name de Chair. It is obviously of French origin, and in its anglicized form has a slightly erotic connotation in French. When my daughter was living in Paris she was known as "la poupée de Chair" — The Living Doll. The family was Huguenot and acquired prominence through Henri IV (Paris is worth a Mass). The first Marquis, Jean François de la Chaire, received his title on the battlefield from Henri IV in 1600. Both he and his son, the second Marquis, held the post of Capitaine des Portes de la Garde du Roi — a position roughly equivalent to that of Captain of the Bodyguard to Queen Elizabeth I, held by Sir Walter Raleigh and the Earl of Leicester, somewhat earlier.

So long as Henri IV was alive, and his Edict of Nantes to protect the protestant Huguenots was in force, the family was safe. But after Henri's assassination one of the family decided to emigrate to England in the 1640s. The descendants of those who remained in France were mostly guillotined during the terror of 1792.

The first de Chair, as the name was shortened in England, no doubt found it difficult to survive as a penniless refugee. My father said the Huguenots lived on oxtail soup, as the ox tails were thrown away by the butchers at Smithfield. As they got more established, many of them went into the Church. John de Chair became Chaplain to George III and caused a stir by marrying Julia Wentworth, daughter of one of the richest men in England, Sir William Wentworth of Bretton Park in Yorkshire. He also owned Trerice Manor in Cornwall, which I happened to own in this century and sold to the National Trust. Perhaps the couple spent their honeymoon there, a happy notion, as I eventually married a descendant of the other branch of the family — Juliet Wentworth Fitzwilliam.

My father, Admiral Sir Dudley de Chair, was one of Jellicoe's admirals, and commanded the Northern Blockade of Germany during World War I. In 1917 he represented the Royal Navy on the Balfour Mission to the United States when America entered the war. In 1925 he was appointed Governor of New South Wales, whither I, perforce, accompanied him and went to school at the King's School, Paramatta, founded as a cadet corps in 1832 by William IV, very early in Australia's history.

My mother's family, Struben, was of Dutch origin, but her

immediate forebears were naturalized English, the first of them having been persuaded to take British citizenship by the parents of an English girl he wanted to marry. "Gad, Sir. We can't have my daughter marrying a foreigner. Eh?" My great-grandfather was one of the founders of the Cumberland Fleet (later the Royal Thames Yacht Club), and took my grandfather, H. W. Struben, out to South Africa, for his health, when he was about 12. He remained there, and married Mary Cole of Inniskillen in Ireland. They moved to the Transvaal in the 1860s, and in the intervals of farming he and his brother started looking for gold in the right place — the Witwatersrand. There was no Johannesburg then and Pretoria, the capital, was then, as it is now, a sleepy town. I have always thought that the family, ostensibly English but of fairly recent Dutch blood, must have suffered some schizophrenia in the disputes between Boers and British. Two of my uncles served in the Union Parliament, in the English faction; one of them as Chief Whip to General Smuts. Two served in the British Army and Navy in World War I; but except for my mother, the youngest of seven children, and her eldest brother, the rest remained settled in South Africa.

Somerset de Chair

My first recollection of any vividness is of a tin sword and a red telescope — they were birthday presents given to me on attaining the age of three. That would have been 22nd August 1914, and my first continuous recollections of any vividness are of expeditions round my home in Berkshire to collect dandelion leaves and nettles for making into salads, when the German U-boats nearly reduced England to starvation. No wonder I grew up rather thin. I was three when the war broke out; seven when it ended. I can even remember being shown a ration card. Then there was a blue writing paper box with a picture of the Houses of Parliament on the outside labelled 'Westminster Bond', which contained brown sugar. It was kept in the bottom drawer of a tallboy in the dining-room, and was produced at rare intervals — forbidden fruit — to be spread on brown bread and butter when we had been very good. My father, who was an Admiral, and the Naval Representative on Lord Balfour's mission to America when she entered the war in 1917, had brought it back with him.

In other ways, I was not conscious of a world tearing itself to bits. That was kept from me. I remember a lot of sunshine, and mild forms of school life. Owing to my mother's preoccupation during the war, I was sent off to school at the age of three. At first to boarding-school! A Lady Molteno kept a girls' school near Bracknell. It was first established at a house called Sussex Lodge, and I remember distinctly sitting on top of a gate and saying to my fellow students (all of the other sex) "Verily, verily, I say unto you . . . " and being hauled down for blasphemy.

Then there was Lady Molteno's daughter, Audrey, aged possibly twelve. The girls were very much afraid of her, but I had the privilege of being invited to play at tents in her bed. The sheets were propped up by a cricket stump. A candle was lit in the darkness of the tent, and a miniature rum cask appeared as if by magic. It was all in the best smuggling tradition.

The school was moved to Newell Hall, so that my three-year-old boarding days ended and I walked to school with my sister, who was five

1

years older than I. She was very much afraid of Audrey Molteno and could not understand how I had the courage not to play ring-a-roses when Audrey wanted everyone to do so.

I cannot remember any classes, but the school certainly gave a production of *A Midsummer Night's Dream* on the lawn. Audrey played the part of Bottom, and I was one of the fairies (humiliating thought). I remember Audrey's voice under a most realistic ass's head, saying, "Scratch my head Pease Blossom." Even at that age I was annoyed at not playing the principal part.

Finally I remember an attic room at Newell Hall with the sunshine pouring down through a skylight, and etching in brilliant outline, the colours of a red admiral butterfly which was clinging to the skylight.

I do not think I remember anything else about Newell Hall, except riding pick-a-back on a girl called Una, with long plaits of bronze coloured hair, and feeling for the first time in my life a most unusual sensation between my legs. I thought she was the most wonderful person in the whole world.

The walk to and from school was along a pleasant dusty white road, between hawthorn hedges and fields. The motor car had not yet developed its insistent demand for hard surfaces.

What excitement when a biplane made a forced landing in a field near Lynwood Chase. Everybody hastened to see this novel contraption with khaki fabric stretched over the wooden framework of the wings; and a pilot in overalls, leather flying helmet and goggles. After some adjustments he swung one end of the twisted two-bladed wooden propeller; and the whole engine, which seemed to be made of half a dozen air-cooled cylinders, spat, barked and started to whizz round with the propeller. The pilot climbed back in and various helpers, who had been holding the thing down, let go, or pulled away chocks of wood from under the small wheels, and away it went.

My sister was very fond of me and took infinite pains to secure my happiness. It is sad therefore, to relate that I attempted to threaten her on two occasions before I was ten years old, once by running at her with an axe, and once with a hammer. Are all little boys like that or was I particularly violent?

Childhood homes loom larger in retrospect than they really are. Nevertheless, I visited Lynwood in after years when it had been sold to some people called Oppenheimer. It was a substantial house, built of brick, in quite a good design. A good upper-middle-class residence, with what would now seem a considerable staff — cook, kitchen-maid, parlourmaid, housemaids and two gardeners. I spent much of my time with the gardeners, watching the electric light plant, with its steady flywheel, being operated, and the testing of the acid in the rows of glass batteries. The house commanded extensive views from the 'stoep' as my mother, from South Africa, called it; really an arched loggia. One day she asked me and my elder brother, Graham, to take a letter to the Downshires at East Hampstead Park. As we approached this lordly Georgian house, gardeners were mowing the lawns, behind horses with leather shoes. "These people must have pots," my brother said. Whatever 'pots' meant, I determined then and there that I required some myself to live in this style. Curiously enough, I bought at Christies, at the end of the war, a set of Brussels' tapestries by Franz Coppens, from East Hampstead, which I hung at Chilham Castle while I lived there, and sold (when I had moved to Blickling) to the Rijks Museum in Amsterdam, which built a special room to house them.

My father had been a shipmate cadet with King George V in the *Britannia*, and the King was loyal to his old naval friends. So I remember some excitement when my parents, in Court dress — knee breeches, stockings and buckled shoes for my father; tiara for my mother, drove over to Windsor Castle, six miles away for dinner. Princess Louise, the King's sister, came to tea one day in a Silver Ghost Rolls-Royce; with its long low flat bonnet, black, with a thin red line round it, and upright coachwork behind. The chauffeur opened the bonnet for me to see the engine purring away. It had to be started up with a crank handle, and a penny put under the carburettor. All these cars would now be worth a fortune, as vintage collector's items. We had a Rover Tourer, painted brown and a small blue Lagonda. But all this was after the war; between 1918 and 1924.

About this time we were taken to Cornwall and I had my first glimpse of the sea — a vast wedge of grey suddenly at the end of a winding lane, between cliffs. My mother acquired an old mill house — Tregony Mill — which she converted into a comfortable seaside house; with white walls, and lemon verbena growing against them; crushed in the hand to an exciting scent. We stayed in a fisherman's cottage while the conversion was going on. The tiny village was called Port Holland, and Dodman Point was near by. There was a collie dog and a sheep-dog which lay in wait for my mother's poodle, Joseph. They leapt for him and tore each other to pieces in a ferocious embrace, while Joseph escaped between them. My mother was to be heard in the moonlight on Dodman Point, calling, "Joseph, Joseph." He returned three days later.

My sister nearly drowned, and my brother Graham won the Royal Humane Society's Certificate for courage in swimming out to rescue her.

At the age of five, I was sent with my sister, Elaine, to a school in Devonshire, at Newton Abbot, called Bradley Wood. On the very first day, I dropped my favourite toy, an iron file, down the lavatory, in peculiarly awkward circumstances. My sister was very sympathetic. I was not the only boy at Newton Abbot. There were several others, and we slept in a dormitory, shining torches into our mouths to make our cheeks glow a barbaric red, and telling each other frightening stories. Owls used to hoot in the woods round the house, and I was graphically told how they came and scratched one's eyes out.

The building cannot have been in a very sound state of repair, for we were awakened in a high storm one night, by the roof falling in and cascades of rain-water pouring down the staircase.

I have the happiest recollections of Bradley Wood. There was a pair of fluffy yellow goslings at the farm. They seemed to me to be quite miraculous. There were also some German war prisoners wearing a vague blue and red uniform, working in a field, and a sawmill at the bottom of a wood. I remember it well, on a particularly hot day, because it was just near the sawmill that certain things in my inside prompted me to start running back to the house. It was up hill all the way and I got terribly overheated and exhausted, but I reached the house just in time.

I can still see myself in late evening of a summer day, standing alone in the walled garden, from which the white house was visible, standing beside a water tank and watching a water beetle denting the skin of the surface without sinking. It seemed to press the skin of the water down as if it were lying on a piece of satin.

There were grass snakes in the garden and I remember holding one by the tail and beating its head against a tree to kill it. I have never liked snakes, although I have come to realise that not all are poisonous, and that one should not always judge by appearances.

The French mistress was incredibly glamorous, and I looked forward to her classes, even at the age of 6, by which time the school had moved into Torquay. During the holidays, there was a girl called Dawn Gillespie, from whom I had few secrets. We were nicknamed Linen and Trotsky, because we were found playing, rather too intimately, in the linen cupboard. That must have been in 1917.

I remember Armistice Day because of rockets being fired at dusk in the town of Torquay, watched by us, from 'Mildura', the school in

Torquay to which Bradley Wood had been moved. Sycamore seeds were falling — it was November, and I was intrigued by the silvery fur inside the seed-pod attached to the end of a wing, after it spiralled down.

Our home was still at Bracknell, in a house named rather grandly, after one of my grandfather's properties in the Transvaal, 'Lynwood Chase'. There was no Bracknell New Town, and the house stood in thirty acres, about a mile from the village. There were pleasant houses near by, one of which was occupied by an elderly friend of my parents, called, Mary St. Quentin. "Call me Squintin Mary," she advised. There were sawdust paths, on which my sister taught me to bicycle. Also a balcony with the balustrade smelling of creosote. Sometimes my brother and I slept out on it. One morning we got up at five o'clock to look for rabbits in a spinney; as he said they were around at that time. We saw none.

Now the house has been demolished and the whole area cleared for the erection of a block of flats. When I saw it I felt assaulted and horrified, as if someone had wiped the slate of my childhood clean away.

"Make way, make way for the Crown Prince of New South Wales."
Thus ribaldly did Saunders clear a path for me upon the hockey field at
my preparatory school. The news had just been published that my
father was to be Governor of New South Wales and after my last term at
St. Michaels, in Sussex, I was to follow him and my mother out to
Australia, by way of South Africa. I went in the company of my sister
who was sixteen and in the care of one of the band of evangelists whom
my mother's special religious convictions (Christian Science)
introduced so persistently into my life.

John Doorley was a 'lecturer' and was travelling about the world
giving lectures. These would last about an hour, delivered without a note
to enraptured audiences. Nobody ever suggested that lecturers or
practitioners were not absolutely conscientious men, who believed everything they said. They had to live up to the full rigour of the law. 'No
Smoking: No Drinking' were two of the main injunctions of the textbook.
'A loathesome weed' the authoress said of tobacco. Coffee and tea also
came in for some harsh words; but one had to draw the line somewhere.

Every day the devout read slabs of the Bible and corresponding slabs
from 'The Key'; as tabulated in a small journal called *The Quarterly*.

Thus you may reconstruct the scene — my sister and I seated
dutifully in the cabin of a ship of the Blue Funnel line, while the sun
sparkled on the waves outside, and I, for one, longed to be on deck. We
were taking over from John Doorley and his wife the parts of First and
Second reader. I had begun to keep a diary at this time and the occasion
is recorded in these terms:

Sunday July 27th, 1924. 'Upon this memoable Sabbath, Elaine
having afore been appointed to the exalted rank of 1st reader, I (how
brave am I?) took up my stance in the inferior position of 2nd reader.
The former reader carried out her part in great style the Bible
readings etc being highly apprechiable. The latter reader's
behaviour on that memorable day, is a secret still.'

6

Not bad at the age of twelve, it seems to me, re-reading the passage now. Looking back on this scene, I realise that I raised the standard of intellectual revolt aboard that ship on that day; and that this signal was a portent, the symptoms of which did not become apparent till much later in life. When I got to the bit about 'The sunlight glances from the church dome, glides into the prison cell,' I interrupted the reading to ask, "Does the sunlight glance off the church dome and then into the prison cell, or does it mean that sunlight is refracted off the church dome, and is likewise capable of penetrating into prison cells?" "What does it matter?" roared Doorley. He was incensed at such desecration and questioning of holy writ. Or maybe he found the care of somebody else's small boy more of a handful than he had expected. At all events he lost his temper and I was corrected for insubordination and I know not what else. This was a lapse from his normal geniality and the rest of the voyage passed happily enough.

I wish all my entries in that diary had been as sprightly. Most of it seems to have been concerned with ship's games and fancy dress dances. 'After dinner we went and persuaded the Captain to let us get up another dance we rounded up all the loafers and idlers who were glad of that species of exercise. We then went to bed after taking orange-ade.' I had begun the trip by saying how ripping Mr. and Mrs. Doorley were. But as the voyage proceeded the preference for Mrs. Doorley and their attractive daughter Katherine became more marked. Mr. Doorley does not get such a good press as before. By Saturday 26th July, the day before the reading episode, the atmosphere is clearly strained in anticipation of the impending storm. 'Games in morning. Lunch. In the afternoon I endeavoured to get to sleep as Mr. Doorley wanted to get me out of the day shine because I kept Miss Pridden awake. But alas Bethia Anderson, Mr. Gibbs, Elaine and others preceeded to kick up an awful shindie under my window. So I made 2 water bombs one of which hit Mr. Gibbs on the white flannels! So he sought my hide afterwards.'

Ah! the exuberance of youth. The sheer high spirits. Could anything be more gleeful than the three huge words, as the ship neared harbour on 4th August.

PACKED   DANCE   BED

My sister and I were being sent out by way of South Africa in order to spend some months there with members of my mother's family. It was thought that a course of uncles would do me good. Aunts would do the same for my sister and of these admirable people there existed no less than six in South Africa. My little grandmother had moved into a new house. Since my grandfather had died, the family home, 'Strubenheim', had been handed over to Cape Town University as the Conservatorium of Music.

My grandfather had died when I was three and I regret that I have no recollection of him. I had been taken out to South Africa at the age of six weeks for him to see me; and I wonder what this practical old man with the keen blue eye and patriarchal white beard saw in his grandson at that age. H.W. Struben was something of a figure in South Africa, partly because he and his brother Fred had discovered the gold in the Transvaal through a brilliant piece of perception when he identified some white rock on the Witwatersrand as gold quartz at a time when gold was only extracted in any quantity elsewhere from alluvial deposits. He had sent his brother Fred home to England with samples of the quartz. The South Kensington Museum assayed them with astonishment.

"Where did you find these? They are the richest samples we have ever tested."

"That is our business," had been the reply.

The two Struben brothers bought stamping mills and all the land in the Transvaal they could lay hands on; employed a large gang of prospectors and in due course struck the Confidence Reef, which made the family fortunes. If one of my grandfather's employees, Walker, had not left him to prospect on his own and struck the Main Reef of the series, we should probably have found that as well. No doubt it would have been bad for us. As it was, with the dislocation of the Boer War and with seven children to share his inheritance, my grandfather's fortune was soon carved up. Being an immigrant from England, although of Dutch descent, he was on the English side in the Boer War. He had been a great personal friend of Cecil Rhodes. Two of my uncles in the Union Parliament could count Jan Smuts among their friends.

It was thus to a family of recognised standing in South Africa that I came as a nephew from England, where the name of de Chair owed what lustre it possessed solely to my father's achievements as one of Jellicoe's admirals and as the new Governor of New South Wales. For his family, reaching England from France as fugitive Huguenots in the seventeenth century, had abandoned the title of Marquis and had been content to secure a precarious footing in the Church. One of them had been Chaplain to George III, while my father's uncle had been Vicar of Morley St. Botolph and an honorary Canon of Norwich Cathedral. It seemed indeed as if parsons swung like criminals on a gibbet from every branch of the family tree. Occasionally my mother's brother, Uncle Charles, devoted to high life and hunting in Leicestershire, would come over to England and when people said to me, "Where does your uncle spring from?" I would reply impiously, "He springs from the African branch of the family tree."

On arrival in Cape Town we went straight to 'Little Granny'. She was a tartar, I am told; but very kind, as grandparents usually are, to her grandchildren. She was an Irishwoman, a Cole from Enniskillen. The tiniest person imaginable, she had borne four of the tallest sons in South Africa. When I saw her she was a regal little figure, all in black, still in mourning for Grandad's death ten years before. Her skin was wrinkled like old parchment and her hair done in a grey bun piled on top of her head. She was just moving into her own new home, Casa Nuova. It was a white building in the Italian style, in the fashionable suburb of Clermont, not far from a house belonging to my Uncle Charles called Nederberg.

The sun shone on these houses all the time. They glowed white, as if there was light in the walls. Over all brooded the majestic blueness of Table Mountain. It went up, from this angle, in smoky ravines to a rounded summit. The table appearance was what you saw from the bay on arrival, at Cape Town, just round the corner. From there it really looked as flat as a table and, joined to it by a dipping ridge, was the Lion Mountain; a crouching lion — so appropriate to the gateway of the Dark Continent, where the lion is still a kingly animal.

Casa Nuova was so new that all the bathrooms smelt of newly-laid tiles, and the whole building had that splendid smell of plaster freshly applied, which wears off in time. I soon acquired a chameleon which fascinated me when its orange tongue darted out at a range of six inches to grab a fly; just like rolled up paper things in a cracker when you blow them out into rude tongues, uncurling in a flash. I used to keep this little fellow in a cardboard box with breathing holes pierced in the lid. Little Granny told me that he would change his colour to that of anything you put him on. I tried him on the Union Jack and he turned a dull grey. Most times he was brownish. His eyes were amazing. They were fixed in round protuberant spheres which could swivel in different directions from each other; so that one eye could squint back over his shoulder while the other might keep a look-out for flies ahead. The incredible beast was not more than four inches long, with a serrated dorsal ridge and a tail which curled up, enabling it to hang upside down. The face was inexpressibly evil and might have sat to any medieval artist wanting to carve a gargoyle high up on Notre Dame.

I was spoilt so long as we stayed with my grandmother or the aunts. My sister's turn came when we began on the uncles. Our next visit was to our Aunt Edith Struben, a maiden lady of massive dimensions and aspect, exactly like the Statue of Liberty. She was an artist and painted water-colours of vivid tones with a masterful use of sunlight and shade, ranging all the way round the world from the pagodas of the Forbidden City to the curving gables of the old Dutch houses in the Cape which she delighted to paint. She owned a house in the old Dutch colonial style, with a high curved-top central gable, and two flanking wings under grey thatch, which was situated on the lower slopes of Table Mountain. The setting there, close up against the two thousand feet of grey and purple rock and scree, rising as if placed before the front door by some immensely Capable Brown, was inspiring. The Horticultural Society chose it for their annual outing and threaded their way admiringly up and down the numerous terraces of flowering gardens which she had created. The disadvantage was that every afternoon the westering sun went behind the mountain and threw a chill shadow upon the house. Aunt Edith had an agreeable native chauffeur who drove her about on social calls and facilitated, while we were there, the business of getting us around. My aunt included among her artistic activities the modelling of Gesso. My earliest recollections included a triptych by her in this: gold and green modelled relief, above our dining-room fireplace, of Vasco da Gama's ships entering Table Bay. She now initiated my sister in the art; but somehow nothing that Elaine did at Luncarty was right. Tiptoeing cautiously across the drawing-room with the lid of a cardboard box, spread with all the acid ingredients and squat bottles of colour loosely corked, she tripped and fell. And great was the fall herof. The paint jars flew eagerly at Chinese screens and acid burned avidly into Persian carpets. It was all over the place in a flash. Aunt Edith smouldered like an awakening volcano. Anon, Elaine was standing at a hot and cold water basin in her bedroom when I tapped upon the window pane. She dropped a bottle and the basin cracked. Our departure to Ida's Valley was accelerated.

Ida's Valley was one of the old Dutch farmhouses, with elaborate gables in curly white plaster work, and the date 1789. Ida's Valley had a homely atmosphere, different from the more sophisticated new buildings of Luncarty and Casa Nuova. There were no hot and cold water basins here. The bath was old-fashioned.

The first thing I did on arrival was to put my chameleon on the bell-rope in my room, 'after adorning it with branches, etc.' Ida's Valley was a farmhouse in the centre of a large estate devoted to growing fruit. But somehow my Uncle Rodbard and Aunt Beatrice always came off worst in the struggle for the world's markets. They grew peaches, which were easily bruised in packing or perished in transport; while near by a man called Pixton, whom my uncle had helped in the fruit farming business, was now thriving on the growing of oranges, which were ripped brazenly from the trees, hurled into a grading machine, twisted into paper by vigorous black hands, and hammered into cases for profitable despatch abroad. Peacocks strolled languidly upon his successful terraces. We were taken to see the oranges plopping down upon rollers which were a little wider apart at one end than the other so that the orange bobbed along until it fell through and was graded in size accordingly. At Ida's Valley the peaches could scarcely be breathed upon.

It was spring when we were in South Africa — early September — and under the fruit trees grew acres of daffodils. These were gathered in the dew of the morning and packed in the old white barns by the 'Kaffirs'* for despatch to Cape Town thirty miles away. I noted on 9th September, 'Got up at 5!! a.m. and helped to pack daffies then made a fire in Aunty B's room.'

Ida's Valley was near Stellenbosch where a young but thriving university was making a name for itself.

Ida's Valley was situated at the foot of Simonsberg.

There is a personality in mountains; and people who live in flat lands are subtly different from those who wake every morning to the changing aspect of mountains. There is a primeval message to man in these great edifices of nature which are clearly so much bigger than anything man can create with his own hands. The skyline of Manhattan or the Pyramids of Gizeh look all very fine when you stand at the bottom of them on the deserts of Egypt or Broadway. Put them beside the Drakensberg and you would rate them infantile. Visualise them against the Himalayas and they disappear altogether. Mountains have moods. Some days the sun sparkles upon their summits and they approach magically close — at other times they are withdrawn in mist and the smoke of torrents. Sometimes they roar as they wrap their winds about them. Sometimes you can hear a pebble drop in the silent crevasses. At all times they present a challenge to man. He must set his foot on their necks, or he can never live at ease in the world, uncertain what goes on in their heads.

No wonder we were encouraged to wrestle with Simonsberg. It was a formidable peak, rising bluely out of the plain. Not formidable at a

---

* Arabic word for infidel; a somewhat surprising word for white Christians in South Africa to have applied to mostly black Christians.

distance; nor even difficult for children to climb with expert guidance. It was 4,000 feet high and we zigzagged about on it all day and very nearly spent the night on it, when we lost the way down. Aunt Beta wrung her hands with anxiety and her moon-like face, under its wispy grey hair, bewailed the loss of two daughters, a nephew and a niece. How would she be able to explain to her sister? Meanwhile we felt grand and gazed, as mountaineers do, upon the toylike towns of people far below. There were low clouds hanging above the horizon of the Atlantic which was now revealed to us. The long white sands skirted the bay towards the distant haze where Simonstown, the naval base, was situated to the north. To our left, obscuring the sea, rose the Stellenbosch mountains; and nearer still, Bosmons Kopje. The foreground was a patchwork of red ploughed fields and green copses. A grey road stretched diagonally away towards Stellenbosch, beyond which was cultivated land, then the sands and the sea. We could see far below us the white walls of Ida's Valley among its trees beyond the lower spurs of the mountain. It looked a long walk back. We returned in the falling dusk and Aunt Beta returned thanks for 'a demonstration'. She had prayed devoutly all the afternoon. I was evidently very tired for I wrote down simply under Saturday 27th, 'Went up Simonsberg. Came home very foot sore.'

We climbed Table Mountain too. This was before the days of the funicular railway to the summit. But Table Mountain was easy enough. General Smuts used to saunter up it in his eighties. We found everlasting flowers on top. These are crisp little pink, white and yellow flowers which seem to be made of stiff paper and keep their colour and texture for weeks afterwards.

At last we moved north to the Transvaal by train over the red Karoo Desert, with its stunted bushes and an occasional meerkat scampering away over the sand, frightened by the roar of the wheels. I was sorry to leave Ida's Valley where Aunt Beta provided me with something of a mother's love and I was thoroughly spoilt, as all sane people like to be. I missed the tiled floors and the cool rooms on the heavy-shaded mornings; I missed the daffodils in the dew and the great whitewashed barn. I missed the large homely pieces of Dutch furniture. Ahead of me lay uncles, uncles all the way. They were hard and angular.

Uncle Frank was six feet four and farmed in the Transvaal near Pretoria. He had vast dairy herds which supplied that city with milk, seven miles away. He had Friesians, glowing black and white, smelling deliciously of cow. A native herdsman stood in the stock yard and called out the names of the cows — Alice, Mirabelle, Anette; and, believe it or not, they trotted up when their names were called and entered their stalls for milking. Uncle Frank had embarked on the building of silos, a new fashion. He cultivated acres of lucerne which was heaved into these concrete towers. Like all men who cultivate the soil he looked worried. I trailed behind him, along the edges of lucerne fields, trying to keep up with his long strides. I fingered a piece of long grass in passing and it gashed my finger like a knife. It was spear grass. "That will teach you a lesson," said Uncle Frank. Later, poor man, he fell from the clouds in an aeroplane, and I visited him at a famous surgery in Edinburgh where Dr. Dott was about to operate on his spinal cord. He was a cripple ever after. I like to remember him striding ahead of me about his estate at Lynwood.

This house he had built for himself and it was well laid out. I thought of becoming an architect and designed a house shaped like a 'Y' with two wings sticking out in front and the servants' quarters in the tail of the Y at the back. I drew plans and showed them to Uncle Frank. He was not encouraging so I switched my interest to farming. I read the advertisements in Uncle Frank's magazines and longed to own a herd of pedigree Jersey cows (which I did one day, to my great pecuniary disadvantage). I yearned for a pair of Berdizzo Pincers (used for castrating cattle).

'I take a great interest in stock and go round the stables every morning. Elaine ill in bed. Sick as a cat!! I wired Aunt B., 1,000 miles away to give Elaine absent treatment.' (The Christian Science way of healing.)

Uncle Frank's wife, Aunt Maisie, was the sister of Sir Roderick Jones, the head of Reuters. They had two small children, Francis and Rosemary aged 7 and 5, which made my sister and I feel older.

It was from these lands and in particular The Willows, an estate near by, where my mother was born, that my grandfather had made his great gold discovery. My mother was convinced that he had known of more gold-fields than he revealed; had planted forests (a habit of his) over gold-fields to prevent his sons becoming too rich too easily. The Willows had been sold, but the Struben family retained the mineral rights. From time to time there were desultory borings; but nothing systematic until 1950, when Mr. Arther Weeks did the job properly and established the existence of tin, antimony, lead, etc. in payable quantities; but no more gold. Even that was discovered 2,000 feet down in 1962.

Uncle Frank took us to see the Premier Diamond mine at Pretoria.

There was a crater in the blue clay which yielded up these gems. The walls of the crater were mined with sticks of gelignite by skilled Kaffirs and everybody withdrew to the summit. We gazed down into the great blue grey crater. There was a roar and a tumble as the explosive went off and chunks of the grey clay fell down the sides of the crater to the bottom. The Kaffirs went scrambling down to load them into trolleys on rails. They scrambled eagerly for if they chanced upon a diamond themselves they were richly rewarded. Dreadful the penalty if they tried to secrete a diamond on their bodies and smuggle it out of the compound. To prevent this they had to live behind a barbed-wire enclosure, for all the world like prisoners. They were X-rayed when they left. The diamond ring is a fierce and artificial business which keeps the supply behind the demand, by vigorous restraints. Uncle Frank knew a lot about the mining industry.

"Cecil Rhodes was in the diamond business," he said, "some of his partners wanted to embarrass him and sent a Kaffir to him with a pure white stone. 'Where did you get this?' asked Rhodes. The Kaffir was non-committal. Rhodes was suspicious; and had the man taken to a room while he telephoned his associates. 'A Kaffir has brought in a fine diamond but its origin is obscure. I should like you to see it.' Rhodes hid the fine stone and produced from a drawer a smaller diamond of poor quality. His associates trooped in. 'What do you think of this?' he asked them. They did not think much of it. But what could they say? They could not ask him what he had done with the good one. They advised him not to buy the miserable specimen and trooped out. That taught them not to play tricks with Rhodes."

On one occasion after the blasting someone had seen a dull glint on the shorn-off face of rock clay and sent a Kaffir up to investigate. He prised out the Cullinan Diamond.

It is a fact that at one time my grandfather nearly bought the farm on which the Kimberly diamond mine was later found; but whether he knew or guessed that there was a pipe of blue clay on the property is uncertain. He had arrived at the farm house and a contract was drawn up with the Boer farmer who said that as my grandfather would be staying the night they could sign it before he left after breakfast. During the evening the farmer's nephew turned up and asked what was going on. The farmer said "I am selling the farm to Hendrik Struben." Whereupon the boy asked my grandfather what there was in it for him; and instead of receiving any encouragement got a kick up the backside for his impudence. The nephew then went to his uncle and persuaded him to cancel the sale.

We descended to the floor of the crater in an iron cage which slid with pulleys on a cable, swaying over nothing; a form of travel I dislike. But we could find no diamonds lying about in the grey rubble of clay rock and returned to Lynwood vaguely disappointed.

We next visited Uncle Robert, a heavy and formidable man who was Chief Whip of the Union Party in the South African Parliament. He had 40,000 acres of land and a house called Bridgewater, which was a long low white house. He was too busy to do more than pat our heads in an avuncular way.

The Union Parliament spends part of the year in Cape Town and part of the year in Pretoria, the capital of the Union. Here we were shown the graceful curves of the Government Buildings erected by Sir Herbert Baker, South Africa's great architect, who was to collaborate with Lutyens in the Government Buildings at New Delhi. There is a sweep and power in bold architecture which can be very inspiring; as the builders of Gothic cathedrals knew. The Government Buildings at Pretoria, with their central curve, and flanking façades are a dignified contribution to administrative architecture which is practically the only building except skyscrapers, factories, and blocks of flats, done on the grand scale nowadays. I remembered Sir Herbert Baker vaguely, when he had visited us during a holiday in Cornwall. South Africa threw up, like some subterranean volcano, two glowing personalities into the stream of our childhood. Herbert Baker and Rudyard Kipling. For Kipling had been sent out to South Africa at the height of his fame for the sake of his health and he had rented a house adjoining the grounds of Strubenheim, belonging to my grandfather. My Aunt Edith, who combined photography in its early days with her eye for artisitic composition, photographed him there; and the glass negative plate has survived in my possession. Kipling became sincerely attached to the Struben family and my mother, who was about fifteen years old at the time, was his especial favourite; so that he wrote often to her with his inimitable brilliance in the course of the years.

Kipling refers very briefly to the family in his autobiography. On page 168 of *Something of Myself*, he writes of his winter visits to South Africa; 'Then, after the Southern Cross had well risen above the bows, the packing away of heavy kit, secure it would not be needed till May, the friendly, well-known Mountain and the rush to the garden to see what had happened in our absence; the flying visit to our neighbours the Strubens at Strubenheim, where the children were regularly and lovingly spoiled; the large smile of the Malay launderess, and the easy pick-up-again of existence.' Well, my mother, being the youngest was no doubt the most regularly spoiled. It is impossible to overestimate the significance of chance contacts in life with outstanding personalities. They cut deeper than blunt figures; they make more of a mark on the immature mind. The difference between a boy who has known Kipling and one who has known James Joyce will no doubt come out in the writings of the man; and the shaping of his personality.

The one personality, whom I never met, who has probably had the greatest influence of all was my grandfather, with his violent temperament, his bold capacity for decision, his flair for buying and selling, and his zest for adventure. Kipling used to say that there was enough material in his life story for twenty novels. The tales of his early experiences, always with some humorous twist, were the stock in trade of our upbringing. There was the story of Grandad stalking the giraffe at which he fired all his ammunition, while the lion was stalking him — to be shooed away with no other weapon but my grandfather's wide sombrero hat. There was the tale of the lion which sprang down upon him as he rode beneath a rock; and of the accelerating effect this had on the pony he was riding; or the story of the cobra under his palliasse in the Kaffir kraal one night which writhed and twisted beneath him in the dark where he lay, prudently aware of his inability to see as well as the serpent in the dark, and waiting with immense strength of character till he was called in the morning and a gun could be sent for.

The tragedy of my grandfather's success was his failure to buy Groot Constantia when he had the opportunity. He considered it, but came to the conclusion, unwisely, that with so many children he needed a larger house and built himself one in the prevailing fashion of the Victorian period at its worst — billiard room and all. Groot Constantia now belongs to the State and is visited by tourists as perhaps the best example of the old white Dutch gabled houses built by the early settlers. These houses which have had a powerful influence on subsequent South African architecture are comparatively rare. Apart from Groot Constantia (where old Governor Simon finished his days) glowing white in the shade, with the old slave quarters and the wine cellars, still in use, behind it; there were the 'very old' farm buildings at Koornhoop; the gable dated 1800 at Parel Vallei, the fine building of Meerlust at Eerste Rivier, which in design might have come from the drawing board of Herbert Baker, but must in fact have been the origin of his work. Even the hen house at Meerlust is sumptuously gabled with graceful curls leading up to the base of a triangular pediment. Then there is Vergelegen. For some reason in the history of the Dutch colony, orders had been sent from Holland for the despoiling of Vergelegen. The wine house, the slave house, the mill and the cattle sheds were to be left standing. But the dwelling-house was to be entirely demolished. Perhaps Van der Stel's old enemy, burgher Jacobus Van der Heyden, who bought a good deal of the property, managed to evade the decree. The Boeren-huis, the farmhouse which stood at the far side of the walled octagonal garden was pulled down, but the walls were left. The mill remained standing and the hen house seems to have survived, although only one gable remains on the front out of three pictured in an eighteenth century print. Mrs. A.F. Trotter writing of it in 1902 said, 'A golden desolateness hangs over the place. Sheets of sunlight, as I saw it, enveloped the house, slanting through gnarled oaks and the small blue-green leaves of the towering camphor trees. Confronted with the old drawings, their young stiffly-set plantations and trim orange groves, you realise with a throb, the change and march of time.'

At Groot Constantia, Meerlust and Vergelegen you find the same farm bell slung on a beam between old white pillars.

I find it difficult to explain the nationality of the Strubens; for they consider themselves purely English, and regard it as only a coincidence that an ancestor, who married a celebrated beauty in Hampshire, settled down in England and became a nationalised Englishman, happened to have been a Dutchman. So far as my mother's family is concerned they regard themselves as entirely English, just as my father's family has long since forgotten its French origin. The fact that my grandfather was born aboard a yacht at a time when his father was a founder member of the Royal Thames Yacht Club (The Cumberland Fleet), and that my great grandfather eventually went to South Africa in search of health and sunshine does not, in the opinion of the family, confuse him in any way with the Boer settlers who came out from Holland. Thus in the ardent disputes which raged over the position and size of the Union Jack in the Union flag, the Strubens were on the side of the Union Jack; yet my grandfather was a close friend of Paul Kruger. Perhaps no distinctions of race are so strongly defended as those in doubt; and if the Strubens are more English than the English, there is plenty of evidence of Dutch blood in their veins, even if it flowed out to South Africa through the filter of English county society in the early nineteenth century.

There were social calls for my sister and me to make in South Africa even at so young an age. Little Granny took us to tea with the Governor

General, Lord Athlone and Princess Alice. There was a staggering array of cakes and buns in my honour; and I disappointed my august host and hostess.

Before we started Little Granny had warned me not to overeat. "You must not stuff yourself at Government House."

So the more Lord Athlone pressed me to eat, the more I felt in honour bound to refuse:

"Have some cake?"

"No thanks, your Excellency."

"Some buns?"

"No thanks, your Excellency."

"A doughnut?"

"N-n-no thanks, your Excellency."

"Well, then. Dash it, at your age. A biscuit?"

"No, your Excellency."

"Your grandson doesn't seem to have any appetite," Princess Alice suggested.

"I think perhaps he is overdoing it," my grandmother conceded, with a frown which indicated clearly that I had let her down. Thus released from the bonds of convention, as I had understood it, I tried to make up for lost time, to the evident relief of my kind host who had begun to wonder if I were ill or what the younger generation was coming to.

To arrive in a land where eight out every ten people he sees in the street are of a different colour to himself, makes a profound impression on a boy. Looking back over one's travels, it is clear that this difference from oneself in the mass of the dwellers in any land is the principal reason for its distinctive atmosphere in the traveller's mind. In South Africa the porters who unloaded the baggage, the chauffeur who drove the car, the servants who waited at table, were all 'Kaffirs'. In those days the problem of racial relations scarcely troubled South Africa. The natives were good-natured, and accepted their lot in life as predominantly that of servants in relation to the white masters. It was many years yet before the Colonial Office in England would begin its policy of granting substantial measures of self-government to the natives in other parts of Africa further north. The relation between white and black is one of the dominant issues of our time. Yet it must be remembered that the white man never came to South Africa as a trustee for the black population, intending one day to hand the country over to them to govern by themselves. That was the British role in India; but never in South Africa. The Dutch and English who migrated to South

Africa went there to make a home for themselves and their descendants. The only natives in the Cape then were the Hottentots; a dying race like the Aborigines of Australia.

The huge native population today is Bantu in origin, from further north, which was drawn south by the prospect of working for the white man. This fact is fundamental to an understanding of the controversial apartheid policy. At a time when everywhere else in the world the native populations are being offered the prospect of self government, sometimes overnight, it horrifies liberal opinion in the United Nations that the Government of South Africa means to keep South Africa safe for the white man. All parties in South Africa are more or less united in this determination, although they differ as to the method of ensuring it. One thing is clear to them all. In a population where there are eight blacks to two whites there can be no question of real democracy. The white supremacy would be outvoted 8 to 2 at once; and the Dutch and English alike find themselves under the yoke of a class of natives whom they have grown up to regard as a helot class. The preaching of the slogans of democracy to the turbulent black races of Africa further north, in the Gold Coast and elsewhere, and the elevation of the importance of the black in relation to the white by Socialist Ministers in Kenya, Tanganyika, Nyasaland, and elsewhere; while an exactly opposite policy is pursued by a Nationalist Government in the Union, has created a dangerous schizophrenia in the African mind. The Africans can scarcely be blamed for not understanding where they stand in relation to the white man. Are they brothers or servants? Or — dare they hope — masters? In this fermenting compost the seed of Communism, fertilised by the twin ambitions of black Nationalism and freedom from white domination, sprouts with alarming facility.

For a long time to come, it seems clear that native policy will diverge in the southern and central parts of Africa. If South Africa could sever itself physically from the north and float a thousand miles away into the Atlantic, there to form a separate continent of Atlantis, its white rulers might live out their lives in peace, enjoying the benefits of a numerous servant class. But in the absence of such a salt water barrier, the South African Government finds itself out of step with governments elsewhere who are merely trustees for native populations and do not suffer in their hearths and homes from the eventual handing over of power.

Perhaps I was vaguely conscious of this underlying problem, even in 1924, as I talked with the Zulu servants. They were not Negroid in face, like the coloured darkies of the Southern States in U.S.A. Here the face was more angular, less jolly, but more proud. They stalked stiffly around the dining-room table, in their white linen suits. The palms of their hands were lighter; almost coffee coloured. As a boy I made friends easily with these servants, especially those who drove cars, like Kippie the chauffeur at Ida's Valley. Yet these were men whose grandparents probably had fought against us in the Zulu and Matabele wars further north, and they had fought savagely and for long with success against the superior equipment of the white soldiers. The proud looking Zulu who worked for Uncle Charles accepted his lot with resignation; and treated his master with respect, if without evident devotion.

There remained the most sophisticated of the aunts and uncles, Charles and Valerie. They gave me a photograph album for my birthday and in it, to this day, I find the snapshots of our visits. There is Casa Nuova, with its squat pagoda-like tower, and jutting *porte-cochère*, the white pillared stoep; all in the style of some great Italian villa on the shores of Lake Como. Very well designed. Nederberg (beneath-the-mountain) ran a little to the half-timbered gable style of building, but it was very comfortable, and from its windows I learnt to look up at my new friend Table Mountain where it threw out a rugged buttress, shadowed with blue ravines. Aunt Valerie was one of three beautiful sisters. The others were married to a Hambro in England and a Horden in Austrialia. Uncle Charles had three lovely daughters, Lavinia, Angela and Diana, younger than me. Now, with Elaine, we were all children, and played under the penetrating blue eyes of Uncle Charles. A swimming pool was being made in the garden and there was a gazebo in the Italian manner; a circle of slender marble pillars, surmounted by a dome in lace-like wrought iron. The grass was tough and rubbery as it is in southern climates, where the soft lawns of England are almost unknown.

Our stay in South Africa was nearly over. Soon we began on the long voyage across the southern wastes of the Indian Ocean. The albatrosses followed us all the way, hovering under the grey Antarctic skies, gliding, shifting against the wind. Every day there was a sweepstake on the day's run; and the Captain made a forecast as to the number of ocean miles he expected to cover. It did not take me long, even at the age of 13 to realise that this old sea dog knew his business and that his forecast was never more than four or five miles out either way. So I formed a syndicate of ten people who entrusted a shilling apiece to my care, which was then invested in ten tickets, squarely bracketing the Captain's estimate. We won every day; and the syndicate paid a handsome dividend. The members held their breath and drew their winnings. The prize money was probably not more than £3 paid out to holders of the winning number. But this, divided among ten people, yielded a regular dividend of 300% on their investment. Thoughtful eyes are said to have watched me descending the gangway when we docked in Australia.

CHAPTER 3

So the girls were lying about in the suffocating shade, while the cicadas sang in the branches of the great Moreton Bay fig tree overhead; and the men went on doggedly playing tennis on the rubbery grass which is all that will grow in Australia. The gravel paths around the tennis court were too dazzling in the sun to be looked at for long; and branched off between clumps of tall brilliant flowers to the harbour's edge. It stretched cool and blue out of sight in both directions; retiring behind a hundred headlands, filling a hundred coves, sprawling inland along a thousand miles of foreshore from South Head to North Head, which were nevertheless only a mile apart. Fort Dennison was a brown turret on an island in the middle distance of the blue water. H.M.A.S. *Canberra*, a lean grey cruiser swinging idly at her moorings, just off shore. Across the water there was Admiralty House, plainly visible, the Sydney residence of the Governor General; and behind it 'over there' the vast sprawling suburbia of the North Shore. Citizens crossed every day to their shops and businesses in the ferry boats. The idea of a Sydney Harbour bridge was being talked about; but there was no sign of it yet. And the men went on doggedly playing tennis on the rubbery grass which sprang up after their feet had pressed it.

The Governor walked quietly up and down the long arched stone veranda, keeping in the shadow, and turning at each end with the ease and pecision of a man accustomed for years to the quarterdeck.

The cicadas sang, their eternal sing song so loud — the crick-crack of tree grasshoppers — that the girls could scarcely hear each other talk. They wiped the perspiration off their beautiful faces and their beautiful legs and hoped they were not sweating through their white tennis skirts and shirts. They were all very beautiful. It seemed as if they grew like pomegranates on every tree, which are only missed in climates where they do not grow at all. There was Morna McCormick, who was all the loveliness and grace and kindness and quiet sense of humour that can be achieved in a single personality. I was fourteen and fell in love with her when she stepped aboard the special coach of the viceregal train and I went on worshipping from afar, but not too far, until I left Australia at the age of 17. There was Bonita Appleton, daughter of an exquisite mother and an Italian father. She had the black hair and brown eyes, the easily tanned skin, and all the vitality of the Mediterranean. She had the right measurements; and she was a torment to me from the time I first saw her till long after I left. Ah, she knew how to tease me; but when a boy is 16 and girl 17, what a world of difference there is. One is at school and the other, is just coming out. Nothing under thirty is of any interest to her until, perhaps too late — when the boy is twenty-eight and she is twenty-nine.

There were the girls; they lay so invitingly under the wide-spreading branches of the great Moreton Bay fig tree, while the cicadas sang. And made up their pretty faces in compact mirrors. They were all beauties. Not merely Bonita and Morna who were my particular sun and moon, but the well-known beauties of the day in Sydney society — Betty Wills-Allen, Pearl Appleton, Gretel Bullmore, Jean Anderson — what has become of them and their beauty? I met Betty and Pearl years later in England and was greatly impressed by their striking good looks, reinforced by staid poise.

It all seems so long ago — and in a different hemisphere, if not in a different world. 1924 to 1929. Is it worth recapturing? Is anybody's adolescence of interest to anybody but himself? Yet in retrospect, it all seems so sunny, so bright, so happy, and so happily removed from the grim realities of the past world war of Britain, that I am tempted to recapture it; the ghostly acres of dying ring-barked gum trees; the long stale yellow grass; and the rotting split rail fences; or the endless miles of brand new rabbit-proof wire netting, with here and there the skin of a snake hanging up on it to dry and shrivelled in the sun; and the rabbits, where they are not altogether extinguished, busily grazing away every bare hillside in the evening sun; and the peculiar tightness and stickiness and massiveness of the heavy fleeces of the merino sheep which you part with your fingers revealing clean yellow wool down to the pink skin, to be judged as fine wool, or medium or strong wool. And the smell of that wool, all greasy, being pressed and squeezed down into the big square canvas bales in the wool-sheds, up country; the corrugated iron roofs blistering under the sun, and the jackaroos, in their blue open-necked shirts, riding around the endless miles of the boundary fences of the sheep stations, in high pommelled saddles with comfortable knee pads, wearing elastic sided boots, and lazily cracking eighteen feet long stock whips from the backs of horses.

The people swarming like flies on the wide Pacific beaches north of Sydney. Wonderful looking men and women in thousands, bronzing in the sun or running out into the surf to mount the great breakers that come combing in from the east.

Or the sunshine on the glossy flanks of the racehorses out at Randwick, where the people go; practically the whole population of Sydney, the whole million and a half, at one time or another; to back the favourite sport of the country.

But one cannot go on, like this, just plugging the atmosphere, trying to evoke fleeting visions of a past 12,000 miles away, waking up to the crashing and banging on the corrugated iron roof of Hill View in the half darkness of the Australian summer night at two or three in the morning — trapping opossums, all snapping teeth, three feet long from nose to tail, to be wangled into a wooden box and the door lid shut.

You may say that when an author begins writing an autobiography he is nearing bankruptcy from a literary point of view. He is dipping into his gold reserve. For that is what his life is to an author. He can let the coins glitter through his fingers but once. He counts the golden hours for the last time.

'A land where bright blossoms are scentless, and songless bright birds', wrote Adam Lindsay Gordon. A land of harsh contrasts. A land where the sun blazes down for eight months of the year on rolling hills of grey grass; where acres of gum trees, ring-barked, wither to silent skeletons in the moonlight, and crumble away to make room for more pastures and more sheep; a land three parts desert, merging through scrub-strewn bareness, where a sheep grazes to fifteen acres; through the well-watered sheep lands supporting a sheep to the acre; to the suburbs of the great cities. Suddenly you are in a vast sprawling metropolis where a fifth of the continent's population lives. There are ferry boats beetling to and fro across the blue sheet of water; there are sails dotted about the coves, and great liners swinging in through the mile wide heads. There are the long beaches of blazing hot sand, like powdered diamonds, where the walls of white surf roar in from the endless blue Pacific and curl and cream in their rush to the beach, dotted with the dark heads of swimmers. Australia: so vital, so sure of itself. Sufficient unto itself; yet so far from everywhere else except the hordes of Asia watching it from just above, as a child is watched in a clearing of the jungle by a tiger.

At the racecourse the gleaming chestnut, bay and black horses under the colourful silks, flashing in the sun, gallop past the triangular winning post, with its broad white line; and the crowd roars. In the viceregal box, the Governor in his grey frock coat and grey topper beams across to the members of the Jockey Club, and they adjourn for a luncheon of cold chicken.

I came to know one part of Australia, New South Wales, very well in five years. I was happy there. I grew up there. I should have stayed there. It is hopeless to transplant an adolescent mind about the world, pulling it up by the roots every five years. By the time I returned to England I was an alien plant, like a prickly pear transplanted and thrusting up through the soft petals of an English rose garden.

Australia is a harsh land; in some ways a crude land. It is raw and

25

young, yet it has an inner vitality which scorns the demure and the self-effacing. It thrusts, it pushes. It arrives. It means well. It is warm-hearted and dreadfully misunderstood. The awful reticences of English life are meaningless to it. Bang the gong and do not whisper 'Dinner is served Madam'.

They swear; but it means not a thing! Not like the lethal expletives brought out on occasion, as through the fangs of a snake, in older lands. Here everything is bloody. *The Sydney Bulletin* carried, in my youth, a poem on 'The Great Australian adjective' — *

> The sunburned bloody Stockman stood
> And in a dismal bloody mood
> Apostrophized his bloody cuddy.
> The bloody nag's no bloody good,
> He couldn't earn his bloody food,
> A regular bloody brumby.
>
> He jumped across the bloody horse
> And cantered off, of bloody course;
> The roads were bad and bloody muddy
> Says he "Gawd spare me bloody days
> The bloody Gov'ment's bloody ways
> Are screaming bloody funny."
>
> He rode uphill, down bloody dale,
> The wind it blew a bloody gale,
> The bloody creek was bloody floody
> Says he "The bloody nag must swim
> The same for bloody me and him,
> Gawd Struth! but this is bloody."
>
> He plunged into the bloody creek,
> The bloody horse was bloody weak,
> The rider's face a bloody study
> And though the bloody horse was drowned
> The bloody rider reached the ground
> Ejaculating "bloody!"

---

* As the period in my lifespan which has elapsed since I left Sydney, cóvers a third of Australian recorded history. I cannot be certain that this is still the great Australian adjective.

No harm in that.

Well, my first impressions of Australia were derived from Adelaide, a young city sprawling in sunshine; and Melbourne an old city drenched in rain. I should have preferred to record my arrival, majestically, between the mile-wide heads of Sydney's harbour. But Melbourne was to be the last port of call. From there we would travel by rail to New South Wales. We were expected to call at Government House, in Melbourne, where the Governor General then resided. He was Lord Forster, and I was told to bow before shaking hands with him. My sister and I presented ourselves at Government House and a regal figure in morning coat appeared on the threshold. I bowed.

"Good-morning, your Excellency," I said. He was the butler and drew himself up stiffly. Inside the hall was an even more majestic figure, swathed in gold braid. I realised that I had been premature so I bowed even lower, and said, "How do you do, your Excellency." He roared with laughter. "I'm only the A.D.C.," he explained. He had large black moustaches, and it seemed to me a mistake not to have made him a governor. We proceeded into a dim drawing-room, where there were people standing about. Behind a pillar I came across a tall and wistful man in a lounge suit. We fell into conversation. I told him of our travels and of the awful mistakes I had made in mistaking the butler and A.D.C for the Governor General. He was very sympathetic and his lean, distinguished face, revealed signs of inner amusement. Presently he was joined by a charming woman to whom he introduced me.

"This is the de Chair's boy, my dear." And he explained to me helpfully, "This is my wife, Lady Forster."

"Lady Forster?" I gulped. "Then you are the Governor General!" But he restrained me in my efforts to make a belated salutation.

"You see," he explained to his wife, "he naturally thought Mulholland must be the Governor General."

Lady Forster was delighted and swept me off to tea, where we worked out together a plan for cross-breeding giraffes and zebras. The idea was mine; zebras being fast, and giraffes having a long neck which would be helpful at the winning post. We agreed to call it a Gezebraff.

In due course we arrived by train at Mossvale in New South Wales. There was something of a mid-western town in American cowboy films about it. In the single street, houses were made of wood boarding and roofed in corrugated iron. There were few shops beyond a general store and a saddle-maker.

The Governor's summer residence was called Hill View. There was a lodge at the entrance drive, and this wound up, under an avenue of fir trees to the crest of the hill, where the rambling house was situated. It had begun as a small stone building, but successive governors had required additions and it was now largely a wooden structure pushing out wings in all directions and at all levels. On the garden side it had a steeply sloping lawn bounded by shrubberies and trees, where a slat fence separated it from the hilly grazing land. The car drew up on the other side where an open space was bounded by the house on the one side and ranges of stables and garages on the other. There was a high tower, containing the water tank. The sprawling wooden building was painted a very pale green, almost white, and the place had a pleasantly welcoming air. After Melbourne, where it had rained all the time, the sun beamed down on the dusty white yard.

There were greetings with our parents, whom we had not seen for nearly a year. My father at this time was at the summit of his powers, after a career in the Navy which had brought him to the rank of Admiral. In accepting the Governorship of New South Wales he forfeited his chance of becoming an Admiral of the Fleet. Actually he had succeeded Beatty as Naval Secretary to Churchill in 1913 and but for a vigorous disagreement with the then young and rather hot-headed First Lord of the Admiralty, would undoubtedly have done even better. He was now crowning a distinguished career, in which he had as many admirers as most men have detractors, by becoming the King's representative in Australia.

My mother had been an auburn-haired beauty in South Africa, when my father, then a Commander on the naval station, had met her. They had subsequently been married in England from her uncle's home, Spitchwick Manor in Devon. My father had then been appointed to Washinton as Naval Attaché and this had been a very pleasant beginning for a married life.

Now they were holidaying in the hills; and had already made of Hill View a home. My mother was collecting odd bits of coloured material, discarded ties, and so on, and working them into a design for a tall screen, upon which phoenixes paraded between the tall pillars of a gateway towards an imaginary palace.

Half a dozen of the bedrooms were on various ground floor levels; and there were not more than four or five above. There was only a narrow little staircase. I had a bedroom, for a while, upstairs. I remember a coloured print hanging there, of a bullock wagon with a long double train of bullocks, sixteen in all, dipping through a ford in a river; the old driver was cracking his whip over their heads. The view from my window was over the humped slope of the garden, with scattered flower beds, towards a stream far down in a hollow at the bottom of a dry grassy slope. Beyond, the grass rose again in hillock beyond hillock towards a blue distance. There were gum trees everywhere, with their scaly bark, flaking off in strips of brown, or grey, or slate blue, or white. The effect of these smooth tree trunks, with their peeling bark, was silvery; and the foliage was feathery, for the eucalyptus leaf is long and thin, very pointed, and dark green. There are over two hundred varieties of eucalyptus or gum tree in Australia. But they all look much alike and are the most characteristic thing about the countryside. The trunk is rather like that of the London plane tree, if one can imagine such a thing in a sunny climate; but the leaves are clusters of thin leaves, casting a speckly shade. Sometimes the gum trees are very large. All round Hill View the land was good sheep grazing country. The fences were mostly made of split rails made from the gum trees. Two rails slipped into large slots in the fence posts.

The first excitement was to hear, in the early hours of the morning, the heavy thump of the silver possums' feet, as they came back from their maraudings and dropped off the overhanging branches of the big pine trees and clumped over the corrugated iron roof to their nests under the eaves. These animals with their finely packed silvery fur and long strong tails backed with fur, short strong legs armed with claws, faces like a sharp-nosed cat, and with long savage teeth, were preserved, for they were in danger of becoming extinct, but at Hill View they were rated a nuisance which kept everyone awake. It was difficult at times to believe that it was not a man clumping heavy-footed across the tin roof. The Minister of Agriculture, who paid a visit to the house to see my father on State business, gave me a special exemption to trap these animals. It was a dangerous contest, for in the dark the silver possum is a formidable animal, all teeth and claws. I tried to lure them into wooden traps with sliding doors; baited with apples. They lunged at these contrivances and passed them by, sometimes swiping the apples out first. Eventually I was reduced to trapping them with rabbit traps. Suddenly at three or four in the morning there would be the heavy thump of the returning hunter. Then he would clump across the roof, only to put his foot in one of my traps, secured by a chain, probably, to one of the drain pipes. A noise like the breaking up of a bicycle shop would follow. The frightened animal would leap about with the iron trap crashing on the tin roof, and the chain dragging this way and that. I would leap from bed, and seizing my flash-lamp, climb out on to the sloping roof. There was no difficulty locating the prisoner. He would be crashing and pounding the place to pieces, and I would shine my flash on him. This would arrest him for a moment. Then I could see him, in the beam of light, his two little ears sticking up, and his eyes glowing red. Then a snarl and a jump at me, lunging to the end of the chain. My task was to get round behind him, keeping nimbly out of range of the snapping fangs, unfasten the chain, and grab the animal by his tail. Only then could he be lowered into the open box, and the lid slid home. At the last minute, as he was going in, the gin trap had to be sprung with a grip of the other hand. So by this time, the flash-lamp had been deposited on the roof, and in the half dark the skirmish would be fast and furious, before the possum was inside the box, and the trap removed. So strong were their forelegs that the jaws of the trap made very little impression through the fur, and it did not seem so cruel as does the trapping of the much frailer limbs of rabbits, which went on, perforce, in Australia a great deal. Once inside the box, the beast would settle down quietly till the morning. There was a small round aviary in the garden, with a conical roof. The aviary had not been used since some former governor had kept birds in there. Into it now I thrust the wily possum. Not long did the first one remain in captivity. He found means of escape, and the edifice had to be checked for breaches. One magnificent specimen which measured over three feet — I sent down to the Sydney Zoo. Of the other three or four which I captured, I do not think one remained in the cage for more than a night. But I liked to think that the warfare discouraged them from nesting in the roof at Hill View and drove them off to more secure homes in hollow trees or the roofs of barns. The silver possum is not to be confused with the little ring-tailed possum, an easily domesticated pet. The silver possum is a tough customer, about twice the size and weight of a wild cat and I marvel, in retrospect, that I was not cut about by one of them in the dark. Certainly my mother, lying in bed and listening to the thunderous din, imagined me clawed in a thousand places. My father no doubt reassured her and explained that it was a good outlet for my energies and a stimulus to resourcefulness.

My sister and I were also given ponies to ride.

It seems in retrospect as if the sun always shone. But that is partly because the longest holidays were spent there, and those were in summer from November till January.

Soon after Elaine and I arrived, Lord Jellicoe, who had known my father for a lifetime in the Navy, came to stay at Hill View on his way home from New Zealand where he had been Governor General. He brought his wild and unruly family who seemed to go over the little admiral like a wave. "It takes me longer to get my family out of the house," he lamented to my father, "than it used to take me to get the whole Grand Fleet underway."

'Lady J', as we called her, was soon mounted, side saddle, on my mother's grey, and set off for a gallop. She showed us a photograph of herself hunting in New Zealand, flying over a barbed wire fence. This, apparently, is done every day in the New Zealand hunting field. Yet is sounds a formidable hazard. Apparently the horses are trained to see and jump the wire.

The Jellicoe children consisted of four daughters and a young son, George, then only about six years old. Prudy came next, a little older, then Norah, a regular tomboy, Myrtle and one other. We took them for long picnic rides — to Gun Rock creek first. There we had found a clear pool in some woods, where there was plenty of shade, and congenial swimming.

In the evenings we played immense games of snooker in the billiard room. This was one of the many extensions to the house, tin-roofed and wooden-walled. It was hung with framed cartoons by Spy of celebrated Victorian and Edwardian figures — all very elongated. There was the usual score board with pointers which could be slid along the score, and clicked up, twenty-five at a time. The scene at night with the six great shaded electric lights casting down a brilliant glare on the emerald green cloth, and the snooker balls; black, pink, blue, brown, green, yellow; as well as the massed triangle of scarlet balls, being broken up by the first stroke with the white, leaves a medley of bright colour in my mind, which takes me straight back to those cheerful games.

Lord Allenby was another visitor. My father had known his brother Claude in the Navy very well. The Field Marshal was a complete contrast to Jellicoe; the Admiral so small, so mild, so cool; the soldier so large, so red in the face, with such a strong powerful nose, and blazing eye.

Governors, of course, are surrounded by A.D.C.s and Secretaries. The worst of all this viceregal entourage from my point of view, was that it inevitably implanted in me at the most impressionable age, the false notion that I was a person of importance. If I went to an agricultural show, I would be photographed; if my sister and I went up in an aeroplane, our picture gazing down upon Sydney Harbour would cover the whole front page of some daily paper the next day. For all this, retribution was waiting for me on arrival at school. But throughout my five years in Australia I was never treated quite as an ordinary boy. It was, in a remote segment of Empire, the upbringing of a Prince of Wales. This unhealthy limelight was all the more damaging because of a supposed brilliance which I seemed to possess; and which made people again and again speak of me as if I were a Statesman in the making. From this atmosphere, which my parents, with their official preoccupation did not do enough to check or correct, I developed a conviction that I was endowed with special gifts, and came, before I was seventeen, to believe that a great destiny awaited me.

It was at Hill View, when I was not more than fourteen, that my father, while he and I were riding across a paddock on the right of the drive going down (I remember the place so well) and moving towards the Fir Avenue, raised the question of my future in life. It was he, then, who suggested that I should enter the House of Commons. I talked so much that it was not a surprising suggestion. "They often say," my father told me, "that it is the best club in London. You meet everybody there, and if you make a mark, there is no knowing where you may finish up."

In my family the idea of some form of public service was so ingrained that it would never have occurred to him or me to discuss a career without some form of public service in it. My brother had followed him in the Navy and was now a Sub-Lieutenant doing his courses at Greenwich and Portsmouth. I would have been entered for the Navy in all probability also, had it not been for my father's appointment to Australia. So the idea, very early, of a political career was planted in my mind. And at school my success in the debating team of which I became the captain, when it won the inter-school debating competition, strengthened my parents in their belief that I should enter Parliament. But it was not until we attended the opening of the New Federal Parliament at Canberra and I first listened to a parliamentary debate, and saw the Premier, Mr. Bruce (later Lord Bruce of Melbourne) rise from the Government Front Bench and address the Chair in a resonant golden voice, "Mr. Speaker, Sir . . . " that the idea of adopting politics as a profession suddenly captured my imagination.

But that was not for another year or two; after I had been at school.

The King's School at Paramatta was the oldest in Australia and had been founded as a cadet corps in King William IV's reign. The boys accordingly wore a uniform which had probably changed but little since then. A tunic of grey with scarlet facings, and cuffs; silver buttons, and blue trousers with a red stripe down the sides; the whole outfit topped off by an Australian Army hat, fastened up at the side, with the school badge in silver. Every boy possessed two uniforms, one for daily use and one for best. There was an attempt at military training as this exempted the members of the school from doing their annual training with the Army. But discipline was not the strongest feature of the cadet corps. Once a young master, fresh from England, was told off to drill them. He barked orders which might have been intelligible to Guardsmen at Wellington Barracks, but failed entirely to carry conviction in Paramatta. The result was surprising. The entire squad squatted down on its heels, to register its disapproval of all forms of discipline and started singing "Ramona, I hear the prison bells a-calling", to the bewildered officer. Going scarlet in the face, he turned about abruptly and marched himself off the field. Australians are not easily handled against their opinion of the fitness of things. Yet, the discipline of the school was severe enough. Before the arrival of Potty Baker, an English international rugger player, as Headmaster, conditions had become very lax. Smoking was common. On arrival Potty Baker sacked nine masters and twenty-two boys. Parents all over Australia wanted to send their boys to King's after that.

The first Government House in Australia had been established at Paramatta, which was fifteen miles inland from Sydney; and the old white colonial house had become the junior house of the school, for boys of preparatory school age. Most of these went on to one of the four senior houses of the school.

I arrived shortly before the main building was reconstructed, and was housed in the large square sandstone building with its jutting porch of four high Grecian pillars. The windows looked down over a playing-field to the river, which was screened from view by willow trees. The school bell hung between tall white posts, on the edge of the terrace, above the playing-field.

But at the end of the gym there was a road, where jacaranda trees flowered blue and flame trees red, in summer, and beyond these, more playing-fields.

Among the willows on the near bank was the boat-house, and in there were training boats with sliding seats. The boats master was Eddie Dorch, of German descent, who had a withered arm, which made him seem a fomidable figure.

I started in boats, as a cox, being very young and small, fourteen; and might have persevered in this line of sport if it had not been for an unfortunate experience. It was not to be expected that the Governor's son would escape lightly in the matter of initiation.

The rowing eights practised down the river some miles away; and here a jetty and pontoon were built out over the mud flats, to reach the water. These mud flats were crawling with wicked black crabs, and I was held upside down and forced to walk, with my ankles held precariously from above through the slats of the pontoon, and my eyes an inch or two from the crawling crabs — forced thus, hanging upside down, and with every expectation of being dropped head-first into the crabs and the oozing mud — forced to walk upside down under the pontoon. To some this may seem a trivial torment, but to me this episode of the crabs still seems exceptionally unpleasant. It savours of the snake-pit.

Yet if this single persecution is discounted, and one other, when I was crammed into a wooden chest, too small for me, while several boys including one odious boy sat on the lid; my life at King's was happy enough.

My desk lid was almost black with age, and shiny as ebony. It had been carved with so many names of previous boys that it was impossible to find an even piece of its surface. Next to me was Rupert de Poister Chance, who was the school's fastest bowler and was therefore an object of respect. The custom of the school was to paper the inside of the desk lid with pictures from magazines, according to choice. And I find the gallery which I established in my own, very revealing. I have two photographs of the desk lid, at different stages of my school life. In the later one we find Pericles, Julius Caesar (side view) and Karl Marx, down the left hand side. Then came a full face bust of Caesar and a Schneider cup-winning seaplane, above a large portrait of Dolores Costello, the reigning beauty of the cinema screen. Next a Focke-Wulf monoplane above Hannibal and Lenin, with a string of racehorses at the bottom; Lenin is obscuring all but the very shapely legs of some other beauty. Next we come to Napoleon, painted by Baron Gros, after Lodi (The Louvre picture), four more aeroplanes, a girl who has fallen down on the ice, skating; one more film star — and an officer of the Household Cavalry (which I later joined), mounted and labelled 'Proud'. Finally, Bismarck at his own desk, in the top right hand corner of the gallery. In the earlier version, Napoleon is still partly obscured by a tube of toothpaste and a number of pens, pencils and screwdrivers. Hannibal has not yet superseded another girl beauty, over whose head is a snapshot of my pet Jersey calf. Bismarck has yet to replace an albatross. My own face is reflected from a circular mirror, under which is a postcard of Sydney Wansey, our champion school runner, winning the half-mile. Between me and Napoleon is a clothes-brush. And Karl Marx has not yet taken precedence over Miss Australia, Beatrice Mills, for whom I felt a considerable admiration. Pericles and the full face of Caesar have yet to supersede a prize merino ram, David, and a girl mounted on zebra. So in 1927 we have only Caesar, Napoleon and de Chair, above an alarm clock, a tin of nugget black boot polish, F.T.C Hearnshaw's *Main Currents of European History*, a slide rule, registering some long forgotten calculation, and what looks like a bottle of hair oil. Is not the whole story written there? By 1928 ambition has taken over.

Napoleon broke into my life through W.H. Hudson's book *The Man Napoleon*. This is meant to be a critical, if not hostile biography. But it fired me with I know not what ambitions. I saw myself, in a grey greatcoat, walking among the wounded, at some subsequent Aspern and Essling on the island of Lobau. I visited Insel Lobau, that flat island, grey with poplar and alder, in the stream of the Danube some years later; but there were no wounded soldiers raising themselves from their stretchers to shout 'vive l'empereur'. Only the soughing of the wind in the Asperns. In the school library, I read the volumes of Rollin's history of the world and thought of Napoleon tearing through these seven volumes when he was a lieutenant at Valence or Auxonne.

The educational standard of the eight 'Great Public Schools' in New South Wales was impressive. The basis of the history teaching was James Harvey Robinson's *History of Western Europe* from the fall of the Roman Empire to the Treaty of Versailles. This vivid history book of 800 pages, profusely illustrated, by the American author of that revolutionary book *The Mind in the Making*, had a prodigious influence on my own thinking. The Kings of England had to take their chance along with Charlemagne and Hugh Capet. Robinson saw the Napoleonic wars as much from the French as the English side; and the whole story of Europe advanced with impartial clarity along both sides of the Channel. I count this an immense advantage, in combating the national insularity of an English upbringing.

The teaching of English, by contrast, was exclusively from English sources. I owe much to the enthusiasm of the English Master, H.H. Harrison who was also my house master at School House. A short, plump, patient man. He took us behind the scenes of Shakespeare's theatre; and helped us to bore into the glossary of *As You Like It* and *Hamlet*. He made us enjoy these plays at the age of sixteen, which is good teaching. The textbook here was W.H. Hudson's *Outline of English Literature*, one of the most fascinating books ever written about the written word. What else should one expect from a professor of English, who was also the author of *Green Mansions*, *The Purple Land*, *Far Away and Long Ago*, *El Ombu* and the rest? A master of pellucid prose, whose book made all branches of writing easy to appreciate.

The public examination on leaving is called the Leaving Certificate, but it was possible to take it the year before leaving if you got into the sixth form in time. I therefore took it twice and was awarded the Broughton Scholarship for the best pass by a boy remaining at school. In my final exams I secured second class honours (a disappointment) in English and an A pass in History. In the previous year I had secured an A pass in Latin as well, based on a fairly intimate study of Horace's *Odes*. But I failed to reach this standard the second time, possibly because of a certain boredom with the *Aeneid*, which was set that year. I was pretty well the only poet contributing to the school magazine so I had little difficulty in winning the school poetry prize. But the surprise came after the leaving certificate, when we had to sit for the Divinity Exam. Potty Baker, an ordained clergyman, was very keen on this, and his weekly divinity talks to the whole school were extremely enlightening. He would stand up on the dais in 'School' and describe the country-side around the sea of Galilee as it was in the time of Jesus — with seven Roman cities and wooded slopes coming down to the water's edge; all so different from the barren slopes, and scattering of villages today, with Tiberias the only town of any consequence. So I made an effort to master the Acts of the Apostles, as I knew that my success in this exam, which was his special hobby, would have a direct effect on his final report. The questions were deceptively easy; and most of the other competitors had answered all six within the first half-hour. Yet three hours were allowed for the paper. For two of these, I was left all alone; but I decided to put everything I could remember of St. Paul's journeys and the meeting on Mars Hill into my answers. Yet I was not prepared for the result when it was posted up on the notice-board: de Chair 94% and the nearest competitor 67%. Potty Baker beamed at me like an affable gorilla, with hair sprouting from his ears and nose, and his little eyes boring intently into me; a formidable figure, with his heavy build of an international forward in the English rugger team, to which middle age had added a comfortable paunch and a new Rolls-Royce. I was awarded the Archdeacon Gunther Memorial Prize. None of these distinctions, except perhaps the divinity prize, required an unusual intellect, but taken altogether, they sounded sufficiently impressive when cabled to the tutor for admissions at Balliol College, in England, to secure my admission without any further examinations. A fortunate dispensation.

My only distinction was to enter easily, and eventually captain, the school debating team which won the inter-school competition; and in the lines which are laid down in youth, we may read the direction of our progress more easily than we realise. Work as we may, to excel in this field or that, we shall find in after years, that we depend for quick results or comparative successes on those talents which manifested themselves most persistently at school — so it is to be the debating team all over again, but next time in the House of Commons (although it is not as easy to captain that side) and there will be more 2nd class honours in English, (*The Golden Carpet*); an A pass from the critics in History (*Napoleon's Memoirs* or *Caesar's Commentaries*); an occasional sprint in Latin (like the *First Crusade*) and to everyone's surprise, perhaps the 94% divinity prize for *A Mind on the March* or *The Story of a Lifetime*.

My mother and father were lent a house at Palm Beach, on the coast a few miles north of Sydney: and here they could relax more than was possible in the semi-viceregal atmosphere of Hill View. Nevertheless my mother had the notion of inviting the Japanese Consul General to luncheon at Palm Beach. She invited him for 1 o'clock and we were all sitting about on the lawn in bathing costumes not long after breakfast when a shining black limousine came along the beach road and drew up in front of the house. From it jumped Japanese in striped trousers and glistening black silk top hats. There was a hurried retreat from the lawn and a peremptory order to me to fight a delaying action to the last round. I ran down the garden steps and greeted the Consul General. He was Tokogowa, a man of immense standing in Japan, which his family had ruled for some centuries as the Shogun Administration until they voluntarily restored the divine monarchy to its traditional pre-eminence. He dismissed his secretaries and chauffeur, and I took him in hand. It was not ten o'clock and luncheon would not be ready for another three hours.

"Before we go in to lunch," I told him, "there is a magnificent view of the bay which all visitors usually wish to see first. May I show it to you?"

"Very please," beamed Tokogowa.

We started the ascent of a small mountain, behind the house. The day was hot and getting hotter. As we got higher and higher we paused frequently at an occasional bend in the track to admire the wide Pacific, which stretched blue in the imagination all the way to Japan. Tokogowa removed his black topper and fanned himself discreetly. His black morning coat was not designed for mountaineering. But time must be killed. It had, in fact, to be tortured first. We struggled on towards the summit, which we reached in about an hour and a half. It was easier for me in bathing costume and sand shoes. From the peak we could see down upon the two-edge sword of sand of which Palm Beach was the broader edge; running out towards a headland which crossed it at right angles.

"Worthy view," said Tokogowa diplomatically. He glanced at his watch. "We shall not be late for His Excellency?" He produced my mother's letter. "See," he said, "ten clock."

I looked at my mother's very clear handwriting '1 o'clock', and saw his point.

"Ah, yes," I said, "10 clock. But you know what life is like at the seaside. Meal-times are rather elastic."

We climbed slowly down the winding track, which took another hour and a half. The delaying action was complete.

On the way down we talked of the forthcoming visit to Australia of the Crown Prince's brother, Nobikitu Takamatsu. I was anxious to meet him, and after being detained for three hours on a mountain in striped trousers, Tokogowa was softened up to the extent of meeting my wishes. An audience was arranged.

Later Tokogowa was moved to a post in Canada but was generous enough to send me from there a set of exquisite dessert finger-bowls in Japanese gold lacquer on the occasion of my wedding which took place four years after this heated stroll at Palm Beach.

I decided on one occasion to surprise my sister with a practical joke. I hired a black wig of slightly wavy hair in Sydney and fixed to my upper lip a small black moustache. Thus altered I presented myself at the lodge gates of Government House, giving my name as Monsieur Marchand.

"Present my compliments to Madamoiselle and say that M. Marchand, whom she will recall, wishes to see her."

Sergeant Swann, the police orderly, looked extremely dubious: and I was constrained to take him into my confidence. I was only thus able to pass on to the front door, which Turner opened gravely to me. He looked even more dubious but his duty, different from Swann's, was to announce me. Certainly he did not detect in the dashing dark-haired dago, the son of the house. He went in search of my sister. There were whispered consultations in the hall beyond. Presently my sister emerged, protected as by a bodyguard by our mother.

"Ah," I cried. "You do not remember Marchand, no? At Nourmoutier, yes? Your very old friend Marchand."

But at this point the puzzled expression on my sister's face and the frigidity clearly marked in my mother's broke down.

Elaine pointed an accusing finger, "Somerset!" and burst into laughter.

Various personages visited Australia at this time and stayed as a matter of course in the various Government Houses. The problem of catering for them alone was serious as when, for example, the Duke and Duchess of York, subsequently King George VI and Queen Elizabeth, stayed before the opening of the Commonwealth Parliament and my mother had to provide food for upwards of 40 people in the front of the house and 60 in the back regions for ten days.

The visit of the Empire Press delegation included many distinguished figures like A.P. Herbert, then Editor of *Punch*, J.J. Astor, part owner of *The Times*, Lord Burnham, then owner of the *Daily Telegraph* and others. Lord Burnham expressed a wish to see a live duck-bill platypus. These are indigenous to Australia and nowhere else. If you can imagine an otter with web-feet and a duck's bill about three inches broad you have the picture. Even in Australia they are extremely rare. However the net was spread far and wide. A duck-bill platypus was brought down from some remote river and placed — where else? — in Lord Burnham's bath. I saw it go in; and swim round with prodigious speed, its broad flat bill level with the surface. It churned up the bath. The door was hurriedly locked from the outside. Unfortunately nobody remembered to tell Lord Burnham that his duck-bill platypus was in his bath, and when the noble lord came in, tired after a day of heavy conferences, and went to his bath, there was a flurry of foam and a skirmish, which nearly gave the newspaper baron a heart attack. Bells were rung; and the platypus was removed to the round fountain pond in the garden around which once more it raced like a destroyer. The remainder of the delegation trooped out there in the morning to see this antiquated beast for themselves; but he was gone. Amphibiously he had clambered or leapt over the concrete lip of the pond, lumbered down the garden and presumably into the harbour. Salt water may have been strange to him; but not so alarming as Lord Burnham's bath. This strange beast, stranded midway in the stream of evolution between a bird and an animal, lays eggs and then suckles its young in a nest after they are hatched. At the age of fourteen, having looked up their habits, I announced loudly at a luncheon party in Government House that they were also known to cohabit. My elders included a friendly anthropologist, Radcliffe Brown, and gravely were the adult expressions strained.

If the duck-bill platypus was rare, the big brown kingfisher, called the kookaburra, was a familiar friend; never far off in the trees, starting suddenly his cadent cackle:

```
          — ku
             — ku
                — ku
   — ku
                   — ku
                      — ku
ku
                         — ku
                            — ku
                               — ku — ku — ku — ku
```

He was nicknamed the laughing jackass; although I believe he got the name from the French word *Jacasser* — to chatter. It is perhaps the laugh of the kookaburra more than anything that gives to the Australian bush its distinctive note, although, like the coffin bird in Malaya with its peculiar tock — tock — tock, varying in number, it becomes so familiar as to be unnoticed. There are some lovely parrots called galahs, like grey doves, with bright pink breasts. A cloud of them will alight on a bush and it seems suddenly to glow with a pink fire.

Australia has not the scenic grandeurs of New Zealand, but the Blue Mountains, well named, might have provided those distant landscapes of receding azure which the Elder Breughel put into the background of his pictures. There is a blue mistiness in these mountains which makes them shimmer in the heat, like mountains in a mirage or a landscape in the clouds, not easily attained on foot.

CHAPTER 5

My parents had decided, generously, that I should take advantage of the long route home, and the six months' interval before I went up to Oxford, to make a wide detour through Europe.

I was unquestionably impressed by Mussolini's rise to power, and everything I saw in Italy was calculated to impress an adolescent mind with the efficiency and superficial cleanliness of dictatorship. Discrimination in these matters comes later, when one has a little more discernment and can look deeper for the essential of good government — orderliness without servitude. I had been reading Mussolini's autobiography on the ship. I was looking forward eagerly to an opportunity, which in those days was not easily obtained, of seeing him; and the height of his fame. It was all to be done through Signor Grosardi, the Italian Consul General in Australia, who had arrived home in Italy at the same time and lodged at the Albergo Reale, Rome. He arranged the audience for the following Monday at 7.15 p.m.

My audience with the dictator when it was arranged for 15th May did not go quite according to plan. When I called for Grosardi in the evening he said in alarm, "You must wear a dark suit."

"But I have no dark suit." I was travelling round Europe with a couple of suitcases, and any suits they contained were light grey. Grosardi became excitable. He was terrified of the approaching ordeal, at which he was to act as interpreter, for he had been in Australia at the time of the Fascist coup and this was his first meeting with the Duce himself.

"One cannot appear before the Duce like that," he wailed. But it was too late to buy or hire a dark suit for the occasion so I said, "Perhaps you could lend me one." Grosardi looked down at his own short and tubby figure, and shrugged his shoulders in despair.

"Perhaps, it would be best," he said.

He produced a black suit, which seemed to be made of thick felt. I tried it on. The jacket could have gone round me twice, and the sleeves which were unexpectedly long, especially with the coat nearly falling off

41

my shoulders, almost obscured my fingertips. The jacket seemed to reach my knees, and the trousers were hitched up high somewhere underneath it. All this was very damaging to my self-confidence, when I had counted on making a good impression as an alert young man, on his way to Oxford. However, Grosardi seemed intent on the sombre colouring required on so auspicious an occasion and, thus attired, I accompanied him to the Palazzo Chigi. We were shown up to an ante-room, where we waited on a gilt backed settee confronted by two Fascist guards who were guarding the door of Mussolini's room. Presently the door opened and the American Ambassador came out. Grosardi was by this time ashen with alarm; and we were shown through the door. At the entrance we paused. The room seemed endless, and, far away, Mussolini was standing behind a desk and bending forward over papers on it. Suddenly he straightened and hurled his right arm up with a roar "A Noi". Grosardi's arm shot up in response and he quavered "A Noi", too. Then he began to trot across the parquet floor towards the desk and I followed as sedately as Grosardi's spare suit, in which I felt like an immature gorilla, would permit. Mussolini's eyes always bulged; but they bulged even harder when this apparition emerged from the shadows. Hurriedly he glanced down at his engagement pad. Commandatore Mameli had squeezed me in between the American Ambassador and the Czech Foreign Minister, Dr Benes. Mussolini had heard of them and was even prepared to take cognizance of them. But who on earth was this? What on earth was this? Grosardi's son, perhaps, wearing Dad's suit? Surely not. He began prowling round the great desk, like a watchful black panther, his eyes fixed on mine.

I had studied Italian every night on board ship for a month, so as to be able to impress the Italian dictator at just this moment. I had even prepared what I intended to say. It was to have gone something like this:

"Sono, veramenti contento d'avere questa opportunita d'incontrare vostra Eccellenza, perche anch'io aspiro alle vita politice — Ho studiato la vostra authobiografia (la quale non e, certamente, che la prefazione della vita vostra) e credo che il Fascismo ha inaugurato uno nuovo capitalo nella storia. Il mondo si stanca della democrazia e della discordia dei partiti. Io spero di diventari Il Capo del Governo d'Inghilterra."

This may not be accurate Italian, but it ought to have shaken Mussolini. Imagine my consternation when he gripped my hand, like iron, and said, smiling with face muscles working like knotted cords, "I am very glad to have this opportunity of meeting you."

This was the first I knew that he had been learning English, but that was as far as his English studies had progressed. And in the general discussion which followed, while Mussolini went round to his side of the desk, Grosardi gripped the opposite edge of it and began chattering on, in voluble Italian too fast for me to follow, an explanation of my presence, as the son of a distinguished Admiral and Governor of New South Wales, on his way to take up his studies in England, adding that I would no doubt be able to impress my youthful contemporaries with all I had seen in Italy, and even that I was going to enter the English Parliament. I injected an occasional "si", or "si, si", which seemed more fluent, and contented myself with staring into Mussolini's peculiar eyes. The white showing all round the brown iris gave him the appearance of continually staring intently ahead. When his face relaxed it assumed an expression of fierce severity with contracted brow. When he smiled there was a visible tautening of all the muscles. When Grosardi drew breath, Mussolini made some appropriate acknowledgements in a slow, clear and decisive voice, and before I knew what was happening he came round the desk once more, and again with a tread that reminded me of some feline animal, led us towards the door, where he took leave of us, with I know not what inner convulsion of amusement. Certainly I felt, on leaving his presence that I had seen a great man; but that may well have been the result of the effective build-up and celebrated name on an impressionable youth. Yet, I think it would be conceded that if Mussolini had not made his one disastrous miscalculation in 1940 when he thought Germany was on the eve of total victory, and if he had remained neutral throughout the war, his position at the end of the struggle between Hitler and the rest of us, would have been that of a powerful neutral and intermediary in the hour of Hitler's defeat. Instead of this he was riddled with bullets in Milan and hung to a lamp-post; which is the common lot of dictators in a land which saw Julius Caesar stabbed to death in twenty-three places. Better, on the whole, the less spectacular career and untroubled retirement of a Stanley Baldwin.

One of the difficulties of writing about foreign places is that the pen is quite unable to convey an idea of their characteristic smells. Yet it is the peculiar whiff, of sour bread, or cooking macaroni, or rotting fruit, or even of sweat in overcrowded, narrow streets, where washing is hung out from wall to wall, that one first senses in Naples. The hotel bedrooms are different to what one has known. The floor is tiled and there is a continental breakfast tray. The coffee has a different, a more aromatic aroma, and there are rolls of bread. The lumps of sugar are in paper wrapping. It is all faintly strange and therefore exciting. The air, even in late April is already drowsy. One's mind is alert to new things, and the eye notices everything. I was collected by a guide under arrangements made far back in Auckland, with Thomas Cook and Son. He took me up to the medieval monastery of San Martino, to see the famous view over the bay of Naples in the evening light. The little iron balcony seemed to hang right out over the city. From the narrow streets far below rose the clangour of the traffic and the shouting of the inhabitants. To the right stretched the blue sweep of the bay. The slanting sunlight picked out the dazzling white sails of the fishing boats returning to harbour. An old square stone fortress at the end of a long narrow causeway stood out in vivid yellow relief against the dark ultramarine blue of the bay. On the hill slopes to my left was the summer residence of the former Neapolitan kings, surrounded by its parks and gardens, standing now in deep shadow. Vesuvius was silhouetted in the setting sun, a beautiful cone, from the top of which the wavering white cloud drifted pink in the evening light. Then the sun went down. A crow glided past me in the twilight, cawing, and alighted below me in the little walled vineyard of the monastery.

Well, if there is one thing certain about life it is that one does not remain seventeen for long. My eighteenth birthday found me alone and somewhat dispirited at a farm outside Tours in a village called St. Avertin, staying with a French dame who took in foreigners, studying the language. There was a Russian called Dëjn and a Dutchman, Vriede. I always feel a peculiar melancholy over unremembered birthdays — and here I was apparently out of touch with my family or anyone who would care to remember me. I tried to persuade a girl in a rather dreary cabaret in Tours to drive up to see the Château of Luynes by moonlight. I had some difficulty in making her understand so unusual a request. She only wanted to sleep with me. She was slightly drunk and came and sat astride my table with her long legs, which my mother would have described as naked to the hip, and repeated insistently, "*Voulez-vous coucher avec moi*?" So I went alone, and climbed the long steps from the deserted village square in the moonlight, and prowled round the château, entering the deep shadow of its four great medieval towers; listened to the strange breathing of nightjars in the surrounding trees; for all the world like a giant's breathing; disturbed suddenly by the warning shriek of an owl as I stepped out into the moonlight. The moat was empty and overgrown with long grass. I descended into it, and paused under the dark arches of the drawbridge, only to withdraw hurriedly when the grass shivered in front of me as a snake wriggled through it. I left the eerie place and went down the broken steps to my car, where the village was still, except for the barking of dogs. It was two o'clock in the morning and I drove back to the farm, entering stealthily so as not to shock Madam Marius, who liked her young visitors to keep proper hours.

I spent an enjoyable month in Touraine, photographing the celebrated châteaux in colour, often waiting a whole day for the sun to come round to some particular façade.

My car was one that I hired for a month, a small two-seater Sigma, and I arranged with the garage in Tours that I could sell it for any sum over 5,000 francs (£50 then) and keep the balance; otherwise I would return it on a hire basis. So I decided to drive to the Island of Noirmoutier on the Atlantic Coast, near Nantes, which I had visited as a child with my parents.

Noirmoutier had changed very little since I remembered it at the age of ten. There were the same fishing boats, returning with their catch in the evening under sails of blue, or red or yellow. There were plenty of French but no English trippers, which is what mattered to me, as I had found it almost impossible to get away from English in Touraine. The only hotel on the beach was still the ramshackle rambling old Beau Rivage, near the 'estacade'. I still seemed to hear from my childhood visit the cries of the hungry diners in the restaurant to the solitary watiress, "*Louise, Louise, ou est Louise?*" The annexe to the hotel was still the same old fort in the bois de la Chaise where I had nearly been bitten by a viper. There was the same wooden drawbridge over the bramble-filled moat and the emerald lizards scuttling away in every direction. Lady Hilton Young had been staying there then with her son Peter Scott, who collected the lizards and was already, at the age of twelve, a fellow of the Royal Zoological Society. Even the plumbing of the fort remained unchanged, with the same acrid smell, from the door labelled Lavabo, which discharged its waste products, with the aid of a can of water, down the ivy on the west side of the fort into the tangled undergrowth. The fort was two minutes walk through the wood from the hotel, where I went for my meals, except *petit déjeuner* in bed. The season was ending and I was given a large room looking over the sea. The beach was separated from me by a low sandy ridge covered with pine trees. There were bushes of wild ripe blackberries on the rock point at this end of the beach; which I picked, leisurely, in my dressing-gown.

There was an American couple called Prince who had built

themselves a house on the island and I enquired if they still lived there. My parents had become very friendly with them on our previous visit and so they immediately asked me round for lunch when I telephoned. Charles Prince was something of an exile from New England and had acid views on contemporary American policy. He had written and gave me a printed copy of two poems about Uncle Sam's attitude to Europe. Prince had an immensely striking personality, and showered me with current journals about debts, reparations, and modern warfare. My mind was already fermenting with all that I had seen on my travels around Europe and this was just the catalyst needed to precipitate my first book. So I began, on the beach, with an old black umbrella shading the pages from the sun's glare, to survey the world from the standpoint of unprejudiced youth. The theme was simple. War was inevitable and after it, the dream of a United Europe. How would the war be fought? Charles Prince provided the answer, with deadly accuracy, from the articles of General J.F.C. Fuller; then appearing in some magazine — breakthrough by the fast moving tank, aided by the close support aeroplane.

I wrote and wrote — and everything was to come true. I should have been hailed as a prophet but I was ten years ahead of the facts and the doves of Geneva were cooing contentedly. What actually happened to the book and its author, when it appeared must be related later, even though the title of the book was specific — *The Impending Storm*.

Sometimes I feel as if Time were like a book which I have read so long ago that I only recognise the events as I come to them and cannot remember what is going to happen later on.

Certainly, I have sensed or expressed trends too far ahead to be easily credible and it has usually been ten or fifteen years before my premonitions have come true; by which time the people who scoffed so deridingly at the time have completely forgotten what I said and are busy congratulating themselves on waking up a week in advance of the event. Thus I wrote in 1929 of the war and European Union.

But of what avail is it to a boy of eighteen who is being mercilessly ragged for talking of the war in the midst of peace, to be able to say at twenty-nine, "Now, I have actually fought in it, so you must believe me." Or to say of the prophecies in 1929 of a United Europe (without Britain) — "These ideas will seem fashionable enough to you in 1949."

But for the time, under these cloudless Atlantic summer skies, I wrote on without prejudices or inhibitions. I had not yet entered the fog of Westminster.

In the evenings there were very pleasant relaxations — for I was introduced by the Princes to some charming and beautiful young French girls of society families who were spending summer on the island. My defences, if not down, were very nearly down and one of these *jeunes filles* in the moonlight upbraided me for not accepting the full implications of the situation. We lay in the sand-dunes, with the gorse bushes above us, and the warm Atlantic sucked at the shore of the island.

This book is an attempt at self-portraiture, not so much for the benefit of the reader as of the writer. For I want to see in it what it is that others have seen in me, which has often been so much at variance with my opinion of myself. And on every page I see the bright smiles of lovely women, embraced with ever-diminishing tenderness. And I begin to wonder whether that was not my doom from the start; and whether I should not have gone through life with beeswax in my ears, instead of lashed to the mast of matrimony. For I love women — all women. As one of the loveliest of them said to me herself, in Hong Kong, they are fascinating creatures, and this preoccupation with women has made me a bad mixer among men; ill at ease in clubs and common-rooms and regimental Messes. It has only been in women that I have been able to confide; and they have always been good to me. Almost without exception, they have never let me down. And this is why I impress women more than men. It is not merely that I am a man. When I speak to women my eyes are lighted by some inner fire which conversation with men all but extinguishes. There is something to me extremely embarrassing about a man deliberately exerting his charm over other men. Yet in politics it is the professional *charmeur* who does not scruple to present himself in the most attractive light, who draws people to him. With me there is a reticence in dealing with other men which amounts to repelling them. At one time I was able to overcome this as a platform orator, and the spell I could cast increased in proportion to the size of the audience. For I have a high and rather excitable voice which is irritating in the conversational style of the House of Commons or on the radio; but does not sound inappropriate in the harsher atmosphere of a mass meeting.

Any boy with fair hair and blue eyes has a good start in life.

I wanted, if possible to sell the Sigma car under the arrangement I had with the garage in Tours; and I heard of a young fisherman on the north coast of the island who was looking for one. I drove there one afternoon and had no difficulty in selling him the car for 5,000 francs

(£50 then). He and his young wife handed over the five mauve notes and I was just putting the car into a shack with a squeeze when the old father came storming along the road.

"What's all this I hear?" he roared.

"I've sold your son a nice car," I explained and showed it to him with its two seats in front and a sort of dickey seat behind in the boot.

"Ah!" he exclaimed, "they will expect me to ride in the trunk at the back. He can't have it."

"But he has already bought it."

"Bought it? *Sacré nom de Dieu*. The boy is not of age. He hasn't the right to look at a car, let alone buy one."

"Oh, well," I said resignedly, "if that's the case," and I backed the car out of the shack with difficulty, handed back the money and drove off.

Outside the Hotel Beau Rivage, next morning, when I was tinkering with the car, to get it ready for leaving, I got into conversation with the local gendarme, who seemed chatty and well disposed. It was a hot day and he leant on his bicycle while I worked. Snowden had been very curt at the League of Nations (S.D.N., they said, meant 'Snowden did non') and the French press was angry with England. Someone had traced the words *Merde pour l'Angleterre* in the dust on my car and I was rubbing it out. I told him about the young fisherman who had not been allowed to buy the car because he was not of age.

"Not 'Majeur'," chuckled the gendarme, "I know that one. He is twenty-eight and about to have a baby."

I straightened up from the engine. "Oh. That's different," I said. "How can I make him stick his bargain then?"

"You must summon him before the Juge de Paix, in that building over there, when he comes on Thursday."

"Who do I get to summon him?"

"You get me to summon him."

"Good. Then please summon him."

When the day came, I attended the court, which was held in a sort of army hut, behind the hotel.

There were more gendarmes, who had come from the town which was the only one of any size on the island, about four miles inland. They called out the name of the young fisherman but he was not present. The Juge de Paix shrugged his shoulders and said: "They never turn up."

In the meantime one of the gendarmes who had been poking about outside came in and whispered to the Juge de Paix who called out: "Is the owner of Sigma car number HD 12486 here?"

I jumped up; hoping that things were moving at last.

"Yes," I cried eagerly.

"Well, young man, you have no *plaque d'identité* on the dash board of your car."

"*Plaque d'identité*? I didn't know . . . . "

"Of course not. Never mind, you can pay the contravention now. It is only a matter of 80 francs. Constable, collect 80 francs from the young man."

Thinking that I was about to receive 5,000 in notes for the car from the young fisherman who was about to have a baby, I forked out willingly enough. But it soon became apparent that the fisherman was sticking to his nets that day; and at lunch-time the Juge de Paix shrugged his shoulders again and closed the proceedings.

This meant that I had to return by way of Tours to return the car to the garage, instead of posting them the money and going straight to Paris by train and on to England.

My book was finished and I felt sure it would shake the world. I said goodbye to Charles Prince, who dangled his pince-nez on a gold chain and smiled indulgently on me, then gripped me by both lapels of my coat, in order to emphasize some point about the Young Plan, and off I went.

I was sorry to leave Noirmoutier, where I had been in much better health and therefore much happier than in Touraine. All the colour plates I had taken of the French châteaux were away at Lyons being processed by the makers; but I had the huge camera with me and this was stuffed in the *coffre* at the back of the car, where the old fisherman had expected to be made to ride by his son.

I drove at low tide, across the road to the mainland and reached the vicinity of Angers by lunch-time. I had seen enough gendarmes for the time and did not want to see any more in Angers, so I stopped at a wayside inn outside, and left the car in the sun. I had just received my soup and was waiting for it to cool, when I heard a 'toot, toot,' on the rubber handled hooter of my car. I leant sideways to peer round the door post and there, sure enough, were two gendarmes beside it. I went out full of forebodings.

"Ah!" said one of them. "You have no *plaque d'identité*."

"I know all about that," I said, "but I paid a contravention for it yesterday."

"Where?"

"In Noirmoutier."

"When were you summoned?"

"Yesterday."

"How could you be summoned yesterday and pay the fine yesterday? The law does not work as quickly as that."

"Oh yes it does in Noirmoutier," and I explained about the fisherman.

"Oh? So it is your own car."

"No. It belongs to a garage in Tours."

"And you were trying to sell it in Noirmoutier?" The gendarmes exchanged significant glances, and their black waxed moustaches twitched.

"I had an arrangement with the garage in Tours to sell it above a certain sum."

"Where is your *Carte d'Identité*?" the gendarmes were getting more fierce.

"*Carte d'Identité*?"

"Every person resident in France for more than sixty days must have a *Carte d'Identité*." (My soup, I thought, is getting cold.)

"But I've only been here fifty-nine days and I am leaving tomorrow."

"Indeed? Then you have your passport."

"Yes," and I produced it.

In the meantime the other gendarme was rummaging in the boot of the car. Suddenly he shouted. "Un apparet," and dragged out the great mahogany camera.

"Where is your *carte de commerce*?" demanded the first gendarme.

"*Carte de commerce*? But I am not a professional photographer. I have been taking coloured pictures of the châteaux of Touraine."

"Touraine!" he said scornfully, "and you came from Noirmoutier and the coast. Where are your photographs?"

"They are all at Lyons at the factory of the Autochrome Lumière Company, being processed."

The gendarmes looked at each other with significance. They bent over the passport together. Finally they straightened up and one said to the other:

"The boy has not landed in France at all."

"Not landed in France?" I protested. "Where do you think I am standing now?"

"None of your lip. You have no entry stamp."

"It must be somewhere," I said and searched for it. The mark had been stamped half over another and the gendarme grunted, as if still unconvinced that I was in France at all. The other one had now hauled out my green canvas suitcase.

"If you open that," I warned him, "it will take you all afternoon to shut it."

"Never mind." The lid sprang open, and he felt round inside. Suddenly his hand gripped a solid contraption and he brought it out. It was a folding trouser press.

"What is this?" he demanded ominously.

What is the French for a folding trouser press?

"*A machin pour presser les pantalons*," I hazarded. (The soup by now must be quite cold.)

"You're coming along with us to the police station in Angers," the senior gendarme said with finality.

"Why?" I said.

"There are spies everywhere," he replied darkly.

"Spies!" This was worse than I had expected. "Look!" I said, "have a look at this," and I produced a letter of introduction to the French authorities, which I had fortunately thought of getting at the same time as my others for Italy and other European countries before I left Australia.

"Ah!" they said, brightening a little. "Why did you not show us this in the first place?"

"How was I do know you were going to take me for a spy?"

'Well, it so happens that we are looking for one on this very road today. He is coming from Nantes and has been photographing the fortifications no doubt. Naturally we thought you must be that one. Sorry, Monsieur." They stepped back and saluted smartly.

"But another time," one of them said, determined to get in a parting shot, "do not park you car in a *carré-four*."

"A crossroads." I looked at the fork in the dusty road where the inn stood at the junction and said, "Oh, all right. I will move it."

When I got back into the cool room, where the soup had a greasy skin over it with a cold metallic gleam, the proprietress ejaculated:

"Gendarmes! In France we say 'to be a gendarme one must be strong and stupid'." (*Forte et bête*.)

After all this I was thankful to reach England; although I look back on those two months by myself in France as a happy time.

It was natural, I suppose, that I should fall in at Oxford with those undergraduates who had been at the same preparatory school as myself in England, like Henry Blyth and Donald Rooke, or at King's with me in Australia, like Sydney Wansey who came up the same term. I also made friends with Broughton Waddy, who had the room above mine on the same staircase at Balliol. And before long I was to be very grateful for the friendships of Henry Blyth and Broughton Waddy, who did not desert me when I was almost overwhelmed by the outraged public opinion of the University.

Not everything was thunder at Oxford. Donald Rooke gathered Oriental students around him, and I found him in his rooms reading *The Wind in the Willows* to a Chinese undergraduate called Choo who reclined in pyjamas and dressing-gown. He also numbered among his friends some Indians and it must have been their influence that prompted me to found a circle called the Sceptics Club, which might have taken as its motto Diderot's dictum that one must doubt before one has a right to believe. We decided to doubt everything; and we took as our model the Emperor Frederick II of Hohenstaufern, the most curious and versatile of monarchs, who established himself with difficulty in Jerusalem where Richard Coeur de Lion had blundered and failed.*

We discovered that in substituting reason for faith we were really Averroists. Frederick II had been Averroe's first great disciple in believing that the human mind, emancipated from theological discipline could investigate the secrets of God, the soul and discover the laws of nature. We were quite confident that, working with untrammelled minds in this way, we would 'evolve a religion that will at least satisfy ourselves'! Ah, youth. All this was a bit above Henry Blyth's head. He was fair haired with a lean face and long nose — not unlike me in appearance at that time. He shared my enthusiasm for photography —

---

* I lived to publish a novel about him called *The Star of the Wind*, Constable 1974.

but made the mistake on one occasion of mentioning my name when trying to do a camera deal with Will R. Rose in the High Street. We used to go for long walks by the river and take photographs of Oxford, which certainly lent itself to the pastime. However, Henry was not above accepting the post of Third Consul in a triumvirate of Averroists in the newly formed Sceptics Club. Soon, however, we had to come down from the clouds to conduct a poster warfare connected with the new Empire Party.

Life began quietly enough, and one sees the usual pattern developing. A promising speech or two at the Union, commended in the weekly report written by the President of the Union, 'Mr. S.S. de Chair (Balliol) in a most able speech, gave us the finest defence of the United States of Europe heard during the evening; it was difficult he said, but worth obtaining, since the U.S.A. was not going to enter the League.' And a fortnight later, 'Mr. de Chair is a promising speaker with plenty of ideas.' But unknown to these good natured people *The Impending Storm* was about to break.

In my ignorance of the publishing trade, I first submitted the book to Messrs Heinemann in its written form, as it came from the pen; and was bewildered and uneasy for days when they sent it back. I then had it typed by Hunts, just across Broad Street, and sent it to Putmans because they had done well with Remarque's *All Quiet on the Western Front*. This time the answer was more helpful; they said (and what balm these things are to a beginner) 'We consider your ideas very valuable and expressed in an exceptionally lucid and effective style.' They thought, however, that the book would be classed as propaganda and as such ignored by the general public; but they advised me to try Messrs Allen and Unwin who dealt with that type of work. I profited by their advice to remove some propagandist stuff about post-war youth in the preface, but in the meantime at a meeting of the Italian Club, to hear a lecture on the adventures of an English Admiral in Genoa in 1849, I met a most unusual girl called Vyvian Eyles; who admitted to having had a Sicilian lover (*lui mi consce completamente*) and was glad to find in me someone at Oxford who knew 'that Hungary exists and that Fascism is a working institution.' She came to tea in my rooms and invited me later to dine with her stepfather, D.L. Murray, an author of long standing and Assistant Editor of *The Times Literary Supplement*, who was staying at Oxford for the weekend. Murray had been writing a biography of Lord Stratford de Redcliffe and was delighted to hear that my father was his godson and had been named after him. After this he was all ears about the book, and if he did not really expect that an undergraduate fresher would be the author of a serious book on international affairs, he was quite prepared to ask his own publishers to read it. D. L. Murray was a benign Pickwickian figure, who beamed cheerily behind gold rimmed glasses; and he gave me the necessary introduction to Messrs. Constable. I received their reply on 20th December:

'We have been very much interested in your manuscript The Impending Storm and shall be very glad to publish it.

'It has been suggested that it might be a good thing to have a foreword by somebody.'

They offered a 10% royalty.

Of course I went up to see 'my publishers' that very afternoon; and if I may interject a word of advice to new authors it would be, don't drop in on your publishers too often. Preferably not at all. They want to see books, not authors; and they know much more about publishing than authors do. How often I must have wasted poor Mr. Kyllmann's time, I cannot imagine, but he was always gravely courteous, and went on seeing me in his office.

So far it was roses all, or nearly all, the way, and I went off for the Christmas vacation full of spirits to stay first with an aunt of Nigel Bowen who had a house in the Boltons, where her husband had collected two Rembrandts and a Frans Hals. Then I went off to friends of the family, the Middletons at Belsay Castle in Northumberland. I used the house later in a noval called *Red Tie in the Morning*, and described my eerie arrival at the Old Pele Tower by mistake, the 'yule cassel', instead of at the later rectangular sandstone building, built very much under the influence of ancient Greece, with pillared entrance and a central court, surrounded by marble statues. Here I was very warmly entertained by Mrs. Middleton, a Christian Science friend of my mother, and the three boys who had been at St. Michael's prep school with me. Old Sir George Middleton was ninety-four and spent most of his time in the library, or being wheeled in a chair. We went to various dances and Hunt Balls — at Hawick where I met the Grey girls, and was interested in the house because it had been the home of Lord Grey of the Reform Bill, and at Alnwick where we arrived late so that most of the girls were booked up. So I felt somewhat out of the revels and spent most of the evening in a library reading Shakespeare's *Richard II* from one of the shelves, while the dancers drifted in and out between dances.

Specimens of the maps for *The Impending Storm* followed me impressively to Belsay where the idea of a book on the next war by a boy of eighteen was viewed tolerantly by old Sir George at ninety-four.

The question of the foreword soon came to a head. Lord Lloyd had been down to Oxford to speak at the Union, just after resigning from his post as High Commissioner in Egypt, in protest at the weakness of the Labour Government. He got a tremendous reception from a packed house. He certainly impressed me, for I wrote 'at last I have found an Englishman that I can admire: Lord Lloyd; a man of dominating will, complete confidence in the infallibility of his principles and an energetic determination to carry them through or fall with them, which is what he did in the face of English defeatism in Egypt.' I wrote to ask him for advice about going out to India on some Governor's staff after I left Oxford.

He asked me to come and see him and advised me to read Indian History, particularly of the John Company period. I wrote to him from Clive Place at Esher where I spent Christmas with my father's brother Oswald and his wife and told him about Constable's suggestion of a foreword. Lord Lloyd agreed and sent Constable's an admirable short foreword. Mr. L.S. Amery who was an old friend of my father, also sent a letter for use by them, describing the book as 'written with courage and originality'. To me he wrote. 'I thought it a good effort, showing wide range of knowledge as well as originality. You will no doubt write still better stuff presently, but I think you have made a most promising beginning.'

With Lord Lloyd's foreword and Mr. Amery's letter Constable's began to plan a spectacular launching for the book. Large placards for bookstalls were prepared by their energetic American publicity Chief, Donald Desmarest, with the banner headline 'FOREWORD BY LORD LLOYD', who was the man of the moment, and Mr. Amery's tribute underneath. If it had not been for a vast, bloated, scarlet-red herring across my path, that is how it would have appeared. Lord Lloyd lost his nerve and withdrew the foreword.

For suddenly upon the political scene burst the impetuous figures of Lords Beaverbrook and Rothermere with their United Empire Party. This seemed to me, in my innocence, right up my street. Had I not just returned from the Empire, and ought not Oxford to raise the banner of such a laudable movement? It did not seem to me that I was doing anything very awful when I telegraphed to Lord Rothermere, asking for authority to open a branch of the United Empire Party in Oxford. I happened to be in London with Henry Blyth that afternoon when the front page of the *Evening News* caught my eye.

'YOUTH ANSWERS THE CALL'; and this was splashed on the front page, then: 'OXFORD UNIVERSITY TO FORM A UNITED EMPIRE PARTY ASSOCIATION'. 'A TREMENDOUS CHANCE'. I felt a sudden chill in my tummy. And there right across two columns of the front page was my telegram in heavy black type headed:

PARTY OF HIGH HOPE

Today Lord Rothermere received from Mr. Somerset de Chair, of Balliol College, Oxford, the following telegram:

'May I have your authority to found Oxford Association of the United Empire Party? Somerset de Chair.'

To this telegram Lord Rothermere sent the following reply:

'Your offer most cordially accepted. The United Empire Party is the Party of Youth. We wish to enlist as many graduates and undergraduates of the Universities as possible. From such members we hope to find suitable Parliamentary candidates. All good wishes to you. Rothermere.'

Mr. Somerset de Chair, who is a son of Admiral Sir Dudley de Chair, Governor of New South Wales, said to our *Evening News* correspondent today, 'the new Party offers a tremendous chance to the youth of the country to get away from the old and useless creeds of the old parties. It is the Party of hope and high endeavour for the youth of the country.

'I have already received scores of applicants for foundation membership of the Oxford Association. The cause is received with especial enthusiasm by Rhodes Scholars, who, coming from far away parts of the Empire, appreciate enormously the benefits of the policy of the United Empire Party.

'The Oxford Association propose to hold a big meeting, in the Union Hall before the end of the present term.'

All this double column front page was repeated in a double column in the *Daily Mail* next morning, and the following evening the *Evening News* front page was again blaring:

OXFORD'S EXAMPLE. Lord Rothermere received today the following message from Mr. Somerset de Chair, whose offer to found an Oxford University Association of the United Empire Party.

was accepted by Lord Rothermere yesterday.

'Thanks for encouragement. Oxford flocking to the United Empire Party standard.'

Was Oxford flocking? They soon were. Not to Lord Rothermere's standard, but to tear my flannel trousers off. It seemed as if the whole university jumped on me from a great height. I had overshot the target completely.

The rag began in the suggestion book of the Junior Common-room. The first front page from the *Evening News* was torn out and pasted in under the date 25.2.30 with the help of the flaps of Balliol J.C.R. envelopes. Across it was written in ink capitals:

B U M P H

and underneath by another hand
NO -------------- TOO ROUGH
Others added comments on the page below,
CAN THIS GO ON?
and
BY THOR NO ANY HOW IT IS ALL COCK AND HOT AIR
The entries flowed on,
Sir,

May I call attention to my able Lieutenant, Mr. Somerset de Chair?

Yours, Beaverbrook.

Sir,

May I call attention to my able Lieutenant, Mr. Somerset de Chair.

Yours, Rothermere.

At Balliol there was a Polish graduate who had just written a learned philosophical book called *Sick Society* in which he sought to prove that society is not a healthy organisation with a sick part, but a sick organisation with a healthy part. So he came in for some of the fun.

Sir,

Perhaps their Lords Beaverbrook and Rothermere might boost 'Sick Society' with gentle persuasion.

Signed, Kraus (Dr. Phil)

Another signed 'Ahmy Gushling' said

> I won't have them poking at him like that beause he's my friend and Mussolini's, and we don't like it. Mr. President will you help me to found a Society for the Protection of Sommy? A sort of society for the Sick.

The entries rapidly grew more ribald and one quite witty, (I quoted it with great success in the House of Commons during a debate on the Empire once).

> That outpost of Empire, Australia
> Produces some curious Mammalia,
> The Kangaroo rat
> And the sheep sucking bat
> And Mr. de Chair inter-alia.

Then a pink telegraph form headed Fleet Street and addressed to Somerset de Chair, Balliol Oxford,

> Best wishes for this evening will stand Carte Blanche for buns beaverbrook bars champagne.
>
> Rothermere.

Underneath someone wrote,

> Sir,
>   The above is a forgery.
>
> Beaverbrook.

So far all this was reasonably good-natured, but there was more oil to be thrown on the fire. The *Daily Chronicle* (Later the *News Chronicle*) wrote to ask me for an article on a Fresher's impression of Oxford. Since the late Lord Birkenhead had referred to the place as degenerate, a furious controversy had started, and the *Chronicle* published my article under the dangerous heading:

SOMERSET de CHAIR A FRESHER OF EIGHTEEN, LOOKS AT THIS 'DEGENERATE' OXFORD

It was prefaced with a short item, 'Mr. de Chair of Balliol, has just published his first book, *The Impending Storm*, which deals with international relations in Europe.'

This article also was pinned into the suggestion book and with it acid comments.

All this while the advance publicity for *The Impending Storm* was gaining in tempo. Oxford was showered with leaflets from Constable, bearing a theatrical photograph of me, looking as like an impending storm as possible. So far no reviews had appeared, and no one could really judge in advance whether the book was good or bad. But Oxford had no intention of waiting to find out.

'ARE YOU FED UP WITH PETTY PARTY POLITICS?' My first poster demanded. 'IF SO JOIN THE UNITED EMPIRE PARTY, ETC.' This we pinned up on the College notice boards. But next morning the bills had all been replaced with others in similar lettering issued by a body calling itself the O.U.A.P.I.M. (The Oxford University Anti-Press Interference Movement).

I went to the printers and got some more copies of these over-printed 'Die-Hards'. And then the war entered upon a new phase.

Sandwich men appeared in the streets bearing enormous placards headed:

ENGLAND'S HOPE
SOMERSET de CHAIR
WANTS TO MEET
YOU
ABOUT THE NEW PARTY
AT HOME
BALLIOL
5 TO 6 P.M. TODAY, FRIDAY
REFRESHMENTS

Smaller versions appeared on all the College notice-boards. In despair I went the rounds (with Henry's assistance) tearing them down. But already the word REFRESHMENTS had got around. I did not see why I should wait in at the time advertised by my ill-wishers and went out to tea. The delighted crowd which had gathered for the advertised reception rang bicycle bells and sang Rule Britannia. But later in the evening some thugs began to assemble in the front of Balliol quadrangle. I emerged into the Broad from my first floor window, dropped to the street and went round to St. Johns to see a don there called Lane Poole who was some sort of relation of my mother's family. To him I confided my unhappiness, for I was beginning to feel very persecuted. "You certainly won't gain anything by running away from it," he told me in effect. "You must face your adversaries. Of course they are always up against originality. The only thing is to ignore it and they will soon give up. If they come into your room just tell them not to be silly fools and get to blazes." By the time I got back just before midnight the door of my room had been securly screwed up and clenched with enormous long nails. The junior Dean, Roger, was waiting in the lodge in an overcoat with the collar turned up.

"Some idiots have screwed up your oak," he said and found me a place in Kenneth Bell's empty rooms to sleep for the night. He lent me a pair of pyjamas. I apologised for giving him so much trouble and explained it was my fault for provoking them by writing a book.

"Why shouldn't you write a book?" he said. "These fellows ought to learn more sense. They aren't schoolboys now."

"I shall no doubt conform to the University soon," I said.

"I shouldn't conform if I were you," retorted Rodger robustly. "Here are some pyjamas. I am sorry you have been troubled. Good-night."

Fortified by Lane Poole's advice I stayed in next evening. I was writing a letter when a drunken mob burst into the room.

"We have come for your trousers."

"Help yourselves," I said with as much dignity as I could, and allowed them to remove the creaseless flannel bags while I went on addressing the envelope. They tore off the trousers in triumph and hung them to the rafters in the great dining hall of Balliol.

Next evening a second party of tipsy undergraduates came up to my room bent on the same errand of 'de-bagging' me. Upon them I turned with dignity and, according to Broughton Waddy, who happened to be with me brewing cocoa, real eloquence. Broughton described it to Henry Blyth as the finest impromptu speech he had ever heard. The gist of my ovation which lasted a quarter of an hour was simple: "I have only two pairs of trousers. One pair was taken last night. If you take the other what happens then? I shall be arrested for indecent exposure." They mumbled apologies and trooped out saying "good-night" and that really broke the back of the rag, although it went on sporadically in the Oxford Press. I wired to the organiser of the United Empire party in London protesting and he wired back.

Sorry if newspaper publicity has caused you any inconvenience. Instructions have been given to stop further references. Quite understand your difficulties.

I also went to see the editor of the *Oxford Mail* which was about to write up the 'at home' party. "If you want to say anything about me," I suggested naïvely, "write about the book. There are two kinds of publicity. Earned publicity and unearned publicity. All this stuff about me is unearned."

"What you mean," he said with a smile, "is that there are two kinds of publicity — the publicity you like and the publicity you don't like." But he suppressed the report.

The Isis printed an entertaining imaginary interview with me under the heading 'Further Interviews with the Almost-Great'.

On the occasion of Mr. S.D. Chair's reception last week, our representative was privileged to be amongst those turned away from the door. So soon, however, as he announced his business, Mr. S. Chare was all, or almost all, smiling affability. "Sit down, sit down", he murmured deferentially, closing the door in the face of two or three Empire widows and an orphan or so, "I am not surprised to see you. In fact, I have been expecting you ever since I forwarded that ch . . . "

"You see," apologised our representative, "we didn't believe you really existed. In fact, we had hoped . . . "

"Pshaw," replied our courteous if slightly nervous host, "didn't you get a trifle of mine I sent to your paper?"

"Well, yes but that was just why . . . . But come, Mr. Clare, to business. We should like to know what you propose to do about Free Trade for Oxford."

"One moment, I do beg you. You will, I hope, accept a glass of Borneo Hock and a yam fritter. Perhaps too a photograph of myself in a pose which is, I fancy, both characteristic and stimulating. Thank you, thank you. I believe you will find the wine quite remarkable." (As indeed we did.)

"And now to business. Is the movement which you at present direct and of which you are, if I am not mistaken, the sole member, affiliated to the already defunct (apparently) organisation publicised by a Mrs. Macdewl?"

"Well, not exactly. To use a little phase of my own, the dawn which then flushed pink is now inspired with a golden glitter. Whose gold it is that glitters, I may not say."

"And how far do you propose to secure the support of the Press, Mr. le Cher?"

"For that I think my personality is sufficient assurance. No de Chair was ever afraid of publicity, you know. The one thing that . . . . but no."

"And what do you mean by Empire Free Trade, Mr. le Chere?"

"Oh, YOU know. At least your readers will. Everybody is to send everybody else what they don't want themselves."

"We gather, then, from present evidence that Australia already enjoys Empire Free Trade, Mr. Chavi?"

But before we had time to say more, a glassy glitter came over our informant's eyes. He, like the Metropolitan, sensed the coming of impertinent questions as to actual facts, and was taking precautions. A moment later, the storm burst.

"Ladies and gentlemen, we are today assembled for the inaugurations . . . "

We left the room.

And there were some humorous versions of imaginary debates in the Union in the Cherwell:

The Society met on Thursday, February 27th, when Mr. Somerset de Chair (Balliol and New South Wales) moved 'that this House approves of Corporal Punishment.'

Opening, Mr. de Chair said that the subject of the debate put him in mind of a new book, The Impending Storm, which he had just written. It showed to European statesmen only too clearly whither (alas!) they were tending. They could take it and salvation or leave it; he hardly deigned to care which they did . . . . The preface was written by Mussolini, but the speaker was modest, he did not expect himself to be writing the preface to any book of Mussolini's not for several years yet. Corporal punishment abolitionists stood for flabbiness, weak-knees, hasty egotistical thinking. What was required was a strong man. Lord Rothermere had singled out the speaker as the steadiest thinker in Oxford, as the leader Youth required: surely the fact that the latter was speaking proved the correctness of the motion. He concluded by quoting a stanza from a poem concerning the tenth anniversary of the peace of

Versailles, with which he had won the school literary prize last year:

> 'Take up the schoolboys' burden
> The curses of them you serve:
> Accepting as thy guerdon
> The whacks you don't deserve.'

Lord Fauntleroy (Honourable Visitor) said that the problem bristled with difficulties. Some thinkers were in favour of corporal punishment, others opposed it. Thought was essential, and a decision not easy. Corporal punishment was in vogue in most public schools, but in few, if any, girls' schools. Frequently the recipient suffered pain, but even this was held by some to be beneficial. The House should devote attention to the matter.

Mr. Lustgarten (the President) then left his chair and poured forth a torrent of awful invective upon Mr. de Chair. So terrible was the vituperation that the latter was observed to cry; then, suddenly brushing aside his tears with a manly gesture, he pointed out to Mr. Lustgarten that he chanced to be speaking from the wrong side of the House. With dignity and with elegance the president crossed to the correct side, and commenced to pay so graceful a tribute to him that Mr. de Chair became palpably radiant: his eyes shone, and, like Odysseus, he assumed yet more godlike proportions. The president then proceeded to discuss Lord Fauntleroy. The latter's temperature is now almost normal again; he has a pleasant room in the Radcliffe overlooking the Tower of the Winds and the nurse is competent. So you didn't make your donations quite in vain.

Good old MacColl doesn't like being called Mr., and won't call us comrades. The hour (he declared) was past and had gone, and there was no reason why the workers should show any mercy. In fact corporal punishment was not enough; many would have to die before the revolution was accomplished. He might well have to kill thousands of women and children, but all was for the best, and far more pitiable things were every day being consummated by the Conservatives and those for whom Conservatism stood. In the school of the future the machine-gun, not the birch, should daily be drilled into the students. The speaker concluded eloquently: "Comrades," he cried, "let us murder the bloody sweaters."

Mr. X.Z. Krisnamayarah then proposed an amendment that capital, not corporal, punishment should be discussed. "I think this would be a capital subject," he said. "In my school O.T.C. I never was a corporal!" A humorous oration.

Messrs Playfair, Ward-Jackson, Irvine, Harrison, Wegg-Prosser, Xinamara, Priddles, Jones (of Jesus), Brodie, Haroun-al-Rashid, Pitchfork, Ramsend and the Rev. Drummond then all rose and PROPOSED different amendments. After some discussion it was agreed to combine all into a single formula, 'that this House admires the splendid lack of self-consciousness of the advocates of the United Empire Party in this University, the spirit of self-advertisement of the promoters of the balloon club and of all other things looming but vacuous, congratulates Mr. Frank Gray upon his appreciation of the sausage-balloon, and Mr. Speaight upon his existence.'

This motion was carried by acclamation at a late period in the evening. The debate was then resumed.

The Rev. Drummond made an interminable speech.

Mr. Pilkinton made an arid speech.

Mr. Weinberg made an inaudible speech.

Mr. Sopote — made a speech.

The hour for the close of the debate having arrived, a division was taken. It was observed that the teller for the Ayes, who happened to be the then Cherwell reporter, made no movement, and examination proved the miserable creature to be dead. What mysterious and unplumbable cause provoked his expiry is unknown; the House adjourned in respect for the solemnity of the occasion without the votes having ever been counted. R.I.P.

C.A.F. (pro AFC — 27.2.30)

When the proof of *The Impending Storm* arrived I sent a copy to the Master,* and expressed the hope that he would give it his blessing in public. But he was at pains to be blunt. 'My dear de Chair. If you begin to be your own publicity agent you get yourself into doing things which you regret. You are too much of a gentleman really to mean that the moral of college patriotism is that it should push one another's books over. Yet that is what you in effect say. I had heard of your book and hoped to read it and I wish you had come and talked to me about it, but you really must not ask this kind of thing of people — at least not in that way.'

With this reply in my pocket, I presented myself at the Master's house with some misgivings. But to my surprise he beamed up at me and said, "I'm so sorry I was such a brute to you, but I had to be." He

* Later Lord Lindsey of Birker.

told me to take a seat and stood with his back to the fire, one foot on the fender. He wore a tweed jacket with his academic gown over it, and baggy flannel trousers. He had a very square head with pale eyes. His attitude was always very informal.

"I was frightfully interested in your book," he said, "there is no doubt that we all want to know what your generation is thinking. The difficulty is that the impression your book gave me was not what I should have thought your generation's attitude was. I think perhaps too you have tried to be too dogmatic. It would have been better just to act as a receiving set for the impressions you get from all the different nations you know. I think you made a mistake in saying that war was inevitable. It would have been better to say that your generation could prevent it. In championing the cause of your generation I don't think the book is conceited enough. You must believe in miracles and they will happen."

The sequel to this interview was two-fold. When the book had at last appeared, the Master came up to my room with a copy of the Review of the Institute of International Affairs, (Chatham House) — to show me the review of *The Impending Storm* by G. M. Gathorne-Hardy, which is I think worth quoting as an indication of the prevailing over-confidence then felt at Chatham House about peace.

'His researches and inquiries have resulted in an attitude of complete pessimism with regard to the prospect of world-peace . . . . But it is not necessary to concur in the author's gloomy prognostication, that "the international problems of the moment can find their solution only in another war", in order to welcome his lucid and thoughtful indication of the points which support his contention . . . It will rest with him and his contemporaries to see to it that the problems which he so clearly grasps are met in a way which will falsify his predictions.'

The Master went on to pay me the compliment of saying that he would like to tutor me in politics himself. So in future I sat at his feet, imbibing subconsciously his quizzical brand of Socialism and submitting my essays to him.

But this was not before I had been through a good deal of mental suffering as a result of my ragging by the University, which also changed its tune, or at least became silent, when the book itself was available in the bookshops.

I was fortunate in the love and comfort of a very old friend of my mother's, Dame Clarissa Reid, at this time, and she invited me to stay with her at a villa she had taken in St. Raphael in the South of France. There I poured out to her my disappointment and anguish at so much persecution — and in the sunshine of early spring and in the delightful surroundings of Provence, I soon got over the shock of my reception at Oxford. But it would not be honest writing if I did not admit that the whole deluge of adverse publicity made me very sensitive to public opinion and made me pause on later occasions before taking courses which were likely to expose me to similar blasts of criticism.

It seemed a long time before the first reviews of the book appeared, (it always does) and although it received a generous amount of space, it did not become a best seller and Constable & Co. who had spent so much in advertising it declined its successor, *The Silver Lining*. They felt that Lord Lloyd, by withdrawing his foreword after a visit to the Raleigh Club at Oxford, when he was no doubt warned not to associate himself with me publicly, had upset the launching of the book on the lines they had planned — and in short that they had lost too much money over it. They had, however, arranged with a new publisher in New York, Richard Smith, to publish it in America. This and the fact that my parents were returning from Australia round the world by way of California decided me to go there for the summer vacation.

The Impending Storm achieved unexpected fame in Hungary where it dominated the front pages of all the newspapers, was translated serialized in the *Nemzeti Ujsag* and published in book form. 'England' wrote Magyarsag, 'has no need to worry for its future so long as it can produce such a prodigy in Somerset de Chair.'

Unfortunately the Hungarian press was not read in Oxford. Nevertheless, after the stormy session through which I had passed before Easter at Oxford, the summer term passed by without incident. I was awakened on a May morning by the sound of laughter and subdued conversation in the Broad, outside my window, and looking out, saw that a considerable crowd had gathered in a ring to watch the Morris dancers. These rustics, in white clothes, with their long trousers tied tightly below the knee, danced in a pattern of six, waving handkerchiefs in a manner reminiscent of the Roger de Coverley dance. They were beribboned and yet artless; and I wondered how long these old customs could continue so unselfconsciously. Later in the day they turned up at Weald Manor, Bampton, where I was spending the afternoon with the Colins. Mrs. Colins was a sister of Nigel Bowen's mother. And Mrs. Innis with whom I stayed occasionally at 28, The Boltons. I was immensely entertained one day when the parlourmaid said to Mrs. Innis, "Colonel Colins called and left a bunch of flowers for you Madam and a bag of manure for Mr. Innis." However, this was apparently no more than Innis, cultivating his considerable rose garden in London, desired. And here were the Morris dancers again on the lawn behind the old grey stone manor house, kicking up their feet in front, and dancing about, with ribbons flying and handkerchiefs waving in the hot May sunshine where the daisies were just skimming the grass, so deep in the heart of England that you could almost feel the pulse of the earth, as the dancers danced upon it.

Henry Blyth invited me to stay with him and his mother at a detached villa in Saltdean, near Brighton for Goodwood. Henry was a keen student of form and counted on making a lot of money once we got to the races. Some prudent instinct prompted me to suggest that we should buy return tickets to Chichester when we arrived at the station at Brighton. The third class carriage was crowded and facing us was a sportsman in check suit who kept doing on his knees a simple trick. This consisted of placing three cards face up, one of which was an ace; turning them down and asking anybody interested to say which was still the ace.

"This is easy," whispered Henry. "We can increase our reserves for the races."

Before I knew what was happening he had staked a pound on the elusive ace; but it had disappeared with his pound.

"Lend me a pound," said Henry excitedly. And that one too disappeared.

With our gold reserve thus reduced we got out at Chichester, the nearest station to Goodwood, and hired a car to the races. We paid for admission to the hill, where we had a magnificent view of the racecourse. Unfortunately Henry's study of the form was misleading and after two races we were confronted with the stern fact that our money was gone. Nor had we eaten since breakfast. There was talk of trading the return halves of our railway tickets, but this I strongly resisted.

"I'll tell you what," said Henry, "we shall have to borrow. There must be some friendly faces here who are susceptible to a touch."

They were hard to find. At last Henry espied a distant acquaintance on the hill who was going into the army.

"He is at the shop," Henry confided urgently as we approached this athletic individual with race glasses glued to his eyes.

"Hallo, hallo," started Henry with forced geniality. "Fancy meeting you here."

"Just came up here to get a better view of the course," said the man uncomfortably.

"Let me introduce my friend Somerset. The fact is we have run out of cash and wondered if you could lend us any," Henry said.

To make matters easier, and remembering Henry's remark that this man worked in some shop, presumably one which Henry patronised, I said:

"What shop is it that you are working in?"

The man's eyebrows rose for an instant above the eyepieces of his binoculars, like birds taking off from a humped ridge, and he walked briskly away.

"Good Lord," cried Henry in despair, seeing our only hope of lunch dropping out of sight down the hill, "didn't you know that Woolwich is called 'the Shop'?"

"Oh! That shop?"

"Never mind, there must be someone else." But there was not, or if there was he avoided us instinctively. Of course now that we had no money to invest, all Henry's fancies came streaking first past the winning post. At the end we filed mournfully and hungrily out of the gates and began the long walk of seven miles to rail-head at Chichester. It was a hot afternoon and car load after car load of successful punters passed us, with a wave. We inhaled the exhaust fumes of their cars. It seemed a long walk, and presently we passed a field of ripe corn.

"We must eat the ears of corn," I told Henry and we plucked the wheat from the tall stems and ate it. There was good precedent for such robbery by the highway, and we trudged on footsore, but in better heart clutching our return tickets. I have not been racing with Henry since then, but I have not often been nearer to the facts of life or enjoyed racing as much when going grey-toppered later on in life, in some glistening Rolls-Royce to Ascot.

*   *   *

I am continually astonished by the degree of inflation in my lifetime; to the extent that I sometimes find it difficult to credit the figures myself. But I can confirm that when I went up to Oxford in 1929, I bought at Esher, from Esher Motors — a garage on the right of the main street as you go from London to Guildford, for £50, an open Rolls-Royce 40/50 h.p. Silver Ghost Tourer of about 1921 date. It was grey and I had it re-cellulosed black, and placed a lalique glass hawk, illuminated green at night, at the rear end of the bonnet. There was a road tax of £1 per horse power, so that the Rolls-Royce was rated at £63; a formidable sum in those days. Thus as soon as a Rolls became slightly out of date there were very few buyers. One way of getting round the tax was to have it licenced as a taxi for £12, but this meant carrying a large metal plaque at the back labelled — 'Hackney Carriage', and I had not the self-confidence to do this.

I did not think of myself as a rich undergraduate, but I can see now that the ability to run a car at all was limited to few. I was in fact receiving £400 a year from my parents, to meet all educational and other expenditures, including holiday travel.

I have described the anguish I felt in my first year at the persecution I suffered over the publication of my first book *The Impending Storm* and my efforts to found an Oxford Branch of the United Empire Movement. But after a year, this upheaval was over, and I was able to enjoy myself in fairly uninhibited ways before I met my future wife in 1931, and became unofficially engaged to be married. I was still a virgin when I travelled round Europe; scorning the lures of the 'painted women' of Vienna and the invitations of the tarts in Tours. I finally succumbed to a professional hooker, who was standing by the elevator of the floor on which I was staying at the Barbizon Plaza in New York, in August 1930; shortly before my 19th birthday. She was dressed in black and looked very smart; much like any other guest. She took me back to my room. It may have been the number of dollars she asked for, that made me impotent; but she certainly did her best. The next day, I thought I would try again with the middle-aged Norwegian maid who was doing my room; and this time I was more successful.

Thus, by the time I returned to Oxford in the autumn, I was eager for more. All the world's a stage and one man in his time pays many tarts. I took advantage of the Rolls to visit London, at least two nights a week — Henry Blyth used to drive up with me most times. We would park the car in some street near Bond Street. There were no parking meters or single yellow lines; or double yellow lines. There was room to park a car almost anywhere, but you had to leave side-lights on, which led to some flat batteries. We would separate and go in search of our evening companions, in the maze of streets between Regent Street and Park Lane. It was not until 1951 that Rab Butler, the most dismal and puritanical of Home Secretaries, removed the tarts from the streets. In 1930 they stood about chatting on all the street corners of Bond Street, under the lamps. On the whole they were extraordinarily good looking. They needed to be. There was so much competition, and they never charged more than £3.00 a time, sometimes £2.00. Most of them had comfortable flats above the shops in Bond Street, Bruton Street or Curzon Street and so on. One simply chatted to one of the girls in a group; or stopped to talk to one walking briskly along the pavement, who would be obviously looking for custom. A brief enquiry as to how much and where, and you would link arms and accompany her to her flat, usually up a flight of narrow stairs, which she ascended first, showing her beautiful legs in silk stockings. Nylons did not appear until World War II. Later on I came to realise that the most attractive prostitutes seldom had to come on to the streets, as they had an established clientele. I got to know two quite exceptional French girls in this way, whom I would not have been ashamed to invite on board a yacht for a weekend party. Indeed I did, after the war, ask one of them, a red-headed French girl called Lucienne, if she would like to come down to the Harebell in the Hamble River for the weekend. She said she would love to; but would lose so much business that she would have to charge me £50.

Henry and I rarely found ourselves visiting the same girl, but there was one called McFee, who had a flat just above Aspreys, I think, whom we both liked. This was before the property developers had made private flats for girls like McFee impossibly expensive. She wore an attractive new leopard skin coat, which she said had cost £3. Leopard skins were not regarded as a very rare or much sought after fur coat at that time.

Broughton Waddy who had a room on my staircase at Balliol, sometimes came up to London with us; but as a Bishop's son and an aspiring clergyman himself, he did not indulge in our pastime. However, on one occasion he was still with me when I was going to visit a particularly attractive tart in Carnaby Street, number 52, I remember, and as I could not shake Broughton off, I said he had better come up with me and wait in the sitting-room. Unfortunately, the bedroom was only divided from it by a curtain, and Broughton teased me back at Balliol later, saying, "But that my lips are sealed, I could a tale unfold, whose lightest word would make your eyes start from their spheres, and each particular hair upon your head stand up like quills upon the fretful porpentine."

On the whole my experience of the ladies of the town before World War II was extremely satisfactory; but there was one exception, which left a deep mark on me. I was walking down Regent Street, not having so far seen any women sufficiently exciting, when I saw walking briskly towards me an exceptionally beautiful one. I hesitated for fear of making a mistake, in case she was some perfectly normal debutante walking hurriedly home, embarrassed no doubt at having to pass so many professionals. However, as we reached each other she gave me a dazzling smile; and I asked her if I could take her anywhere. She said we could take a room at the Regent Palace Hotel in Piccadilly, just round the corner. I was absolutely trembling with excitement. My luck seemed too good to be true. She was so beautiful, and so well turned out. She wanted £4.00 but I felt the extra £1.00 was well worth it in the circumstances. She helped me to register, and we went up to the room allotted to us. She had a short umbrella, which she laid on the mantelpiece. The sort that cost about 4/6d at Marks and Spencers in those days. She said she would just pop along to the bathroom. In those days not every hotel room had one opening out of it. So she asked me for the £4.00 in advance — this was quite usual — and she tripped gaily off to the bathroom. I started to undress, thinking what a tale I should have to tell Henry when we met for dinner and drove back to Oxford. If we were after midnight I should have to climb up the drain pipe outside my room, which was on the first landing to the left of the main entrance. I was thinking that it was rather extraordinary and not a little sad that such a well brought up and beautiful girl should be forced to seek a living in this way, when it dawned on me that she had been gone rather a long time for the usual preparations in the bathroom. I glanced at her umbrella, which was still where she had left it, and felt reassured. But she never returned. It was a confidence trick and I should have guessed that she was a little bit too good to be true. I must have waited three-quarters of an hour before I finally convinced myself that she had fooled me into parting with £4.00* plus the cost of the room (about 12/-) for the outlay of a cheap umbrella. She was not a disgrace to her profession, or at least not to that trade, because she was obviously not a tart, but a confidence trickster. On the whole during these years when I was desperate for relief, and had to find it at least two or three times a week, I found the fraternity, or rather the sorority, unfailingly kind and conscientious. But then at 19, fair-haired and fit, one is possibly quite attractive oneself. I remember the girl I had drinks with in the night club in Budapest. I had asked her to take me home. She said, "Don't do it. Tonight it is fun. But *Morgens haben Sie den Krank*." (Tomorrow you will have caught the disease.) I never had any occasion to worry about my health in London with the West End tarts, because they were fastidious and lived in luxurious surroundings. And AIDS had not even been heard of. Also the sort of girls one met at dances were supposed to arrive at the marriage bed as virgins, so they were not much help.

I gave up frequenting tarts after they were swept off the streets. The whole business went underground somewhere in Soho, and I never felt

* Half my weekly allowance for food, clothing, education and travel.

inclined to penetrate those sleazy strip-joints. I think that the decline of the British Empire coincided with the removal of these healthy distractions from the heart of London's West End. When you start sweeping things under the carpet you end up with a really sordid mess. But during my second marriage to Carmen, and my time with her before it in 1947 and 1948, she accepted from the beginning the need for my regular diversion, and in Paris gave me one as a birthday present. On another occasion in London, dressed in her Paquin gown from Paris, she accompanied me, when herself indisposed, to visit the red-headed Lucienne in a flat on the third floor of George Street, Hanover Square, next to St. George's Church. She had a superb figure as well as long red hair down to her shoulders, and used to come to the door in her high heeled shoes and nothing else. (I always think of her as Petra — rose red titties, half as old as mine.) Lucienne had a peep-hole to see what kind of visitors she was receiving, but she was not in the least disconcerted to find Carmen with me. Indeed she offered to entertain her as well. But Carmen took advantage of a horsewhip which she found lying around, to work off her feelings on me, while I was too preoccupied with Lucienne to protest. I reproached her on the way down to Virginia Water for hitting me so hard.

I said, "You told me that you would love me forever."

"Forever is a long time," she replied. But for all that, until she ran off with a naval officer, who was navigating my yacht, Carmen and I had a very full and happy relationship. She certainly understood men.

I was separated from her when I visited the Far East to lecture to British troops in 1948, and I remember a memorable night in Bankok; which every man should visit once in his life.

I gave up visiting tarts before my third marriage in 1958. Not only were the tarts disappearing from the streets where they had paraded under the eyes of fairly benevolent bobbies, but the field was being increasingly invaded by amateurs.

I wrote a short story about a newspaper running a competition to see if a virgin could get as far across England as in Alfred the Great's time, with a bag of gold and arrive with both commodities intact. The difficulty was to find a virgin.

The only time I tried my luck with a professional tart again was when my third marriage was breaking up and I found myself in Taiwan, having flown there from Hong Kong, to see the Imperial Museum, to which Chiang Kai-shek had taken four train loads of Chinese works of art in 1948.

I came to Taipei after visiting the Cambodian Temples of Ankor

Wat, and Ankor Tom, in 1969, while my third wife, Tessa, was on her way to visit her sister in the Solomon Islands.

I had been told that the whole business of refreshment had been reduced to a fine art in Taipei. So on arrival I asked the taxi-driver, what the form was. He said he knew just the girl and would collect me from the President Hotel, after I had given drinks to a friend of Allison Werner. The driver took me down to the commercial part of the town and left me for a minute while he went to collect his friend. He said she worked in a department store. I had got rather tired of waiting an hour or so for women who said, "Don't nag me, it will only make me slower," when they were dressing or making up to go out. So I thought I would not have to wait long in Taipei. But after three-quarters of an hour, parked beside the kerb, the driver reappeared and apologised for his friend taking so long. It did not seem to me that she could be all that enthusiastic, but no doubt she had been roused from bed and told to dress. The idea was for me to take her to an Italian restaurant (of which the proprietor was no doubt a friend of the driver) for dinner and then back to my room at the hotel. Eventually she appeared — a pleasant Formosan of no great beauty or distinction, apologising for being so long, — her hair, etc. She could have been one's wife. The driver left us at the door of the Italian restaurant, where I treated her to the best meal they could produce. Over coffee I said that I was looking forward to some more of her company; and she explained that she was indisposed; but thanked me for the excellent dinner, and said she would telephone a Japanese friend of hers, who would oblige. She went into a call-box; and emerged to say her friend was on the way. The Japanese girl turned up in a few minutes and joined us for coffee. She was reasonably attractive, and the Formosan bade us good-night at the entrance of the hotel. There was a houseboy at a sort of reception desk on the landing upstairs who, I thought, eyed my companion with some disapproval. The Japanese girl had been punctilious about making me sign her in at the reception desk downstairs, as they are very carefully watched and controlled. Considering I had only just flown in from Hong Kong after spending ten days with one of the most attractive women in the world (my third wife) I acquitted myself fairly well with the Japanese girl! After we had taken a bath together, she left about 2 a.m.

Next morning the houseboy on the landing said, "That girl last night, very disappointing — no? Very small breasts. Why didn't you ask me? I send you girl with big breasts." So I reflected ruefully, that is the form in Taiwan; I could have saved myself a lot of trouble and a long wait. Since then I resigned myself to the amateurs who were becoming daily more competitive.

CHAPTER 7

Monday, 14th July 1930

A fog hung close about the *Bremen* as she neared the Western shores of the Atlantic this morning.

As the time of arrival is continually postponed I grow increasingly apprehensive as to what will be happening to dear Pearl* who has written that she will be down to meet me.

Suddenly beside me a voice that makes my heart jump and beat madly — "Here you are" — "Pearl" — "Somerset" a slight hesitation then an ecstatic embrace and the softest kiss I have ever known. She was the last to see me off from Sydney harbour a year ago last March. We held a long yellow streamer together till it broke. Now it is joined up again. Has she changed? What of her dramatic rise to theatrical fame in *The First Mrs. Fraser* on Broadway, what of her £50 a week salary? No, she is simpler than ever and being so far from everyone, almost as glad to see me as I her.

We take the subway into New York, exchanging views and opinions as hard as we could go; Pearl talking in her high rapid bird-like voice. Her brain moves so fast. It sparkles all the time. She has reserved a room for me in a newly completed hotel, The Barbizon Plaza, near her club. The price is very reasonable for New York only 3 dollars 50 for room and breakfast (this latter an innovation here). "You must try to get all other standards out of your head while you are here. Prices are simply awful. You know my salary — well I manage to put half of it away every week but the rest simply doesn't get anywhere." She comes up to my room which is not ordinarily allowed for a woman, to see me safely ensconced. It is lovely; a private bathroom (all rooms in New York have). I throw my coat on the bed and tip the bellboy who brings up my bags, generously. It is all too wonderful. We look down at the street only ten floors below. Pearl — "Isn't it too marvellous to think you are here." Somerset, "!!!" I hug her again. I can't help it, but I only get the cheek

* Pearl Appleton

74

this time. We are to have dinner at her club.

She points out the Park Central Hotel where a big gangster was shot not long ago. Broadway looks very dingy by daylight compared to the other clean stateliness of the skyscrapers on 5th Avenue. These are less congested than I expected. Moreover the sidewalks on Broadway are all broken and dirty under pent-houses. While we are at tea Phyllis* says we must be perfectly clear on one point; that all expenses are to be shared equally 50/50, at the time of paying, and that I must not have any extra expense on her account. She also warns me against buying anyone flowers, as they are a prohibitive price compared to anywhere else — obviously a hint not to bother sending her a bouquet at the theatre.

Until recently I was supposed to be in love with her sister, Bonita, to whom I had been writing reams without response.

On Friday we had an exciting lunch at Sardi's, the famous theatrical restaurant. 'Boy' Halloran and an American, Bill Westbury who had been brought along because he had a car, were with us. All of us (not counting the American) arrived exuding excitement. It was our lucky day. Metro Goldwyn Mayer had come forward agreeing to Pearl's demands for a whole year's contract. Boy had been offered an excellent part at a bettter salary in a new play, and I came in loaded with five columns about me, (including a portrait reproduced from Pearl's copy) in that very afternoon's leading New York papers — 3 columns with the photo were in the *Telegram* headed 'Oxford Freshman, 18, famed as Author Forsees New, Major War in Europe.' And stating elsewhere 'the young author admitted that he will extend his stay in New York to be near an old friend. She's Miss Phyllis Elgar, the second wife in *The First Mrs. Fraser* now one of the legitimate attractions on Broadway.' *The Sun*, begins, 'Author, 17, here with a mission. Somerset de Chair from Oxford sounds a call to the youth of the world.' The jovial cartoons around Sardi's seemed to beam down upon us. After a drive up Park Avenue, they dropped me with these press introductions at Simon and Schuster, publishers on 4th Avenue to whom I then offered *The Silver Lining*, as Richard Smith who published *The Impending Storm* here, though a charming friend, is not very well known as a publisher. In the meantime a snag was found in Pearl's producer O'Brady who refuses adamantly to release her from her contract in *The First Mrs. Fraser* unless M.G.M. will pay 5,000 dollars for it. This is not cleared up yet, and so I have to leave for San Francisco without her. On Saturday after

---

* Phyllis Elgar was the stage name by which she was known in New York.

trying the New York branch of Kodak without much encouragement, I took the invention for viewing cine motion picture films through the lens of the camera — without projector electric light or screen — and for which I had applied for a patent before leaving London — to the Zeiss 'Kinamo' camera. The manager was most intrigued and called up the mechanic (a German) to look at it so that he could make a duplicate of the changed part, asked me to send him a copy of the patent specification and said he would send the adaptor straight to the works in Germany, who would make me an offer for the rights if it was practicable.

Wednesday, 30th July 1930

Westward ho! and Family hi! San Francisco after a gruelling four days in the train from New York, during which I wrote some more scenes of my play, *Alive*, and met a commercial traveller in silks who showed me the ropes on arrival and lent me the use of his room at the Sir Francis Drake until I located my family at the Mark Hopkins.

A hearty embrace from my sister, Elaine, and I am led into the breakfast-room where Mother is breakfasting with a short, nuggety little man with grey hair, searching light blue eyes and a tanned skin.

She introduces me to the little man, who has been standing up unobstrusively, while we reunite. Now we shake hands. "This is Major Burnham," my mother says. "The greatest scout that ever lived. My word, when you hear of some of the things he has done. You will have to read his book. He has been reading yours. Lord Roberts and Rhodes both sent for him when they were hard put to it with the Boers. He knew Grandad."

After my humble mode of living with Phyllis in New York it made me feel rather like the prodigal son coming back, at about the time he did eat of the husks that the swine did eat. However, it was evident that the family, after months of travelling in viceregal state, needed husk treatment badly. Accordingly as the shadows of night were falling and the cold breeze was blowing up from 'The Gate', I forestalled the family going into the hotel dining-room for a ten dollar meal and led them, with the exception of Mother who had remained upstairs, down to the nearest drugstore where I sat them on four stools against the counter and stood over them as they consumed milk shakes. And they loved it, feeling all the while they were doing something they shouldn't.

"My Aunt," said Dad, "wouldn't the *Daily Guardian* (of Sydney) give something to see us in here." And, thence on foot — the heretics had the audacity to try to take a taxi — to the beautiful Fox Theatre, next to some in Sydney, the finest I have seen (not excluding New York). It was Greta Garbo in *Romance*.

A long drive brought us into the redwoods, groves of towering red barked trunks which were seedlings when Kufu was getting to work on his Great Pyramid. At picnic lunch Major Burnham immaculately dressed, ate nothing, arguing that food only made one slow, and it was hunger that made a man energetic. We got him to talk more about his experiences while we chewed chicken drums. He told the story he could read from a deserted camp, how an Apache Indian would lie up on a rock, surveying the country for ten days at a time, never moving from his point of vantage, living only on a little wheat and dried meat, lighting a fire of two twigs at night and shielding it with his blanket, to warm himself during the cold night.

Monday, 4th August 1930

Hollywood — Our introductions took the whole drove of us into The United Artists Studios to lunch with Mary Pickford in her bungalow on the lot. She is very charming and petite, but not very pretty to look at in ordinary day clothes. Yet it is significant of her firm success that, presenting the appearance she did when I first saw her, in the cine film I made of her, when she came outside with Mother and Elaine afterwards, she looks simply lovely. The party at lunch was interestng. Mary Pickford, petite, polite, even a little pathetic, as Atlas must have seemed after he had been carrying the universe on his shoulders for a few thousand years. At the other end of the table was Schkenk, Norma Talmadge's husband (divorce, it is rumoured, impending) and a very big figure in the film world from the business point of view, a Jew of course. So was Sam Goldwyn, another film magnate, sitting opposite me. Syd Graumann who looks very like Charlie Chaplin must look in real life came in and stayed to talk to Mother about the famous 'Chinese Theatre' which he built. All five de Chairs are present at the table, and Mother apologizes to Mary Pickford for inflicting such a drove, to which Mary replies a little wistfully, "Why no. If only I had some children I should be so proud of them I should want to show them to everybody."

In the meantime we all walk round to one of the indoor sets on which they are working. Mary says she has given up work on her film as she isn't satisfied with it and is going to sign on for a contract with someone else for the first time in fifteen years. During that time she has been her own manager. The atmosphere in the lofty tin building is very peaceful.

78

There is no rush excitement, no shouting. Dwarfed by the lofty scaffolding and hanging draperies (to dull the sound) is an interior scene in a castle, complete on three sides, but without a roof. Arc lights are ranged round the top and a lamp shines through the fireplace from behind. We are sitting in a row on canvas backed stools labelled Miss Pickford, Mr. Ziegfield, etc. Mary is between me and Mother, and explains to us what is happening. Presently a ravishingly beautiful woman, an English girl and from the first an obvious thoroughbred, dressed in a long white satin dress and made up with a warm sun-burned complexion and lacquer red lips, is brought up and introduced to us as Miss Laye, the heroine of *Bitter Sweet*. She says she is terrified as it is her first film, but feels all nice and tanned by reason of her make-up.

"What is the piece called?" asked Mary.

"Lily," replied Miss Laye, "but I think it's a silly name. I expect they'll change it before it's put on. I'm afraid I must be going now," and saying goodbye she moves off to her little dressing-room behind us in the set.

"It's really Lili, a French name," Mary said after she had gone. "I know what she must be feeling like, her first time. Its just like jumping into ice. I think I had better not be here when she goes on as I'm afraid it might make her a little nervous." And no wonder, for a girl, even Evelyn Laye, to make her first film in front of the great Mary Pickford. So Mary moves off, Graham escorting her back to her bungalow, when the scene is set.

Friday, 8th August 1930

"Goodbye, then, until Friday." Those had been Miss Pickford's last words to me. And sure enough her big Phantom Rolls-Royce came for us at The Ambassador at about 7 p.m. and drove us out to Pickford, the beach 'Pickfair' at Santa Monica beach. Mary had rung up to say that she herself would be a little late, but that we were welcome to go ahead and bathe in the pool if we wished. This we decided not to do as we were already in evening dress (dinner jackets). Mary was not long after us in arriving and, after shaking us warmly by the hand ran up to change and came down again looking perfectly lovely with her golden wavy hair and pink dress. Hitherto I had only seen her in a tight hat. The beach house was small but plentifully supplied with rooms, and furnished with great taste. Mary sat on a stool with her back to the fireplace talking to Dad and me about the film she was going to make next, *Kiki*, in which she was to play a French part. She said that the only time she undertook to speak on the radio, in New York, she completely lost her nerve and began to stammer. Next day she got letters of sympathy, and parcels of wholemeal bread from people who said she must be needing vitamins, being away from her home and so on. But when she had to speak in French, she felt entirely self-possessed and spoke with great fluency. She hoped that *Kiki* would be a success accordingly. In *Coquette* she played a southern part and consequently had to assume a southern accent, which people abroad took to be her normal voice and thought her very common. In reality her voice is very pleasant and soft. But she said, "The talkies have made a great change. In the old days of the silent screen, when I was shown in Germany, I was a German to them, or in France a Frenchwoman. Now I am only an American and they don't like me any more." Presently Douglas Fairbanks arrived with a couple of friends, and at once fell into a genial conversation with Mother and Elaine. At dinner I was up at his end of the table and listened to him. He is very jovial but shows the signs of advancing years. He says his nerve isn't what it was. The other day he tried to do some stunts on the wing of an aeroplane, and didn't feel a bit comfortable as he would have done years ago. From the other end of the table I heard Mary saying that when she was at Fontainbleu, the guard insisted on her sitting on Napoleon's throne. At first she refused as she thought it absolute sacrilege but the guard said, "No you must. He was just your height." At which I chimed in, "Yes he must have been. He was just five feet two."

"Well I'm five feet two in my heels," said Mary, "and Napoleon's throne was the only chair I've ever sat in, and had my feet on the ground." Then she imitated the way Napoleon always used to sit with his head bent on his chest even when he was talking to people. It wasn't till after dinner when the ladies went upstairs, and the men drifted out on to the veranda that Doug began to get really reminiscent about his films. He had told Dad and me before dinner about how he had been held up by a burglar a few nights ago (as a matter of fact we had read about it in the paper) in the very room where we were standing. He showed us the curtain where he crept upon the man and where the revolver had been stuck into his ribs. And how the man emerged to find it was Douglas Fairbanks and said, "Jesus Christ it's you. You know we hate to do this to you."

And Doug said, "That's all right, what do you want?"

"Some dough."

"All right, I'll go upstairs, only please don't follow as you'll wake the missus."

"Now don't you try to pull any of your stunts on us," said the burglar. "We've seen you on the movies." But Doug gave his word. He was terrified the man would want to go upstairs, as all Mary's jewels were lying about on the dressing-table. Even then the man shadowed him upstairs and made him put the money (100 dollars) on the stairs. There were two others outside the window too. Now Doug told us of some of his exploits in making his films. "In *Robin Hood*," he said, "we spent months and months on research work, and I had a committee of my very English friends like Dickie Mountbatten, to vet everything we did so as to make sure it wouldn't be disagreeable to England, seeing that it was her legend. Then I had an Indian teach me archery for five months. Do you remember the scene where I jump on to the top of the curtain and slide down to the bottom? Well I didn't know what was going to happen the first time so I got all the cameras going and let fly. It turned out to be as easy as pie and all the kids round the studio were doing it next morning. Well, you only saw the times I hit it off. It's only a few inches wide and on the move you know. But the greatest difficulty we had was over the tournament. You remember the tournament in which I have to unhorse Sir Guy of Gisbon for the Lady's honour and all that? Well, after all her stirring words about honour, etc., we thought we must have a really effective collision and the best way to do that was to do just what they did in the old days. So I got all dressed up in armour and padded up and we had another chap, a big cowpuncher, fixed up in medieval armour too and he said 'What do we do now?' So I said 'You level your lance at me and I'll do the same at you and gallop full out at each other with the cameras going and see what happens!' And we did, and the lances were splintered and both of us shot off like rockets. Only, when the film was shown it just looked like two men leaving their saddles. So then I told the cowpuncher to miss me with his lance, and I'd try knocking him off. But that only turned out like a man falling off his saddle which wasn't any use at all after this woman's stirring appeal. So we were at our wit's end. Then one of the mechanics suggested that we calculated just where the horses met and fasten a bobbin of piano wire just that length to the horse, and another wire to the saddle and another to me, and to use a rearing horse too. Well, we tried that, having nearly broken our necks doing the proper things, and sure enough it looked marvellous on the film. Just when the horses met, the bobbin of wire ran out and the horse was pulled over backwards, the saddle flew off, and the rider crashed on to the ground. Then it really did look worthy of the lady's honour."

Doug told us many stories like this about the *Black Pirate*, when he split the sail and so on. He said he didn't think much of the talkies, but thought some young man would come along from right outside the business and see what it really meant. "The only thing so far," he said, "that's come out of the talkies, is Mickey Mouse, there's real genius behind that."

We visited Major Burnham in his own home at Passadena; a house curiously piled up on different levels, with much plain wood boarding inside. Upon one such wall hung an old repeater rifle; a precision weapon of about 1896.

"That is the rifle with which I shot the M'Limo," he said.

"Tell us the story," I urged him.

He reached up for the rifle and handed it to me to examine while he picked up the tale again.

His early adventures during a black uprising in Rhodesia, seem to me to be of such absorbing interest and so relevant to more recent conditions, that I have decided to reproduce his account here, of which, as the Speaker of the House of Commons says when reading the Queen's Speech, for greater accuracy I have procured a copy.

"It was in 1896," Burnham said, "on the 25th March to be exact when I landed in Cape Town. The Matabele had risen again and there were two cablegrams from Lord Gifford on behalf of the British South Africa Company — which administered what is now Rhodesia — ordering me to rush off to Bulawayo, regardless of expense. The swift and easy conquest of Matabeleland by a handful of pioneers in the first war had misled the new colonists into believing that the black question was settled for all time. It is almost impossible for the white race to grasp, even in a slight degree, the motives actuating the black. There was one inscrutable factor which even the wisest of the officials did not fully take into account — the ancient power of the priesthood. Here were people given more liberty than they had ever known before, the slaves all freed, labour paid in corn, lands held in safety, and taxes lighter by far than those levied on any white man in the empire. But let one cabbalistic word be whispered in the ear of a servant by an emissary of the M'Limo (the mouthpiece of God) and he became as a bit of grass swayed by an invisible wind. All the white man's kindness and the benefits of good government were swept from his mind. Faint rumours drifted into Bulawayo that the Kaffirs were restless and gathering in great numbers in the hills. Native servants were absent at night and red-eyed and listless by day. It became known that great dances, like the

Ghost Dances of the American Indians, were going on in the mountains and caves of the Matoppos. We learnt afterwards that the M'Limo, the great high priest of the Matabele natives, had commanded through the smaller chiefs that on a certain night of full moon, all servants should rise against their white masters all over Rhodesia. In every case the entire family should be killed. The massacre was to be complete; not one white man woman or child was to be spared. What upset the M'Limo's plans was the zeal of certain young warriors on the Insesi River, forty-five miles from Bulawayo. Instead of waiting for the full moon, they began killing the settlers three days in advance. The whites, hastily fortified themselves, but it was a desperate situation and hundreds were massacred. At Bulawayo we were a frontier community of a few thousands shut up in a wilderness five hundred miles from a railroad. Our sole means of communication was ox teams, and at this very moment we had to be scourged with rinderpest, which attacks all cud-chewing animals. Whole spans of big, strong Dutch oxen dropped dead in the yokes, and their precious loads were left to be looted by the natives. More than eight thousand animals died in three weeks along our only line of supply — the road to rail head at Mafeking. Some of the last of this great line of wagons managed to reach Bulawayo with staggering dying oxen, just before the native uprising. Our little daughter Nada, not yet three years old, died from the hardship of the siege."

It was the death of his little daughter that made Burnham merciless when he came face to face with the M'Limo, whom no white man as yet had set eye on. Major Burnham resumed his story.

"One day in June 1896, a young man called Armstrong came through the lines. He said that a certain Zulu who had a Matabele wife had betrayed to him the location of the M'Limo's cave in the Matoppos. The reason for this treachery was personal hatred of the M'Limo. Armstrong had come to propose to me that we go together, find this cave and kill the M'Limo and put an end to the source of all our troubles with the natives.

"General Carrington then gave his instructions to Armstrong and me and impressed upon us that we were not ordered on this enterprise, but that it was entirely a volunteer venture on our part. His final words were 'Capture the M'Limo if you can. Kill him if you must. Do not let him escape.'

"There was small need for that last injunction. Constantly before my enraged vision rose the picture of my wife vainly holding to her breast our dying Nada.

"Armstrong had secretly arranged a rendezvous for us with his mysterious Zulu informant. By turning a rock in a certain way, he arranged a sign indicating the time and place for the meeting (a method of communication also in vogue among our American Indians). After the sign was set, we undertook the difficult task of a preliminary scout to locate the M'Limo's cave from the description given by the Zulu. There are many caves in the Matoppos; fortunately, the one we sought was not many miles distant from Mangwe. The country was full of trails.

"Our first effort, made at night, failed to locate the cave. So at break of day we tried working along on foot, screening ourselves from observation with bunches of grass when in the grass and with branches when in the scrub. In this way we got a general idea of the mountain that held the fateful cave. It was a rough granite pile, perhaps a thousand feet high and three-quarters of a mile in length. Over its dome-shaped mass great boulders lay scattered, many of them the size of an ordinary house. Bushes, scrub, and grass grew in every crevice where there was a handful of soil, though there were many masses of granite as devoid of vegetation as the Pyramids.

"At last we found the entrance to the cave, about half-way up the mountain, in a mass of detached boulders among some scrub, and from it a zigzag path descended to the base of the mountain where there was a level space of hard-beaten clay used as a ceremonial dancing floor and wide enough to accommodate a thousand natives at one time. In front of this floor we saw about one hundred Zulu huts of a shape used for ceremonial purposes and not ordinary dwellings, for, unlike the Matabele and Mashona living huts, these were thatched with grass clear to the ground.

"The prospect of ever gaining entrance to this cave unobserved appeared hopeless. Over the numerous trails were passing many goat herders and women carrying grain and supplies to the villages that lay further on. At any moment, we might run into a party of fully armed warriors. Our method of procedure was for Armstrong to hold the horses well hidden in a clump of scrub or deep in the six-foot grass along the spruits while I worked out on foot a route for the next advance and another safe spot to hide the horses. When this was done, I would return to Armstrong and we would advance, carefully brushing out our horse-shoe marks as they crossed the trail. In this way, we kept our mounts available for quick escape in case we should run into a band of warriors. We observed the boulders and the bush that marked the end of the zigzag trail, and we believed that by coming in from the south-east end of the mountain and covering ourselves with grass, we could then slip from boulder shade to bush screen undetected. Favoured by a breeze that would make all things quiver slightly, we could even cross certain bare spots that were in full view of the village at the base of the hill.

"Having ascertained so much, we returned to Mangwe and awaited with keen impatience the arrival of our Zulu informant. He duly appeared, having read the rock sign, and he then gave us the promised details of the M'Limo's plans. This cave, we were told, was not the residence of the M'Limo but his temple, and the god would certainly strike dead any man except the M'Limo who should put his foot inside it.

"Our Zulu now held us in the hollow of his hand.

"We left Mangwe before dawn, following the route scouted before and repeating our previous methods. We hid our horses in a clump of scrub and high grass as near the village below the cave as we dared. We tied their heads high and left no metal to clink or gleam on the saddle. From this cache, by utmost caution and favoured by the hoped-for breeze, we gradually worked along the side of the mountain to the cave above the zigzag path. Though often in plain sight except for our grass coverings, we were unnoticed by the numerous goatherds or by the women who were preparing the huts for the feast to come, fetching quantities of native beer and filling the earthenware jars. After two hours spent in slowly working along the short distance from our cached horses, we managed to skip inside the great cave; moving at once into deep shadow, so as to see out clearly without being seen. Soon we would discover whether or not we had been duped. After watching for more than an hour, we saw the Ring Kops coming from the huts at the foot of the kopje, just as the Zulu had said they would. The path leading to the cave made several turns and at these turns were poles smoothed off to serve as seats. The Ring Kops stopped at these stations.

"Then I saw with surprise that a man striding in advance of the others was not a Matabele at all, but a pure Makalaka, one of the ancient people of the country. He separated from the Ring Kops and kept on alone, moving higher and higher up the path to the cave; pausing at certain points along his ascent to make cabbalistic signs and utter prayers, as if he were a high priest preparing to meet the god supposed to dwell inside the cave and for whom the great M'Limo acted as mouthpiece. We learned later that, when anyone would speak at the entrance of this cave, those outside would hear a booming of the voice, faint at first as if at a distance, and then growing much louder. This echo or ventriloquial quality was used by the crafty M'Limo to awe the

Matabele into deadly fear and the implicit belief that they heard indeed the very voice of their god.

"Now I gazed fully upon the M'Limo as he was about to enter the cave. He was a strong, active man, perhaps sixty years old, with short cropped hair; rather sharp-featured for a Negro, and of a mahogany tint rather than the Nilotic black. His face was forceful, hard, cruel, and very wide between the eyes. He was not dressed in snake skins, charms, or any of the ordinary equipment of the witch doctor; neither did he have about him any article whatever of white manufacture.

"Here was the author of all our woes. Because of him, my little daughter was dead and the bones of hundreds of brave men and good women were scattered on the veldt by hyenas. Carrington's command, 'Capture him if you can; kill him if you must,' rang in my ears. The moment had come for action; but after all, it was young Armstrong's skill that had located our arch-enemy, and I knew Armstrong intended never to ride back to Bulawayo until the M'Limo was dead. I whispered, 'Armstrong, this is your work. When he enters the cave, you kill him.'

" 'No,' he replied. 'You do it.'

"So as the M'Limo came in I made a slight sound and gave him his last chance to turn the white man's bullet to water. I put a bullet under his heart.

"It would have been impossible to capture him alive, even if we had chosen, for we were almost within gunshot of a black regiment, and the country swarmed with armed natives. At the crack of my rifle, we sprang out of the cave, stepping over the M'Limo's body, and ran down the path toward the huts, the nearest way to our horses. There was no further need for secrecy in our movements.

"The roaring echo of the shot within the cave, booming and bellowing after us, and the frightful apparition of two armed white men dashing out of the temple of their gods were too much for the old Ring Kops. They sat for one instant frozen with terror at their stations and then fled. In their excuse, be it said, they were armed only with knobkerries, and the young herders who were helping the women prepare the dancing floor for the next day's ceremony had only their assegais. Our real danger was from the armed regiment in camp at the north end of the kopje, about half a mile away. Running toward our horses, I shouted to Armstrong to help me fire the huts. Pulling out a bundle of thatch and lighting it, we set fire right and left and sped on. The yelling of the natives having stirred up the fighting regiment, we circled around our horses, fearing an ambush, but found our mounts still concealed and undisturbed. Fortunately for us, the African native is far less observant than the American Indian.

"Yet for two hours we were hotly pursued and had a long hard ride and a running fight over rough ground, until we were nearly exhausted, but the savages abandoned the chase after we had crossed the Shashani River. On looking back we saw a huge sheet of flame and volumes of black smoke rolling over the granite dome above the cave and knew our work was well done. We arrived at Mangwe at 6.30 p.m., caught the military wire, and sent our report in to Headquarters."

The killing of the M'Limo ended the Second Matabele war, and Major Burnham's bullet, fired from the rifle I now held in my hands had done it. The *Illustrated London News* carried at the time a vivid drawing done 'from a sketch by an officer with the Imperial Forces' of the escape of Major Burnham and Mr. Armstrong after the killing of the M'Limo in his cave in the Matoppos. But nothing ever impresses the British for long and after giving this spirited American a D.S.O. for winning one war, and making dramatic contributions to two others (The First Matabele War and the Boer War) the British public turned wearily to the next hero.

CHAPTER 8

On my return from America where I went during the long vacation to meet my parents, I began my second year at Oxford, with the added dignities which that implies in a place where the memory of man does not extend beyond three years.

My sequel to *The Impending Storm* had not found a publisher. It was cast in the form of a dialogue between delegates to a youth conference at Vienna; and fell between fiction and non-fiction. Accordingly I redrafted the book as a straight non-fiction book, like *The Impending Storm*. I may have been a presumptuous and irritating youth, but there is no doubt that I was ringing the right bell regularly in international affairs every time at this period. I noted on 2nd May, 1931, (my second year at Oxford) that 'I changed the significance of the whole book by introducing Russia and Bolshevist influences in the East generally as an external factor looming over the insignificant disputes of Europe.' And I have never written any more books on international affairs, for the reason, to be frank, that they would be repetitive.

I had met, in the meantime, E.J. O'Brien; who edited annually an anthology of Short Stories for Jonathan Cape. He lived in North Oxford and had written, also, a novel called *The Dance of the Machines*. He read my manuscript and advised me wisely to delete some passages on Tibetan occultism. When amended, he forwarded it to Cape with a surprising letter, (which I saw afterwards at Cape's office):

Dear Cape,

Here is an interesting M.S., I think. The author seems to be another Disraeli. He is at Balliol and his political activities display an amazing degree of energy. The master of Balliol thinks he will go a long way. His father commanded the submarine blockade during the war. He has already published one book with Constable. He throws out the typically Disraelian touch that we should put this one out under the name of "The Hon. Member for Y."

Yours,

E.J. O'Brien.

87

88

Cape wrote, 'A book of this nature runs a considerable risk of receiving good and lengthy reviews in the press without any equivalent response in the way of sales. However, I am so impressed with the book that I want very much to publish it and am prepared not to let the question of possible sale influence my decision and the book should certainly be published and that is sufficient reason.

'I will admit that my eye is definitely fixed on your future work and I hope that this book will be the first of a number of titles which we shall publish for you — '

This led naturally to his publishing my next book, also written at Oxford. I took to my boardship habits again of working from midnight till five or six a.m. and turned out a political extravaganza called *Peter Public*. Cape agreed to publish this over the pseudonym of 'The Hon. Member for X' and got it up to look as like Bernard Shaw as possible. I wrote, for the dust jacket, an author's note:

Democracy is meant to be Government by the Public. The word Public does not mean Demos (who is mad), nor The Proletariate (who is a fool), nor even the Press (which is simply a windbag). But something of all these and a good deal more which is usually regarded as being beyond the public pale altogether — such as The Intelligentzia, The Aristocracy and the Capitalist class. But it is these last who really create the abstraction called Public Opinion. And the Press is only their mouthpiece to bluff Demos and the Proletariate into thinking they were thinking for themselves while they are really thinking what has been thought for them.

The play was a play of Abstractions, of which the Public, a hairy neanderthal individual, but not such a fool as he looks, was the chief character. It did not have the success we hoped for. The *Irish Times* attributed it to Shaw and in South Africa the *Cape Times* singled it out as the literary event of the year 1932. But the cautious English reviewers adopted the attitude of the critics in Fanny's First Play, which I quoted on the title page. 'If it's by a good author it's a good play, naturally. That stands to reason. Tell me who the author is and I'll place the play for you to a hair's breadth,' and the failure of this, following upon the poor sales of *Divided Europe*, notwithstanding the excellent reviews of that book which he had foreseen, diminished Cape's ardour for publishing my work. Nevertheless he drew up a contract for a first novel on Napoleon's early days — and I was astonished to discover when the manuscript was delivered that he was not bound by the contract to publish.

By the time *Divided Europe* was published I was a senior under-graduate at Oxford and took care in the preface to acknowledge the Master of Balliol's assistance with the proofs. There was no de-bagging this time. Oxford was content to make peace with me as an unorthodox success. In an article in the Cherwell, Lionel Gelber, a Canadian Rhodes Scholar, reviewed the book under the title of 'The Case of Mr. de Chair and Mr. O'Brien.' 'Toby' O'Brien was the president of the Union, and I think the review is worth quoting as a final assessment by Oxford on one of its products who did not follow the usual *cursus honorum* of secretary, librarian and president of the Union:

Divided Europe. By Somerset de Chair.
Jonathan Cape, London, 1931. Price 5s.

It is time we considered the case of Mr. de Chair. He has pursued none of the conventional modes of achieving a notable public career at this university. Yet, unavoidably, he confronts us. Impressed by this, perhaps a trifle disturbed, even Mr. E.D. O'Brien has been constrained to step down from the Presidential dais to review his latest book (vide the Isis, November 4th, 1931, p.15). Could there be surer evidence of his success? It was Charles Dickens who evoked the well-known American essay 'On a Certain Condescension in Foreigners'. Is Mr. O'Brien going to call forth some later rendering — let us say, 'On a Certain Condescension in Union Presidents'? It is becoming increasingly clear that we have not read the last of Mr. de Chair's prolific works. Some day, inevitably, he will publish a volume on the current state of English politics with sketches of contemporary Young Men of Promise. Or probably Mr. de Chair will soon be writing reminiscences of his sojourn in Oxford (it has been done before!) and one may predict how intriguing a record it would be. Surely then, if we were to be given no preference, we should choose to be described venomously since it is far better to be attacked than not to be mentioned at all; for from one thing the good Lord must deliver us and that is from being ignored.* Such forebodings may sound premature. But Mr.

* Well, Lionel. Here is your book.

de Chair, it is evident, will soon wield a formidable pen. It is just as well, even if slightly late, to be a little prudent.

Still, one may venture the opinion, however bizarre and timid, that in the long run Mr. de Chair's way is the more hopeful one. Unsound in several respects, the author of 'Divided Europe' must always arrest attention by the deep and energetic nature of his convictions. He gives promise of developing an imaginative capacity for generalisation as well as an instinctive ability for going to the heart of the matter and avoiding irrelevance. Attempting to unite the interpretive method of Prof. Alfred Zimmern to the ideals of Lord Lloyd, the combination is not altogether happy. Moreoever he expresses himself in an awkward prose; a style which nevertheless, is occasionally illuminated by a striking phrase. His historical equipment is sometimes inadequate for the task to which he has set his hand and one must pause before accepting either his analogies or his aims. But Mr. de Chair is significant not because of his defects, which, if he keeps his mind open he will swiftly outgrow, but because of the extraordinary merit of his faith. Alone among his fellows at the University he has seriously attempted to think through and organise his reasoning upon, some of the major perplexities of our age. In an Oxford generation which accords fame to the iridescent froth of the Union and the light inanities of the weekly journals, it is a relief to turn to a man who believes in something sincerely and intensely and can present his credo with force, knowledge and clarity. Fired by convictions so wide and sweeping with a personality so dynamic, there can be no doubt that ultimately Mr. de Chair's voice will be heard in the land. One can only trust that with the passage of the years he will have forsworn some of his present certitudes, some of those heroes and doctrines which are curiously inconsistent with his vision of world stablity. It would be a matter for regret it, above all, he failed to retain that warm and thoughtful fidelity towards the Empire, that abiding concern for the welfare of his country and the prospect for mankind which is his unique distinction. Lionel M. Gelber.

The summer vacation of 1931 saw me staying at the Dormy House at Wentworth where my mother and father were converting an old farmhouse near the golf course. Old 'Billy' Hughes, the First World War Premier of Australia, now a dynamic octogenarian monkey of a man, was staying at the Dormy House and inscribed for me a copy of his book

— *The Splendid Adventure*, (which he described as a review of Empire relations within and without the Commonwealth of Britannic Nations). He appreciated better than any statesman in the Commonwealth since Cecil Rhodes or Joseph Chamberlain what a splendid adventure the evolution of the Commonwealth was. But he was wrong about India; which he thought incapable of practising Parliamentary democracy.

My parents had entertained the late Lord Salisbury at Government House in Sydney during an Empire Mission; and took me with them, when Lord and Lady Salisbury asked us to luncheon at Hatfield. The elder statesman showed us round his house after lunch, with all the charm and courtesy of the Victorian age in which he had grown up; and when we took our leave at the front door, we were startled, when he opened it, to find three or four people sitting on the doorstep. He murmured apologetically, "Ah yes, the public; it is their day."

Now they have every day except one: and if some members of the public arrived on a Monday and saw through the magnificent lace-like wrought iron entrance gates the present Marquis strolling in the grounds, they might murmur with equal resignation, "Ah yes, the owner; it is his day."

Thus quietly, within a generation has the social revolution come to England; and Russian *emigrés* or the descendants of guillotined French nobles may well stare in wonder at a people with such a capacity for adjustment.

It was at Wentworth that I first saw Thelma Arbuthnot. I had strolled across the links to Bears House, where a friend of my brother, Deborah Jenkinson, was giving a tennis party. I walked into the drawing-room, through the french window. There were half a dozen girls in the room and, in the centre of them, one who bore a remarkable resemblance to a film star called Norma Shearer. As soon as I saw her I said to myself, "That is my future wife." The girls accompanied me across the links to the house, which, in the stage of conversion, seemed the work, to Thelma's eyes, of a millionairess. The old tithe barn was to be the main hall, with a minstrel's gallery and room opening off it. The old dwelling-house of the farmstead formed an annexe across a central sunk garden, beautifully designed, which opened on to larger lawns through a high moon-gate, characteristic of my mother's ideas of garden design.

A few days later Deborah Jenkinson rang up to ask me to join a party she was giving for a dance in London. I was not very enthusiastic until she mentioned that 'Norma Shearer' would be there. And there, then, was I. We dined first at some women's club, and Thelma turned up in an ancient family car, driven by an ancient family chauffeur. The car was important because its mustiness and decrepitude, even its respectable but by no means extravagant make — an Armstrong-Siddeley — conveyed indelibly to me the background of a family fallen on evil times. Thelma had very lovely grey eyes — cooler in temperament than any I had admired since Morna McCormick in Australia, whose type she wholly resembled. Graceful, dignified, charming — the opposite in every way to the vivacious brunettes with whom I had been so preoccupied in Bonita, Pearl Appleton and even Dot Collins in California. Here was a woman worthy of living up to — if I could.

We danced at the Goldsmith's Ball — and sat out in a little square where a fountain tinkled; and a policeman padded by smiling benignly. Afterwards the family car drove her to some flats where she was staying with Deborah up near Lord's cricket ground; and I was tactfully to be dropped at my own address by the chauffeur afterwards. She curled up in my arms and we felt like marrying; although I made no attempt to kiss her, nor did she expect me to. Everything had conspired to give me the impression of a girl of respectable family — her mother, whom I met at the dinner party, was a woman of tremendous dignity and restraint in matters of dress and jewellery — but seemingly of a family of no particular wealth. And this I believe was important to my attitude, for rightly or wrongly, I am not adapted to the role of a dependent husband. It came as a violent shock, when she collected me in her old, touring 12 h.p. Standard motor at Wentworth one day and drove me over to her home, Merrist Wood. This was not, as I had gathered, a small house on the golf course at Worplesdon, but 'The Hall', the big house of the village, before the golf course was built. We drove down long winding drives, past cottages on the 1,000 acre estate, through wrought iron gates, past garages and stables, only too evidently repaired without regard to cost, past neatly painted black iron park fencing, where their cattle grazed, past some of the seven ancient gardeners mowing acres of lawn, past oak woods undergrown with rhododendron, until we swept up to a great house, built in the Tudor style by Norman Shaw in the last century. And there was Mr. Arbuthnot, pottering fretfully about looking as dyspeptic and dejected as I was always to see him. He was tall and stooping, with a very high, intellectual forehead, and a drooping moustache. He was in a permanent state of gloom. The prospect of a suitor coming over for tea added immeasureable depths to his gloom. There was a genial old butler, Bradley, in a stiff wing collar and morning suit and a footman, wearing the family livery, with a blue uniform and a wasp-striped black and yellow waistcoat with brass buttons. All this was very formidable to me — and although not unwelcome, quite unexpected. We had tea in the hall, where the wood was of pale, yellow oak, very new. Mrs. Arbuthnot sat in front of the silver kettle and glittering tea things and Mr. Arbuthnot soon went off groaning and muttering to his study, where he sat with the door open so as not to miss any of the conversation. His mother had been a woman of great brilliance and he had been one of a very large family. So large had been the family that the plans to send him into the diplomatic service or the Greys had been abandoned and he had gone on to the Stock Exchange, of which he was never really proud, although he became a respected figure on it, and he got more and more depressed, the more money he made. He began making about £40,000 a year in the rubber boom and then when he began making less he got even more depressed. In the meantime, Mrs. Arbuthnot had inherited a considerable fortune of her own from her father, Lambert, whose firm, Lambert & Butler, had been one of the principal firms in the group formed into Imperial Tobacco. All her £1 shares now stood at £5 and that added appreciably to everybody's gloom and made them more determined than ever to keep ancient motor cars going till they fell to bits. It took me a long time to realise, even then, that their fortunes had not all gone. No doubt Mr. Arbuthnot did feel in some obscure way a very poor man and a financial failure when he could only leave a quarter of a million on his death, to add to his wife's considerable assets, which, through careful husbandry and frugal way of living, had increased continuously.

To such people the prospect of their daughter marrying an undergraduate with no visible livelihood or settled career appeared appalling.

She had more relations than I had believed possible. They might have sat to Galsworthy for *The Forsyte Saga*. They were all there — the men of property, with connections in the City; and marriageable daughters. There was a great touch of Soames Forsyte about Arbuthnot — if only he had been more robust in health. Fundamentally Harold Arbuthnot was a sick man — and died after an operation in 1945, having lived to see the end of his second war. Ill-health had prevented him taking an active part in the first — and that had been a cause of depression. Mrs. Arbuthnot was a woman of fine principle. She said that she should have married a bishop. She was a pillar of the Church, and having made up her mind to accept me as a son-in-law, never turned her back. And although always somewhat astringent in outlook, was a devoted mother-in-law, and soon became a magnificent grandmother. I respected her and grew very fond of her, and I think that the feeling was reciprocated. I am sure that she understood me much better than her daughter did; and she was the only person who knew her daughter as well as I did. She was, I am sure, deeply averse to the divorce which finally separated us, and opposed it till the end. She saw, beyond the pressures of immediate emotion, the stress of a world war — the effect of wounding and operations on the sensory nerves of a young husband. And she saw the future of her grandsons as an important factor in a balance of interests. When the marriage finally came to an end, I felt very keenly the loss of my mother-in-law's friendship.

I spent my 21st birthday, working from 5 p.m. to midnight as an unpaid sub-editor on *The Times* newspaper, a useful experience, while one of the staff was on holiday in August. And where was my 20-year-old fiancée on this occasion? Collecting me at 5 past 12 in Printing House Square to go on to some night-club? Not a bit of it. She was with her parents in Surrey explaining what a diligent young man I was. I had already turned down the post of honorary attaché at both the British Embassy in Instanbul and Paris, as they did not want a married man.

I obtained a contract to write a novel on Napoleon as a young man in Corsica, and we went there for our honeymoon. I wrote 60 pages of the novel there; and this was never regarded afterwards as faithful. (The novel was published eventually under the title of *Enter Napoleon*.)

Then we studied for the diplomatic service in Paris, living in a small flat, where the scratching of my pen was not escapable, eating in cheap restaurants with French taxi-drivers as we did not seem to have enough money; then in London (a flat at the top of several flights of stairs in Halkin Street) and in Vienna, where the winter was very savage and the snow froze like steel on the tramlines as it fell. I had a painful series of operations without anaesthetic on twenty-two of my teeth, many being cut open to the nerve to remove the old fillings and replace them. 'Extension for Prevention' was Plöchl's only English phrase. I believe he was practising to become a Nazi dentist in Buchenwald or Dachau. He gloried in causing me pain. I staggered out into the biting winds of the Vienna streets. We studied — and Thelma shared the lessons here as in Paris — indeed it could be said that she never left me out of her sight for two minutes in either capital for twelve months — we studied under an Austrian woman called Frau Mitrofanov. She had married a Russian. She made us translate the whole of Raine Maria Rilke's lovely book *Die*

Hände vom Lieben Gott, and we became reasonably proficient in French and German.

Being so near Hungary, where my first book had caused such a stir, we decided to go down to Budapest by car.

On the eve of our departure for Budapest we saw a play in Vienna called 'Thirteen at Table' in which the leading actress wore an impressive evening dress called the Cleopatra dress, which differed from most in that it had an opening in front which descended nearly to the waist but was clipped together further up to preserve the decencies. We looked up the name of the dressmaker in the programme and the shop agreed to make a duplicate for my wife within 24 hours. We had to wait while it was finished and were somewhat delayed in our departure. We drove down the Danube basin in our old white Isotta-Fraschini sports car, which had a musical hooter, suitable only for very young people such as ourselves. We had arranged to stay at the St. Gellert Hotel and when we arrived at the end of a five hour drive, we found it difficult to approach the hotel on account of a large crowd. We asked someone what the crowd was waiting for.

"We are waiting for Somerset de Chair," came the astonishing reply. As soon as we entered the hotel, accordingly, and were identified, we were surrounded by press photographers and reporters, who swarmed up with us to the suite which had been reserved. There they began upon the interview, which was reported enormously in all the papers next day.

From then on our stay in Budapest was organised for us by Istvan Antal, the government's director of Public Relations — as if we were visiting royalty — there is no other way to describe it. We were made to appear in a box at the opera; we were given an audience with the Regent, Admiral Horthy; we had tea with the elderly Archduke Franz-Joseph and his wfie; and met his son; we were taken to a play called *Janos* by the author, Lajos Zilahy and went on with him and his exquisitely beautiful wife, Piroshka, to a night-club called the Arizona Bar where the dance floor revolved; and where the gypsy musicians came and played their heart-rending music to Thelma, till there were tears in all our eyes. I was taken to the studio of a leading Hungarian sculptor, Lanyi, to sit for a bronze bust for the Hungarian Parliament museum; (it was bitterly cold in the studio and my cheeks look drawn and haggard in bronze to this day with cold and the strain of the visit); I had an interview with the Prime Minister Gömbös and was taken round the desolate mudflat settlement of refugees on the shores of the Danube by the organisers of

Caritas; and saw the pathetic hovels in which the exiles from former Hungarian lands were living. Ever at our side was Ladislas Toth, editor of the *Nemzeti Ujsag*, a mournful dark-eyed little man with hooked nose and drooping moustache. He wore in his buttonhole a badge with an O surmounted by a crown, the symbol of the monarchist party which looked forward to a restoration under Prince Otto of Hapsburg. And it came as a shock to me to hear, years later on the radio, of his being arrested by the communists at the trial of Cardinal Mindzenty and made to step forward and hear, (with difficulty no doubt, for he was very deaf) a 'sentence' of ten years' imprisonment for plotting to restore the Hapsburgs. It is certainly difficult to think of the twin cities of Buda and Pest under a communist regime. Nor could the legend of the thousand-year-old Crown of King Stephen be expected to die easily in the land of the Magyars. Sometimes I receive travel brochures — sent to me, who knows, by some official who remembers my visit — and in its photogravure pages are depicted the holiday resorts of the communist proletariat in the old hotels on Lake Balaton: and I wonder if this is the probable destiny of the world — the People's world, grim and grey, but without hereditary privilege. The Kings were on the way out after the First World War. They were being followed by the aristocracy before the Second. Then the bourgeoisie began to go — they are not going quietly. And the people remain.

To return after such a dazzling experience in Hungary, to the routine of German lessons in the Salesianergasse in Vienna seemed an anticlimax. It was easy to read into the acclaim of Budapest a portent for the future — but where? In Vienna there were occasional distractions. Baroness Boi-Orosdy, an old friend of Dame Clarissa Reid appeared from Hungary and invited us to dine at the Bristol. Among the other guests was the most beautiful woman of her generation in the world. Her husband, a sleek armament manufacturer called Mandl sat passively with Baroness Boi-Orosdy, while I danced with her. I had never quite believed in violet eyes, but she had them. And her voice had a mocking lilt as she said, "How beautifully the moon shines upon the balcony tonight." But that apparently was all the English she had learnt. She had begun learning it for a film. Among the guests was her former admirer Prince Starhemberg, whose ancestors had defeated the Turks upon the heights of Kalenberg overlooking Vienna and saved Christendom (until the advent of Stalin). Starhemberg ran a semi-private army called the Heimwehr; and aspired to imitate Mussolini as an Austrian dictator. He had run short of armaments and these were now supplied by Mandl;

and Hedy Lamarr, now married to the arms king, looked with unswerving gaze out of her violet eyes across the table at 'Bub' Starhemberg. Two other members of the party were Graf Semsey and his wife. Semsey was the Hungarian Minister in Vienna, a genial bear of a man, who told me that at Caporetto he had been in command of a platoon in the Austro-Hungarian Army, when a battalion of Italians came marching along. He fired into the road and they halted. They put up their hands and he ordered them to surrender.

"You can't capture us," the Italian Colonel declared indignantly, "we are on our way home. Besides, there are nearly a thousand of us and only thirty of you." So they compromised. The Italians laid down their arms as they filed past on the way back to Italy. Not dissimilar stories were to be told by British officers after Wavell's victories in Libya over Graziani's army in 1941.

We went up to Graz with the Semseys to hear Starhemberg make one of his rabble-rousing speeches. Although an aristocrat, he spoke in a raucous, slangy voice, which roused a lot of applause. But the pocket Chancellor Dolfuss was strong enough at this time to keep the Heimwehr within bounds; and use it for the more unpopular duty of suppressing socialist trouble when it came. And it came sooner than we expected. We were staying with a couple called Syfert, who had a flat in one of the large converted mansions in Prinz Eugen Strasse, overlooking Schwarzenberg Palace and gardens. Ruldoph von Syfert was a civil servant; but made no secret to us of his Nazi sympathies. He was one of the respectable Austrians, and they were many in 1934, who looked to union with Hitler's Third Reich as the solution of Austria's difficulties. They looked all the more eagerly when the Social Democrat Revolution broke out. We were playing bridge with them, in the ornate drawing-room, with its high stove in the corner and its double set of windows firmly shut to keep out the bitter cold; when the electric light suddenly went dim, flickered and went out. The workers had closed down the powerhouses. Presently the lights came on again, feebly at first, when the troops moved in but we were not aware of this at first. Yet there had been a strange atmosphere of tension in the streets all day. The dogs had begun barking everywhere hysterically. When we realised that something was amiss, we went out in the darkened streets and made our way towards the Schotten ring. All the streets leading into the inner part of the city were barricaded off with barbed wire road blocks and sentries in the grey-green uniforms of the Heimwehr stood on guard. An armoured car, manned by soldiers in their heavy German-type steel helmets, rolled past on their way to the Karl Marx blocks of workers' flats on the outskirts of the city, where the revolutionaries had their headquarters. Artillery was moved out there too; and presently we could hear the booming of the guns. All through the night there was spasmodic machine-gun fire. Once it seemed close to the Schwarzenberg gardens. Towards morning, Thelma got out of bed to look out of the window and was surprised when a bullet sang into the masonry above it. It was probably fired by some government soldier on the watch for the emergence of a gun from an unexpected quarter. But by morning the city was quiet. The revolution was over and the leaders of it, Schmidt and Braun, had escaped by car to the frontier. Within a few hours Vienna was back to normal and posters appeared everywhere, '*wer had die Heimat geschutz? — Der Heimatschutz*;' which was a boast by Starhemberg and Vice-Chancellor Fey who was closely in league with him, that the country had been saved by the Heimwehr. But the abortive rising of the Social Democrats strengthened the demand for the German Nazis to come over the border. Within a few months the gallant little Chancellor Dolfuss was shot in a Nazi coup and the way cleared for the march into Austria four years later.

I wonder what happened to 'Rudi' von Syfert, always so polite, clicking his heels together to bow and kiss my wife's hand with the traditional Viennese greeting, "*Küss die Hand, gnädige Frau.*" And what of Fritzie Von Seifert with her shock of bronze hair and her bridge parties and trays of sweetened biscuits and tea at eleven at night? Or of Wolfgang her son, of whom she was so proud; destined, no doubt, for the shock troops of Hitler's assault upon the world? I do not believe that the Seiferts dreamt of world conquest. For them Hitler meant the salvation of Austria by the simple, bloodless process of the amalgamation of the six million German speaking Austrians into the Great Reich. And, living from hand to mouth, in a capital from which the old Hapsburg provinces had been torn after the First World War, the Anschluss was a plausible theory. That Austria was but the first of a planned series of conquests may not have occurred to the easy-going Austrians who made it possible.

An old friend of my father, Mr. L.S. Amery, a distinguished Minister in many Conservative Governments, was lecturing in Vienna and I took the opportunity to ask his advice upon a chance which seemed to have occurred of entering the House of Commons.

"I would not go in too young," he advised. "It is far better to wait until you have gained some experience and made a success of some other occupation first."

But at twenty-three one does not pay much attention to the advice of wise men. Charles Rhys, who was Member for the Guildford Division of Surrey, in which my wife had been born, had just announced his intention to resign his seat, and it seemed that Thelma's connections there might prove useful. So I wrote to Lord Stonehaven, the Chairman of the Party, whom I had known in Australia when he was Governor-General. He replied that Sir John Jarvis had already been selected for Guildford but advised me, on returning to England, to call on Sir George Bowyer, at the Conservative Central Office.

Pessimistic about my chances of passing the examination for the Diplomatic Service in July, we set out for England, driving as if the devil were after us, with only one stop at Augsburg. We reached Merristwood late on a foggy night after a thirty-six hour drive across Europe, 750 miles non-stop from Augsberg and 1,100 from Vienna, taking turns at the wheel. It was not the best way to arrive, unheralded, at Merristwood; and we were very tired.

Sir George Bowyer, a Conservative Whip, in the House (subsequently Lord Denham) was dealing with prospective candidates at the old Central Office in Bridge Street overlooking Palace Yard. He smiled tolerantly at my youth, and listed the constituency candidatures vacant, among them S.W. Norfolk.

"I like the sound of that," I said.

"So do a good many others," he answered me with a smile, but could see no harm, and no possible danger of my being selected, in adding my name to the list they were to interview.

I discovered that the chairman of the S.W. Norfolk Association was a Vice-Admiral, which seemed propitious, who lived at Narford of which he was Lord of the Manor, having retired from the Navy in 1924. My father wrote a note, quietly, to express the hope that I could serve under his flag. Admiral Fountaine had this letter, no doubt, in his pocket when he brought a committee consisting of a brace of squires, various farmers and a seed-merchant from the lowlands and fens of Norfolk to see what the Central Office had to offer. They considered the particulars of the various candidates on their way up in the train and scratched my name off the list at a glance; aged 23. They liked the particulars of a Lincolnshire farmer aged 40. With him and other aspiring politicians I found myself sitting in a waiting-room at the Central Office. I took Thelma with me, but it was not the fashion of selection committees in those days to interview the wives as well.

When I entered the small room I found half a dozen lean men around a green baize table, and filling almost all the remaining space an enormous Admiral who came towards me, with a broad smile creasing his great face, and a twinkle under his bushy brows. With grave courtesy he showed me to my seat; and the interrogation began. I had brought with me copies of *The Impending Storm* and *Divided Europe* which I handed across the table. Jack Wormald, a spare military figure with an army moustache, began to peer into *Divided Europe* incredulously. I told them that I had been reading up the history of Agriculture and quoted a line about the various things an agricultural worker boasted he could do in Tudor times:

" 'And I can do my master too
When my master turns his back.' "

Major Swann liked that.

"They still do," he chuckled. He farmed in the Fens. But the difficult one was Gordon Parker, the seed-merchant who had ambitions to be the Member himself and was secure in the allegiance of many farmers who sold their corn to him. He had been largely responsible for the resignation of the sitting Member, Sir Alan McLean.

Admiral Fountaine leant forward, helpfully, and asked me for my views on India. It was the question of the hour. Self-government or not? I plumped for self-government.

"But didn't you know," he said, taken aback, "that our association has just passed a resolution deploring any attempt to give self-government to India?"

"I did not know," I laughed, "but I am sure you are wrong. Consider for a moment the Simon Report — " of which I proceeded to give them the gist.

"Communal trouble?" hazarded Jack Wormald.

"Don't you know that nearly all the soldiers are recruited in the Punjab?"

What on earth this was supposed to prove, I have forgotten, but it had a good effect.

"It is quite obvious," smiled the Admiral, "that you could argue the hind leg off a donkey." And with the most affable of smiles he showed me to the door.

I had offered to bring Thelma in, which seemed to amuse the committee immensely. "She was born on the back of a cow," I assured these agriculturists.

She looked up questioningly when I emerged.

"No good at all," I said, "I disagreed with them about India."

"Never mind," she consoled me, "there will be other con-
stituencies." Nevertheless we drove back to Merristwood in somewhat
low spirits, Thelma regretting, not for the last time, that I had not put
my point of view a little more tactfully to a committee of this kind.

There was a telegram for me on arrival.

'You have been unanimously chosen to stand for
S.W. Norfolk.   Fountaine.'

I see now that all this came about too quickly and too easily.
Following upon the acclaim of Hungary it seemed to open the door to
spectacular advancement in the British Parliament; and I saw myself
soon brushing aside the people at the head of our affairs, like Ramsay
MacDonald and Stanley Baldwin, who seemed to me to be antiquated
statesmen. I had absolutely no conception of the complexity of political
life in England or the violent jealousies with which progress of any kind
inside the parties is beset. I had not even been old enough at the last
election in 1931 to vote and the first time I would ever cast my vote
would be for myself.

In the meantime we were invited to stay with Admiral Fountaine at
Narford, who had indeed written to offer us the loan of the Red Lodge
on the estate, until we found our bearings. But at our age we wanted and
thought we had found our own home.

Narford was my first experience of a really big house. When we
drove up to it, the building seemed immense. And Mrs. Fountaine
drifting about it, in wispy garments, like a good-natured gypsy,
admitted that she never dared to count the number of bedrooms. The
house was built in George I's reign, of brown brick and stone, an
unusual colour; and had been added to ponderously, in the Victorian
era. The high tower over the porch and the great music room were
Victorian. Beyond the house stretched a vast lake; seemingly like the
upper reaches of the Amazon, for it appeared to be surrounded by
forest. It was all in keeping with the Admiral; who rose from a doze in a
chair by the fire as we were ushered by the parlourmaid into the 'saloon'.
This word which is used of great houses in Norfolk — (The Duke of
Windsor speaks of the saloon at Sandringham in his memoirs) — is one
which normally evokes a very different picture. The 'saloon' at Narford
was remarkable.

The walls were covered by the only surviving set of mural paintings in England by Pellegrini with scenes from classical antiquity. The piano was cluttered with the working parts of various wireless systems which the Admiral had made himself; and his desk contained a litter of slide rules, logarithm tables and unanswered letters. The marble fireplace was adorned with two finely carved marble lions, but between them was an assortment of old calendars, invitations to social functions, tobacco jars, lighter spills, letters, and oddments which must have run into scores. The log basket was full of logs, which protruded over the top and had gashed a hole at some time in one of the Pellegrinis. The occasional tables held mountainous accumulations of old reference books. One sofa by the wall was devoted to the back numbers of *The Morning Post*; in one corner a green and yellow parrot squawked in a cage; and from all this the Admiral emerged like a benevolent giant to take us for a walk by the lake. He was rather top heavy, and walked with short strides. Someone had lent him a very fierce bulldog and this he now tried to take for a walk also. It was the only thing on earth of which Carlo Fountaine lived in some awe. A short lawn beyond the house sloped down to a graceful stone bridge, where a stream fed the lake. We crossed the bridge and walked along the bank. There was a certain number of stinging nettles, and the full view of the lake broadened on our left, revealing a small church on the opposite shore. The lake was in fact only sixty acres in extent, but sixty acres of water, surrounded by trees, looks a lot more than a similar acreage of land.

Narford, off and on for the next ten years, was to become a second home to me and Carlo a second father, so it is difficult to recapture the first sense of strangeness and indeed wonder which the place inspired. We were shown to our rooms by Mrs. Fountaine and the head-housemaid and these rooms, scarcely above the ground floor level, which certainly had not been redecorated in living memory, looked out upon an attractive clock tower, which stood above the entrance to an asphalt tennis court. Beside the bed was a novel by A.E.W. Mason called *The Sapphire* with an Oriental woman and a leopard on the dust cover. That book remained there for ten years, so that I was able to finish it on subsequent visits. The bath was in a small cubicle down a dark corridor and was about four feet long and completely rectangular — an early experiment in baths, very probably.

Tea was at a round table in the wide bow window of the dining-room, overlooking the lake. This room was magnificent, with fluted Doric pillars, ornamented in gold, and surrounded by busts of the Caesars in porphyry and marble. The chimney piece carried a carved marble plaque showing the legend of the young woman offering her breast to an old man in captivity to keep him alive, her head decorously averted. There were magnificent Georgian side tables, with lion masks in gilt; and the room owed not a little I gathered, to Mrs. Fountaine, who was an heiress from New Zealand and said that when she came to live there the rain was coming through the ceiling of the dining-room, which was propped up by fir trunks. The house had been owned by Sir Andrew Fountaine, one of the most famous of the eighteenth century dilettantes, and owed to him the fine collection of Italian works of art which it contained. A special room, behind a glass panel, had at one time housed a famous Majolica collection.

Carlo said, "Duveen offered my father £50,000 for it. So he concluded that it must be worth double. He sent it up to Christies and got £110,000 for it."*

Tea was hailed by Carlo with shouts of "tea-booze" and Mrs. Fountaine drifted in from somewhere in the back regions where she had been dealing with the cook or the flowers.

Carlo showed me 'the geography' of the house, as it is so often charmingly described. It was down a few bare stone steps, from the serving room door of the dining-room, past a horrifying black iron mantrap spread-eagled to the wall, and looking every time you passed it, as if it would snap with a crash of its great steel teeth, and bite your whole head off. The plumbing was wonderfully antiquated but belonged to the mechanical age.

There was a short cut, beyond the geography and a gun room, where an arsenal of weapons was kept, and a billiard room leading off it, past the passage to the kitchens, and up some dark stairs, to our half-landing and rooms.

To do justice to Carlo would require a book — but possibly this is the book. He had laid down three pipes of Taylor's '24 when he left the Navy (equal to about 144 dozen) and a bottle of this ruby vintage came up every evening to be decanted without ceremony by the Admiral into one of the cut glass decanters. This in turn was poured into very large claret glasses; so that the fumes came up in pleasing volume.

"That's got a nose on 'um," Carlo would chuckle, pushing the decanter towards me across the corner of the shining mahogany table after the ladies had withdrawn. But at this time I did not drink, and so

---

* When a solicitor who was a fellow trustee with Carlo's father for the Amhersts at Didlington absconded with the trust funds.

he would in all probability drink the whole bottle himself, if we were alone. Later on in life I came to the conclusion that there was something wrong with this picture, and helped him to lower the level in the decanter. There never was port like the Taylor's '24 at Narford. Certainly Taylor's '24 drunk anywhere else lacked its splendid quality. The Narford cellar was famous and an impious legend said that after Carlo had taken King George V down there to examine it after dinner one evening, Queen Mary had gone in search of them after breakfast.

"How," I asked Carlo, "do you choose a good port when it is raw? How do you know what it is going to be like in fifteen or twenty years' time?"

"Strong and black and sweet and makes you drunk. That's the test, when you come to lay it down."

Carlo had been commander of the *Lion* under Beatty at the battle of the Dogger Bank, and it is generally accepted that he saved the ship by ingenious arrangements when she was holed below the water line. As a disciplinarian he had been loved and certainly respected.

"Ship's police," he would exclaim after dinner, placing his thumb down on the table, "that's the secret. Ship's police. You must know what is going on. When I joined the *Lion*, I found about a hundred cases up before the Commander. Give the first three 30 days and let the rest go, I said. That shook them. No one knew what he was going to get after that. No more argy-bargy, like with the last Commander."

Then there was the matter of Carlo's inventions. He was possibly an inventive genius. He spent the last three years of his life working out, designing and making at that desk in the saloon at Narford, a new type of slide rule for calculating the angles of triangles. And he was one of the few men alive who could discuss relativity intelligently with Einstein, and in German. In the Navy he was said to have invented a half-pint telescope, which contained rum; and could be raised to the lips as well as to the eye. The firm of Blake who made hydraulic rams consulted him regularly about their appliances. They would write to say that a hydraulic ram installed on the *Zambesi* was giving trouble and after studying the measurements of its siting, Carlo would write to say that if they examined the induction pipe 300 feet from the point of intake they would find it badly pitted; and it was so. The rams at the end of the Narford lake were of course installed under his supervision and gave forth mysterious sounds; very like the tom-toms of the Congo basin. He had been interested in establishing perfect time-keeping clocks in the cellar, which would enable Greenwich mean time to be checked by

Narford time; but a bricklayer engaged in the cellar on other work had backed his rump into one of the clocks and the work of years had to be abandoned. Carlo made an expressive gesture about this workman, a gesture which he normally reserved for civil servants; he gripped an imaginary head by its imaginary ears and gave it two or three swift jerks, clockwise, as if to screw it off. Words were unnecessary. At the mere mention of a bureaucratic official of any type, Carlo's great hands would reach for the imaginary ears and click click, twist, twist, off would come his head.

The object of our first visit to Narford was to present me to an adoption meeting in the Assembly rooms at Swaffham. Carlo took one look at our long white sports Isotta-Faschini car and advised us to leave it out of the picture. We drove with him in a sedate blue Hillman saloon car, driven by the chauffeur handyman Ellis who was not generally thought to have enough work to do. Mrs. Ellis, (the head housemaid) did all the work in that family. There were five hundred people in the Assembly rooms and the platform was gaily flagged with Union Jacks. The agent was an ex-naval Petty Officer, and knew how to deal with Admirals and their sons, without losing any sort of independence or self-respect. His name was King. A clean-shaven man with a square face that had contemplated in its time the Persian Gulf and the Arctic Circle. It gazed, now, contemptuously at Gordon Parker's bullet head, hoping for the best.

I got a rousing reception, and Carlo said we had already chosen a house in the division before the meeting, which brought laughter and cheers. I made what I thought was a good speech, saying that S.W. Norfolk must remain an island of common sense in a troubled world. But what raised the temperature was Carlo's bellowing speech afterwards. Pointing at me, and leaning on the Union Jack, he roared, "I served under this fellow's father, and a finer Commander never stepped the quarterdeck."

My first speech to the assembled Conservative Party was at the Conference on India when Baldwin secured his 3 to 1 vote of support for self-government (which I supported). Pointing a finger at the elderly Lord Salisbury and at Churchill I cried, "While you old tigers are fighting over the carcass of India, the jackals of Socialism are entering your lairs and stealing the cubs." But the cubs were not old enough to vote until 1945.

Swaffham was a congenial town for our headquarters. Its Georgian houses were loosely spaced about an ample market-place. Here it seemed as if a dog turned over lazily in the sunshine once a year. And legend clung to the town. Upon the pews of the church were the figures of a pedlar and his dog. The townsfolk had commissioned a young nephew of Sir Howard Carter, the ill-fated Egyptologist, to make them a sign, of the pedlar and his dog; and this was erected at the Lynn entrance of the triangular market-place. — The story of the pedlar was contained in the medieval *Black Book of Swaffham* preserved in the church:

At about the time when the first ploughs were being made by the plowrights who, as Plowright & Son, still made ploughs upon the market-place in my time, a tinker at Swaffham had a dream. He dreamt that if he went to London Bridge 'his rewards would exceed his pains.' He journeyed thither on foot, peddling his wares, and accompanied, presumably, by the legendary dog. It must have taken him some days, through Saffron Walden and the picturesque towns of East Anglia, before he reached London. There he enquired after London Bridge, which he will have found to be a bridge surmounted by shops and booths. He walked up and down this busy thoroughfare all day. But nothing happened, and he must have looked a puzzled countryman staring about him in the great metropolis. Towards evening a shopkeeper who had been watching him with amusement, asked him what he was doing there.

"I had a dream," said the tinker, "that if I came to London Bridge my rewards would exceed my pains."

The Londoner laughed, possibly slapping his thighs and sharing this good joke with his neighbours.

"If I paid any attention to such nonsense as dreams," he told the tinker, "I should be in a place called Swaffham by now; because I dreamt that there was a tinker there who had an apple tree in his garden under which is buried a pot of gold."

"How right you are," said the tinker, brightening up a bit. "I will not waste any more time here." And he returned to Swaffham, in Norfolk, walking probably more swiftly than on the outward journey.

When he reached Swaffham, he waited until nightfall, and dug under his apple tree. He brought up a pewter tankard, full of gold coins. The coins he secreted, but the tankard he placed upon a shelf in his booth. One day a learned man, possibly the Vicar, stopped at his shop and noticed the tankard.

"May I look at that?" he asked. "It has a Latin inscription on it."

"By all means."

"Under me is another twice as large," translated the learned man.

"What it must be to have a classical education," said the tinker, and waiting until the learned man had departed, dug under the apple tree and brought up a second and larger tankard full of gold. He even dug deeper; but this one had no inscription on it.

Some time later, the churchwardens and others were collecting money to repair the church, and they called on the tinker, not despising the pennies even of the humblest parishioners. The tinker gave them eight hundred pounds to build a new transept; and that is why he figures to this day with his dog, in carving on the pews.

Snore Hall, a small Tudor house on the edge of the Fens would in many ways have been an ideal house for the Member. It was unpretentious and placed in the heart of the liberal-nonconformist part of the divison which had always felt neglected before. Old Harold Arbuthnot was willing to advance the £4,000 Col. Pratt would want for its purchase if Admiral Fullerton did not take up his option on a lease. But the Admiral, hearing of our occupation, arrived with Lady Fullerton (a daughter of the renowned Jackie Fisher) and they marched all over us, siting the radiators for central heating and making it clear that they meant business. So we had to look elsewhere.

Nevertheless it was a happy summer in that little house. Chaffinches perched just outside the warm bathroom on a holly tree. The apple blossom from the huge apple tree fell on to the linoleum of the big bedroom floor. We bought furniture sparsely from Harry Reed in Downham Market and round about.

We went on to an even larger house called Weasenham — there seemed to be nothing in Norfolk between the halls and the cottages; except for the rectories. The house belonged to Dick Coke, a red-headed man who lived in a smaller house in the village and worked all day in his beloved woods, which were planted with rare rhododendrons. He posted up odd notices for the benefit of trespassers who wanted to pick the blooms:

PICK NOT NOR STEAL
THEY PLEASE OTHERS
BESIDES YOU.

So here for the time being we were ensconced in a respectable abode, built on very solid lines, even if the door was labelled ANO DO 1905. Here the Conservative dance was held, and Carlo, bulging with a stiff shirt front and white tie, sat on the massive knee-hole desk in the panelled library, thumping the desk with his fist and saying, "This place suits you down to the ground." He was probably right and if I had stayed there I should probably still be the Member for S.W. Norfolk. The rent was not excessive even by 1934 standards, £2 a week. However, the books on houses had opened a new world of domestic architecture to us. The first thing that arrested our attention was the frontispiece of Volume II. At first sight it appeared to be the entrance of the very house in which we were living, but at second glance the adjoining brickwork looked about 300 years older and more mellow; and the oak door, although exactly the same in all other details, bore the legend ANO DO 1620. It was the main entrance gate of Blickling Hall. And learning that it had been lent by its owner Lord Lothian, to the future Prime Minister Stanley Baldwin who was in poor health, we decided to leave cards, as was appropriate for a candidate and his wife, upon the leader of our party staying in the county. In fact he had been lent the house as a retreat 'to think about Mrs. Simpson'. This was in 1934.

We drove over to Blickling and, as I turned the corner of the great approach of yew hedges which line the drive and saw this incomparable house of old rose brick flanked by slender turrets and graceful outbuildings, I had the same feelings I had experienced on first seeing my wife. "That is my home." But it was owned by an 11th Marquis and lent for the moment to a Prime Minister. Where in all this was Somerset? But there and then I resolved to make it my abode. Nothing less than this would do and nothing more than this, surely, existed.

The novel on the young Napoleon, begun in Corsica and finished in Paris, ran to some length. When Jonathan Cape, to my astonishment, rejected it in spite of the contract, I sent the manuscript to Frank Swinnerton and his opinion was very favourable. He read it in the extended version and said, "As a picturesque account of young Napoleon and his environment it is delightful. The whole book is charged with romance. I read the manuscript in two goes, half at a time, and was interested throughout."

In the meantime, the difficulty of placing it had led me to reconstruct the book. I cut it down savagely and divided it up into 52 short chapters, which were likened, when it appeared, to cinema shots in a scenario, each complete and visual. The book was to have been called 'The Young Man from Ajjacio' and I changed this to *Enter Napoleon*. Ethel Boileau, a popular authoress who lived in Norfolk, was a friend of my aunt Beatrix White. In due course my aunt came to stay at

Weasenham. So also did my cousin Derek Studley Herbert (her son by a former marriage) and his wife Nina Seafield, who resembled and continued for a long time to resemble at every stage of her life the late Queen Victoria. Ethel Boileau came over to Weasenham at the instigation of Aunt Beatrix, fell with alacrity on the young Napoleon and offered it to her own publisher, Hutchinson; who was not, perhaps, the most distinguished publisher of the realm, but had certainly sold large numbers of Ethel Boileau's books. They seized upon it also and in due course I received at Weasenham an advance copy of the book, bearing an extremely effective dust jacket, upon which Lieutenant Bonaparte was to be seen bestriding the town of Bastia like a young colossus. Hutchinson obtained Swinnerton's permission to use his letter about the book; and the 'blurb', not uninfluenced by myself, suggested that the author was almost as remarkable as the subject. As Rudyard Kipling was a friend of my mother and had known her since she was a girl in South Africa, I sent him a copy, in the hope that he would give it a boost, with the result shown in his letters to me reproduced in the Appendices.

In due course I became the Member. After visiting all the people recommended by King in all the villages in the division, and filling columns of the local press with reports of speeches 'Mr. de Chair at Saham Toney', 'Mr. de Chair replies to Mr. Dye', 'Mr. de Chair and the sugar beet subsidy', etc. etc., the day suddenly arrived when Ramsay MacDonald and Stanley Baldwin thought it popular to renew their mandate. Mussolini had attacked Abyssinia and for the first time, in a country which had embraced the Peace Ballot and refused to rearm, it was possible for Baldwin to appeal to the electors, promising even at this late hour, 'no great measure of rearmament.'

Three months before the election a son, Rodney, was born to Thelma and myself. I was addressing a meeting of Women Conservatives at Humbletoft, (where Sir Alan McLean's brother lived) outside Dereham when the news was telephoned from the nursing home in London. I told them the story about the local postmistress who was horrified when the vicar wired for instructions as to the wording and measurements of a banner to be erected on the stage at a nativity play in a neighbouring parish hall and received the startling reply 'Unto us a child is born, six feet long, four feet wide.' The Conservative ladies roared with delight, and waving to them as they showered their congratulations I rushed back to Weasenham, collected all the roses in the garden into a bucket and drove headlong for the nursing home in Welbeck Street. Women are difficult to understand. It had been made abundantly clear to me beforehand by all the women involved that I should only be in the way, and, not knowing the exact time when the birth could be expected, I had fulfilled my engagement to speak to the good ladies of Dereham in my constituency. But roses by the bucketful could not apparently atone for my absence when it came to the point. (When the next son was born I was at the races at Ascot, but that being within an hour's run of London brought me on the scene, after an appropriate delay, amid every sign of approval.)

The arrival of a son and heir three months before the election reduced the more serious matters of Abyssinia and rearmament to second place. At every meeting in every school room there was the same question, "How is the baby?" and the hecklers were discomfited. My majority was 4,116. The eve of the poll took us along the fenland dykes in a November fog, and my father and mother, trying to keep up in a car behind with a driver not familiar with the roads, nearly landed in the Ouse. After the declaration of the poll, I said to the cheering crowds, "I love every square inch of S.W. Norfolk and every voter in it. And shall work just as hard for those who voted against me as for those who voted for me." And I meant it. When, ten years later, the tired Parliament, its life extended to double its normal term by the war, was dissolved and we appealed to the people again, Norfolk went left in a landslide which carried the safest Tory seats away. But my constituency which had always been one of the most doubtful, did its best to push me uphill against the landslide. 15,321 voted for me and 15,374 against. I was out on a recount; but in the light of all that happened it was no meagre testimony to my ten years' stewardship.

When I first entered the House of Commons, Walter Elliott was standing in the Members' Lobby expounding in his booming and benevolent voice to some newcomers: "The House of Commons is the sounding-board of the world." There was seating accommodation in it for 325 out of the elected 615 Members. I was advised by my predecessor, Sir Alan McLean to stake a claim to the seat he had occupied, about midway along the third bench above the gangway, behind the Government Front Bench. He did not warn me that seniority had edged him sideways towards the middle and that the reverse of the process would edge me right off the shadowy end of it. In any case it was necessary to be there bright and early on the opening day, to lay a card with your name on it, reserving the seat for 'Prayers'. The doors (now known as the Churchill Arch since the reconstruction of the Chamber after the blitz), were to open at 8 a.m. When I got there, I was astonished to see Lady Astor and Jimmy Maxton, well-up at the front of the queue, having been there at some unexpectedly early hour. Apparently these old Parliamentary hands took this undignified scramble seriously. When the doors opened there was a wild rush and I, being very young and athletic, had no difficulty, hurdling over the front benches, in landing in my chosen seat well ahead of my nearest rival, Captain Plugge. This man, newly elected, for Chatham, had all the solidity which was to be expected in one who had built up Radio Luxembourg; and he cannoned into me with a jar which nearly rocketed me off the padded green leather bench. He tried to shift me forcibly sideways.

"This is my seat," he said in high and acid tones.

"I am sorry," I explained, "but I got here first."

"That may give you a claim to it for today," he squeaked, "but I am prepared to get up at half-past six every morning to get it in future."

"In that case," I said, "you will probably get it."

All this at one or two minutes past eight on my first morning. But we were both new to the House, very new. The real ugly crush began before Prayers in the afternoon, and as I sat tenaciously on the seat to which I had staked a claim, a procession of increasingly senior members forced their way between our knees and the backs of the seat in front (the P.P.S. bench), grinding our toes forcefully into the carpet. Plugge persisted in the belief that there was room for both us; when in point of fact he needed two seats himself, not half of one.

Colonel Ropner, very brick red in the face, and of long standing in the House, said meaningly as he was standing on my feet, going by, "There is plenty of room still in the Members' galleries."

I felt that the time had come to take a hint, couched in such broad terms, and levering myself with difficulty out of the squashed row of dignitaries, and not in any case particularly enjoying the business of being suffocated between Captain Plugge and Sir Edmund Brocklebank, I trod a few of their toes into the carpet, and went up to the Members' gallery opposite, where I had a better view of the Front Bench. Even these celebrities fared little better. Ramsay MacDonald, recently Prime Minister and now Lord President of the Council, sat nearly opposite the Despatch Box; but his lithe form, topped by his waving grey hairs, was gripped, as in a vice, by the robust square headed figure of Stanley Baldwin and the lean steel of the Chancellor of the Exchequer, Sir John Simon. Ramsay MacDonald could not move an elbow to right or left without their consent. He could scarcely breathe; except at the head of the stairs at Londonderry House, where I had seen him not long before, supported by the glittering Marchioness, in all her diamonds, and the queenly figure of Lucie Baldwin.

In the corner of the Front Opposition Bench, below me was the white spun-silk of Lloyd George's fine hair, crowning a pink and noble face, of which the twinkling and flashing eye, now directed upon the Front Bench, was obscured from me by his white brows. Across the way, however, in the corner seat of the Front Bench, but below — how far below, an inch? — below the gangway — sat the massive brooding figure of Winston Churchill. His aquamarine eyes roved somberly over the newly-elected assembly, recalling perhaps his own first entry on that stage. Anon his gaze rested reflectively on the side of Baldwin's impassive square head. Immediately opposite him and separated by strips of red-bordered carpet, across which it would have been out of order to step, for fear of coming within swords' lengths of each other, was Jimmy Maxton, whose grey hair seemed to hang almost to his shoulders, like the dashing cavalier that at heart he was. Beside him crouched his faithful I.L.P. — McGovern, Hector Buchanan and Campbell Stevens. They made up a great deal in eloquence, for their deficiency in numbers. All came up from the Clydeside, and spoke rich Scots, a joy to hear. Never shall I forget Jimmy Maxton on the diet of the poor, exposing the 'Porridge Swindle'. It was filling, but not apparently, as I thought, sustaining.

Two rows behind Winston, in the corner of the third bench below the gangway sat Nancy Astor in a black tricorne hat, reminiscent of a highwayman, slim and erect on her chosen and hard won seat. Next to her, in the seat reserved by tradition for ex-Ministers sat the thin, distinguished figure of Sir Austen Chamberlain, in morning dress, glistening top hat and monocle. He looked along the Treasury bench to where his brother Neville, the Minister of Health, sat wirily aloof from those who pressed upon him. Most eyes were fastened, however, upon the Caesarian face of Sir Samuel Hoare,* who as Foreign Secretary, had to a large extent dominated the election. For this had been fought on the issue of Abyssinia and Mussolini's attack upon it. Now that we were pledged to collective resistance to aggression and, simultaneously, to no great measure of rearmament, how was the desired objective of saving Abyssinia to be achieved? Perhaps Sir Samuel Hoare would soon provide the answer.

Into this 1935 Parliament came Mr. Speaker's procession, heralded a long way off by cries of "Mr. Speaker — Mr. Speaker". He was preceded by the mace, borne, upon the shoulder of his clerk, and he was accompanied by the Chaplain of the House of Commons, in black and white and purple robes. The Speaker himself strode firmly under robes of swinging black and gold, and his dim grey wig increased his air of majesty. This was Mr. Speaker Fitzroy. The Members rose to their feet at his approach and bowed to him as he passed from the bar of the House to the table, where the Chaplain turned to read the prayers, and the Speaker stood at the other side of the table.

"Setting aside all private interests and partial affections," intoned Canon Don, and at a given moment the Members all turned about towards the backs of their benches and not kneeling, for there was no room, they recited the Lord's Prayer. Then, after the final Amen, the Speaker mounted his throne, where he seemed even more elevated under its embroidered canopy, and a shout went down the long corridors of Parliament, echoed by voices further and further away. "Speaker in the Chair." The day's work had begun.

There is a regular pattern in our Parliamentary affairs. The House

---

* Subsequently Viscount Templewood.

meets to hear the speech from the Throne. Black Rod taps loudly on the doors, and advances to request the presence of this honourable House (here a nod to each of the front benches in turn) in the honourable House of Peers. The two sides of the House file out, in a crocodile of half sections which bracket the Prime Minister and the Leader of the Opposition, led by Mr. Speaker, to stand at the bar of the Lords and listen to the Sovereign reading the speech prepared for him by the Prime Minister. Then the whole procession retires to the Commons, and the Speaker, rising with the speech from the Throne 'of which for greater accuracy I have obtained a copy,' reads the whole thing over again.

After this there are usually formal speeches by the Prime Minister and the leaders of other parties in provisional acknowledgement of it; and the House adjourns early to study it. Next day the debate on the Address — an humble address — thanking the Sovereign for his gracious message, is hotly debated and goes on being hotly debated for three or four days.

Now, this is by far the easiest occasion to make a Maiden Speech; for there is absolutely nothing that can be out of order in debating the Loyal Address. If the subject you wish to discuss is not in the Loyal Address then it ought to be and you say so. To open the debate the Government usually select two of their most promising newcomers, to move and second the address. It was customary in those days, if the mover and seconder had been members of the forces, for them to wear full uniform. Wavell Wakefield thus appeared in Air Force uniform to perform the honoured task, which he did with all the gusto of a celebrated footballer.

I should have liked the opportunity myself, and thought that as the youngest member of our Party in the House, I might have been thus far indulged. The Baby of the House was a Socialist member, Malcolm MacMillan who had got in for the Western Isles, and at twenty-three was a year younger than I. However, I should have had no uniform to wear — and would have had to speak in Court dress — black knee breeches and court shoes, with a thin sword at my side. Nevertheless I decided to make my speech; for I had evolved a plan to deal with the unemployed by organising them into an honoured body to be called The National Labour Reserve, and employed on conservation work, like the system of Civilian Conservation Camps later introduced by President Roosevelt in America. This plan I had submitted when I was studying for the Diplomatic exam, to Mr. Amery who had warmly approved of it. He had forwarded the plan in turn to Sir Godfrey Thomas, Secretary to the Prince of Wales, who also seemed interested in it. But when referred to the then Minister of Labour, Sir Henry Betterton, the official reply had been that it would be regarded as a para-military organisation and that "England, does not love standing armies." (Macaulay). Now was my opportunity to put the plan forward from the floor of the House.

The House is usually very kind to Maiden speakers and spares them the worst agonies by giving them precedence in the order of debate. I took this to mean that if I spoke on the second day, I would be called first, after the end of questions. I jumped accordingly to my feet, "Mr. Speaker, Sir." But to my horror the Speaker called out, "Sir John Simon," who was already on his feet. Well, I reflected, after all he is Chancellor of the Exchequer. So I had to listen to him for about an hour. When he had finished I was on my feet again in a flash, only to be dashed back by the Speaker calling on an ex-Minister from the Labour Front Bench. Then, ye gods, Sir Archibald Sinclair, leader of the Liberal Party was called. This was too much. I got up and walked out. Why, hardly anybody remained in the House by now. They had all gone out to tea; whereas Wavell Wakefield had spoken to a crowded and buzzing House. I returned to the Chamber later in the evening when it seemed to me that it was filling up again. But now the Speaker turned a deaf eye to me. I rose in vain. Presently one of the Whips came and sat beside me. "You silly fool," he said. "Why did you go out? The Speaker was going to call you fourth after the leader of the Liberal party."

"I thought Maiden speakers had precedence," I answered coldly.

"Not over Front Bench speakers. Anyway, he is prepared to call you forth again tomorrow, which is more than you deserve."

The question was where to speak from. Winston Churchill seemed to have found a commanding nook in the corner seat below the gangway on the Front Bench and, provided he wasn't sitting in it at the time, that seemed to me as good as seat as any. There, accordingly, much to the amusement of some, I moved after questions next day and awaited the Speaker's word. The House again emptied after the two Front Bench speakers and the Liberal speaker, Major Gwylim Lloyd-George was doing his best to clear the House right out. I watched the retreating backs of Members as they reached the bar, turned to bow to Mr. Speaker and then push their way through the swing doors. At this point, however, an unexpected figure appeared at the bar — Winston Churchill and gazed incredulously at the young figure seated in his accustomed place. When I saw him, I moved to make way for him, but with an artful sense of the humour of the situation, he pressed me to remain where I was, and seated himself beside me.

"Are you going to make a Maiden Speech?" he asked.

"Yes," I replied, "and I wish you would give me some tips from the store of your great experience on how to make a Maiden Speech."

"Well, you know," he said, "the conversational style."

"They like that, do they?"

"They not only like it, but have thrived upon it, alone among the great Parliaments of the world."

"Your former Naval Secretary is sitting up there in the Distinguished Strangers Gallery," I told him, indicating my father aloft.

Winston looked up, smiling. "Your father? I remember him very well. Now, I am afraid I must leave you. Good luck." And he withdrew from the Chamber. Two rows behind me, however, Leo Amery in the seat of an ex-Minister was waiting to hear my speech on the plan which had interested him so much. In the meantime a Member sitting on my bench, interested, possibly, to know what Churchill had thought of my taking his accustomed place, had engaged me in conversation, and I never noticed that Gwylim Lloyd-George was sitting down. Several Members naturally leapt to their feet to catch the Speaker's eye, and in some discomfiture he had to bellow, "Mr. de Chair," to attract my attention. This was a bad beginning and I have never felt that my Maiden Speech was impressive. Instead of concentrating on the main plan for a National Labour Reserve, I added a plea for a joint share by the self-governing Dominions and ourselves in the administration of the dependent Colonial Empire — and I even made a case for the introduction into our affairs of the Referendum, as it is used in Australia. I affected a certain deference to the House at the outset. "The jungle is large and I am small." But it was fortunate for me that I drew a place shortly afterwards, for the first and last time, in the ballot on going into Committee of Supply. This enabled me to introduce a motion of my own in the middle of the Navy Estimates — and this speech, much more coherent, better established and worked on with the help of the First Sea Lord, Chatfield, was thought by most people to have been my Maiden Speech. It caused something of a stir because of my reference to what had hitherto been treated as a secret — the asdic for locating submarines. The speech also sought to disprove the popular theory that fleets were doomed to annihilation by the advent of Air Power. On balance my case was upheld by the experience of war. It is always a good thing in the House to become identified with some particular subject, so that the House turns instinctively to you on occasions, instead of dismissing you at all times as a bore. And, as what one Admiral in the

House, Sir Murray Sueter, described as an hereditary expert on naval matters, I might well have concentrated on them. I did ask some pertinent questions in the House on the development of gliding bombs and wireless controlled torpedoes, but received the assurance that development on traditional weapons was adequate.

The Press reported my plan for a National Labour Reserve, and Leo Amery stepped down from his bench to congratulate me on it. But I had a feeling of having put my foot on a step that was not there, and plunged into darkness. There were too many other Members, as usual, making speeches on the Loyal Address, for anyone to bother much about mine.

In the meantime Christmas was approaching and I was swept up in a new and violent emotion.

My Aunt Beatrix,* ever sensitive to success, and proud of her young nephew's entering the House, now invited my wife and me to dine at her flat in Charles Street. She rang me up.

"The Premier is staying with Derek," she had told me without preamble, just before the election apparently at Cullen.

When we reached Charles Street her son Derek had evidently finished entertaining the ex-Premier for he and Nina Seafield were of the party. There was also an unusually attractive woman of uncertain age, standing up in a long white evening dress, and resting her elbow lightly on the mantelpiece. Her honey-coloured hair was rolled across her head in an unuusual tiara fashion and she gazed penetratingly into my eyes.

My wife and I were very tired by all the exertion of the election and the strain of making my Maiden Speech — to which of course she had listened many times before it was delivered, and had then waited for hours in the Ladies Gallery to hear. Nancy Astor had approached me after my speech, to come down and have dinner with herself and some Christian Science Lecturer who was in the building. But when I said that I had my wife up in the gallery, Nancy Astor's enthusiasm for having me dine seemed to wane. "Better run along and look after her," was all she said.

Vivienne Wooley-Hart's reaction was quite different. "Better run along and look after me," was her line. She too was American and looked not unlike Lady Astor. She had been married to Count Bernsdorff, of the Austrian Foreign Office in Vienna in 1914, which should have dated her, but for some reason did not. For one thing, she made no attempt to conceal it. She told me a lot about her life in Vienna after the war.

---

* The late Mrs. Geoffrey White.

118

"We were very poor by that time, and having nothing to do, we used to go along to the morgue just to amuse ourselves. One day, a real hot baking day, Bernsdorff and I were walking along a street near the morgue, when I felt a cold shiver and looked up. There was figure coming towards us. It was wearing a heavy greatcoat — and I thought, 'That's odd, wearing a great heavy coat like that on a stifling hot day.' But a cold wind seemed to come with it, and as it passed it turned and gave us one look out of its — well, it just had no face. It had a skull. Evidently the corpses didn't relish our looking at them in the morgue."

I found Vivienne Wooley-Hart very stimulating and as I was dead tired and had lost my voice completely with a cold, or laryngitis, I just gazed at her and drank it all in. When I did speak it was in a husky voice on account of the cold, and she was patently attracted by it.

After dinner the women withdrew and Geoffrey White, an Edwardian figure with a grey moustache and a stiff shirt front, gathered us around his end of the shining mahogany table. None of them had paid much attention to me as I was so young and, on account of my vocal chords and the Wooley-Hart, somewhat silent. So Geoffrey asked me some leading questions about the new Parliament. To get into Parliament in those days cost a certain amount of money and was regarded as something of a social achievement. All chairs were accordingly switched slightly in my direction. After we had joined the ladies, it was decided to go on to the Ritz to dance, and tables were reserved for us all there. Derek was in high spirits in the taxi and his remarks slightly shocked my wife's delicate ears.

Once we were seated at the tables and the champagne was flowing, I found the Wooley-Hart sitting beside me. We danced and I whispered German into her ear.

"*In dem Leben eines jeden Menchens gibt es eine Sieten Gasse,*" I said.

And she laughingly replied, "*Wie du Dinge errinerest ist fabelhaft.*"

"I have just bought an island in the West Indies," she went on. "I met some old Bozo who said he wanted to sell his island and I said to him if you will sell it for what that old lugger of yours that goes with it, cost you, I'll buy it. And I bought it. Why, it's lovely. You just lie there looking at the blue sea and the palm trees. Why don't you and Thelma come and stay with me there?"

"It sounds alluring. But there is Parliament."

"Don't they have a recess soon?"

"They do."

"You talk to her about it."

We returned to the table and I danced with Nina Seafield. I made some remark in praise of Vivienne Wooley-Hart.

"That old t-t-trollop," burst out Nina. "I don't know what you can see in her." Nina was very like Queen Victoria. She paused to greet a couple on the dance floor, of which the woman seemed to me remarkably dark and beautiful. She was Essex Drury; later Lady Monsell.

Thelma had not failed to notice the ease with which Vivienne and I had got on to terms of intimacy, and her exhaustion, not merely after the election but after the birth of our son Rodney as well, was such that she was in no mood to treat the event in a good-humoured fashion. But when we were invited by Vivienne to dine with her for the Chelsea Arts Ball, Thelma had no valid reason, beyond her own instinct, for refusing. So we went. It was a fancy dress occasion, and we hired from Clarksons costumes in which we turned up at 56 Princes Gate as Lord Nelson and Lady Hamilton. Everybody else seemed to be in pyjamas or pirate bandanas. Vivienne wore a leopard skin. We felt overdressed. The house was unusual in that the front rooms were decorated for Vivienne in black glass and chromium while you passed from all this into a Louis Quinze dining-room where her aged and mildly amused husband, Wooley-Hart, was dining by himself. He did not take part in any of her festivities — which had included recently an enormous party during which a live pink elephant had been introduced into the illuminated gardens behind the house. Now the whole party of us went off to a preliminary dinner at a restaurant down the road in Knightsbridge, where I found myself beside Vivienne and a good long way from Thelma. Opposite to me was a man dressed as Pickwick or something of the sort with grey cloak and high collar up to his ears. He was the editor of the *Tatler* and his memory did not fail him when he saw Vivienne. "I like my love with a W-H," he chuckled. "Am I right?"

"You are," she cried, "and let me introduce you to your future Prime Minister."

"Good God," his eyes bulged at me. "Are you another of those young men who want to be a big shot? I'm always meeting people who want to be big shots."

There was a certain amount of dressed crab and wine — before we went on to the Albert Hall. Here a box was reserved above the dance floor where one or two thousand couples revolved to the music. The place was gaily decorated with mural designs of gods and goddesses embracing under grape vines and somehow I was dancing with Vivienne at midnight when the lights went dim and came up again with the New Year. It seemed an occasion for salutation. But the spectacle, witnessed or guessed from a distance, was not well received at home. Before we got home Vivienne took some of us on to the 400 in Leicester Square and there in her leopard skin, which somewhat startled the inmates, she danced with me while the band played 'Dancing cheek to cheek'.

I suppose it was inevitable after this that Vivienne should come down to stay with us in Norfolk for a weekend. Thelma invited an old friend Elspeth Thompson-Walker to even the numbers. Evelyn had been one of the girls in the drawing-room at Bear's House when I first met Thelma. Apparently I had said to Elspeth: "You are one of those modern young women who will have synthetic babies." All this and a good deal more Vivienne was interested to hear from Elspeth. I saw little if anything of Vivienne alone, but she found a moment, walking in the garden, to say, "You're not the sort of man who could survive on one woman. All this Poppa and Momma stuff." With which potent observation she returned to London.

This may not be a very subtle approach but is calculated to tickle the vanity of a young man. By now Thelma was giving a firm negative to any invitation to the island in Bermuda. The only question was whether I went alone. Soon the bedside lamps began to fly about the room, to be picked up in fragments by astonished servants next morning. Suddenly Thelma herself departed — and I wandered into an empty bathroom where the scent she used still lingered on a damp bath towel. I had never contemplated an alternative as harsh as this and drove through the night to Merristwood, her home, where she had been born, and whither in the manner of all enraged brides, she had withdrawn. The house was dark and shuttered on my arrival in the early hours. I climbed up a drain-pipe and entered her room by the window. Within a few days Vivienne Wooley-Hart was on the high seas, bound for her sun-kissed island in the Caribbean and I resumed the preoccupations of a Member of Parliament. The affair had not lasted long — a few weeks. I received a letter or two, but burnt them unanswered. I was throwing one on the flames of a fire in the Aye Lobby of the House, when Leslie Burgin passed, soft footed; murmured 'smokeless fuel'; and was gone.

Beatrix had intervened, sensitive at having introduced us under her own roof, and urging her friend not to destroy her own flesh and blood's future happiness. As for me, I transmuted the base metal into prose — placing Vivienne squarely into *Red Tie in the Morning* as the Duchess of Lynwood; a by no means unflattering portrait. 'Not one of the Great

Ladies of England, but one of the Small Women of America'. And it was of her that I was thinking when I wrote 'A woman's prime is not the period of her freshest beauty but the moment at which her beauty and experience are combined to the most deadly effect.'

This book and *Buried Pleasure* tell the story of my life in a series of Chapters of Autobiography. But like most autobiographies its early drafts were significant more for its omissions than for what they say. Most people are out to give a good account of themselves, and readability suffers. They are offering you what American restaurants describe as the ultimate dinner — a huge steak; but without the pepper and salt that makes it go down easily.

Most authors, if they want to write about their marriages, have to get divorced two or three times before they can write about those delicate and dangerous episodes, without inhibition. Most husbands spend a lot of their lives traversing very thin ice, and when they fall through it, the water tends to be very cold till they reach the bank and clamber out, looking for the next pond.

So it may now be possible to add a little pepper and salt to my account of the Wooley-Hart episode, when I was married to my first wife — Thelma. I wrote a novel (unpublished) for her benefit which might have been entitled 'I can explain . . . . in 80,000 words.' She found them very touching and very nearly forgave me for an episode which nearly broke up our marriage. One might have supposed, after reading those 80,000 words, that my relations with this exotic nymphomaniac stopped short of sullying the sheets of the marriage bed. Alas, dear reader, that was not so.

After the New Year's Eve Ball at the Albert Hall, the party got into various cars and taxis to go on to the 400 — then the leading night-club in London. I have referred to the impact of Vivienne's leopard skin, in that dimly lit establishment; but what I did not refer to — husband's amnesia, no doubt — was that Vivienne and I managed to separate ourselves from the rest of the party leaving the Albert Hall, and call in at her place in Princes Gate. Her elderly husband, whom we had last seen sitting with a rug over his knees, eating fish, alone, at the dining table in the Louis XV dining-room, had long since retired to bed. The glasses and bottles, in the modern part of the house, had been tidied away by the sort of priceless servants still to be found in 1935, and they had also gone to bed. Uncertain whether any of the other guests might step off to relieve themselves on the way to the night-club, Vivienne and I shut the dining-room door behind us, and she lay down promptly on the thick pile savonnerie carpet of the exquisite dining-room. I was in such a hurry that I found Nelson's sword a slight impediment, and also had some difficulty unfastening my white knee breeches. As Vivienne wore nothing at all under her leopard skin, contact was soon made, and the whole procedure lasted about five minutes, before I was buckling Nelson's sword on again, and we were arriving to join the rest of the party at the 400. Arriving indeed, before many of the others. Here endeth the first lesson in deception.

The second lesson was on Box Hill. Thelma and I had been looking at a drop-head coupé, by Thrupp and Maberley, on a Humber chassis. I took an opportunity to take this out for a spin; after we had bought it for £800, nearly new. The leather smelt as only the leather of newly coach-built cars smelt in those days — rich and rare. I picked up Vivienne and drove her down to Surrey — this must have been in mid-winter, because she left for Bermuda in March at the latest. Anyway, it was a clear perfect day, and we had the furry motoring rugs, given to Thelma and me as wedding presents.

I do not know why we chose Box Hill; presumably because of the view; and the privacy from which we could see anyone approaching.

Vivienne was a woman who enjoyed a very varied experience of men. To say that Thelma, a fairly inexperienced young woman, whose brushes with Italians in Maseratis and Alfa Romeos had been fairly brief, could not hold a candle to Vivienne Wooley-Hart, would be unfair. It is unfair to expose a candle flame to the competition of a blowlamp.

There is no doubt that at this point, Vivienne was interested in me; and she did in fact marry again three times later in her well advanced life, although she always retained the name Wooley-Hart, possibly because he was the richest of her seven husbands. I visited her in 1970 or 71, with my own third wife, Tessa, and two of my children, when she was staying at her farm in Connecticut. By this time she was over 80, and surrounded by young men in their twenties. She had a small apartment on Park Avenue in New York, which she described as just a jewel-box. She had taken to oil painting, quite well, at the farm. She lamented having sold off 500 acres of it, before land prices boomed, and was left with the patch of ground on which the house stood. We ate barbecues by the light of oil torches on tall sconces in the garden.

I think she was highly entertained to see me after a lapse of 35 years. But I could not help remembering my father's warning that if I married her, she would be an old woman, while I was still in my prime.

However, when one is 24, flushed by some slight success, and sexually starved during a long pregnancy, the hectic in the blood certainly rages. I only slept with her one night in the house in Princes Gate. It took a bit of diplomacy before I got away and found an excuse to escape from Thelma, even for one night. We arranged that I should go ahead to Princes Gate, and she would join me there the following night. So I found myself in a room on the third floor, and had to wait until Muggy was asleep in his own room before Vivienne summoned me down to a sort of boudoir, where a Louis XV daybed, with gilded head and foot, was made up for occasional use.

The first shock was to find that the sheets were very thin and had already got torn in places. This somewhat disconcerted me, as my foot kept on pushing through a gap in the sheets, and getting caught up. This annoyed Vivienne, who was possibly also embarrassed by the torn sheets, in the otherwise luxurious house. Also she felt that it was time she extended my education a bit, and I may have been too impatient to be a satisfactory pupil. She certainly opened up inviting prospects.

"You can beat my bottom till it is black and blue," she suggested "but not here. It might wake Muggy up." On the whole, I was relieved when Thelma arrived next day and we were able to inspect the house in Buckingham gate belonging to the Apsleys, with their recent portraits by de Lazlo. We decided to rent it — just the other end of Bird Cage Walk from the Houses of Parliament. That night, Thelma and I slept together in the room on the third floor at Princes Gate; and shortly afterwards, my Aunt Beatrix cornered Vivienne and told her to lay off me. Vivienne made a final appeal by telephone to me at Weasenham, in Norfolk, to join her in Bermuda; but by this time, with Thelma monitoring all calls on another extension, as usual, I was somewhat guarded in my endearments and declined the invitation on parliamentary and constituency grounds. So endeth the third lesson, not very successfully, in marital deception.

CHAPTER 10

It was a dreary winter and suddenly all the great names died out of England in a night. Beatty, Jellicoe, Kipling, the King. There was great pomp in the King's passing. I stood in the bitter cold of Westminster Hall with the rest of the Lords and Commons to pay homage to the dead King on his catafalque; guarded by his Life Guards, leaning, white gloved, upon their swords.

Thelma did not want to return to Weasenham, and we accelerated our move into Necton, another house in the Norfolk constituency. It was now a desolate place — the great trees all gone, and wreckage in their wake. The lovely orangery demolished. We employed a builder from Dereham in the constituency to redecorate the house and renew the plumbing. He said ruefully at the end of it all that he did not get two halfpennies for a penny out of the contract. Nevertheless the house was bright within by the time he had finished, and here we spent the spring and summer when not in London. We required a house in London, and had rented, first the attractive house in Buckingham Gate belonging to the Apsleys, where the bugler of Wellington Barracks woke us too early and the traffic changed gear outside the door; then bought the long lease of a house in Eaton Place. In Norfolk we were always welcome at Narford, the home of Carlo Fountaine, Chairman of my Consistituency Association, and there we went to bathe in the lake on Sundays. Carlo would row us out of the boat-house and round the wooded point, sliding his oar into the water if it squeaked; and near the beating tom-tom hydraulic rams — with their repeated thump and hiss of escaping water — we would dive and swim from the boat. Carlo would float for long periods, like some risen Loch Ness monster. Afterwards there would be cold supper spread in glorious array; cold duck, cold chicken, ham. Enough for all who might come. The Fountaines had two young boys, Andrew and John, then perhaps fourteen and ten years of age.

This is in no sense a history book; but some account must be given of the various crises which arose in this Parliament, for the MacDonald-Baldwin government and the Baldwin-MacDonald government rested upon the jellied mass of the Conservative majority; of which I was but a prawn in the aspic. There is first the enigma of Baldwin himself. He appeared to have no driving force, unless to steer carefully in the wake of public opinion proves some capacity for steering — one is inclined to be tossed about in a rough wake. Yet he seemed to hypnotise the House when he spoke. Winston Churchill could thunder from his place below the gangway about the pace of German rearmament and urge the need for long-term planning in munitions. "In these sombre fields, Mr. Speaker, in the first year you sow the seed. In the second year you harrow. And it is not until the third year that you reap the harvest." Or to us: "One healthy growl from you young people would alter the history of the world." At the eleventh hour we gave one healthy growl and altered the history of the world; on the night of the Norwegian disaster, but we left it very late. In the meantime Baldwin was entrenched behind all the ramparts of patronage and official sanctity which go with office. The Whips said of Winston that he was a spent force — had taken to the brandy bottle — would take up any line if he thought it would get him back into power. And Baldwin would make speeches about the sound of the corncrake in the field and the whetstone against scythe which made every Tory squire behind him shed a tear in his secret heart. Yet with it all he was one of the most astute foxes who ever breathed. No Prime Minister ever looked more like Oliver Cromwell. Indeed, as I write, a portrait of Oliver gazes down from the wall and if you cut his hair, removed the black armour and put him in a blue suit with a pipe, you could label it Stanley Baldwin and nobody be any the wiser. There was a maddening streak of piety in Baldwin. And he had an instinct for public opinion, which in a democratic age was holy. No sooner had Parliament been elected than the news leaked out that Sir Samuel Hoare was doing a deal with French Foreign Minister, Laval, to hand over a slice of Abyssinia in the hope of calling Mussolini to a halt. Those of us who had campaigned at ninety meetings against Mussolini's ruthless aggression and vowed to halt it by collective measures, were all aghast. In the lobby Members clustered round old Sir Austen Chamberlain, who doffed his top hat to mop his brow and said, "I'm like the old parrot. I'm not allowed to say anything. But I can think a hell of a lot." Baldwin sensed the rising storm; and without a moment's hesitation threw his Foreign Secretary overboard. At the Despatch Box, he rubbed his stomach in a soothing circular motion and said, "I sanctioned the plan. But if I had known what the public would think, I would not have sanctioned it."

Very different was the voice of Sir Samuel Hoare, now speaking from that third bench below the gangway beside Amery and Austen Chamberlain. Often there were tears in his eyes and his pathetic appearance was increased by a strip of sticking plaster across his nose. He told of his attempts to get the other powers to act in agreement with us. Nobody but ourselves had moved a man or a gun. He held out his horn-rimmed spectacles and waved them up and down slowly to emphasise his points. He retailed his meetings with Laval. There was a slight titter when he said that he had left Lady Maud and the baggage in Paris. "Who was the baggage?" whispered an impious member. Sam Hoare proceeded to explain why he had felt it better to save the bulk of Abyssinia than to abandon it all. It was the argument, specious, and soon to become all too familiar in relation to dictators, of buying them off with scraps of territory. Whatever may be said against the 1935-45 Parliament in its middle life, it did not approve of appeasement at the beginning; and Abyssinia was temporarily absorbed into the Italian Empire. There were lurid reports of the use of mustard gas.

But with hindsight it is clear that all we achieved was to throw Mussolini (who had fought on our side in the First World War) into the arms of Hitler, with incalculable consequences for us in the Mediterranean and Middle East. And at the end of it all Haile Selassie's dynasty ended in the massacre of his whole family, and its replacement by a Communist State subservient to Moscow which could not even feed its own people. But in 1935 we were indignant and oblivious of the possible consequences of our actions. One should be sceptical about the politics of indignation; notably in the case of South Africa today (1987).

If Stanley Baldwin was quite unable to cope with the King's enemies abroad, he knew just how to use them at home, when the unfortunate monarch overstepped the bounds of domestic propriety. The news that the beloved Prince of Wales, now King, wished to marry Mrs. Simpson struck England like a wet fish in the face. I was in the bath at 92, Eaton Place when my wife came racing up the stairs with a newspaper, and shouted, "This woman must go!" All over England wives were racing upstairs with newspapers. We had heard of Mrs. Simpson, in the columns of a weekly magazine called *Cavalcade*, which was no respecter of persons. But no one had given serious thought to the possibility of her becoming Queen of England. Only a few weeks earlier my wife had sighed with awe and sympathy at the spectacle of this wan young King, still uncrowned, seated in his doublet and hose, upon a single throne in the House of Lords at the opening of Parliament while Lord Londonderry held the glittering diadem before him on a velvet cushion. He had looked, my wife thought, so pathetic and so sweet. Now there was nothing bad enough to be said about him. The Welsh, who a week before had cheered his appearance in the Principality, now turned from him in puritanical loathing. I too was deeply shocked. But if a Member's duty is to represent his constituents, there would never have been any doubt as to my duty. From the hour of my arrival on Friday in Norfolk till I returned to the dramatic events of the House during the following week, there was a ceaseless murmur of anger and dismay. There were certainly no long views about the danger of tampering with primogeniture and the hereditary principle in the matter of the Crown.

In the Commons Baldwin sustained admirably the role of the patient father dealing with an erring son. Everything he said seemed more in sorrow than in anger, while the young King, driven nearly hysterical by private torments and public uncertainty, had no platform from which to defend himself. Yet he did not go undefended. And here we saw, although we did not recognise, the true greatness of Churchill. For he was already far from power and favour. And now stood up, in the teeth of the angry Commons, who all but tore him to shreds, and pleaded for time and sanity before so drastic a step as the removal of a King be taken. We were deaf to his blandishments. And it was not long before Baldwin himself appeared at the bar of the House, bowed to the Speaker twice as he approached and said, "A message from the King, Sir, signed by his own hand." There was no triumph in his voice. A certain smugness, perhaps. And then, coming past the table he handed to Mr. Speaker Fitzroy, the short document of Abdication.

There was legislation to be enacted; for even with our unwritten constitution you cannot just brush aside a Monarch with a roar of "ayes". But the machinery of Parliament, so ponderous at other times, now whizzed like a guillotine. And Baldwin, so lethargic in all other matters of state, moved now with the strength, the speed, and the suppleness of a panther. It was his hour. Or perhaps his second hour, for he had acted likewise in 1926 at the time of the general strike. He awoke twice from long slumber like a giant refreshed. And if there is one thing that can be said of the statesmanship of Stanley Baldwin it is that he brought us, as a united nation, within measurable distance of the Second World War.

Apart from the moments of high drama, all-night sittings often provided the best entertainment. The old Chamber of the House was a singularly unhealthy place in which to spend a lot of time — the air conditioning brought in with it the dust of ages and the heating rushed up through coconut matting on which Members had ground their boots for hours — the effect, said the wags, was to give Members hot heads and cold feet. And the light blared down balefully from large squares of glass high up in the roof, decorated with the roses of Lancaster and York. From every pillar some gargoyle from the turgid imagination of Pugin glared down upon you from wreaths of vine leaves and grapes. And all stained to the darkness of Victorian night. Lying along the Front Bench below the gangway, in the small hours of the morning, was Victor Raikes, with a white order paper over his eyes to shield them from the glare on high. Arthur Greenwood was speaking from the Opposition Despatch Box.

"Is it in order, Mr. Speaker," he demanded, "for an honourable Member to be lying in a recumbent position?"

Slowly Victor rose, hingewise to a sitting posture, removing the order paper from his face and retorted, "That is better than lying in an upright position." Then lay back amid the laughter.

When the Labour Members had tired of keeping the Government awake, a task which required a formidable effort in 1938, they wanted to go home towards five in the morning. But by this time the Tories had got their second wind and David Margesson, the Patronage Secretary, (as the Chief Whip is still officially called, without a smile or trace of irony), rose from the Treasury Bench in a cut-away morning coat and kept the House going for an hour or so himself.

We came thus in good order and good time to the events which preceded the Second World War. I had become very isolationist in my views, believing that Hitler, if left to himself, would dash himself to pieces on the Russians. I believed that guarantees to Roumania and Poland could save nothing in Eastern Europe, while committing us to a struggle there which was not worth the bones of an English Grenadier.

"Let us quit the cockpit of Europe," I cried. "Let us turn to the fertile plains of our own Empire and try to secure its development." These words, torn from my speech in the Commons, were flaunted right across the top of the front page of the *Daily Express* next morning. This was the sort of reporting I understood. I asked to see Beaverbrook; and was received by him in a lordly house; down the marble stairs of which his doctor was descending with shaking head.

"I have warned him," said the doctor, "to get away to the sunshine in a dry climate."

The Beaver — (need I describe this wizened little monkey of a man whose guts were so many coils of electric cable?) — received me, seated in an armchair beside a dictaphone. With this machine he fiddled all the time and, so sinister a man was he reputed to be, that I eyed the instrument warily, by no means dismissing the possibility that it was being used as a recording device to report the entire conversation, whereby I might subsequently be discomfited.

He coughed pathetically, "They want me to go to Arizona," he croaked. "And I'm going. But I've left word to keep the presses grinding for you. I liked your speech. If you like, I will run you a campaign of speeches. Of course they will say you are Beaverbrook's stool-pigeon. All you can do is to deny that with fierceness and passion. At first you will be disappointed in your audiences, (he pronounced it ardiences) but that's only at the beginning. What do you say?"

What was I to say? I could thus have become a national figure overnight — the apostle of Isolationism; of which Beaverbrook was the Lord. But the idea of denying the connection, Peterwise, with fierceness and passion, was not in my character. Yet to be known in the House as a Beaverbrook stool-pigeon undoubtedly spelt exclusion from all official advancement. I said I would prefer to work on my own, but in so far as my speeches fitted in with his own designs, I hoped the Express Newspapers would give prominence to them. The next one was to be made in the Connaught Hall at Newcastle, and the Beaver, visibly weary of his asthmatic affliction, repeated that he would keep the presses grinding and saw me to the head of the stairs. Whether it has been the result of this inconclusive meeting or because my interest in imperial affairs naturally led me along lines approved by the Beaver, it is a fact that I always enjoyed a good press from his newspapers while he was alive. I did not see the old wizard again until after the war, when our Party had been soundly thrashed at the 1945 Election.

In 1937 I made hay with Conservative orthodoxy in *Red Tie in the Morning*. And this hilarious satire, in which a young Tory Member, John Armour, tries to help his old friend, Sir James Peabody at a by-election by standing in dark glasses and moustache as an Independent workers' candidate to split the Opposition vote, only to find himself elected (on two sides of the House) was ecstatically received by the reviewers. If reviews could make a best-seller, this should have sold well, but Stanley Baldwin was expected to give up the Premiership after the Coronation, and he appeared in the novel as the Prime Minister, Mr. Wormwood Scrubs who went to the Lords at the height of the armaments boom as Lord Gall and Wormwood. I had the quixotic notion that it would be unfair to lampoon him after he had resigned, and so I insisted, against the publisher's advice, in having the book published just before the Coronation. The book got the right sort of reviews, and one of them, reviewing the bizarre career of Mr. Snooks-Badajoz, said, 'Mr. de Chair, one feels, would make a stimulating dictator.' But the Coronation ironed all else out of the newspapers, and at the end of it, the public mind was as a blank page. Ronald Cartland, one of the most promising young Members on our side, who was unfortunately killed on active service in the war, said that an old friend, whose opinion he valued most, had said of the book, 'If Disraeli had been alive today and had set about writing Vivian Grey what he would in fact have written would have been *Red Tie in the Morning*.' There was one incident about this book which illustrates the unexpected pitfalls which beset an author's path. The publishers submitted the typescript to their counsel for libel. Learned counsel in this instance was my friend in the House, Quintin Hogg.* He instantly pronounced the book most libellous. There was first, he pointed out, the Duchess of Lynwood — clearly meant to be Nancy Astor, (a comparison which had never entered my head). Then there was Sir James Peabody, a keen if absent-minded student of Theucydides with a very pushing wife. Did the author not know that Sir Somebody else with a very pushing wife had also been a keen student of Greek History and had failed miserably at a by-election? (No, I had not known.) Then there was the girl Marjory Graham. If she existed also in real life, there might be most libellous consequences. (No, she did not exist in real life.) The publishers were slowly reassured; and in any case the Coronation trod on the book as if it were a beetle on the route of a Durbar.

There was, in the thirties, an unusual dread of war. This was partly founded upon books like *The Shape of Things to Come* by Wells, and an exaggerated notion that war would literally end civilised life on the planet. It is surprising how many people who dreaded war in 1936 enjoyed it when the thing happened. But to judge the 1935 Parliament, it is essential to absorb this fact; that there was an absolute revulsion in Britain and France to a resort to war in order to stop any dictator, whatever he did. There was an immense amount of self-deception and wishful thinking; and both Mussolini and Hitler traded on this. They realised that they could push us to extraordinary lengths without risk of serious action, until they hoped it would be too late for us to act at all.

* Later Viscount Hailsham, Lord Chancellor.

Now that we know so much of the story it is easy to point to Hitler's reoccupation of the Rhineland in 1936 as the moment at which Britain and France should have reacted firmly and forestalled the whole march of events. Hitler, it is said, promised to resign or slit his throat if the occupation were resisted. Since then we have put the blame on the French, who were said to be unwilling to move. And the French have put the blame on us, saying that we would not support them. There, nevertheless, was the decisive moment and, from two benches behind, I watched Anthony Eden explain in worried but unruffled tones the grave events which were unfolding. Did he comprehend the full implications of Hitler's first overt step beyond the Versailles borders? If so, should he not have staked all on rousing the two nations bordering the English Channel to resist? This was the turning point. The path of statesmanship was clear. Resist. By the time Neville Chamberlain took over, there was very little else to do but appease, if only to gain time. It was his predecessor, Baldwin, who pointed in 1936 the path which was to be followed with accelerating servility in 1938, to Godesberg and Munich. Eden resigned in due course, over the government's reluctance to impose oil sanctions against Italy. But it was over the Rhineland that he might have resigned with more effect on the course of world events. Later, with the departure of Eden and his faithful under-secretary Cranborne, the Commons was all a-buzz. Rounding a corner of the aye lobby I nearly collided with the short stocky black-jacketed figure of Churchill. He had his hands in his jacket pockets.

"Well, Mr. de Chair," he asked, "are you going to make a speech?"

"I did not think I should have a chance of catching the Speaker's eye," I replied.

"On the contrary, you would have an excellent opportunity, for nobody has made up his mind yet which way to turn."

And, feeling that he had put up a good supporter, he passed genially along the lobby. The 1922 Committee of Tory backbenchers was at that moment in session upstairs in room 14, thrashing out the problem. I went into the Chamber and approached Mr. Speaker's Throne, asking him if he would put my name on his list. He looked keenly at me, like an eagle eyeing a dove; and nodded. I stood up in my place soon after and caught his eye with fatal ease. I spoke warmly in support of Neville Chamberlain. After that Mr. Churchill, for quite a while, passed me in the lobby without urging me to speak.

How did it come about that a young Member of twenty-five in that Parliament ranged himself under the banner of Neville Chamberlain rather than of Churchill? There were many reasons. Both my father and Carlo Fountaine (my constituency Chairman) were of the Jellicoe school in the Navy and Churchill was more or less identified with the Beatty school; moreover their experience of Winston had been when he had come early to office as First Lord of the Admiralty and was regarded as too self-confident and ambitious, ("Regarded himself as a mixture of Lord Nelson and Lord St. Vincent," said one of them) and thus subconsciously my mind was wary of Winston. Secondly I was susceptible to all the influence which an administration, powerfully entrenched, knows how to exercise over a fresh Member. I was prepared on occasion, and did, to stand up against the dictate of the Whips' Office, where David Margesson ruled like a teak-faced Red Indian and secured a very wide measure of subordination. But I was as sensititive to their authority as a new boy in school, however spirited, is likely to be under the senior prefects. Thirdly I had a strongly religious bias — and Neville seemed to me like some old prophet out of the Old Testament. I believed in the possibility of miracles and divine intervention — and when at a dire moment a telegram was passed along the Treasury Bench, in the middle of Neville's speech, containing a last minute invitation to meet Hitler in Germany, I was one of the first to believe that peace had been vouchsafed to us. I too probably waved my order papers; while Winston frowned darkly at the credulity of so many responsible people. I had entered the fog of Westminster and I did not see clearly things which would have been evident to the youth who wrote *The Impending Storm*. I could even on the very eve of war reassure my constituents with the feeble joke about the Rome-Berlin Axis that the dictators were always grinding their own axis. When I said there would be no war, I was voicing an article of faith. But the corollary was equally severe. Once war came, the whole basis of faith in Chamberlain collapsed and was replaced by a cynical detachment. Yet if it be proved by the long jury of future historians that those who supported Chamberlain at the time of Munich were 'guilty men', as we were so freely called in the 1945 Election, then I was certainly one of the guilty men. One more explanation for the support which Neville secured in the House must be advanced. After the extraordinary flabbiness of Baldwin's administration, and the appointment of such men as Sir Thomas Inskip as Minister for Co-ordination of Defence ("One of the most extraordinary appointments," exclaimed Churchill, "since Caligula appointed his horse a Consul"), the House felt a definite tightening of the reins of government as soon as Neville took over. This new and firmer grip at once reassured them, without their pausing to ask in which direction the formidable old man was driving.

When the Munich crisis broke upon the country in the autumn of 1938, the nation was bitterly divided. Every family and house party was riven to the point of coming to blows. For those who scorned the waved paper and the 'peace with honour' cry of Neville at the airport — so different from the circumstances in which Dizzy had returned from the Congress of Berlin in 1878 — those people who were not taken in by Hitler, raged with a baffled energy at the gullibility of the mass. The argument in the autumn of 1938 was not 'we must have another year to prepare' (although that was inherent in the Munich Settlement and is its only justification). The cry was 'Peace is saved.' And the snarling reply was 'No. War is but postponed.'

That autumn and the Munich crisis, saw my wife and myself with our single son, at a charming Elizabethan house in Norfolk called Breccles, just beyond the border of the constituency. Our own house at Necton was let for the summer while we were in London, as our finances could not run to maintaining two establishments all the time. Moreover Breccles was an exciting house where the haunted room had been liberally decorated by some long-dead monk in blood. It was of Tudor brick, with an impressive row of seven gables on the north side, and was owned by Venetia Montagu, the widow of Edwin Montagu whose name was identified with the Montagu Chelmsford reforms in India. She very kindly agreed to let the house to us for six weeks at a moderate rent, and we took over the service of her butler Clements, a model, I have often thought, of what a butler should be. He was slightly grey-haired. He had an air of dignity without pomposity and deference without servility. The gardens, surrounded by old Tudor walls, were very lovely; planted out with scarlet zinnias in great profusion at that time of year. The house was approached from a by-road, by way of a short oak avenue and an old brick archway, topped curiously, like the dromedary, by two curved humps. The old oak in the house was mostly stripped and limed; and over it all presided an unusual smell, connected possibly with the seven large dogs which normally leapt about it. There was a little shooting round the house which had 160 acres with it; and away to the west rolled the breckland, over which it was possible to ride Judy Montagu's pony. Here our solicitor, John Barstow, and his pretty wife, Diana, stayed with us at the height of the Munich crisis; and gravely was the legal imperturbability strained by the arguments we advanced for Chamberlain. At this time, also, Chips Channon, who had been P.P.S.

to the Under-Secretary for Foreign Affairs, Rab Butler, told me that I was going to be given office. Chips was a dapper sparrow who lived at No. 3 Belgrave Square, next door to the Duke of Kent and had become totally absorbed in the social whirlpool; and the exertion required to remain at the vortex, and not be vomited up to the circumference of the same now preoccupied him. He seemed to know everybody. He had at one time written a book on the Ludwigs of Bavaria and decorated his dining-room in the style of some rococo palace. There, at the glass mirror dining-table, he entertained the celebrities of the day or those who were expected to become celebrities. He prided himself on knowing everybody and everything. What he probably had in mind was that his brother-in-law, Alan Lennox-Boyd, had contemplated, on being appointed a junior Minister, making me his Parliamentary Private Secretary. If Alan ever thought of such a thing I had probably not made the tactful reply when, over a game of cards at Camfield, under the driving eye of old Queenborough who liked to see the young politicians up and doing and with Whitney and Daphne Straight making up the party, Alan had asked me if I would ever consider being a P.P.S. and I had replied, "Good heavens no!" Anyway, when Chips took me aside in the House, and put his arm through mine, which was no doubt intended as a sort of social accolade in public, and said "You are going to be given office," I thought that I was about to be summoned by the Prime Minister and made an Under-Secretary. I walked between the bracken turning gold on the breckland in Norfolk and thought how very well everything was working out. But I heard no more of under-secretaryships or P.P.S.-ships; and was soon caught up in the great treadmill of the Army machine.

Fortunately I had not waited for Munich or Czechoslovakia before joining the Army. On the day that Hitler marched into Austria I marched into the Knightsbridge barracks. I had long fancied myself in a plume and a cuirass; and a friend in the Irish Guards, Harry Elliott, who was at the War Office, explained to me the advantages of the Supplementary Reserve. He consulted the Army List and it appeared that although the Foot Guards had a number of Supplementary Reserve officers, the Household Cavalry had not yet accepted any. Yet there was no technical reason, beyond the fact that they had an unusually large number of officers on the Reserve of officers, why they should not take on one or two in the Supplementary Reserve.

Charlie Romney, in Norfolk, was enlisted in support of the application; and Harry Elliott said that Lord Bridgeman at the War Office, who had heard me speak in the House, was willing to help at that end. In due course I was invited to luncheon with the Colonel at the Officers' Mess in Knightsbridge. It was necessary to create a good impression. I went to a suitably Edwardian tailor in Savile Row; and was fitted by the old man (Scholte) himself. I felt somewhat ill-at-ease; but marched forth, in a few days' time, feeling like a knight in armour, if one can feel like a knight in exceptionally narrow drain-pipe trousers of dark blue cloth; and, with a bowler hat (prescibed by Harry) and a tightly furled umbrella, I swung as jauntily as possible through the gate in the railings of the Officers' Mess in Hyde Park. There were a good many officers in the Mess, in blue frock coats with black frogging and overall trousers with a broad red stripe down the sides, above wellington boots with spurs. They had just come in from stables and were sipping drinks before lunch. The Colonel was Bertie de Klee but he was shortly handing over to Lord Weld-Forester, a mild and charming man who was something of an ornithologist and lived in Shropshire. It was 'Weld' who took me in hand, and sitting on the fender seat, with back to the fire, asked me to join him and called to the Mess waiter for a drink.

Although I had been a Member of Parliament for three years, every aspiring subaltern will agree with me that this vetting by the Colonel and officers of a regiment is a bit of an ordeal, and when it is one of the two premier regiments of the Empire, and is the Sovereign's personal mounted guard, it seems more alarming than usual. Yet Weld was such an unexpected person to be encountered as the Colonel designate of a warlike regiment, that I was immediately disarmed. Nearly all the officers then serving in the Blues were surprisingly unmilitary. They were quiet and for the most part cultured young men, very different in their outlook from the robust horsy officers of their fellow regiment, the Life Guards. Except, possibly, for the second Colonel, Joe Lane-Fox, whose only advice to me on joining the regiment was "Don't mix port and champagne and don't have your wife in the morning, in case you meet somebody more interesting in the afternoon." This is not to say that they were not very good soldiers. But they lacked to a marked degree that paralysing thing — the military mind. Weld, the bird-watcher; Henry Abel Smith, a man of a political rather than a military mind outside of routine Army matters; Eion Merry, shy and quiet; John Kitson, a lanky youth of literary tastes, descended from the builder of Hengrave but no longer connected with the house; Bones Sudeley, so very shy as to be positively diffident, oddly cast in the role of Adjutant; William Amherst, polite enough to be a third secretary of Embassy instead of the popular conception of brash cavalry captains; Micky Dillon, red-haired and moustached, with his slight hesitation of speech and Irish charm of manner. At the lower end of the table John Thynne and Edric Nutting, the least bellicose of men. Among such officers, helping themselves at the sideboard and seating themselves about the dining table, it suddenly seemed no ordeal at all. I was seated on Weld's left for Oswald Birley was also lunching on the conclusion of his portrait of King George V as Colonel of the Regiment, which hung on the wall opposite me; a most pleasant picture of the King wearing the heavy blue cloak, with red lining, of the Regiment. I talked freely of politics and the House, about which Henry Abel Smith was much better informed than I. Nevertheless I had a feeling that all was going well, and I left after a cup of coffee in the ante-room, feeling that if one had got to join the Army in March 1938 in preparation for the war, (and this was my answer to my constituents in 1945 who said I supported Munich) I could not hope to do my soldiering in more congenial surroundings or among more congenial officers. What they thought about the new recruit is anybody's guess. Knowing that I was an author, they probably had dire misgivings, belonging as they do to the school of thought expressed by their then Colonel-in-Chief, who said, "People who write books ought to be shot," but they certainly went out of their way to make me feel as welcome and at ease as possible. Certainly it is possible to notice that a change had come over the subject of this book — at least outwardly. The young man in a bowler hat and starched collar, twirling his umbrella as he enters the Cavalry barracks, is hardly identifiable as the same youth who strolled hatless up Bond Street, with the typescript of his latest play under his arm, to collect his fiancée from Almond's Hotel where she was staying with her mother. And to whom is this change in outward appearance due? To the fiancée, I suppose. Subtly and without my knowing it I had been groomed for the Blues, like some unbroken horse from the bogs of Ireland which is gradually subdued and polished, till it walks black, glossy, and sedately down Constitution Hill to the Changing of the Guard. I was happy enough; and entered upon my new life, for which I virtually obtained leave from the House of Commons, with unfeigned zest.

My application had first of all to go before the Sovereign, who scrutinises all commissions in the Household Cavalry. I was then told to report one day to the Adjutant's office, where Bones greeted me, and took me up to the Medical Officer's room for a physical check. Bones Sudeley was very fair-haired, almost albino, with hair cropped very short. It seemed almost an agony for him to speak at all. Like all the officers not on duty he got into plain clothes as quickly as possible after luncheon, and took me in a taxi to the regimental tailors, Rogers, in Maddox Street. Here I was fitted for a variety of uniforms — blue frock-coat and blue cap with gold braided peak and scarlet band; overalls, blue patrol jacket, for dining in the Mess; two sets of khaki uniforms; British warm and riding breeches. The stars on the shoulder tabs were unusual in the Blues, having a red cross in the centre of the garter; and in the gold braid version of this for blue patrols, they looked very fine. Bones took me from Rogers to Maxwells in Dover Street to have my wellington boots made. I already had a pair of brown field boots; dating from my days in the Cavalry O.T.C. at Oxford. It was not considered necessary, for a four month period of training, for me to acquire the full dress outfit of buckskin breeches, huge black jackboots, gold cuffed blue tunic, cuirass and helmet; as these could be borrowed if I had occasion to wear them.

In fact I only had occasion to wear review order twice. Once when taking over the 24 hour King's Guard at the Horse Guards from another officer who needed a substitute; and once at a levée in St. James's

Palace. I went in borrowed plume.

I was allotted the services of Bones's personal servant, Church, who would look after my uniforms and have them laid out in an empty room at the Officers' Mess overlooking the park; which was given to me. It had a bare floor and contained some plain deal furniture; but there was an iron bedstead and mattress upon which I was thankful to rest at times, so gruelling was the course of training prescribed for new officers. The main training is in the Riding School and I was detailed to join the 6.20 a.m. ride. This meant rising at Eaton Place a few blocks away at about 5.30 and driving round to the barracks. The riding school is in the barrack yard, and is a dim building, with a floor of soft stuff, around which the new recruits were cantered in an energetic file. I had also been allotted a second servant, or groom, in addition to Church who was my first servant. And the groom's job was to have my black charger properly groomed, saddled and bridled, and mounting this beast, I entered the riding school, where the 5.20 ride was just finishing. The riding instructor was Corporal-Major Poupart, who won prizes for jumping at Olympia and elsewhere. I remained in the centre of this ring, patting my horse's neck, while he brought the expiring ride to a halt; and dismissed them to stables.

"Would you join the rear of the ride, Sir?" he said to me with a deference which I found immensely soothing, having expected to be bellowed at like any recruit.

Poupart was a lean, clean-shaven man, who was of course, a remarkable horseman; and it was a pleasure to watch him in the saddle.

"I don't know how much riding you have done, Sir, but as you know, all officers have to pass out of riding school. You will find it quite pleasant." And eyeing my grip on the reins and the dip of my heels in the field boots, professionally flicked his charger round to the middle of the soft floor.

"Ride, trot," and we began to joggle round the room.

"Don't rise in the saddle, there, Mr. de Chair," he called out firmly. I did not think I was doing so, although the temptation to do so was considerable. The style of trotting was arbitrary, for in ceremonial parades nothing would look more comic than a number of helmeted heads bobbing up and down like pistons all over the escort. Thus the Household Cavalry were trained to ride at the trot, jolting on the pummel of the saddle, in a way which takes some getting used to.

"Ride, canter." With a good deal of kicking, the new recruits got their mounts off to the canter, and once again Corporal-Major Poupart was beside me.

"Sir."

"Yes, Corporal-Major?"

"Do you know how to canter off on the off-fore?"

"No."

"Sit well back on the left seat bone and apply pressure behind the girth with the left leg."

All this was said in a subdued and respectful tone as he cantered beside me, then he wheeled his charger to a halt in the middle and bellowed to the Ride.

"You look like a nice bunch of daisies, I must say. All cantering uncollected and sprawling about. Ride trot. Now then collect your horses. You're going round clockwise. Very well, you're going to jump off with the off-fore foot. Otherwise you will trip up, and you've got to canter collected, that means the off hind and fore feet move together and the near hind and fore together. Now let's see you start off a little better. When I give the order to canter, sit well back on your left seat bones, and press with the left leg. Don't kick them in the belly. Just press, firmly. Now, ride canter."

The trouble was, of course, that the horses were so accustomed to these manoeuvres that it took a remarkable man to prevent them answering the riding master's word of command correctly. However, by putting us into a figure of eight and bringing us on to the anti-clockwise track, Poupart gave us a chance of wearing out our right seat bones and prancing off on the near fore.

I found it very soothing, cantering round the dim barn-like building on the rotten floor where the horses' hoofs thudded softly. Presently the doors were thrown open and brushwood and rail jumps were brought in. The ride was halted.

"Make much of your horses," ordered Poupart. Instantly there was a noisy patting of the lathering necks. What a charming word of command, I thought — to make much of your horses.

The jumps were erected at intervals and the ride was sent over them, at first, one by one. "Mr. de Chair first." This was a bit of an ordeal, for there would be no small joy if the officer bit the dust on the first round. However, the jumps were not formidable and my charger was well accustomed to taking them in his stride. So up and over and round I flew, bringing my mount to a stand in the middle, making very much of my horse.

When all had been over the jumps, Poupart gave the order, "Walk, march," and led us out into the yard, under the high brick arch into the park, where he held up his hand to the approaching traffic and led us across, like a duck with her ducklings waddling behind, to Rotten Row. Here we went through the motions again, and as we were cantering along, a quiet voice behind me said, "Don't hold your stick like a fishing rod. Two or three inches above the hand is all you need show." It was Eion Merry, the Equitation Officer.

I looked around, startled, and adjusted the knotted leather covered cane in my hand accordingly. He smiled reassuringly.

"How do you like your first morning in riding school?"

"Very pleasant, so far," I replied.

"Drop back a bit and we can talk. We can catch the others up later."

Eion Merry was prematurely grey-haired, which gave him a slightly melancholy appearance, but he had great charm and was a very conscientious officer. He would not have been relied upon to watch rides at half-past five and six in the morning if he were not. He gave me some quiet instruction on holding my reins better, and encouraged me with some praise.

"You will find it rather a bore having to go through all this. But we all have to do it."

"How long does it take before you pass out?" I asked.

"The recruits have to do nine months, but then some of them have never ridden before. I expect you will pass out with the rest of this ride in a couple of months' time."

That was encouraging news, and we cantered up to join the rear of the ride, who were now walking along past the Serpentine. It was a very early spring and all the trees were unexpectedly darting green buds. The sun sparkled on the water, where the ducks quacked lazily. It seemed a good life and I suddenly wanted to become a soldier. Yet in the back of my mind was Kipling's advice, from the good book, 'Whilst thou have breath of life in thee, bind not thyself to any man.'

After riding school I had twenty minutes for breakfast, and the bacon and eggs went down eagerly, chased by the coffee before I dashed up to my room to change out of my boots and breeches, into P.T. pants and vest, rushed across to the barracks yard, ran up fifteen flights of iron stairs to the gymnasium just in time to join the class. Here I leapt and jumped and swung like a chimpanzee with the best of them; then ran downstairs, across the yard, into the Officers' Mess and arrived in my room panting, to find Church with a wry smile at the purgatory designed for officers, proffering me the next change of kit, dungarees, I think, for small arms instruction in some lecture room high on the opposite side of the barrack square. There I spent an hour fingering the familiar bolt of a Lee-Enfield rifle or being explained the intricacies of the new bren-gun. Back to my room and a leap into the short leather wellington boots, into the heel of which the rowelled spurs were thrust with a spring clip; into the skin-tight blue overall trousers with the broad red stripe.

"Excuse me, Sir, if you would lift your chin a little higher," and Church fastened the high collar of the long blue frock-coat. "The young gentlemen always find the training a little fatiguing for the first few days."

"I am glad to hear it, Church."

"Don't forget your white gloves and stick, Sir. Your cap, Sir."

"Thank you Church."

Thus accoutred, I descended to the ante-room where the subalterns on the stroke of 11.25 were getting up to go over to stables.

"Still alive?" laughed John Thynne, as we strolled out together.

As we came into the stables, the Corporal of our troops cried, "Troop, shun!"

"Carry on Corporal." And the men bent again to the task of grooming their horses.

Five minutes later the Squadron Leader arrived and the senior subaltern called the Squadron to attention.

Most of the officers changed before lunch and left after it in a hurry to get to some race meeting. I had to attend another recruits' lecture, followed by drilling on the square, and got back to my room by half-past three, where I threw myself upon the bed until I recovered. When I was Orderly Officer it meant dining in the Mess as well, and there might easily be no other officer dining in at all; or perhaps one of the young subalterns.

John Thynne and I sat thus one evening at a round table in the wide bow window of the dining-room. As Orderly Officer I wore over my blue patrol jacket, a white leather belt, with a red lanyard in the middle of it, attached to a black pouch on my back embossed with the Royal Arms, surviving, I believe, from the days of some musket loading equipment.

Dusk was falling over the trees in the park and the Mess waiters lit the candles on the table.

"Is it true," I asked, "that you are not allowed to mention a woman's name in an Officers' Mess?"

"If we didn't mention women here, there wouldn't be much conversation," John replied laughing.

At some period during the evening the Orderly Officer was expected to do the rounds of the stables and visit the guard-room. 'Expected' is the right word, for he invariably did the rounds on the stroke of midnight. He would go to the guard-room and the wary sentry would bawl, "Fall out the guard." Then, accompanied by the Corporal of the Guard carrying a lantern, he would go round the stables, where the stable guards would jump to attention as he marched briskly by. I loved the solitary duties of the night round, with the horses champing slightly in their stalls, dragging at their head chains and pawing the tiled flooring. But this long wait at the end of a hard day's training seemed very long and it would be a sleepy officer who would at last let himself out with a key from the side door in Knightsbridge to go home. The gates of the park would already have been shut, and Church would therefore have driven my car home for me earlier. I was allowed, as a special dispensation, to get another officer to answer for me after midnight, otherwise I should have had to sleep in the barracks.

The new life in the Army led to new friendships. Eion asked us to dine and we met his lovely wife, Jean; who seemed, in diaphanous yellow-green chiffon, an aqueous, underwater figure — who would not have been out of place in Keats's *Endymion* among the naiads. There was Harry Legge-Bourke, the inner core and conscience of the regiment, as he was later to be of the Conservative Party in the Commons — even when throwing pennies at Herbert Morrison the Foreign Secretary, across the table of the House. Jean Legge-Bourke became a very close friend of Thelma's and there was much coming and going between the nurseries, for the Legge-Bourkes had a son Bill, of Rodney's age; known even to his parents as Bill Bourke. The shyest, most retiring and least military of all the officers was perhaps Philip Morris-Keating, who also had a lovely wife, as vague as she was exquisite, with ungovernable red hair and an expression of wonderful sweetness — until she cut me dead in the paddock at Ascot after years of friendship, for the crime of divorce. All these wives in the Blues seemed to be beautiful. One of them, Susan Ward, had claims of being one of the most beautiful women in England, with her flawless features and magnolia skin. But it was no longer the fashion, as it had been in Edwardian times, for fashionable ladies to seek the limelight in a sort of rarified beauty competition. The poisoned chalice had passed to the bathing belles, and the lovely women in society shrank from the suggestion of beauty as if it were an insult, except at very close quarters. The essential thing was not to be overheard being beautiful.

Life in the spring and summer of 1938 passed by in an atmosphere, for us, suggestive of St. Petersburg in 1913. At Ascot the Blues had a tent of their own, guarded by a Corporal of Horse in full review order, with burnished helmet, scarlet plume, gold-braided blue tunic, white buckskin breeches and black jackboots. Never was a tent easier to locate on the far side of the racecourse; and in that dim marquee, tea with strawberries and cream could soothe the most harassed punter. I became very fit; and at the Royal Norfolk Show one of my constituents failed to recognise me.

"I wondered," he said, "who this young subaltern of two-and-twenty could be."

I had my duties as a Member of Parliament to perform but those were the days of the great majorities and after a vote of confidence for which a three line whip had been issued — 'Your attendance is most particularly requested' underlined three times — Stanley Baldwin himself had to write a circular letter to Members on the government side, pointing out that on this occasion no less then 122 of the government's supporters had been absent from the critical division. Those were the days when the House was still counted the best club in London and advocates of the higher life, like Philip Dunne, Charles Wood and Loel Guinness, could not be counted on the fingers of all the hands in the Whips' office. Yet there were all-night sittings at which some of these young bloods were to be seen eyeing the clock with wistful sighs but little signs of fatigue. When one of the Labour Members said to Stanley Baldwin, "Don't your fellows object to staying up all night?" he replied with rare breadth of mind: "If they weren't here they would not be in bed."

Lord Queenborough at seventy had more energy than most people at twenty. I met him about this time at a dinner of the Chamberlain Club* (of which I was the secretary) at which Neville was the guest, in honour of his father's memory, which the club existed to celebrate. Old 'Q' asked me to bring my wife down to Camfield. It was a pleasant white house, somewhat in the American Colonial style, with a good deal of weather-boarding. The grounds were not impressive, and Queenborough made his guests slave in them, himself leaping high in the air with his secateurs beside Lady Mallaby-Deely and shouting,

* It still contained many of Jo Chamberlain's supporters in the 1904 Tariff Campaign.

gleefully, "Oh, aye, aye." She was shrouded in newly acquired but attractive widow's weeds. Yards of black tulle, through which Queenborough was constrained to peer keenly. The house itself was extremely luxurious. The bedrooms were heated to an almost oppressive degree; and the curtains, of the heaviest possible material, with the deepest possible pelmets, admitted little fresh air at night. The bathrooms, lavishly equipped with hot towel rails, bath salts, and scented soap in cellophane wrappings, opened out of the bedrooms. Beside the beds were bottles of Evian water. The walls were hung with oil paintings and the pale close-fitted carpets were overlaid with silky Persian rugs. It was a cushioned atmosphere, faintly overhung with the aroma of Queenborough's expensive cigars. He included us in his house party for the neighbouring dance given by the Salisburys at Hatfield for Robert Cranborne's coming of age. It was a soothing sight to see the old house ablaze with light and the young couples sitting out in the Long Gallery with its gilded ceiling floodlit.

In his study Queenborough discoursed energetically and lucidly on politics and racing; he was a keen racehorse owner, although not to the same extent as his daughter Dorothy Paget. He had a young brood of children, now growing up, by his second wife who was also dead. They were a lively element in the house. Here Queenborough entertained the more active young politicians and made them all join one or more of the clubs and organisations in which he was interested. Me he placed firmly on the Council of the Royal Society of St. George and drove me, at intervals for years, to do good works for it. One of them was the formation of a library for youth. We were to select and issue biographies of the more adventurous Englishmen to Boy Scouts, Boys' Clubs, Rovers and others. I was made Chairman of the Library Committee and under his compelling eye, at a luncheon given at the Perroquet for three, Victoria Sackville West was recruited to it. We relaxed next door, after he had departed, at a film on the Northern Territory of Australia, before she drove off to the Chelsea Flower Show. Arthur Bryant was also flogged, from afar, by correspondence dictated by Queenborough in high spirits and speed, to add his name to the Committee. I procured the services of E.P. Smith (the M.P. who wrote plays as Edward Percy) and William Collins, the publisher. The cohesion of the committee extended to one meeting, but their names, on the syllabus of books to be issued, were impressive and before we had finished with the project, Queenborough had lashed to the wheel the Archbishop of Canterbury, Field-Marshal Montgomery and the heads of various distinguished bodies, interested by him in instilling a spirit of adventure into the tired youth of England. There was also the Knights of the Round Table; from whom I received a badge, at his instigation, of a visored knight. But I fear that I never attended one of their illustrious dinners, and after a decent interval let my subscription lapse. He also tried to interest me in joining the St. Stephen's Club opposite the House of Commons, to which it was connected by a division bell and an underground passage. But to this request I shut a blind eye. Chips Channon said he had stayed one weekend with Queenborough and it had cost him £25 in subscriptions. I did however let Queenborough put me up, in later years, for the Royal Thames Yacht Club, of which he was Vice-Commodore, and on the walls of which hangs a very lifelike portrait of this tall, thin, energetic old Englishman, with silver hair and one eye rather red-rimmed. With all his zeal for making people mount behind him on his sometimes rather Don Quixote-ish hobby-horses, he was loved by all, and his passing was a blow to many. Perhaps in some celestial fields he is still leaping high in the air with his secateurs; and signing up the apostles for some club, connected by some mysterious passage to who knows what infernal chamber. He had himself, in youth, as Almeric Paget, been a Member of the House of Commons; and had earned his own peerage. The family title was Anglesey.

After having admired Blickling so much from outside, it was a pleasant surprise when Lothian invited us to stay in the house. He had known my mother, as a Christian Scientist; and I had corresponded with him about the staircase and other details of domestic architecture.

He frequently held conferences at Blickling, principally reunions of Milner's young men; or meetings of the Round Table, where Commonwealth problems were thoughtfully discussed. He liked to group around him conflicting currents of thought; and I found myself bracketed with a Christian Science Socialist, Alfred Edwards, also in the House, and a Liberal woman candidate for Parliament. Our views over the dining table just about cancelled out; although Edwards was a capitalist and eventually left the Labour Party in protest at the nationalisation of steel. Lothian asked me to define Neville Chamberlain's foreign policy and I can remember thinking a bit and then summing it up in a phrase which was at that moment a novelty and was meant to be flattering: "Appeasement in Europe." It was left to Churchill in after years to refine the policy; appease the weak; defy the strong.

If Blickling had satisfied my most romantic conception of the English house, viewed from the road, its interior was no less satisfying. The Jacobean house had been largely reconstructed inside during the Georgian period by the 2nd Earl of Buckinghamshire who was British Ambassador to St. Petersburg. A magnificent Russian tapestry of Peter the Great at the battle of Poltowa had been presented to him on leaving, by Catherine the Great, and gave its name to one of the lovely drawing-rooms on the first floor. The Georgian influence had lightened the soufflé, and Lothian had been fortunate in the help of his sister Lady Minna Butler-Thwing and Nancy Astor who was a very frequent visitor. They devoted much time and thought to bringing the furnishings and decorations up to date; while placing the collection of pictures and furniture to advantage. Thus the whole house had an air of quietly sophisticated distinction, and from the garden room, hung with

146

tapestries reproducing Tenier's pictures, Lothian gestured through the
mullioned windows at the flower beds, rising in July to fountains of
colour, and declared, "There is high summer for you."

In the dining-room, we stood together once, looking down the drive,
between its retaining parallel of gabled out-buildings dated 1624, and
the giant shelving clipped yew hedges, towards the road, where a farm
cart, drawn by a plodding shire horse, crossed the vista.

"I like to see things passing," he said. "It gives a pleasing touch of
informality." And added, without any obvious connection, "I do not
believe any man can go through the hell of public life unless he has some
degree of personal ambition." He turned from the window with a sigh.
"I do not suppose I have ever spent more than one consecutive weekend
in this house." He looked at that moment like a deceptively benevolent
sparrow hawk that had perched on a telegraph wire.

The visit to Blickling strengthened my resolve to live in the house
one day, possibly after Lothian's death, but I naturally said nothing of
this to the owner. A year later, however, came the announcement that
he was appointed Ambassador to the United States. A column appeared
in *The Times*, with a picture of Blickling, stating that he intended to let
the house while he was away, to a tenant who would have a proper care
for it. There was some history of the house; how the manor had
originally belonged to King Harold, when he was Earl of East Anglia;
how it had been in the house pulled down before the present one was
built that Anne Boleyn was born; and how the present building was
regarded as one of the most beautiful as well as the most stately homes
of England.

I had for this sort of purpose, broadly speaking, no money; but I had
unlimited faith. Blickling was to me holy ground, and I felt confident
that I was meant to have it; and that the money would, as usually, be
forthcoming. I wrote to Lothian asking for the tenancy while he was
away and he readily put me in touch with his agents in London,
Farebrother, Ellis & Co. Heads of agreement were drawn up and
agreed, and these proved of great value after the war, when the house
was finally leased to me by the National Trust to whom Lord Lothian,
before he died of blood poisoning in Washington, bequeathed the
house. For, by the time the heads of agreement were agreed, in August
1939, and I had heard from Mr. Farrel of Farebrother, Ellis to this
effect, war was nearly upon us.

Consulted about the move to Blickling, twelve miles outside the
constituency, Carlo Fountaine beamed and said, "You will have to drive

further to the meetings, that's all."

Miss O'Sullivan, Lothian's pessimistic grey-haired and blue-eyed secretary, an Irish Catholic, who was very helpful about the arrangements for our projected taking over at Christmas, 1939, said afterwards that she had always thought war was inevitable and 'nobody but a lot of barmy Christian Scientists' like ourselves and Lothian would have dreamt of leasing the house in 1939. She thought that we were entering upon a period in Europe, of wars of fanaticism, comparable with the Thirty Years War. But she completed the cataloguing and card indexing of the 12,000 books in the library for all that.

The Second World War came in the end with deadly fatality. Lord Ironside, just back from Poland, visited us at Necton in Norfolk, and standing his immense height and impressive grizzled head beside the empty fireplace in the blue drawing-room said to our astonishment, "Only a miracle can stop it now." Outside, Daines was mowing the lawns and marking out the two tennis courts. In a day or two, the tennis players in white flannels and the young mothers with their sons of three and four tumbling about on the grass, crowded into that drawing-room and listened to the radio announcer as the news of Hitler's attack on Poland came over. Even then it seemed remote, as if this peaceful English garden in late summer could not be torn up and the house wrenched about and demolished and finally erased as if it had never been; all of which was to happen because that morning Hitler's Panzers were crashing through the Polish Corridor.

We took the babies to the sea for a bathe at West Runcton (for Peter had been born in June, 1939). And as we drove up from the sand-dunes on the evening of 1st September, and entered the dense woods of Felbrigg, along a sunken lane, the car radio announced peremptorily, "All officers of the Supplementary Reserve of Officers must report to barracks immediately." This was the moment which in the lives of so many happily married young couples broke the continuity of their joint existence, wrenched them apart and flung them to distant corners of the earth. And then with mocking smile the fates threw them together again, almost unrecognisable if they had been through many hospitals, and said, "Now begin again where you left off." But that was not always possible, and along with the broken limbs and lost lives, are the broken marriages to be chalked up in some Hell's Kitchen to the debit of Adolf Hitler.

CHAPTER 13

At my father's suggestion I kept a diary from the outbreak of the war; and I kept this until I went into action, when I became responsible for the official War Diary of the Column despatched from Palestine to relieve the British Colony in Baghdad; and subsequently that of the 4th Cavalry Brigade sent from there to capture the desert Fortress of Palmyra in Syria. No doubt any faithful account of life in Britain during the high summer of 1940 will one day be of interest to a generation which took no part in these events; for it will interest them to know how ordinary people comported themselves under the threat of invasion while their destiny was being fought out for them by a few pilots in the sky above their heads. At times these battles appeared to be no more than vapour trails in the blue, with the remote chatter of machine-gun fire. Now and then a Messerschmitt would hurtle with a thud into neighbouring ground and a pilot, if lucky, emerge to surrender.

Being of a romantic disposition I wrote some lines of poetry about these heroes; for even to those of us who witnessed their performance, they seemed fabulous people.

> These battles seemed so high and far away
> Wings of pure silver throbbing in high air
> And the brisk rapier of machine-gun play
> Rasping so easily, that they seemed to dare
>
> Happily, like the warfare of a song;
> As if the gods upon Olympus tried
> Their swords against the bronze, sounding a gong,
> Which echoed far below them when they died.

For the rest, we went about our business as best we could, each shouldering perhaps more than one man's burden, so that as the summer wore on, and the duties of guarding reservoirs or royal residences and training soldiers crept round the clock to a full circle, some of us fell down from sheer exhaustion; and were ordered away for brief spells of leave by regimental Medical Officers. I was able thus to visit the Island of Gigha off the west coast of Scotland; which I had taken over freehold from my sister who was unable otherwise to dispose of it in wartime. Not for nothing was Gigha, with its silver sands going down into transparent emerald waters, known as the Jewel of the Western Isles. The Minister, Dr. McLeod, was a famous man not necessarily wasted on a parish six miles long and two miles wide, in mid-ocean. He had written the song 'The Road to the Isles' — by Tummel and Lochaber and by Rannoch I will go — for the lads in the First World War; and was glad to see me home in due time from the Second. He would preach in the Gaelic and his silvery voice was music to hear, albeit the meaning of his words escaped me.

I acquired this island for what my sister had originally paid for it, but after some reorganisation it was to prove the foundation of my fortunes, such as they are. For when I was home from the wars and wanted to settle nearer London, I was able to sell the Island handsomely to a malted milk manufacturer, Colonel John Horlick; and the castle which I bought with the proceeds was in turn sold for more than double what I paid for it and the arithmetical progression continued for a while, within the orbit of historic houses; until I could lecture blindfold on the subject at 25 guineas a time, when I felt so disposed, which helped to pay for their central heating.

But during 1940 I was only able to visit Gigha twice, for a week at a time.

I had little time for my parliamentary duties; but went up to London from Windsor to vote on occasions. When Winston made his famous speech on the Few in the Battle of Britain, I was only able to find a place on the steps between the benches opposite him on the other side of the House. I watched him shift his weight from one foot to another and say:

"Never before in the field of human *endeavour* has so much been owed by so many to so few."

The word 'endeavour' was changed later for 'conflict', but I am sure the evening newspapers carried the original wording. When Hitler invaded Norway and the Labour Party tabled a motion of Censure on Neville Chamberlain's handling of the war I asked my Colonel, Lord Weld-Forester, if I could have leave to go up and vote.

"Which way are you going to vote?" he asked unconstitutionally.

"Against the Government," I replied.

"You can certainly go in that case," he said. Such was the feeling at the time.

Some forty Conservative members serving in the forces arrived upon the same impulse and nothing the Whips or Cabinet Ministers could say to us before the vote was taken could deflect our resolve to defeat the Government.

I was dining with Stuart Russel (soon to be killed in action) when Sir John Simon, the Lord Chancellor, paused at our table and said, "May I ask which way you young people are going to vote?"

"Against you," I said.

He sat down somewhat deflated with us and said, "Of course I do not question your right to do so. But may I point out some of the Constitutional implications of your action? If you succeed in bringing down the Government, as you very well may do, the King cannot send for Mr. Churchill or Lord Halifax. He would have to send for Mr. Attlee or Mr. Greenwood. Is that what you want?"

"If you are going to stand on Constitutional niceties at a time like this," I replied, "you will be sending out a three-line Whip when Hitler arrives at Dover."

The atmosphere inside the Chamber grew very tense and rowdy as the time for voting approached. Churchill was at the despatch box defending the Prime Minister. Amery, a right wing Tory ex-Minister yelled, when Greenwood rose to speak, "Speak for Britain." The Whips and Junior Ministers under the gallery near me in the corner (this was before the old Chamber was blitzed) pointed to the Opposition who were baying like hounds while Churchill was saying, rashly, that all ships in the Skagerrak will be sunk, "How can you vote for a rabble like that against a man like that?"

I said, "I am not voting against him. I am voting against you and you and you," pointing at three of them in turn. It is not surprising that in these conditions those of us in uniform who marched into the Lobby with the Socialists were described as parachutists who had landed behind the lines in Conservative uniforms.

Good fortune favoured our enterprise, as the Government survived by a margin small enough to secure Neville Chamberlain's resignation while allowing the King to send for Mr. Churchill. Thereafter an entirely new impulse was given to our affairs and although the danger mounted, a sense of pride and determination in being in England during the Battle of Britain animated all.

It seemed at one moment in September as if the Germans had actually started their invasion. The code word 'Cromwell' was sent out;

and I remember in the Mess Peter Williams of the Life Guards, who happened to be the senior officer of the joint Household Cavalry Regiment present, and was sitting at the head of the table, announcing, "Gentlemen, the invasion has begun." But it was a false alarm and the crisis passed.

In October I was ordered out to Palestine in command of a draft of three officers and forty men from the Training Centre.

Getting forty men on a draft from Windsor in the dark hours of the morning and marching them all aboard a troopship at Liverpool to As Zib in Palestine is anxious work. They were lined up in the blacked-out gymnasium and addressed by Tommy Clyde, acting Adjutant.

"From now on Mr. de Chair is in charge. That is all I have to say."

There was a road diversion on the way to London on account of bomb damage, and we only had five minutes to spare at the station. Time to commandeer the Salvation Army canteen hut to give them a cup of tea. The congestion aboard the troopship was desperate. Designed to accommodate 1,600 *The Duchess of York* was carrying over 3,000. The men were slung below decks in hammocks, six inches apart, head to feet. I had to fight from 4 p.m. till 9.30, merely to hold their quarters from other officers trying to seize accommodation for their drafts. I had two officers from the regiment with me; lanky and bespectacled Dennis O'Rorke, an Irishman of culture and sensitivity, with whom I played chess languidly in the cabin in the tropics. We lay on opposite bunks with the chess set ferried to and fro for alternate moves, on a string attached to pulleys. John Shaw was the third officer of the draft, a blunt hunk of a youth, who borrowed our clothes and shoelaces without scruple, was put to bed by us in a far from sober condition on occasion; but was one of the first officers in the regiment at the receiving end to win the Military Cross, for blundering into and far beyond the enemy lines. We were fortunate in having a cabin to ourselves. This came about because an embarkation officer at the gangway, when he saw the name 2nd Lt. S. S. de Chair sprang up and said, "Are you Somerset de Chair? You came and spoke for us once." He had been the Conservative agent in some constituency. He immediately struck a brigadier and two colonels off the top rung of the accommodation ladder, and gave us a cabin with an outside porthole in the gangway facing the Commanding Officer's cabin. One of my machine-gunners was on the draft, Trooper Grose, who consented to act as batman, and prevailed upon some steward to let him bring us coffee, toast and marmalade in bed for breakfast.

There is a lot of bullishness about a troopship in wartime. The Commanding Officer tries to find work for all to do, which often seems unnecessary. But we were spared the usual fatigues. I had the men up on the after deck and said, "There will be a lot of unpleasant jobs to do on this ship; but they will not be done by the Household Cavalry." And I explained why. At the first meeting of heads of drafts, the C.O. said somebody would have to man the anti-aircraft bren-guns. Up spoke a mad major, with a few fingers off and a monocle, called Wintle, and said, "I will be responsible for the anti-aircraft defence of this ship; I and my 17 Yeomanry officers."

"Splendid," said the C.O. Wintle had just been released from the Tower of London, in which he had been incarcerated for 'assaulting Air Commodore Boyle and saying that all officers over the rank of Group Captain in the Air Force ought to be shot.' He had tried to get them to fly the French Air Force out of France before the surrender; and was defended at his court martial by Field Marshal Lord Ironside, who said he had been bothered a good deal by Wintle about getting overseas on active service. Wintle was now getting overseas. But he soon realised that 17 Yeomanry officers cannot or will not man six anti-aircraft guns, two men per gun, during all the hours of daylight. So he sought me out in my cabin.

"I will provide the officers," he said, "if you provide the men. You and your two officers can remain with them in a supervisory category and for training purposes. As for me the voyage will be simplified — Wintle, Major, duties, bugger-all." And so it was arranged.

Everything went well until we got into the tropics, for the troopers' tropical kit had all been seized from them before departure by some genius in the quartermaster's store. I discovered just in time that there was a quartermaster deep in the ship's hold who had a few tropical kits to issue, and managed to pass the draft through the sweltering hold, to collect them in time. Khaki serge in the tropics is not amusing, but we did not like to wear our own till the troops had been issued with cotton drill.

The first port of call was Freetown where the battleship *Resolution*, holed at Dakar, lay listing to one side, with the gaping hole tilted clear of the water.

Freetown is surely the hottest spot in the world; a town on sloping green hills, beside a wide and rapid river. All night a tanker lay alongside refuelling; and I listened through the porthole to a rich dialogue in Scots, between the crew of the tanker and the man on deck above me; in such technical terms as, "Do you suck or do you blow?" When the tanker pulled away I tried to sleep; but was awakened by a stampede of running feet overhead; and splashes in the water. I looked out of the porthole. Lifebelts were plopping into the dark water far below, and shooting astern with the current. There were cries of, "Man overboard! Man the lifeboat!" There was a great splash as the boat dropped from the davits; much shouting in the night. Then all was quiet again. Two hours later a voice in the gangway outside the C.O.'s cabin. "No hope I'm afraid, Sir. We have wasted two hours. We've done everything we can. Thought I ought to let you know." Poor fellow. There were numbers of soldiers sleeping on deck under the stars on account of the foetid conditions in the hammock flats below; and this one had apparently got up and walked overboard in his sleep. I tried to doze off again. There was the sound of an engine chugging alongside and a hail, "*Duchess of York*, ahoy. Have you lost a man overboard?" Cries of yes. I leapt to the porthole. In the beam of a searchlight was a small tug, with four or five Africans standing about, their dark faces gleaming in the light and their teeth flashing in great white smiles. Wrapped in a grey blanket at the foot of the mast was a dejected man with dark hair. A naval officer in white duck shorts and tunic came out of the wheelhouse and stood languidly against it. "We picked him up at the bar. He had drifted nine miles." A voice called back, "There is a gangway being lowered on the other side," and the tug chugged out of sight. The searchlight was switched off.

The convoy, escorted by the cruiser *Southampton*, on which a long artificial bow wave, very impressive at night, was painted, steamed on towards Cape Town. There we got one night ashore; and I rang up an astonished Uncle Charles, my mother's brother, who asked me to come out at once to Nederberg. The family, Aunt Beta and others, were gathered in to hear the latest news from Britain. It was a relief after the congestion of the troopship to wake up on a crystal clear morning and breakfast on the white-colonnaded loggia at Nederberg, where the pillars were half-smothered in creeper, framing the majestic spectacle of Table Mountain. Warm blue shadows in the ravines and the sharp outlines of rock where it rose above the lower wooded slopes. The soft voices of native servants in the back regions could be heard calling to each other; and from the garden came the soothing chop-chop of shears clipping the high hedges. Soon Uncle Charles, dapper and blue-eyed, came in from his morning ride. The black boy began laying a table for tea and cakes, a South African morning custom. I visited Luncarty.

Aunt Edith was dead, leaving the house on the slopes of Table Mountain to be bought by any of the family for £10,000 or sold for that sum. It had been bought by some people called Usher, who had enlarged it inside without spoiling the charm of the exterior, with its thatched roof, and high white central gable. The owner was away but her darkie housekeeper who knew Aunt Beta to be a friend of the Ushers, let us see over it. I noticed an original Jacobean court cupboard in the hall; and approved. One glimpse of the Victorian front of the old family home — Struben Home — was enough.* But Ida's Valley seemed more charming than ever. I had forgotten how completely like an old farming homestead it was, with its surrounding estate; with all the charm of an unspoilt old world South African residence; the great curly gables were glowing white in the sun. It was Herbert Baker's opinion that the gable at Ida's Valley dated 1789 was the finest in South Africa. I noticed that the old brass door handles carried dates like 1781 on them. Mary's husband, Jack Dendy was now in uniform, a 2nd Lt. in the Engineers, garrisoned at present at the Castle in Cape Town. Later he was to see active service in East Africa. Charles Malleson was retained at home to run the farm. Aunt Beta was very busy as head of the committee which was providing hospitality to the passing convoys. And from all accounts when I got back on board, the hospitality was beyond anything the troops had ever experienced. They were driven everywhere like lords; and danced the whole night through. Dennis O'Rorke who had left half his heart in England with some beauty, left the other half in Cape Town overnight. At Ida's Valley, Mary took me up to a dam by the fir woods to bathe, as the temperature was 84° in the shade. She had two lovely Russian borzoi dogs which bathed with me from the clayey bank. I rather regretted not having bathed in the clear swimming pool at Nederberg. But I was much refreshed and washed the clay off my feet in the outside bathroom on the ground floor at the house.

Everybody on board felt the tonic of the brief stay in Cape Town and we settled down to the next long cruise up the east coast of Africa, to the Red Sea. I had begun writing during the voyage, and completed 15,000 words of a novel on Oliver Cromwell as a young Member of Parliament at my own age (29). This is the only part of the novel which survived, as the earlier part had all been dictated and the single typescript was destroyed by a bomb which demolished the publishers in London. So

---

* We gave it to the University of Cape Town at Rondebosch of which it became the Conservatoire of music.

some of this part alone appeared in a book which I called, *A Mind on the March* under chapters called, 'The Death of Queen Elizabeth', 'The Last of the Elizabethans (Raleigh)' and 'Oliver Cromwell's Maiden Speech'. Now, after leaving Cape Town, I started to write a novel in the style of John Buchan, of fifth column activity in the Western Isles. There was a lot of Gigha in the book, and I called it *Moon in Kintyre*. There was nothing profound about the book, but the writing of it revived the scenery of the Western Isles for me during the tropic days. I discussed the plot with an R.A.S.C. officer called Gael with whom I shared a table in the dining saloon. He amused me by saying he had some tough fellows in his unit — North Londoners. "I heard that they ate razor blades and things. But I did not believe it until I had one of the men brought up before me. He solemnly proceeded to eat a razor blade, chewing it to powder before swallowing it. Then he took down an electric light bulb and ate all of that, except the brass part. He had been in a circus."

The novel may not have been of great merit and was, like *Dungeons in the Air* (which was about a young Member of Parliament in domestic difficulties over an American woman), never published. But the astonishing thing about *Moon in Kintyre* was that I wrote 50,000 words in four days. I added to my diary, 'If I can keep it going for another 30,000, the novel will be completed, full length.' Unfortunately novels are not gauged solely by the number of words — although one might almost think so to read some publishers' contracts, providing that the next book 'shall not be less that 80,000 words.' The difficulty was to find a typist aboard. Of the feminine variety there were none. Had there been, I doubt if she would have had much time for typing. But the ever-resourceful Major Wintle soon produced a clerk in some R.A.S.C. unit, who did his best; and bashing away in the Purser's office, produced a copy on airmail paper, so that I could sent it home quickly. I found Wintle, when I sought him out for this purpose, sitting in his cabin staring moodily through his monocle at a pile of square cards. I asked him to explain. "On one side of each card is written a word in English. On the other its equivalent in Arabic. You stare at the English word and try to remember the Arabic for it. When you turn it over you soon find out if you have remembered it right. The beauty of this scheme is that you cannot cheat yourself." When he heard that I was studying Russian he produced a pile of similar cards, inscribed on one side with Russian words.

All this helped to pass the time until we reached Aden. Fierce crags of barren red sandstone enclosed the smooth blue water. Wintle who, as Welfare Office aboard, managed to get himself ashore on some errand at ports like this and Freetown where nobody else was allowed to land, got off in a boat with the Adjutant and Garstead, the Quartermaster. But they were not back by the time the ship was due to sail at 11. It waited till ten minutes past and sailed without them. Everybody thought it a great joke. But a few hours later, the small cruiser *Caledon*, which had taken over escort duty, brought them aboard, laden with soap, topis, tracer ammunition, and £1,000 in cash for the troops.

We sailed on towards the Straits of Bab el Mendeb, within sight of British Somaliland. This was now in Italian hands; and the anti-aircraft bren-guns had to be manned continuously. No Italian bombers appeared. The R.A.F. in Aden had chastised their aerodromes across the Red Sea. At the beginning of the war the Italians had sent over 9 bombers and the ack-ack guns had shot them all down. After that they came over so high, at 25,000 feet, that their aiming was contemptible. Soon we were passing Eritrea — the whole convoy moving swiftly over the moonlit sea. Next day we coasted up the Red Sea, past Italian Eritrea but there was still no sign of the Italian Air Force. Only the bracing news on the wireless that their biggest battleships had been sunk in harbour at Taranto.

I had begun to write a poem before leaving England, a habit that had almost lapsed since my schooldays. This was about the destroyers in the spirited action at Narvik.

'Slowly the lean grey shapes formed in the mist.' Dennis O'Rorke liked the opening. And there was one line, at least, which commended itself to Altounyan, no mean poet, later. 'Death is a lesson that is hard to learn.'

I went in search of the ship's printer, who did the daily menu cards, as if we were American tourists in peacetime. He printed twelve copies of Narvik for me, on House of Commons paper, and I gave one to the Purser (in whose office the novel was typed) one to the C.O. and another to a congenial spirit called Arnold Breen. On arrival at Suez various staff officers came aboard; among them an Engineer Staff Officer looking for specialised knowledge. Breen said they were all lined up and asked to state their qualifications. A voice at the back:

"Please, Sir, I used to do tunnelling."

"All right. There is a job for you at Wadi Halfa."

Another voice, "I worked at roads."

"Mersah Matruh for you."

When it came to Breen's turn they said, "What do you know about?"

"Admiralty, Probate and Divorce," says Breen. The man began writing it down, "Admiralty . . . " then looked up. "What?"

Breen said he had been a barrister. So they gave him a job in an office with 'In' and 'Out' trays. Breen was enjoying all this immensely as he was already assigned, through the medium of his godfather, Dill, the C.I.G.S., to the Intelligence Staff.

"However, I have taken both jobs," Breen says to me, "so that I can choose which I like best." That was the last I saw of Breen; but heard of him later, administering some province, I believe, in captured Abyssinia.

At Suez a harassed Transport Officer had to see 6,000 troops off the convoy in one day; and we were entrained for Haifa. We were soon routed out at Kantara, where the East stole upon us in the guise of Arab wallahs, flitting about in the moon-shadow of the palm trees, in white gowns.

"Fountain pen, Mister. Very fine pen." The police shooed the Arab boys away; but we bought their dud pens.

At Acre I paraded the men for the last time, and delivered them intact at the Orderly Room — a low wooden hut. No mean effort delivering the same number at Acre as set out from Windsor via Liverpool, Freetown, Cape Town, Aden, Suez, Kantara.

It was rather like getting out of a concentration camp, when the truck took me and my soldier servant, Grose, off to our final destination. The truck left the coast and began winding upwards on a red earth road into the hills. We passed a village in the dark, completely surrounded by barbed wire. We were on the Northern Frontier of Palestine. Beyond the wire was Syria and Vichy France. Darkness was closing in swiftly now. We pulled up among huts. There was a brisk challenge. Orders were shouted and a sentry peered into the driver's seat.

A Corporal of Horse came up and saluted — then led the way into the Squadron Mess. A bright aladdin lamp lit up a cheerful scene of drinks and books, a wireless and two or three officers sitting easily around in wicker chairs, smoking. They wore Crusader jerseys over open-necked shirts but had changed into drill slacks for the evening and wore no belts. Eion Merry got up to greet me — a little greyer than I remembered him. But the same pipe and the same slow smile. The stars were the same too — three Blues' stars on each shoulder — not newly lacquered stars of gold radiating from the Red Cross in its blue oval of the Garter, such as the newer officers wore. His lacquer had worn off with seniority and the gold was brightly polished — carefully, by his servant Lightbrown, so as not to chip the blue and red in the centre. The only other officers were Bobo Roxburghe* — a dark version of what Henry the Eighth might have looked like in youth — bold and bluff, with black hair and black moustache and black eyes. Rather Spanish perhaps. Full of personality — he was bound to have a humanising effect on the discipline of any Squadron. Tony Murray-Smith was Second-in-Command, not in the least put out by an occasional stammer. Valerian Wellesley** — fair-haired and blue-eyed. Finally Max Gordon, a recent arrival at Windsor. Nothing much was known of him beyond the fact that he seemed a keen soldier. This was the Blues Squadron, guarding the Northern Frontier and they made me feel very welcome. Indeed I felt almost dizzy with excitement and I suppose to those who have been isolated up in the hills for weeks merely patrolling the frontier to report hashish smugglers and suspicious breaks in the 'wire', the arrival of a new officer from England, slap out in five weeks, and so, well ahead of the latest sea mails, bursting with information about the bombing and the Battle of Britain — yes, I suppose it was something of a change.

Bobo showed me a room in the sleeping hut that had been vacant since Charles Wood*** had gone off to a Driving and Maintenance Course at Sarafand. Hanging behind the door were Tony Murray-Smith's gleaming white sheepskin coats. He said the bedouin wore them in the Hebron district. They were put in there for the smell to wear off. I savoured the sour smell of the East in them.

There was a period after Juela, of familiarising myself with the Holy Land. At Sarafand, where I was at once sent to do a Driving and Maintenance Course, I could hear the jackals howling at night in the sand-dunes; and I made the pilgrimage to Jerusalem; but not before I had been taken by Bobo Roxburghe and Bill Allen to the Piccadilly Night-club in Haifa, where the owner, a Yugoslav called Freund sat at a table with his lovely wife and her Russian admirer. She was not to be lured into dancing with officers, according to Bobo. I danced round the room with Mrs. Freund talking Viennese and passed Bobo's table with a wink. When I got back he blew the air out of his lungs in astonishment, nearly screwed the hair off the side of his head and ordered two bottles of champagne to pay the bet.

* Duke of Roxburghe born 1913, died 1974.
** Later Marquess of Douro and Duke of Wellington.
*** Later Lord Irwin and Lord Halifax.

Palestine was already noticeably divided between a predominantly Jewish part and an Arab hinterland. Even in Jerusalem the modern Jewish quarter was sharply divided from the Old City, with its winding alleyways, with shaded booths, and its bazaars — the street of sandal makers, the street of spices; and the fish market. There were old men with brown and wrinkled faces, beneath turbans of green and white and red; the green being no doubt the fillet of the Haji, of the man who has been to Mecca. I spent a year in and around Palestine.

While I was at Sarafand, learning on the red and beaten soil under the harsh Mediterranean glare, more about the inside of a motor vehicle in a fortnight than I had learnt in ten years as a motorist, the regiment had moved to Tiberias. Here around the inland sea, three hundred feet below coast level, and warm, accordingly even at Christmas, the regiment settled down to pass the rainy season, when even Kings cannot go forth to battle. I found the Officers' Mess in a neat little white villa, which had formerly been a Jewish pension. The troopers were quartered in a rambling hotel, where the owner, Mrs. Feingold, retained a private suite approached by the fire escape ladder. When off duty, the officers used the annexe to the Windsor Hotel in Haifa, not far away as a sort of club. The Windsor annexe was a small white house on the lower slopes of Mount Carmel overlooking the bay. I had heard a good deal since my arrival of a woman whom I will call Louscha Sevinsky. She was not without illustrious admirers. She had come to Palestine, originally from Marish-Ostrau in Czechoslovakia and with her smouldering grey eyes and rather high cheek bones, she looked very Slavonic and would not readily have been recognised as Jewish. She had married a Palestinian Jew, who was a Civil Servant, and they lived in a square flat-roofed villa, with an incomparable view. When I met Louscha I had the advantage of being able to talk German, as she knew no English at that time.

There are some brave souls who are no doubt ready, at any time of the day or night, to leap into the cannon's mouth; or charge gleefully through machine-gun fire without thought of hearth or home. But I was not one of these. I was very devoted to my wife in England and proud of my young sons in the nursery. It had been almost a physical wrench to leave them all at home; and I suffered much sadness. Yet it is essential if a man is to become a good soldier that he shall go through a hardening-up process; so that he will not, when the trumpet sounds, be thinking all the time about surviving to get back to the loved ones far away. Nothing is more helpful to this hardening of the heart than a period of preparation for battle far away overseas in a distant land. Letters when they arrive after months in some Army sorting office in Cairo, are out of date and contain no answer to letters sent home and similarly delayed. Cables to the Middle East took as long as two months, the airgraph service had not started; and England seemed as far away as the moon.

"War being what it is; and soldiers what they are," my wife had said, sagaciously enough, as we drove through the gates of Great Fosters for the last time. "But there is no need to tell me about it." Here, however, we come up against the occupational disease of authors, writing. They cannot keep away from the bottle — of ink. And so it all comes out. Even a reader of average discernment, without knowing the author, would say of *The Dome of the Rock* that it was based on some knowledge of the Middle East. Indeed the critics said that it was 'vivid with authentic colour' and so on. How then to account, without grave suspicion, for the grey-eyed Louscha Sevinsky? Idle to point out that the novel also describes people in Abyssinia (which I had not visited) and that all characters in fiction are composite. This one was composite of far too many attractions to pass unnoticed. Within two months I had learnt to speak German perfectly — but with a slightly Czech accent.

I was keeping a diary at this time, and was well aware that in the event of my not returning from some battlefield, the diary would end up on my wife's lap in England. She would not fail to notice the appearance of Louscha Sevinsky in Northern Palestine, where she lived, but also staying with her sister-in-law at Tel Aviv, when I was doing a course near there. Louscha's last words to me, recorded on Sunday, 18th March, 1941 were that I should not go gadding about in bars by myself, but wait until I collected her for dinner. However, walking along the sea front with her sister-in-law past the Gat Rimmon Hotel, the sister-in-law said, "What is the betting that your friend's car will be here?"

Mrs. Sevinsky said, "Oh, no, he is not that kind of man. He doesn't sit about in bars."

"What is the number of his car?" asked the sister-in-law.

"476," replied Mrs. Sevinsky.

"Well, there it is!" laughed her sister-in-law.

'Of course,' records my diary, 'Mrs. S — took me to task over this when we met, and I had to begin asking myself what Rima (my wife) would think about all this. Would she be pleased to think that someone was "keeping an eye on me" and protecting me in this ludicrous fashion, or would she, on the contrary, get the wind up that Mrs.

S — was too interested in me by half? After a bit she calmed down, and we were dancing when Tony Murray-Smith came in with a Polish girl he met when he was down here on a course, and about whom we have teased him a lot. There were two other people in the party. Tony hailed me gleefully and a little tipsily, and was obviously struck dumb by Mrs. Sevinsky. He said, "Is Somerset behaving himself properly?" and she replied, "Somerset! I don't know him by that name. I only know him as Mr. de Chair." Not strictly true, but very good for Tony.' One day, perhaps, my diaries of the war will be published, but not just yet. On another occasion, when we were dining at Pross's in Haifa, Valerian Wellesley came over to our table. As I had no intention of letting Valerian and half the regiment know who she was, I introduced her as Baroness Skoda, late of the Skoda Works in Czechoslovakia, (recently expropriated by Adolf Hitler, along with the Sudetenland in 1938).

A diary entry on the previous Thursday: 'I drove Mrs. Sevinsky, at her suggestion, to have tea at Nathanya. We took the car down to the cliffs at the end of the street overlooking the sea. It was windy, but fresh and delightful after the city atmosphere of Tel Aviv. A ridge of sandy cliffs runs along the coast at Nathanya, and the beach is down below. There was a wind up and the sun shone fitfully in the late afternoon. Long lines of breakers were sweeping in to the beach. She had brought no coat or hat, and was wearing a pale blue frock, so I lent her my British Warm, with its four stars on the epaulettes. She looked enchanting in the heavy fawn army coat, with her high, Slav cheekbones and wide, blue-grey eyes, now alive and vivid like the sea, at other times slow-burning and dreamy. (I tore up a photograph of her like this when I was wounded and pushed the pieces out of the ambulance into the desert near Palmyra. I thought it better for the picture not to be found on me, for Rima's sake.) She looks very like Marlene Dietrich at times, I recorded, and she remarked that the scene as the two of us walked along the windy cliff, she in her light blue dress, with the heavy army coat over it and her hair blowing about, and I in khaki service dress and cap, was like some incident in a film of Marlene Dietrich's. It was too late and too cold to walk more than a hundred yards or so, and we drove to the Eden Hotel, where we had tea. The atmosphere was so European — the proprietor by the name of Epstein, with books on art in all the ages — such an atmosphere of culture. He talked to us for a long time, never apparently taking me for an Englishman at all.'

These and other passages scarcely do justice to some intimate scenes in the moonlight between the Horns of Hattin, where Saladin defeated the Crusaders: or high up on the hills above the Sea of Galilee, where the swine, having great faith in their leader, followed him to their deaths. Louscha was no mean lover, and was inclined in moments of ecstasy to thrash about with the frenzy of a snared rabbit:

"*Wirkt das auf Sie, wie auf Mich*," she would ask; and was specific in her requests: well, well, no wonder I regard my time in the Middle East as among the happiest of my life, except when actually being shot. The first three sonnets in SONNETS FOR SEVEN SIRENS, in my *Collected Poems*, were inspired by her.

> Alone to look on her, made men desire
> And those who knew her felt a slumbering fire
> Steal through their arteries, as when a lyre
> Has felt the brush of fingers cross its wire.

Or again:

> Why blame the miser in the dead of night
> If he withdraws his sacks of gold by day?
> If I possessed a jewel of such fame
> That men would torture, kill and lust for it
> I would not wear it in the glare of noon,
> No, I would watch it by the candle's flame.
> So, all night long I am content to sit
> And watch your beauty in the crystal moon.

(English Lyric Poets, Vol. IX)

> Eros, the strongest of all gods and laughter
> Conceived her in a flash of ecstasy
> And Venus taught her, in her infancy
> The ways of beauty, which she used thereafter.
> Pan and the Naiads bathed her lovely face
> In the translucent wooded pools of night.
> Her witchcraft stole from the Blind Muse her sight
> And Bacchus, dazed with wine, felt her embrace.

And it was of her I was thinking when I wrote the poem which prefaces *The Silver Crescent*:

Let the day's unnumbered treasure
    Render up its gold.
Let the night's unnumbered leisure
    Yield what it may hold.
When the moon is silver crescent
    Let me make a prayer,
That the beauty of the present
    Stay with me a year.
When the moon is gone for ever
    And the night is dark,
Let us make a pact to sever,
    Stamp upon the spark.

Louscha, who, for all I knew, was possibly working for British Intelligence to keep an eye on us or for the Haganah (ditto), or both, asked me what the Household Cavalry Regiment consisted of. I replied, "Horses and Lords." Flattered no doubt by having poems written for her she said *"Ich glaube Sie sind mehr als ein Lord."*

Before I left for Iraq, we stayed with friends of hers in the beautiful Italian Hospice at the head of the Sea of Galilee. As it was Italian property it was sequestrated during the war, and unoccupied except for the curator, an Englishman married to an Arab woman.

Louscha looked after my car and surplus baggage while I was on campaign; and on my return came to see me in hospital at Jerusalem, where her hysterics were somewhat disturbing in a ward full of officers, and extremely exhausting.

"Ihr armes krankes bein," she wept. We only met once more after that, in the suite of Mrs. Hamburger, wife of the Manager at the King David Hotel, where she came a long way to say goodbye. But I wish I had kept that photograph of her wearing my army greatcoat, and carrying my leather-covered swagger stick.* I even thought it prudent to destory the negative when I returned to Scotland, as my wife was not above examining those too. Thelma was, however, to her credit, one of the few authors' wives who bothered to read their husbands' books in manuscript; and when the typescript of the *Dome of the Rock* arrived, she was reading this in the brown drawing-room at Blickling. It hurtled through the air, scoring a neat hit on my left ear. She died in 1974.

*   *   *

* After this book had already gone to the printers I had the idea of writing to an old friend in Israel, Reggie Kidron, who was the Israeli Chargé d'Affaires in London in 1950 and had brought his lovely wife Nora to stay with me at Blickling. He looked exactly like one of those dashing young men in their flying machines, with huge black handlebar moustaches. He could have passed anywhere, and probably did, as a British Wing Commander. He was a mine of information on Middle East affairs and enabled me to appear more of an expert on the subject in the House of Commons than I really was. So now I wrote to him care of the Foreign Office in Jerusalem, to ask if he could trace an old wartime friend of mine called Louscha 'Sevinsky'. I gave him the correct name and asked him to find out if she still had her copy of the photo of her I took wearing my army greatcoat on the beach at Nathanya. He replied that he had no difficulty in doing so, and gave me her address and telephone number not a hundred miles from Haifa; and he said that she would be sending the photo, as she would not want a picture of herself wearing a British army greatcoat floating around Israel. I said, "I can't think why not, as we were all fighting Adolf Hitler at the time." Louscha herself replied, and when I telephoned her she gasped, "I'm going to fall down!" Since I knew her, she had learned to speak English. She was now a widow. As soon as she got my letter she posted the picture (which is reproduced here) and one or two others. I asked her to stay with me and my new wife if she came to England; and she reciprocated with an invitation to visit her in Israel. The friendship, in short, was still intact. Louscha did in fact stay with us for ten days in September 1987 at the age of 75 (when I was 76) at Bourne Park in Kent, St. Osyth Priory in Essex and in London. She could not understand why my fourth wife had a title (Lady Juliet de Chair) while my third wife, Tessa, who took her around the sights and shops of London and drove her to the airport, had not got one. She said with splendid malapropism, "No one would know that you are not a Lady." Louscha brought us slap up against the realities of the Holocaust by revealing that her father had been killed, shot at 3 metres range, his face blown off; her mother was incinerated in a hospital for Jewish women which was deliberately set alight; and her sister, whom she was going to visit near Strasbourg, had to wear special shoes because her toes had been cut off in an experiment by Dr. Mengele.

But we are back in Palestine in 1941.

I was again in Eion Merry's Squadron and for a week our horses were picketed on horse lines down in the square of Tiberias in the Arab quarter. The Jewish houses were all up on the hill where the air was fresher, and the ground, if not already built on, marked out with iron pegs in building land at 400 mils a dunam (or quarter-acre). There was an Arab mosque down by the water front, and a pleasant café on the edge of the lake called the Lido where the officers in gabardine drill uniforms could sip drinks while looking pensively across to the barren ravines in the Gadarine hills, down which the swine had tumbled. We were known as the Gabardine Swine. After a week, Eion's Squadron of Blues and Eric Gooch's Squadron of Life Guards, were sent twenty miles down the Jordan Valley to camp at Beisan.

We rode all day down the valley in heat which was astonishing in this deep cleft in the earth's surface; and found our camp site beside a Byzantine mosaic of the Tree of Life and a conical hill in the wadi beyond, where seven civilisations had deposited evidence of their occupation in turn. The University of Philadelphia had sent out an expedition to excavate the tell before the war; and had sawn off the top, like an egg neatly sliced. The valley was littered with the capitals of marble columns, and the rains, washing off the mud in the horse lines, brought up Roman coins. With Eric's approval I formed an archaeological society.

A land which has boasted the immaculate conception of the Saviour of the World, has, perhaps, already exhausted in advance its power to astonish. Can one be altogether surprised, however, that those to whom was first shown the whole Book of Isaiah on scrolls said to be over 2,000 years old and found in sealed jars in a cave, supposed them to be forgeries? By comparison the manuscript of one of Shakespeare's plays, written not more than 350 years ago would seem an easy discovery.

Violence and not peace appears to be the surest preserver of records. Only in times of trouble do people seal up copies of Holy Writ.

Much has been buried in Palestine in the overthrow of civilisations. Nowhere is it easier to excavate the stratas than at Beth Shan. This town occupies a strategic position at the junction of the Jordan Valley and the Valley of Jezreel. It has been seized and held by the Egyptians, the Persians, the Greeks, the Romans, and the Byzantines, by anyone, in fact, claiming to exercise authority over Northern Palestine. Here Saul was buried. Hereabout Jezebel laughed from her balcony at Jehu, driving furiously, and was eaten by dogs. Alexander the Great built upon it Scythopolis, one of the ten cities of the Decapolis which he founded in the Levant.

In 1940 it was called Beisan; a dusty Arab town. The portals of the police station were flanked by Greek marble columns, which was not surprising. The University of Philadelphia, after sawing off the top of the tell neatly, made cuts vertically in the course of the excavations. They shared their finds with the Department of Antiquities in Jerusalem and half their finds went into the Rockefeller Museum at Jerusalem accordingly.

On the further side of the wadi and directly overlooking the tell, stood a church in Byzantine times and the exquisite mosaic flooring of the Tree of Life was wonderfully preserved. On the slopes below this were innumerable graves in the hillside and as the winter rains washed away the earth, new tombs were coming continuously to light.

Every morning the Orderly Officer rode out of the camp with 300 horses, on 'Watering Order'. This was a trot down to the Jordan and round about, to exercise the animals. They jogged along in half sections, each trooper leading a bare-backed horse beside his own mount. There was a tendency to follow the same route every day. I noted one morning, as the heels of the horses ahead of me went over the ground, that something white was beginning to show through the red and beaten earth. Next morning it was clearer, and the next time I went out with the Watering Order, the key pattern of a mosaic border was beginning to be laid bare. I diverted the rest of the horses and formed, that afternoon, the Household Cavalry Archaeological Society. It seemed the easiest way of getting the thing excavated. But now 16 troopers volunteered for an exciting pastime and with a lorry, spades, brooms and water I led them to the site. Half an hour's enthusiastic labour cleared fifteen feet of Byzantine mosaic flooring, not so spectacular as the Tree of Life flooring near the horse lines, but quite intriguing enough to fire the enthusiasm of the newly formed archeological society. Thereafter every Wednesday afternoon, which was a half-day, we held a meet beside the Tree of Life and would proceed to excavate in an ever widening circle.

Some of our finds were forwarded to the Archaeological Museum in Jerusalem, who declared most of them indifferent speciments of Roman pottery, of which they already had examples. One bowl of Persian work, a shallow black earthenware bowl with a starlike pattern moulded on the underside, they offered to buy for the sum of 400 mils (about eight shillings). This went to the finder and the finders of most of the other articles were glad enough to sell their discoveries privately for similar sums. In replying to our enquiries, the Department of Antiquities pointed out strenuously the provisions of The Archaeological Excavators, Palestine Act, etc. etc. and seemed to deplore so much amateur zeal. I pointed out, however, that the co-ordinated enthusiasm of a score of amateur archaeologists was better than the unbridled lust of 300 Cavalry troopers prodding about on their own, and with this view the museum gloomily concurred. They had known about our mosaic.

I also got the leading N.C.O.s enthusiastic about a production of *Twelfth Night* in the wilderness and went over to Tiberias on occasion to buy embroidered velvet from puzzled Arabs for Elizabethan doublets, to be made up by the regimental tailor. The Squadron Corporal-Major Evans, who was a man of enormous girth, played the part of Sir Toby Belch to the roaring delight of the troops. My own Corporal-of-Horse, Margan, played Malvolio and Corporal-of-Horse Peach, as temperatental as any opera star, was coaxed to shave off his moustache and play the Countess Olivia. He clung to his moustache for a long time. "But really, Corporal-Major," I expostulated, "we can't have Countesses with moustaches." So off it came. During one rehearsal it blew such a gale in the Jordan Valley that half the tents were torn up and blew away. I tried to introduce a donkey for light relief in the final production. But we could not heave it up on to the stage without being kicked to death. Instead Trooper Regan, dressed as an Arab, brought the house down at regular intervals, crossing the stage whenever the Shakespearean dialogue seemed a bit above the heads of the audience, touching his forehead and saying "Saida" to the cast. It was a great success; and Sir Toby Belch consumed, if I remember right, a dozen bottles of beer during the final performance.

I also edited a magazine for the troops, which I got printed in Jerusalem called 'The Far Cry from the Middle East'. A photograph competition was held and the winning entries were admirably reproduced. The magazine was sold to the regiment at cost price, 30 mils per copy; but thanks to a substantial demand from other units in the 1st Cavalry Division, it was possible to pay for the entire cost of production and show a small profit for the regimental P.R.I. funds. It was for this magazine that I wrote the story of the Night Guard in Jerusalem at the trial of Jesus. I was trying to convey to our own troopers the forceful parallel of their own position with that of the Roman soldiers in AD 33. Some two or three years later, an American author adopted the same theme, in a novel called *The Robe*. My own story was republished in 1945 in *A Mind on the March*.

In the course of publishing the magazine I had to visit the Jerusalem Press in Jerusalem several times. In the shop window of an antique dealer called Ohan, opposite the King David hotel, I saw what appeared to be a larger than life bust of Bacchus, apparently in stone. On entering the shop I was startled to find that it was a double-headed figure, the other side of which was the lovely face of his girl-friend Ariadne. They were joined by vine leaves and grapes. After many visits and many cups of black coffee, I entered into a contract with Ohan, under which I paid a ten per cent deposit and gave my executors 18 months to pay the balance and collect it if I did not return from the battlefield.

While all these activities went forward in camp, I was also ranging further afield and beginning to secure some knowledge of the Arabs living on both sides of Jordan. During a big exercise by the 1st Cavalry Division in the Jordan Valley, I was sent off on my own, on the third day, with an escort of three men and my horseholder to see if a ford could be found for a Squadron over the river, which is at all times dangerous for horses to swim, on account of its swift current. I rode hard for forty minutes, passing long low oblong black tents, of goat hair, under which the bedouin squatted. I asked the way to Mahadan Al Saghir — a ford indicated on the map; and came straight down to it. I found a dark skinned bedu in white robes and aqual, sitting disconsolately on a white horse in the edge of the river. There was an Arab boy standing near by. So I cried, "Across?" in Arabic. The bedu expressed surprise but turned his horse upstream in a discouraged fashion, holding his feet high. The animal began to get deeper and deeper in the water. Leaving my escort and horseholder on the shore, I followed the bedu and soon the swirling current was racing under my heels and the horse was only able to keep his footing on the bed of the river with difficulty. After a few yards, the bedu turned in a curve to the right and, plunging into shallower water, we came up the further bank into Transjordan. He had shown me the exact route to follow in crossing the ford. I hoped that he would also lead the way back but he went on his way into the wastes of Transjordan and, thanking him, I spurred my horse back into the current, following the reverse route with some precision; as it is only too easy on these occasions to be washed up in the Dead Sea. I had found for purposes of the exercise, an alternative crossing to the Sheikh el Hussein bridge.

We were confined to camp over Christmas (1940) because of five diphtheria cases reported in the camp. There was a cry for china plates to give the troops a palatable Christmas lunch in place of their mess tins.

Bobo Roxburghe went into the Arab village at Beisan, while Tony Murray-Smith and I raced up to Nazareth in my car (a Packard which I had just bought second-hand from the son of the Arab Mayor of Haifa). Nazareth was perched up in the hills, approached by a steeply twisting road. There were some superb convents in the Florentine style, now taken over as hospitals; and there were houses, behind walled gardens, also reminiscent of houses in the hills above Florence. There was still the old Arab quarter, with its narrow street, looking probably very much like the Jewish town of Jesus' childhood. Our intention was to get the 350 plates required from the Naafi, but we found it closed. A small Arab boy offered to guide us to the Manager's house. The lad jumped on the side of the car and we drove right up the further hill to the Manager's house. But he was out for a walk and we had to wait till he got back. I stared impatiently at a signpost labelled in English, Arabic and Hebrew, 'Nazareth Town' one way; 'Tiberias' the other. There were, in war, mercifully no tourists. But what if not tourists on a celestial scale were we? The Manager returned at last and sent a man down with us, who spoke English. He gave us all the plates he had got — thirty. He then showed us a route for the car into the Old City, down ever diminishing streets, along one which finally had a trough in the centre, until we came to what he called the Square — an open patch of earth between the houses. The yellow plastered buildings had blue shutters and carved bargeboards in old weathered wood under the gutters. The impression of Florence returned more strongly than ever. More than once, in the narrow side streets, I peeped into a carpenter's shop, where men were working at the making of blue cradles and rough agricultural implements. We came to a crockery shop where the owner, an Arab, wanted 165 piastres (about 33/-) for a day's hire of 300 plates of all colours and sizes. He settled for £1, which was reduced to 15/- when Tony learnt by telephone that only another 150 plates were now needed. They were placed loose in a large oval tin bath with handles and carried down the tortuous streets by two old Arabs who had little idea of time or the urgency of the approaching festival meal. It was already past noon and we had to get them back to Beisan camp for the midday 'dinners', which had already been postponed. I pointed out to Tony that the petrol tank was empty and that it must be filled up before we got back, but he said, "The gauges on these American cars are always wrong." We had 25 miles to cover in 25 minutes. We bounded down the steep, twisting road from Nazareth, like mountain goats, the plates chinking merrily in the tin bath on the back seat of the car, which was fortunately well sprung.

"So long as you keep this car, you have got your passage home," Tony observed. Five miles from camp the car ran out of petrol. A lorry from a Jewish agricultural settlement came by and the tin bath with the 180 loose plates was heaved aboard it, and Tony rushed on with the driver to deliver the goods. A few minutes later one of our own ambulances, returning from taking our diphtheria cases up to Nazareth lent me a two gallon can. I got back to camp in time to find that the men had finished their sumptuous repast. Perhaps they would have preferred it half an hour earlier from mess tins. Later, we returned to Nazareth in order to take back what could be collected of the plates and listened on the way to the voice of the King broadcasting his Christmas message. I recorded, 'It was moving in its simplicity, in its direct appeal to the homely things in life, in its understanding of the real sorrow of war — the separation of people who love each other.'

Of Boxing Day, I wrote, depressingly enough:

'Marooned in a desolate plain, far from the consolation of their families, cut off from the amenities of life, confined to camp by diphtheria — There was a football match between the two Squadrons played on the ground at Beisan, but the Arabs were more interested in two troopers dancing the boomps-a-daisy, and in that Don Quixote of the other ranks who, springing bare-back upon a mule, rode slowly and majestically across the baked earth football ground under the hot Christmas sun, while the players belaboured his mount in an endeavour to get it off the ground.'

There was a visit of officers to the N.C.O.s' Mess, at which large quantities of beer had to be drunk, and a return visit to the Officers' Mess, where a dart competition was held. Corporal-Major Evans told incredibly lewd stories, made us all play two thumbs, two fingers, two legs, stand up, sit down, stand up, turn round, sit down, keep moving, and dominated the entire party.

At dinner in the tent where we sat each side of a long trestle table with four plain candles stuck on upturned egg cups to recapture some glamour of the candle-lighted Mess tables in England, the talk turned upon the death of King George V. Many of those sitting at the table had taken their turn of duty on guard at the catafalque in Westminster Hall. These are the officers who stood rigid as statues in their blue or scarlet uniforms, with helmets, plumes, white gauntlets, buckskin breeches and jackboots, as the endless procession filed by. Bobo said that he and Henry Abel were in the picture of it which appered in *The Times*. Tony said that the best time was on the first night, after everyone else had departed, and they were left alone in the hush of Westminster Hall, with the upturned lights, guarding the coffin. Eric Gooch said that while he was on guard he noticed a little man in plain clothes standing under the archway (which leads down to the Fees Office). He found out that he was the detective posted there to watch over the crown. An amusing idea Eric thought, with four Life Guard officers and the Yeoman of the Guard all posted round the coffin. While he was on duty they came in the dead of night and took the crown away to have it mended; the top had fallen off in the procession and a Grenadier had picked it up and put it in his pocket. Tony bears out what Kipling says in his story of the Gurkha brothers at Edward VII's lying-in-state — the incessant passing of people's legs made you giddy if you looked at them for too long.

Next morning I went down to the Jordan alone, to write to my wife. I sat on the bank near the Jisr al Hussein. A large kingfisher, larger than the English variety, brilliant blue but with a black face, breast and wing tips, flew leisurely, in dipping curves, across the river, which rushed past brown and turbulent. A heron winging his way slowly upstream saw me and turned away with a sudden flapping of his huge wings. Across the water a sentry in khaki helmet with a spike on top, peered curiously at me from the castellated buff frontier post. The khamsim had been blowing all day — a fine drifting of desert dust. A bugle rang out from the little fort.

I began writing poetry again; of the people of London,

> Let me attempt with all my power
> To hold the trivial in check —

and of Greece,

> Perhaps some whisper from the Parthenon,
> Still lingers on the air
> Of Greece; of Salamis, of battle won.
> If not, how could they dare —

Then, riding alone, around the deserted tell of Beth Shan, which under the name of Scythopolis had also been one of the ten cities of the Decapolis set up by Alexander the Great, I thought sadly of more lines, looking further ahead after the sudden hour of victory —

Who are the remnants of the field, poor men?
They are not happy, not the ones who live.
For them the uphill road begins again.
Happy who gave all that they had to give.

Some of these poems were printed at the end of the limited edition
of the *Golden Carpet*, and later in the war when I went up to the
Chiswick Press in North London, where the pages of hand-set type were
being printed for the Golden Cockerel Press, I found a sad little
compositor, staring through the thick lenses of his steel-rimmed
spectacles at these lines.

"If you will forgive me saying so," he confided to me, "those words
mean more to me than anything in the book. That is just how I feel. I
was in the first war."

No doubt the better poetry was to come later, born of pain and
hardship and disappointment; or of love in sad circumstances. It was
Melville in *Moby Dick* (for whom and the sea he had a deep respect),
who said that the pattern of life must be three parts sadness, just as the
world is three parts under water.

There is a religious emphasis in some of the poems like the 'Sea of
Galilee'. It was an experience of tremendous significance to me at this
time to stand upon the shore of this inland sea, and gaze over the same
blue unruffled surface that once had soothed the brow of Christ. I was
intensely interested in the marble ruins of the synagogue at Capernaum
where He had preached His first sermon; and if my assessment of these
events has altered as the years have advanced it has not diminished my
interest in them nor discounted the privilege of walking in the footsteps
of a Master. All this also is clearly reflected in *The Dome of the Rock*.

My poetry, of which four examples appeared in *The Far Cry*,
attracted the attention of the Brigadier, a powerful giant in whose mind
there were deep undercurrents. More often than we realise in our youth,
we are studied from on high, by eyes unseen to us and my visits to
obscure Arab Mukhtars in hill villages, or to the bedouin tents of
Transjordan, where the sheep, heaped high with saffron rice, was laid
before me as an honoured guest, began to suggest to Joe Kingstone the
presence in his brigade of an unorthodox officer. I had seen him once at
Juela, huge, red-faced, with those pale and penetrating eyes that I had
last seen in Allenby and seem to be a distinguishing mark of great
generals. He had cross-questioned me closely about the bombing in
England, and gone away pensively. When I tried to call out the guard as

he departed, he said softly, "Don't bother with that nonsense for me." Thereafter I viewed him with some respect. And at Nazareth, on a football ground outside the town, he was surrounded at half-time by a group of officers from our regiment which was playing in the match. I stood on the fringes of the group, not volunteering athletic views; and over the heads of the group, I found the Brigadier's eye resting on me and slowly it closed in a wink.

My first visit to an Arab village did not commend itself to my Squadron leader, Eion; for I was out on patrol and he had asked me to call on the Mukhtar for ten minutes. You cannot without grave discourtesy, on a day which transpires to be a Muhammadan feast day celebrating the Hejira, pop in and out of an Arab's house as if you were making a call in a telephone booth. There are grave courtesies to be exchanged. Besides, it takes a long time for the coffee to be prepared. So while I sat cross-legged, wearing my spurred boots and breeches, (which made the posture exceedingly uncomfortable) upon cushions on the floor against the wall, a crescent of the Mukhtar's male relatives was formed on each side of me and the Mukhtar sat in the curve of the wall, to my right. A brass tray piled high with red-hot ashes was produced and brass coffee pots with weird spouts set to heat in the ashes. The Mukhtar removed his saliva and shook it from his fingers into the ashes. While the coffee was being heated, orange juice was brought in tiny glasses sprinkled with a pattern of coloured flowers. It was a small house and the quiet room was very low; but Jabbul was a squalid village, perched high upon a crag, accessible alone to men on foot or horses. It came on to rain and I thought of Eion down in the valley, waiting impatiently astride his horse. The Mukhtar's friends were amused by the Italian broadcasts which spoke of disturbances in the Beisan district, where we were sitting. "Who should know better than you," they said, "if there are disturbances in the Beisan district?" But they did not pretend to dislike the Germans as they disliked the Italians. The Arabs always respect strength and they smiled covertly when I suggested that we would soon do to the Germans what Wavell was now doing to the Italians in the Western Desert. The rain came down harder outside the low ceilinged room in which some dozen Arabs were sitting. One of them was quite red-haired, a descendant possibly of the Crusaders, with a little red-headed daughter of three and a half. When the coffee was ready, I said, "Daime," in gratitude, when a cup was first handed to me, instead of waiting until I had finished it and set it down. They heaped extravagant compliments on me, which I returned in the most flowery phrases I could think of. Eventually I felt the time had come when I could say that, much as I should like to spend the whole day with them, the two troopers of my escort outside had to be back in camp by a certain time and I must reluctantly tear myself away. There was a great leave-taking. The Mukhtar came out and shook hands with me on my horse. I started off with my escort and horseholder to join my troop outside the village; and descended the steep track to find Eion, a sodden victim of Anglo-Arab relations. After this I encouraged Eric Gooch, who was commanding the two Squadrons at Beisan, to pay a ceremonial visit to the Mukhtar. This time we gave him plenty of warning as, on my arrival unheralded, the Mukhtar was to be seen hurriedly getting brocaded cushions out of cupboards in my honour. I went with Eric Gooch.

What was the impact of this army on the Middle East? Let us tell the story of the Major and the Mukhtar. Eric looked very like God. His boots shone like polished metal and the grips of his breeches gleamed canary yellow in the morning sunlight. He rode with his moustache flaring up on each side of his fine face like the bow wave of a battleship. He was escorted by a khaki cavalcade which wound down the sides of the steep rock-strewn wadi and up the further slopes towards the village, perched on a crag. The Mukhtar was there to greet him; a brown-skinned, thin little man, wearing his white head cloth, fastened by two circular black cords, and his long robes. The Major took his seat cross-legged on the cushions spread out for him upon the floor. He did not understand a word the Mukhtar said. But he had an interpreter who understood everything. Coffee, flavoured with a rare spice from the Hejaz, was offered to the Major at frequent intervals in little cups. Sweetened orange juice was brought to him in gaudy glasses. He bowed his head most charmingly and asked the interpreter to convey his compliments to the Mukhtar, who replied, "Sharraftuna" — we are honoured. At length lunch was borne in. Trays of chicken, pigeon, and lamb, onion, tomatoes, and potatoes — huge dishes of saffron-coloured buttered rice. And bread in sheets like chamois leather, on which the Major spread his food and ate happily with his fingers, squeezing the buttered rice up into a delicious ball in his hand. And all the while, the Mukhtar and his male relatives sat aloof, watching, for no Muslim would think of eating until his guests were satisfied. At length, the Major could eat no more, and water was poured over his hands. The food was taken away and he was given sweetened tea in glasses. And then, between puffs at his cigarette, the Mukhtar told his story. His son, who had carried a gun in the troubles, had recently been released from prison. He was to report once a month to the police. And then, suddenly, the same malodorous persons who had got him shut up (enemies in the next village) had now whispered against him and the son had been told to report three times a day. He could not till the Mukhtar's fields, and everybody laughed at the Mukhtar because in all the village, his land alone was not sown. He hoped that the Major would intercede for his son. The story had taken a long time to tell. And the Major knew all about it before. He knew, in fact, that the case had already been sent forward for review. So he said, with a basilisk expression on his face (for he did not believe all that the Mukhtar had said) that the papers were being considered and he hoped that the Mukhtar would soon have his son with him. The Mukhtar said that he put his trust in God and the Major. There seemed to be no adequate answer to this, so the Major took his departure. The following evening, the local Police Inspector came into camp as usual and sat in the Officers' Mess tent, sipping a whisky and soda. He mentioned that the case of the Mukhtar's son had just come through and that the son had been released the same afternoon. In the estimation of the Mukhtar, the Major had gone to the top of his very exclusive class.

While we were seated in the Mukhtar's house, an impressive figure had entered — a tall man, with a golden beard and blue eyes. He cast his shoes, like the others, in the depression for this purpose, inside the door, and took his seat against the wall without a word. His arrival caused an electric tremor to run round the group, but nobody stirred from his place on the floor. The man wore the smooth round white hat of a Ulema, from the top of which protruded a circular scarlet crown, which is the mark of a priest. He had blue eyes of extraordinary power. Presently he got up and went out, as it was the Muhammadan Sunday, ostensibly to call the faithful to prayer. Eric was interpreted as saying that he hoped no one would be deterred by our presence from attending. This was greeted by loud and genial laughter. We thought at first that he was the priest from Kokab, a neighbouring village. But when I questioned Fullbrook of the Palestine Police, he could think of no priest in the vicinity who answered to this man's description. Years afterwards I saw a photograph of this man and recognised him at once. He was the Mufti of Jerusalem himself, then in hiding, who came and sat there boldly in the room, listening to the two British officers, saying nothing, but creating by his very presence such tension in the atmosphere, and departing without a glance of respect towards the guests. Jabbul was a Husseini village where it would have been easy for him to hide. He was at that time regarded by the British as a rebel leader, and appeared shortly afterwards in Berlin where he was much honoured by Hitler. He crossed frontiers in the Levant with the ease of a ghost. His startling appearance in that hill village prompted some lines:

> They were there on the floor of the Mukhtar's house,
> On the floor of the house in Jabbul.
> Carpets of Isphahan, carpets so rare
> On the floor of the house in Jabbul.
> And a Prince came from Kokab,
> And sat by the wall
> On the floor of the house in Jabbul.

In March, 1941, I was sent to an intelligence course in Cairo.

At the 63rd General Hospital, outside Cairo I found Harry Legge-Bourke, in a blue hospital jacket, sitting up in bed, rather dazed, with a three-inch piece of shrapnel, extracted from his arm, lying on the table beside him. He had been dive-bombed in Greece where he was liaison officer to Jumbo Wilson. The noise of his motor bike had deafened him to the roar of the Junkers 88 diving at him near an ammunition dump, and the Junkers 88 had deafened him to much else since. I could tell him, to his evident relief, that his wife Jean and his boy, Bill Bourke, were remote from the domestic brand of bomber in a small house called Cairnviskoye newly converted, on the Island of Gigha, near my own wife. We were on the way out of Greece, much accelerated by the sort of prodding given to Harry from above. Now Rommel was pounding across the desert towards Egypt.

I was overtaken by fever in Cairo and the officers of the course wanted me to see a doctor. I feared incarceration at a critical time in some hospital and rang up a Christian Science practitioner instead. She gave me silent treatment, and I might have recovered, had she not said on the telephone that we must learn to love the Germans, who were also God's creatures, and want to free them from tyranny. My temperature rose sharply and I nearly threw the telephone away. I calmed down in time, and was rescued from a sense of depression by Elizabeth Coke from Norfolk who came to tea, and invited me to dinner, where I met her brother David, a fighter pilot, flown out of Greece; doomed, as were so many of his gallant band, to die in other skies, in combat over desert troops. Elizabeth's husband, Tommy,* was now at

* Later Earl of Leicester.

Mersah Matruh, getting a close up view of the German Army; and life seemed insecure. Elizabeth who had been at school with my wife, dined and danced with me at Shepherd's Hotel also, then something of a centre in the Orient, where British soldiers in uniform were viewed with awe. Now Shepherd's has been burnt out in a night of dreadful fire and riot when Englishmen, whose power alone saved Egypt in 1941 from the Nazis, were disembowelled at the Turf Club and thrown by fanatical Egyptian nationalists upon a bonfire. When I think thus of Elizabeth and I, she one of the great ladies of England and I a wandering minstrel, dancing in such self-confidence upon a floor so soon to be charred in anti-British phobia, a chill shivers down my spine; and I wonder what other unseen, unexpected turns the wheel of destiny holds in store for us. Certainly power is not easily held in diluted quantities. You must be great — or you are nothing. Indeed you may be disembowelled and burnt upon a pyre.

At the foot of the Great Pyramid, in the Mena House Hotel, I found Quintin Hogg* with the green lanyard of the Rifle Brigade. He joined me for an hour, and over the Turkish coffee at my table, we dissected the House of Commons pretty thoroughly. I noted in my diary: 'The greeting was I think mutual. He is the only really brilliant young M.P. out here and one of the very few in the House.' He had been dining with three other officers of the Rifle Brigade, camped in the desert hard by. He left with them, and was shot in the knee soon afterwards and returned, for good and sufficient reasons, but perhaps a little unstable as a result of his experience, like the rest of us, to the House of Commons later in the war. Quintin Hogg, Randolph Churchill, and I were all, broadly contemporaries at Oxford; and I do not think that it was a bad vintage. Unfortunately we all suffered from the effects of violent handling in transit, during the war, and the vintage would take a little time to settle down. Some of our contemporaries avoided the more violent shocks and appeared fresh as daisies at the end of it all, moving Prayers and other Parliamentary devices to attract attention, and were soon the unsullied ornaments of the Tory Party in office. When I met Quintin after the formation of the first post-war Tory Government in 1951, of which I had hoped to see him, another F.E. Smith, Lord Chancellor, he said somewhat ruefully, "I should not have been able to accept a position in the Government, on account of my work at the Bar; but I was very mortified not to be offered one." I was not even in the

* Later Lord Hailsham.

House at all.

But we are back, ten years, in 1941, separating at the base of the Great Pyramid, and going each our several ways to a rendezvous with lead which, like stolen goods, is difficult to handle at the receiving end.

In Cairo I found an Isphahan carpet, much torn, and took it up to Ibrahim Ali Pasha, the Minister of Health, a noted collector and connoisseur of carpets, who knelt upon it, in his office, untwisted its fibres and pronouced it 400 years old.

I also visited Luxor, which I had long intended to reach.

Ibrahim's face was black and his gown was bright blue. We drove sedately in a two-horsed carriage, trotting to Karnak. The sun was blinding, but there was a light breeze. Ibrahim kept laughing, "You are so lucky, Lieutenant. Yesterday it was so hot I could not walk. Today you have nice breeze. You come a little later it will be too hot. And the moon, Lieutenant, you have the full moon tonight. You are lucky, Lieutenant."

Karnak was unbelievable, a forest of stone, approached by its forbidding avenue of ram's-headed sphinxes. Within the huge walls a hundred and thirty-four pillars, lotus headed, and etched in exquisite designs, stood like trees which had succeeded in growing up to the sky. I lay in their sultry shade. Do these colossal efforts to impress posterity reveal an inferiority complex? Dwarfed by the giant colonnades, the divine form of the Goddess Mut was yet on surer ground.

Ibrahim Achmed had taken me first to a govenment office where — you are so lucky, Lieutenant — the permit to visit all the temples was issued free to me as a soldier: a concession on the part of the Egyptian Government to visiting troops, which I appreciated.

I shall not forget the return to Karnak by moonlight. A road, newly opened — you are so lucky, Lieutenant — followed the bank of the Nile all the way from Luxor. We trotted along, with the moon glittering on the fronds of the palm trees and a gentle breeze blowing off the river. We came to Karnak again, and walked along the grotesque sphinxes in the moonlight; a hard, silent, inscrutable Egyptian moon. Then for an hour or two, wearing only a thin cotton shirt and shorts, I wandered among the great pillars of the temple — roofless now — and the moon shone through the pillars, making weird patterns on the stone. Quaint Egyptians slept in odd nooks, guarding the place, and went ahead, clopping on the stone floor with sticks to frighten away snakes and scorpions. Ibrahim had brought with him his last strips of magnesium ribbon — you are so lucky, Lieutenant — and suddenly the black shadows flared and glared white hot and the incandescent light shone on

180

Photograph by Angelo
Budapest 1934

Venice 1929, where I met a young American girl with her mother, Mrs Maxwell. When I called at their hotel to take the daughter for a ride in a gondola the mother greeted me with: 'Good Morning Glory', to which I could only reply 'Good Afternoon Tea'. Hence the title of this book. Miss Maxwell and I duly passed under the Bridge of Sighs.

Hitherto unpublished photograph of Kipling in South Africa, circa 1900-1902, by the author's aunt, Edith Struben. (Negative on a glass plate). Probably taken at the 'Woolsack'.

Thelma Arbuthnot. A resemblance to the film star Norma Shearer was noticed.

Wedding at St. Paul's, Knightsbridge. October 8th 1932.

Lunch with the Arch Duke Franz Joseph (jr) in Budapest 1934.

Bronze bust of the author by the sculptor Deszo Lanyi executed for the Hungarian Parliament museum.

The 23 year old candidate haranguing the faithful in front of Narford Hall, home of the Chairman, Admiral Fountaine (right foreground), and Mrs Fountaine, on steps, and C. S. King, agent, left foreground. Oliver Lyttelton (Lord Chandos) to whom I was later parliamentary Private Secretary described me in his memoirs as "something of a rabble rouser". When I protested he said "you should not mind if your oratory is compared with that of Marc Antony rather than with Sir Herbert Samuel".

H.M. King George VI inspecting the Household Cavalry Regiment including the four Supplementary Reserve Officers on the right: Somerset de Chair; Arthur Collins (later senior partner of Withers & Co.; who divorced me three times), Jakie Astor, later a distinguished member of the Jockey Club, and Tommy Clyde, who survived the war.

Across the Jordan
Major Eric Gooch, DSO, the Life Guards, commanding A and B Squadrons of the Household Cavalry at Beisan and 2nd Lt. S. S. de Chair MP, Royal Horse Guards; with Inspector Fulbrook of the Palestine Police, visiting the Emir Mohammed Salah in Transjordan, December 1940.

Louscha 'Sevinsky' on the beach at Nathanya, March 1941.

Brigadier John Joseph Kingstone DSO (and bar), leader of 'Kingcol' which captured Baghdad, 1941, and rescued the British hostages in the Embassy.

*Glubb Pasha DSO, commander of the Arab Legion in the advance on Baghdad and Palmyra.
Photograph sent by Mrs. Glubb from Amman for use in connection with 'The Golden Carpet'.*

S. de C. at Luxor on the head of Rameses II.

Entering Baghdad. The Sargon Gate of Korsabad.

Before Palmyra.
Portrait of the author by Anna Zinkeisen.

Ibrahim's black face and bleached the bright powder-blue of his gown as
he confronted the proud, advancing figures of Ra and Mut, who had put
fear into the hearts of his ancestors five thousand years before.

* * *

Three weeks later, two English Members of Parliament stood in the
blinding glare of the yard outside the gymnasium at the Kasr Nil
barracks, which in Arabic means the House of the Nile. We wore
gabardine drill uniforms so that we might almost have been mistaken
for the 'Gabardine Swine' of Cairo; we were certainly not gymnasts.
We were young Army officers attending a short intelligence course
and the lectures were delivered in the gymnasium. The two officers
discussed the significance of a message which the shorter of the two,
Henry Hunloke, had received from Jerusalem, ordering him to return to
Force Headquarters there. "It looks like trouble in Iraq," said Henry,
who dealt with Iraqi matters from Force Headquarters, which were
pleasantly situated in the King David Hotel. There was trouble
everywhere. Rommel had just arrived on the Egyptian frontier for the
first time and a message sent back by our troops, 'Germans arriving in
Alexandria tomorrow,' had caused some misgivings, until it was
discovered that there was an error in the signal which should have read
'German prisoners arriving in Alexandria tomorrow.' Henry departed in
a hurry and I was left for another day or two to stay the course. I too
thought there was something impending and had concealed the effects
of a fever which I seemed to have acquired at Luxor which made my
teeth chatter in the heat, but I was afraid of being incarcerated in some
military hospital when the Brigade in Palestine to which I was
Intelligence Officer got orders to move. I had acquired a Studebaker
saloon car in Cairo and had it painted grey; it had already stalled twice
in the dead of night and I doubted its ability to get me across the
Sinai Desert to Palestine. I was accompanied on the return journey by
another officer doing the course, Dawkins, who was rejoining the
Yorkshire Hussars.

We reached Ismailia without mishap and were startled by its
greenness: like driving unexpectedly into Kew Gardens. Soon we were
out in the much travelled Sinai Desert. The black tarmac road crossed it
like a pencil stroke across a deal board. It was absolute desolation; and
presently the engine began to resound with an ominous clonking. I
pulled up. A revealing trail of oil behind the car told us all that was

necessary. From the bottom of the gear box black drops dripped sluggishly on to the road. I lay on my back under the car, where the heat of the engine was added to the heat radiating from the road so that I was like a sandwich of roast beef, and tried to tighten the bung plug with a spanner and a hammer. There were still about 90 kilometres to go before we reached the Egyptian-Palestine frontier post, where oil might reasonably be obtained. We rattled on. Soon we overhauled a battery of twenty-five pounders: Australian gunners. We pulled up where a lorry was ditched in the sand beside the road, and agreed to take word ahead to the officer in charge, farther up the column.

At the frontier was a scarlet and yellow Texaco sign and a brown wayside caravanserai, where we bought oil in gallons and poured it down the throat of our trembling vehicle. At Beersheba we drove up to the Police Post, to register. The policeman said that the Customs Office was next door, where one could observe the formalities of entering an Egyptian car and pay the appropriate duty. But the Customs post was bare, and I had to settle for the duty much later, when I arrived wounded in Jerusalem. We drove up the shabby street of Beersheba between its mud-coloured houses, to a Y.M.C.A. hostel, where we were given lunch. It was a cool place, curiously English in this borderland of the wilderness where Moses' followers had arrived thirsting for milk and honey.

We took the road from Beersheba to Gaza; there was a good deal of military work going on, to improve it, and the sandy diversions were tricky. It was nightfall before we passed the cross roads at Beit Lidd, where I would have turned off to my own camp, had I not got to deliver my companion to his own regiment in Karkhur, farther on.

Brigade Headquarters at Nathanya had been a peaceful, or, at least, a dignified spot when I had left them on the day before Good Friday; I am writing of 1941; but now the place was in a turmoil. Andrew Ferguson of the Life Guards, commanding the composite regiment of Household Cavalry, was still acting brigadier and a scheme was planned to keep us out all night on the move. This was a bad time to reach camp after fever and a three hundred mile drive from Cairo. But it was the first time I had experienced the activity of a Brigade Office truck on the move; and learnt many lessons. I was given a motor bike to reconnoitre otherwise impassable routes and arrived back in camp, when the scheme ended, shaken in mind and body. After this the luxury of a brand new staff car, for my exclusive use, seemed too good to be true.

Something was afoot. New equipment was falling on us from

Ordnance like hailstones, which rebounded on to subordinate units. Cleansed 2-gallon petrol cans, painted black and marked 'water'; and canvas bags, quaintly reminiscent of the traditional goatskin bag of desert travellers, called Chargules, hinted at a desert crossing. But nothing was certain. Syria was still the focus of Brigade attention; and I worked feverishly to mark the talc covering of a large map of Syria, with chinagraph hieroglyphics in blue, to show the position of Vichy forces there.

Suddenly Joe Kingstone descended in all his might from Haifa, where he had been acting as divisional commander, and resumed command of the Brigade. Brigadier John Joseph Kingstone, large and red, drew us all into conference in the wooden hut where Brigade Headquarters messed, and we learnt all. A column was to be formed, for which the code name was to be Kingcol — Kingstone's Column — under the general auspices of a force called Habforce which was destined to relieve our beleaguered Air Force garrison at Habbaniya on the Euphrates. Raschid Ali, whose revolt was a week old, had nearly succeeded in overwhelming them, but they were still holding out.

General Clark, who had been commanding at Force Headquarters in Jerusalem, returned to Division at Haifa, and would command Habforce. Rumour had it that the redoubtable Archie Wavell had arrived up in Jerusalem from Cairo and fixed George Clark with his one eye, "You go and capture Baghdad," he had told Clark. "What with?" had been the reply, for in all Palestine there was nothing but the 1st Cavalry Division, some regiments of which were at long last being relieved of their horses and given some old Morris trucks to get on with their 'mechanised training'. To recall the words of our Prime Minister, they had at least been mechanised to the extent of losing their horses. Wavell was not perturbed. "That is your affair," he had retorted and returned to Cairo. (Wavell subsequently told me that it was Winston Churchill's idea to send a force from Palestine. Wavell pointed out to him that it would leave the Holy Land absolutely denuded — but the Prime Minister shouldered that risk; and it was well justified.)

Iraq was a new orientation to all of us. I regretted not having carried out a plan to drive there on a week's leave with John Doxford (like myself, a lieutenant in the Blues) when I was with the regiment in February. Nothing in the way of really useful information seemed to have been laid on from Force Headquarters for such a contingency. I dashed up to Haifa and lunched with Edric Nutting, of the Blues, who was divisional Intelligence Officer; and he imparted to me all that he knew. He was frantically sorting piles of maps; and I took away the bulk of them, which were destined for the units of Kingcol. This was to include the combined regiment of Life Guards and Blues; two companies of the Essex Regiment. These were the infantry and were mounted in old trucks snatched hurriedly from some of the remaining cavalry regiments. (I remember the expression on the faces of the Greys at Rehovot, who parted gleefully from their long-faced friends on a Thursday, congratulating themselves on being about to see action as an armoured unit, only to see all their horses come back on the Saturday.) The 237 Battery of 25-pounders, under Major (Daddy) Wright gave us the certainty of outranging the Iraqis with their 18-pounders. There was an independent anti-tank troop of 2-pounders; a field troop of Engineers; and a section of the 166 Field Ambulance. On arrival in Transjordan we were to pick up eight Royal Air Force armoured cars and Glubb's Desert Patrol — black-faced Arab Legionaries, wearing pink gingham headdresses and flowing buff robes, who were recruited from all over the desert, and would provide us with guides to the waterless desert beyond Rutba.

This desert had never been crossed by a conquering army; and it was something of an undertaking to be self-supporting in petrol, oil and water for a fight with two brigades of the Iraq Army lying in wait for us on the Euphrates on the farther side of the desert. However, we planned to give them the slip and get round to succour the Habbaniya garrison by way of a trestle bridge which they were hastily erecting over the broad flood race at the southern end of the great Habbaniya lake.

Our new staff cars (American) were being driven straight off the slips at Suez and racing up to us. Grose, my soldier servant, who was to be my driver, viewed the new car as if it were a bride adorned for her husband; and took it up to Haifa for a quick camouflaging. He had some hot driving that week, and ended by taking my own saloon up to a garage, known to both of us, for safe storage.

Peter Grant-Lawson, the Brigade Major, impressed on us the importance of sending all our heavy baggage away to storage, and of taking the minimum in our vehicles; since every corner would be needed for fuel, water and food.

The column's rendezvous for the start was Beit Lidd crossroads, and we drove out of our camp, beside the sandy Mediterranean shore at Nathanya, early on the morning of 11 May 1941.

When we finally drove out of the camp, I asked Grose, as a matter of interest, where the men thought we were going. "The Regiment think they know," he replied. "They got it from a Don-R from Division that we are going to Durban to look after prisoners of war. The Brigade Headquarters people are certain that we are off to Abyssinia as Internal Security troops."

"They gave us a proper gruelling," added Williamson, my cipher clerk.

"And where do you think we are going?" I asked Grose. He had the best opportunities for finding out.

"I think Syria," he replied. So the secret had been well kept.

We drove by way of Jenin, to Beisan, that outpost at the junction of the Jordan Valley and Plain of Jezreel, where I had floundered in the mud of the rainy season and dug up many traces of the succeeding civilisations whose power politics had necessitated the control of this strategic point — our own the latest of them. We halted at Beisan, for the first of the twenty-minutes-every-two hours halts, and sucked oranges which an Arab Walad sold us from his basket, and gazed past the ancient Tell of Beth Shan; across the Jordan Valley; to the desert hills of Transjordan, whither we were bound. Our old camp was deserted. The wooden army huts, completed too late to be of much use to us, and the long building of the Naafi canteen, just completed in time for my production of *Twelfth Night* before I left the place, now stood deserted on the red and beaten soil, with its patches of green grass on which the same old Arab shepherd's flock still grazed with tinkling bells. Even his chestnut mare was there, her fetlocks hobbled, so that she hopped, clanking, across the meagre grass.

After our halt, the column crossed the narrow gauge railway line of the old Hejaz Railway. The grey trucks, marked with the initials H.R., stood in the little station at Beisan, with its warehouse, where a visiting cinema had been known affectionately to the Blues and Life Guards as 'the Thirty-mils intermission' on account of its frequent breakdowns. We turned north up the Jordan Valley, where the heat of April, in this curious cleft of the Earth's surface, was like an oven. I passed Henry Abel-Smith, second in command of the Household Cavalry. His truck was broken down, and he stood, hotly, in his shorts and open-necked bush shirt, already braced in martial fashion with webbing equipment, compass, cartridges, revolver and all. He peered dubiously from under the green shade of his sola topi into the dark recesses of the engine. Like most of us he had done his driving and maintenance course at Sarafand, and knew more about the engine than his driver. Evidently his scrutiny was effective, for he soon dashed past me; only to be met with a few miles farther on, peering even more dubiously into the engine, and so on, all the way through that steaming valley.

The Jordan is a swift-flowing and treacherous stream, not easily fordable. It is surprising that the Axis aeroplanes, which occasionally raided Palestine, did not go for any of the three bridges which cross the river.

We now crossed the river at Jisr Majami, near the pylons of the hydro-electric works, and began the ascent up the winding dusty road to Irbid, which we reached in the afternoon. After Irbid, a cluster of hovels, we came upon a good tarmac road, which took us happily out on to the main desert plateau of Transjordan. We camped for the night at Mafraq. The units of the column were dispersed over such a wide area that we seemed like a convoy suddenly halted in mid-ocean, stretching to the horizons. To the south of the road was the Iraq Petroleum Company's wired-in settlement; where water could be obtained.

Mafraq is at that point of Transjordan where the Syrian frontier comes down to an obtuse angle, in the corner of which is the aerodrome and railway junction of Deraa, where Lawrence was taken prisoner in unpleasant circumstances. Now it was a potential landing ground for German aircraft, only five miles from our camp. Fortunately German aircraft only began to appear on Syrian aerodromes, bound for Iraq, two days later. So we slept undisturbed; and started early on the next lap of our march, which would take us to H.4 on the Haifa pipe line this side of the frontier with Iraq. Not until then could we expect to come to grips with the Iraq Army, who were in occupation of Rutba fort, the next post along the oil pipe line. But Glubb with his bedouin Patrol, in light Chevrolet trucks, armed with Lewis guns, and Cassano's Air Force armoured cars were skirmishing there with a guerrilla leader, Fawzi Kuwuckji, who had, in 1936, led the Palestine Rebellion. He was an able general.

Joe Kingstone took me with him, next morning, ahead of the column. Joe drove himself, in spite of the presence in his utility van of two drivers, and I followed in my yellow car, driven by Grose, and with one of my cipher clerks, Williamson. Williamson's was a rugged personality, good for campaigning. He had served on the North-West Frontier of India in his time.

Soon we were entering the Great Black Lava Belt. Surely this must be the most barren area of the earth's surface. As far as the eye can see in every direction, extends a wilderness of black basalt boulders, polished in the sun's glare, like gun-metal. These smooth boulders are so densely strewn that it is impossible to step between them. No sand shows a golden gleam through the chinks. For mile after mile you pass through this black nightmare of a land. Later, when I was back in England, lame from a bullet in the Syrian campaign, and serving for a short time in M.I.2 at the War Office I was asked if this lava belt could be considered tank proof off the road. (Rommel had just arrived at Alamein, and it was legitimate to wonder where he could be stopped if he got any further.) There are not many parts of the world of which one could say, unhesitatingly, that it is tank-proof off the road. Parts of Northern Palestine, with its vast pumice rocks, across which even horses have to leap like cats, can fairly be so described. But I had no hesitation in saying that the Great Black Lava Belt of Transjordan was tank-proof off the road at any carefully selected point, and I was glad to have confirmation of this later from Brigadier John Shearer, who had been Director of Military Intelligence for the Middle East when I was there.

At a bend in the road Joe halted his utility and stepped out, asking me suddenly to show him, on the map, where we were. This was his way of testing me. Fortunately, a wide patch of sand from which the black stones had been carefully cleared, gave me the clue I needed. It was a landing ground marked A.25 on the map, where the road bends at a broad angle towards the north-east — and the Iraq frontier.

We emerged from the barren area at last — I wondered whether any explorer could have traversed it before the smooth tarmac road had been laid across it in our engineering generation. I doubt it. This roadway was unfortunately not finished beyond the Transjordan frontier by the time we needed it in May of 1941. Its future course across the worst and widest strip of waterless desert between Rutba and Ramadi, was indicated, as yet, only by piles of stone collected for the projected work. We would have to rely on our crude maps of this desolate region, on which a red line curving in unexplained places marked the 'Obligatory Air Route' which pilots had to follow, and coincided broadly with the time-worn maze of tracks known as the Old Damascus Road. Along that legendary path we would fight our way to Baghdad. But with our arrival at H.4 on the frontier of Iraq, where soldiers and airmen jostled each other at a bar in the cool Mess to get at some sparkling liquid, our Approach March may be said to have ended. Kingcol camped off the road seven miles beyond H.4, at a point marked on our maps as the Wadi Tarifa. Next day it crossed the frontier into Iraq and did not halt until it had relieved the Air Force garrison at Habbaniya and struck onwards through the flooded waters of the Euphrates to rescue the British Ambassador and the British colony beleaguered in their Embassy; and to capture Baghdad itself.

PART II
BAGHDAD

Who can discern the future in the past,
Or in the woven fabric of a rhyme
Follow the needle of the present time
Threading its way to hold the pattern fast?
When it is done, the Golden Carpet made,
On whose wide floor will the great work be laid?

CHAPTER 15 *Glubb Pasha*

T.E. Lawrence says in one of his letters that a year in the Middle East counts for ten anywhere else. I know what he meant. When I try to recall my time there it seems crowded with so much incident and colour that it is difficult to select what is really significant. 'I have camped amid the timeless scenery of the Bible; floundered in mud in the Jordan valley during that season of the year when even kings cannot go forth to battle; found myself in deserts and floods; and, if I may say so, it is not an everyday experience for a Parlimentarian to find himself being carried blindfold at dawn into the city of the Caliphs, there to have the bandages stripped from his eyes and to see, across the fast waters of the Tigris, the domes and minarets of this fabled city which is associated with the memory of Haroun Al Raschid.'

That was how I expressed it to the House of Commons on my return; and it seems to me, re-reading the passage, that as I stood there trying to call to the tip of my tongue only the most vivid impressions during my absence, I unconsciously selected the most significant experiences. But I did not want my *Golden Carpet* to follow merely in the dust of the desert. Only a man of no imagination could fail to be sensitive to the associations of the Holy Land which was the gateway to my journeys in the Near Orient. Even a soldier can visit Palestine as a pilgrim; whether it be to the ruins of the Decapolis, the Holy Places or the Crusader Castles. He who goes with an air of expectation will not be disappointed. I was partly hoping to resurrect Lawrence against his proper background and I picked up some unexpected threads of his story.

Lawrence says in a letter to Robert Graves that one of the only three people he really cared for was an Armenian called Altounyan. Altounyan certainly cared for Lawrence and was on the point of departure from Aleppo to meet Lawrence in England when he heard of his death and was shocked into writing around the memory of his friend 119 of the greatest sonnets in the English language since the time of Shakespeare. I saw much of Altounyan when I was convalescing in

Jerusalem after the events chronicled in these pages. He read his poems to me and, as he did so, his walnut face became suffused with an inward radiance. He scorned my rendering of my own poems for I read them self-consciously as Englishmen do. He told me much about Lawrence, whom he had first met at the Carcemish dig in 1911. At that time he had thought Lawrence an insufferable young prig, and it was not until after the war that they became friends.

By that time, according to Altounyan, Lawrence had learnt the art of submerging himself in a group (which pleases the group). He had also come around to the conclusion that nothing but poetry really mattered; and it was thus that his interest in Altounyan was awakened, for Altounyan sent him some 20,000 lines of poetry (which have not been published) and Lawrence was impressed. They met and they corresponded. When Lawrence left the Air Force, his intention, according to Altounyan, was to return to public life and his head was full of plans; possibly it was for this reason that he skidded into disaster. Altounyan thinks that Lawrence's return to public life would have taken the form of his associating himself with Winston Churchill in the capacity of political aide-de-camp. The combination would have been formidable and at a time when the future war Prime Minister was waiting for his cue in the wings and was crying to the stolid youth behind the Baldwin Government, "One healthy growl from you would alter the history of the world," the assistance of so romantic a young figure as Lawrence might have foreshortened the shadows of fate, which were lengthening as the sun of peace went down.

Not all the threads of Lawrence's story which I picked up in the Near East were free from the dust of the road. Elphinstone, who had spent eight months of the first war with a Kurdish tribe (to whom he was known affectionately as El Finstoon) and met Lawrence when Damascus was captured, threw a new light on the abrupt departure which appears to have been wrung from a reluctant Allenby at the close of the *Seven Pillars of Wisdom*.

Lawrence had begged Allenby's permission for the bedouin to occupy Damascus, but they massacred the occupants of the Turkish hospital and hurled the bodies through the windows. Allenby arrived, saw the sickening pile of corpses, said 'enough', and Lawrence was given a single ticket home. This would account for the abrupt acceleration of the timetable which took Lawrence from Damascus to Cairo in a week at the close of the campaign, but does nothing to diminish the part played by Lawrence himself in the success of the Revolt which ended, as he had prophesied, only at Damascus.

Indeed, loyalty to his Arab comrades would have made it impossible to close his narrative with such a scene as Elphinstone describes. Elphinstone was the kindest of men and certainly no detractor of Lawrence, whom he saw subsequently as an orderly room clerk at an R.A.F. station in India. He told me how an Indian havildar sergeant in his regiment, on entering Damascus, saw what he thought to be the prototype of all Fifth Columnists — a man swathed in Arab robes, driving in a battered old Rolls-Royce armoured car — and promptly arrested him. The prisoner's embittered protests were lost upon the Indian N.C.O. who insisted upon taking him before 'his officer'. Not till then was it realized that the doubtful bedu was Lawrence himself.

In this book appears the figure of another Englishman, closely identified with Arab aspirations — Glubb Pasha. He was happily denied the leisure of wounds which gave me time to write in the middle of war itself. But I can imagine no more fitting context for the character of Glubb than the story of the Iraq campaign and the crossing of the Syrian Desert to surround and occupy the fortress of Palmyra, where Glubb and I co-operated — for Glubb was totally lacking in pomposity and gladly came to me (as Intelligence Officer) with such information as his 'girls' could give him of our objective.

I have not attempted to see the story as others saw it; for to do so would be to rob it of all vividness and authenticity. It will, however, be found to accord in every particular with the Offical War Diary of the flying column known as the Advance Striking Force, which captured Baghdad.

Alexander the Great went through Turkey and the German military textbooks laid it down, obligingly, that Baghdad could not be captured from the west.

We were a motley crowd. His Majesty's Life Guards and Royal Horse Guards jostled along in their army trucks beside the bedouin of the Arab Legion — Glubb's Desert Patrol, swathed in garish robes, who raced about in light trucks armed with Lewis guns. We even embraced eight Royal Air Force armoured cars. Tough stuff, these boys. They had left Sidi Barrani in the Western Desert on Thursday and were reported in action against the Iraqi guerrillas at Rutbah on Saturday, a thousand miles away. They were all rogues, God bless them, for whom the war had come as an eleventh hour reprieve. They were the sort of men to whom legend clung like the cloak of Mephistopheles.

The Flying Column was called Kingcol after its Brigadier, Joe

Kingstone. Some said he was the best fighting Brigadier in the British Army. He could be very frightening. Likewise he possessed great charm, so that people did things for him which they would not do for other men. He was a great leader and his face was very red and his powerful sharp nose jutted out beneath the green shade of a sola topi or (in the early mornings) under the peak of his red-banded khaki cap. At breakfast on the desert he often wore the latter and the blue jacket of his pyjamas above his khaki shorts, which all added to the colourfulness of the expedition. Cassano, who commanded the R.A.F armoured cars, was first met with at H.₃. (It took me a month of campaigning, as Intelligence Officer to Kingcol, to discover why the Iraq Petroleumn Company's posts on the pipe line were called H.₃, H.₄, T.₁, T.₂, or K.₃; they were on the pipe lines running respectively to Haifa, Tripoli and Kirkuk.) Cassano's face was thin and sallow. He resembled Mephistopheles in every respect, with a thin pointed nose, arched black eyebrows and mocking dark eyes. I see him now, when we were back at H.₃ after sharing every variety of adventure, preparing for another campaign. An oil lamp illuminated the intent faces of five of us at Poker: Dick Schuster (who was our Signals Officer), soon to be killed by a French bomb; Ian Spence, who had been on Jumbo Wilson's staff in Greece and now acted as Joe's special Liaison Officer; Peter Grant Lawson who had ridden in the Grand National and had the military mind — and lastly myself. And there was Cassano leaning forward in the lamplight, as if he were the devil himself, and saying in a long drawn out whisper, "Go-the-whole-hog." All this fraternisation came later.

Now H.₃ was merely an outpost on the way to Rutbah and Glubb was somewhere ahead of us, feeling out the enemy in the wadis of the desert. Joe and I had left Kingcol behind us and meant to see Glubb before nightfall. We had hoped to catch up with him at H.₃. But of Glubb there was no sign. The Brigadier sent Cassano ahead with the armoured cars, and we drove on, in the gathering darkness, with a protective troop of Lumpers (Joe's word for the Blues and Life Guards) bumping along behind us and keeping up as best they could. It was long after dark when we reached Rutbah and found ourselves passing various low mud buildings and barbed wire entanglements. Joe discarded his protective troop on the desert outside the town and we drove on until we came to the great fort, whose dim outlines loomed up against the stars. Here there were trucks, armed with Lewis guns, and cars outside the gates. As we drove up to these and dismounted, the lofty oak doors swung open and in the glare of our headlights we could see the tall white-robed figures of the bedouin framed in the darkness of the archway. Their black faces glinted under pink headdresses. They were swathed in cross belts of ammunition, of which the pointed bullets gleamed like necklaces of shark's teeth. Long silver-handled knives sparkled in their girdles. Many had rifles slung over both shoulders. From this throng stepped a short man in buff drill uniform, with a yellow keffiyeh fastened to his head by the double ropes of a black silk aqal. One side of his jaw appeared to be dented in (wherefore he was known to Arabs as the Father of the Jaw) and he had a little sandy moustache. This was Glubb — Abu Hunaik.

He led us into the courtyard where a propelling stink and the tangled wreckage spoke eloquently of the recent engagement. As we passed under the archway, the figure of Lash (second-in-command of the Arab Legion) loomed up, his dark tanned face recognisably British under the white headdress. I asked him if he were returning direct to H.₄, and he consented to take back a message form which I had prepared on information given to me by Cassano about the fall of Rutbah. Lash, being a picturesque type of soldier, accepted the added duties of a despatch rider without comment, and his white form was promptly swallowed up in the darkness.

I hurried after Glubb and the Brigadier, past groups of bedouin who were standing in easy attitudes of relaxation and talking to one another in their uncouth tongue. I caught the phrase 'Dahbit inglesi' as I followed the Brigadier and Glubb into a darkened hall which must once have served as a canteen, for there were little tables and chairs scattered about it. A candle, thrust into the neck of a beer bottle, shed a flickering light up to the rafters and illuminated the intent shadowed faces of the three of us.

Glubb sat himself down, with his feet up on the table, while Joe Kingstone towered over him, a vast red-faced mountain of a man, glowering down at the incalculable soldier who had many ribbons on his tunic and who wore, also, on his shoulder tabs, crossed swords and two stars of a peculiar design which Joe Kingstone had never seen before. Nevertheless Joe Kingstone meant to command the expedition.

"The first thing I want to know," he said, "is about the water. Are any of the wells working?"

Glubb seemed rather bored by all this talk of water. His men were accustomed to carrying little water over long distances.

"There is a pump still working outside the fort. Another one up on the hill was knocked out, but we could ask Gresham about that."

Gresham was an engineer-lieutenant, working on the Haifa- Baghdad road, and we had sent him up during the afternoon to investigate.

I had taken an instant liking to Glubb, and asked where Fawzi Kuwuckji had gone to after he withdrew from Rutbah.

"I think he has gone down to Fort Nuqaib or the Wadi Tebel," Glubb replied, "that is what my men tell me, but the Air Force could find out." (Which they did later and confirmed the report.)

I handed Glubb a message from Force Headquarters asking what forces had defended Rutbah and whether the tribes had helped the enemy. Glubb produced a piece of foolscap paper, which was ruled into columns headed with small Arabic printed script and wrote in bold pencil capitals: 'Forces defending Rutbah consisted of about one hundred police, mostly Desert Police. On 9th May, however, Fawzi Qawukji, with machine-guns, came to Rutbah. On 10th May he fought an action with R.A.F. armoured cars, as result of which he retired east in evening and contact has not been re-established.'

This did not answer both questions, so I added with Glubb's approval 'No tribes co-operated in defence of fort.' Glubb commented, "You can say that the tribes are amicable." So I concluded 'Tribes amicable', initialled it and added the time of origin as 21.30. Glubb scrawled his peculiar signature at the bottom of the page.

"You talk too much," the Brigadier said to me. He always teased me with this reproach. I suppose it arose from my political training; although I often believed myself to be capable of remarkable silences. We went out to examine the pump over the well in the courtyard. We lit matches in the darkness. There was a large iron wheel, with a handle, which I turned, but nothing came up.

As we crossed the courtyard the Brigadier and I fell into step.

"This fellow thinks he is King of Saudi Arabia," Joe said, "I am going to get him out of the way as soon as we leave here. The trouble is that I don't know whether he is senior to me or not."

"I thought he looked like a lieutenant-general," I said unhelpfully.

"Well, you go ahead. I am going to have a word with our friend Glubb."

We had reached the main gateway, and Joe stepped back to speak with Glubb.

I do not know what he said. The conversation was short and sharp, whatever it was. They were to become firm friends as the campaign developed, but tonight they were like a couple of prima donnas billed to perform in the same opera, who meet behind the scenes for the first time, and were eyeing each other with some misgivings.

Glubb and the Brigadier emerged from the fort and the three of us crossed the open ground outside, stepping over a dead goat which stank to high heaven. We were joined by Lieutenant Gresham who assured the Brigadier that the pump was working and that the water had not been polluted. He pointed to the square outlines of a 10,000 gallon tank silhouetted against the night sky.

"I want an armoured car slapped down here and it is to stay here all night," Joe said, and told me to find Cassano. "He is somewhere across the aerodrome." He pointed vaguely into the darkness in front of the fort.

I went back to the fort to collect my car, and Joe called out, "You will find me outside the town where I put the Lumpers. We can sleep there."

I roared across the aerodrome, feeling tired and angry. Cassano was not enthusiastic about sparing an armoured car. He suggested a tender; but I assured him that when Joe asked for armoured cars he did not mean tenders.

"I don't expect he knows the difference," Cassano observed, and sent an armoured car.

I found the Brigadier and Ian Spence, the Liaison Officer who had been making arrangements for the night with Gerard Leigh of the protective troop. The staff cars were parked on a hard little plateau surrounded by the desert. Here and there the flicker of a spirit lamp pin-pointed the vehicles of the protective troop whose sentries had now been posted, and who were settling down to an evening meal. Joe and Ian were already finishing their food and I joined them, while my leathery-faced driver, Grose, and that even more leathery individual, Williams, set about lighting our primus stove. They prepared tea and other things. I never probed into Grose's arrangements. So I was not as surprised as the Brigadier when Grose dished up some sizzling sausages and baked beans and followed these with some pineapple chunks for me in his mess tin. This luxury could not be expected to last, but Grose had laid in supplies (of which the back of my car was full) at H.4 which was the last civilised outpost.

Joe referred darkly to a racket, added unkind comments about household cavalry and went off to lie down on his camp bed for the night.

I had a little canvas safari bed, which rolled up like an umbrella when not in use, and, when stretched, cleared the ground by three or four inches. It was delicious to lie upon. Grose had unstrapped my valise and even rigged up a little canvas basin on its trestle and poured some water into it, for there would be plenty more next day.

I lay down, but I did not go to sleep immediately, for now the desert moon was rising, large and round and bright as a silver dollar; and two long-legged lifeguards tramped noisily round the encampment in a ceaseless circle.

"I can't think what they want to bring us to this sumthin' place for," one of them said. "I wouldn't give two sumthin' mils for Transjordan; and as for this sumthin' place I wouldn't give one sumthin' mil for it."

But for me it was the beginning of the fabulous days. For the first time I had leisure, since the scramble of departure, to think of the adventure; and I dozed off recalling a last bathe in the glassy swell of the Mediterranean, when I had taken an hour off from the turmoil of the camp at Nathanya and gone down through the nullahs to a sandy beach, and stood alone in the water, while the round sun peered down through a hazy sky and there was no sign of human life or of a habitation anywhere. I wore no clothes, and I might have been at the dawn of time, where the waters lapped the shores in silence and there was the beginning of life.

CHAPTER 16   *Rutbah*

We were startled into wakefulness, soon after four, by the roar of an approaching column. The protective troop believed firmly that the whole Iraqi Army had arrived. For who else could it be? The head of our own column, upon the calculation of that meticulous staff officer, Sir Peter Grant-Lawson, Bt., could not by any reckoning arrive before eight in the morning. Yet here was the Household Cavalry, with the Blues Squadron out in front, coming in like a bat out of hell, after one of the finest pieces of cross-country desert navigation in the dark imaginable, as Joe was reluctantly forced to admit. Bobo Roxburghe, leading the advance troop, was responsible for this. The Household Cavalry were supposed to be advance guard to the whole of Kingcol, but on this, as on later occasions, they looked ahead rather than behind, and the rest of the column came in unprotected four hours later. 'Galloping A' Squadron (as Corporal-Major Evans called it) had not arrived three minutes before they were dispersed and bivouacking for the night. It was a picturesque sight, the cooking fires of the vehicles flickering all over the desert, like glow-worm lights. As this had once been my own squadron I went in search of its leader, Eion Merry, that grey-haired, dark-skinned Red Indian of a man, who was known to the troops as Old Misery. When he smiled, it was like dawn breaking in the East, and he was charming. I had risen on the sound of vehicles by night, for I saw that the Brigadier was rising, and nothing impresses an early-rising Brigadier more than an even earlier Intelligence Officer. I was never able to repeat this enthusiastic performance. But now I walked down a declivity and found Eion, coated all over with dust, sitting on a camp bed beside his 15-cwt. truck and pulling off his boots. He looked up in astonishment, and smiled his rare smile. "Fancy finding you in Rutbah," he exclaimed.

We spent two days at Rutbah, filling up with water, holding brigade conferences. Our operation orders were duplicated illegibly on a Roneo machine in the office truck. Joe provided a sentence on the 'intention', and the order began with a paragraph supplied by me about the enemy.

The rest was all Peter and, contemplating his industrious efforts, I was sometimes driven to define the military mind as a grasp of everything but the essential. Peter was known to the regiment as Piggy or Sir Pig, possibly because his initials were P.G. But out of delicacy he was not usually addressed by this nickname.

I had a lot of information pencilled in a green notebook about the Iraq Army. Most of it, collected by our 'cloak and dagger merchants', was collated at Force Headquarters in Jerusalem and passed on to me by that quiet owl-like creature, Edric Nutting, of the Blues, who was Divisional Intelligence Officer. The rebel leaders belonged to a secret society called The Golden Square, of whom the chief was Salah Ud Din Sabbagh. Fahmi Said commanded the Iraq mechanised forces.

"Remember," Edric had said, when we discussed all this over lunch at Pross' in Haifa, "that Fahmi Said is bloody idle."

The Iraq order of battle ran to pages in my notebook. It consisted of four divisions, one of which was guarding the oilfields up at Kirkuk, another containing our Indian forces at Basra, and the other two holding the Habbaniya-Baghdad area which we hoped to pierce.

While we were at Rutbah, disturbing intelligence reached me, which I passed on to Joe. Seven unidentified aircraft had passed over Aley, near Beirut, heading for Iraq. Another seventeen were reported to be refuelling at Mezze. We knew they were Germans. Was this the advance guard of the 22nd Airborne Division which I knew to be ready for action? Was it going to be sent through Syria to assist the Iraqis, to whom lavish promises of German assistance were hourly made by Axis propaganda? Or would the 22nd Airborne be used against Crete? It looked rather as if we were for it. Then Squadron-Leader Dudgeon arrived in a Blenheim from Habbaniya where our Air Force cantonment was surrounded by Iraqi forces, and told me that one of our pilots on reconnaissance over Mosul had been fired at by a Messerschmitt 110.

"Are you certain?" I asked.

"Yes. There was no possibility of mistake. He looked round and saw the thing ten yards away."

The situation inside the cantonment was less obscure to us since I had seen Pilot Officer Belgrave, a fair-haired Intelligence Officer who also flew out of Habbaniya to report to us at H.4. In addition to the ordinary Air Force flying and ground staff, with their aeroplanes and a few old Rolls-Royce silver ghost armoured cars, there were 1,500 Assyrian Levies under Alastair Graham; and a battalion of the King's Own Royal Regiment which had been flown first from Karachi to Basra and thence over the heads of the Iraqis into Habbaniya. The Iraqis, who had at first closed in on the cantonment, were now driven off the plateau by sheer low-level bombing and were content to hold Ramadi and Falluja, the two towns above and below Habbaniya on the Euphrates.

The sooner we got on the better. Glubb appeared at our conferences, but the Brigadier had not warmed to him yet. We crowded into and around the brigade office truck, a cumbrous affair of sloping awnings, with a narrow table down the middle. There we assembled our component parts; all the clanking levers of our Heath Robinson machine — Andrew Ferguson, with his mournful dark eyes and dark head of hair, and a complete hiatus in his speech. He would open the mouth in his long olive-skinned face to comment on Joe's plans, but only air would emerge and Joe would lose patience. If, as often occurred, some heedless despatch rider, naked to the waist, would drive up to the truck on a motor bike, Joe would rush out at him snorting like a Bull of Bashan. He did not like noise in the vicinity of Brigade Headquarters; and nudity invited sunstroke.

Andrew Ferguson had a restlessness which was the despair of the combined Life Guards and Blues; but lent to what might otherwise have been a staid and horsy regiment the flicker of a marsh flare. He had been acting Brigadier when I arrived at Nathanya to find that he was driving the Brigade Headquarters to distraction with every form of physical training and infantry practice superimposed upon their ordinary function of running the brigade. Knowing my Andrew and that the only way to deal with him was to let his suggestions roll off like water from the duck's back, I changed the programme in subtle ways. Knowing my own restless spirit at Beisan when the publication of *The Far Cry*, the organisation of an archaeological society, lessons to bewildered troops in German, French and Russian, and a full-dress performance of *Twelfth Night* (with scenery by Trooper Bardon) had not sufficed to exhaust my energies, he had added to my responsibilities, as Intelligence Officer to the 4th Cavalry Brigade, those of Brigade Welfare Officer, Passive Air Defence Officer and Camp Commandant at headquarters. In this capacity I hurriedly diverted physical training (which included a collection of lowering officers at 6.30 a.m.) into 'running to the beach and swimming exercise' at which at *least* one officer must be present (the alternative hour being 4 p.m.) My attempts to change the rest of the tactical training programme into an experiment in disguising Brigade Headquarters as a bedouin encampment were interrupted by my departure for Egypt — not, however, before I had sought out my old friend Inspector Fulbrook (one of the biggest rogues known on the side of the law), and asked him to borrow from our mutual friend, Emir Mohammed Salah, six goat-hair tents, which I arranged to collect in two army trucks. I returned from Egypt (after studying intelligence during General Rommel's first advance into the Western Desert) in time to bid goodbye to Andrew, who was returning to the regiment, while Joe came back from Divisional Headquarters at Haifa to command the present expedition.

A mild contrast with Joe and Andrew was Daddy Wright, who commanded our prize exhibit — a battery of 25-pounders. For there was to be hitting-power in Kingcol too. Daddy Wright was a slow, modest little major, reminiscent of the Great War; slow, but greatly to be relied upon. Two companies of the Essex Regiment, who had particular reasons for proving their martial ability (which they did) were included under Major May. These, with His Majesty's Life Guards and Royal Horse Guards, completed the lorried infantry strength of the expedition. They were the P.B.I. of the outfit. May was a smooth-faced man, with dark hair, and an excellent opinion of May. We had sting in our tail also, in the form of an independent anti-tank troop firing 2-pounder guns. They were commanded by a lean, dark-faced lieutenant who sparkled with competence and inspired confidence in all of us; but they never seemed to be needed and so I forget his name. Perhaps it was Barraclough. Finally there was the field troop of Engineers under Cheeky Boy Oldham. The Brigadier named him Cheeky Boy on the first day, and I remembered him as a Canadian lieutenant, entering my cabin in a troopship, when the portholes were sealed in the hours of black-out, and smoking a vile-smelling pipe, until I was rude: which made us the best of friends when we met unexpectedly on the desert. Young 'Doc' Arundel appeared at our conferences representing a section of the 166 Field Ambulance.

I recall the scene at Rutbah — all these units of Kingcol scattered in roughly homogeneous areas over the desert, down the middle of which, leading to the town, ran the unfinished embankment of the Haifa-Baghdad road. It was just high enough to present an obstacle to cars. Brigade Headquarters was somewhere in the middle of all this; like a hub to which the spokes of the wheel came. Our own cars were dispersed in a circle fifty or a hundred yards from the office truck: the Brigadier's utility; the Brigade Major's utility (in which Dick Schuster, the Signals Officer, also drove); Ian Spence's lean greenish staff car; and my own, a pale yellow. Three other officers, who were not members of the fighting group, caught up with us from time to time: the Staff Captain (Corpo), a massive man of competence; a melancholy youth named John Hampton; and that sorrowful little man, Toler-Aylward, who combined in action the thankless tasks of Camp Commandant and Mess President. These men were the background of our daily lives; we depended on them for our smooth functioning, rather as a projectile depends on the smooth working of the barrel and breech block from which it is fired. Loping along in the rear of all our doings came 'Fish' Ackroyd of the Light Aid Detachment. He salvaged the vehicles which fell by the wayside; and arrived long after, cool and lanky, to spread calm into the feverish atmosphere. He was the first to go unshaved.

All these were to Joe Kingstone as a family, and when, as at Rutbah, we were all assembled, he sat down at the trestle table which Corporal Barnes continued to carry on the Mess lorry, and while we ate, we eschewed military talk. Joe loved to kill flies, and it was interesting to watch the deadly stealth with which his great hand would descend silently upon a fly and squash it. Others tried. My own lightning strokes always failed to achieve the same result. Ranges of blue hills closed in upon the horizon, setting limits to the desolation.

While we were at Rutbah, a pair of native interpreters, for whom we had been crying, arrived from Force Headquarters. Edric Nutting deposited both and returned in a hurry to H.4. One was tall and one was short. They had lost all their equipment on the way. The taller was a sallow-faced fellow, with the beginnings of a moustache, and he complained bitterly of having nothing but the khaki shirt, shorts and topi in which he had been abandoned to us. He went by the unexpected name of Reading. So I kept him and sent the little one over to the Household Cavalry. Reading soon had an opportunity to practise his craft, for a suspicious tribesman was sent over to me from the House-hold Cavalry. He had been found wandering through their lines, and carried ammunition. Reading (who was an Arab, and knew Iraq almost as well as his native Palestine) soon discredited the man's excuses. The prisoner stood there, on the desert, shifty-eyed, in his swathes of black clout, while Reading broke down his alibis. The man claimed to have been engaged by the Haifa-Baghdad Road Company, but he carried no pass. Moreover he was not a local tribesman, such as might find work in the neighbourhood. He came from the Shammar tribe, to the north-west of Baghdad, which was suspicious. Furthermore, he carred £12 in Iraqi money which was incredible for a casual labourer then. I was copying down the markings of his ammunition, when Joe, ever suspicious of too much intelligence, sidled up to listen to the interrogation.

"Hand him over to Glubb's Girls," Joe advised, "they'll get all the information out of him which is required."

As we were soon moving off I did so, but regretted it later, when I heard that they had shot him out of hand, after removing his money.*

"Poor little sod," was Joe's comment when I told him, for he, too, had a soft heart.

Joe's attitude towards intelligence was discouraging. "Don't you worry about the enemy," was his view, "we will find out all about the enemy when we run into him." Peter Grant-Lawson, the Brigade Major, was even more explicit: "Intelligence doesn't matter a — ." I was just contemplating adopting, as my battle insignia, a carafe of brains being dashed out on the sand, when a signal came from Force Headquarters (where El Finstoon reigned intelligently and Henry Hunloke, a fellow M.P., watched over Iraq) ordering me to send duplicates of all my intelligence summaries and reports to them direct.

We were two days at Rutbah, filling up with water and making plans. It seems longer in retrospect and we were glad to start on the real beginnings of our hazardous enterprise. Already Baghdad, 300 miles away, was beginning to have a lure — and it cast a spell over all of us. We knew that if we persevered and went eastwards far enough, we should eventually find ourselves inside the City of the Caliphs. I talked at breakfast about Joe Kingstone as The Peacock of the Dawn. "Peacock of the Dawn!" snorted Joe, but he was pleased; and indeed it was just possible to see him in the slippers of Haroun Al Raschid, with myself as a second Ishak, pencilling ballads about the conquest. Henry Abel-Smith of the Blues maintained stoutly that Joe had insisted on my coming to Brigade Headquarters in order to be his poet laureate. He had, according to Henry, read and reread my lines in *The Far Cry* and summoned me to his court.

There is one other personality in this story who must be mentioned. He was a civilian called Brooks, who owned jointly the firm of Brooks and Murdoch, Engineers in Iraq, and who was to become a valuable guide and friend, as far as Habbaniya, never obtruding himself, but always at our elbow for consultation. To me he came as a sixth sense, for he knew what lay ahead of us. He was quiet, grey-haired. He lived, so he

---

*I am sorry to spoil your story, but the tribesman was not shot, nor did we steal his money. I am afraid this was a fable. Glubb Pasha.

told us, at Mujara, where the trestle bridge was being built for us. It seemed a curious place for a man to choose as home. But then, I reflected, it is just this sort of Englishman that makes our brand of imperialism possible. You simply cannot decree in advance that engineers should go and live in places like Mujara. It can only be absent-mindedness that makes them do it. And so Brooks, in a blue saloon car, became one of our party; one of the Brigadier's family.

I prepared maps for Joe, on which he indicated to a brigade conference the whereabouts of the enemy. I tried to mark their positions in blue (when the heat did not melt the chinagraph pencils completely). It was decided that the Household Cavalry should lead off as advance guard to the column, with a truck load of Glubb's Girls to guide them. Speed and density, as worked out by Peter Grant-Lawson, were to be fifteen miles in the hour and twenty vehicles to the mile. The real advance now lay ahead of us. We were faced with the waterless stretch of desert, about 200 miles to the shores of Lake Habbaniya, which was fed from the Euphrates. But Ramadi at the north-west corner of the lake was held by one or possibly two brigades of the Iraq Army (two proved to be the number) and was also surrounded by natural floods. A long culvert on the road between Ramadi and Habbaniya had been blown up by the Iraqis; and we received messages from Habbaniya that an alternative trestle bridge over the flood race, south of the Lake at Mujara, which was now in the hands of our troops operating from inside the cantonment, was being hurriedly constructed to take us. If this trestle bridge were bombed by the Germans before we got across, we would not be able to relieve the Air Force garrison at all.

I was to lead the Brigade Headquarters with the rest of the column following. This would have been easy if the Household Cavalry had remained within sight, but we had scarcely cleared the eastern bridge over the wadi beyond Rutbah, in the grey dawn, when their rearmost vehicles were gathering speed in clouds of dust on a mysterious course to the northwards, drawn on by the incalculable will-o'-the-wisp bedouin who were their guides. The pleasant thing to do would have been to put on speed myself and disappear with them, but upon my speed and density depended the cohesion of all that followed. So I told Grose to keep the needle at twenty-nine kilometres, and at this speed we went on like fate, with all the Iraq Desert ahead to choose from.

Williamson, who sat beside Grose and took turns at the wheel, talked incessantly. It was impossible to suppress him. "I used to be with the Brigadier in the Bays," he told us. "I was in his squadron too and I remember once on manoeuvres in the North of England, we wanted to get across some land farmed by a sort of German colony. At least the farmer to whom the Brigadier spoke answered him in German and told him we could not go through."

"What did the Brigadier say to that?" I was curious.

"Oh, he just knocked him down flat," said Williamson with relish.

(I teased Joe about this one evening and at first he would only admit to an argument with the German, but eventually veered round to an admission that he rather believed it had ended in his knocking the man down!)

I sat in the back seat with my oil compass, hoping that the metal of the car would not deflect it in any particular direction, and placed it on the map. I had spent the previous evening working out, according to the Old Damascus Road marked on these ancient maps (which ignored the beginnings of the Haifa-Baghdad Road), the various stretches of desert to be covered on different bearings. There were only two ways of navigating: either to keep the foundations of the unfinished Haifa-Baghdad Road in sight (which might at any time lead us on to

206

impassable ground), or else to adhere to the compass bearings which I had worked out from the old camel-track marked on the map. I decided upon the last course, but I soon began to curse the rugged explorers upon whose imaginative researches these maps were drawn. They would see some range of hills shimmering away in the heat and ask the first bedouin they passed how far away they were and would as likely as not receive for answer the information that they were two camel-days' going distant. This would be translated on the tips of the fingers into a rough distance, and a line would go down on the chart. Our experience approaching Rutbah had already opened our eyes to these facts. I relied, however, upon the blind instinct of the herd (behind me) who, seeing the leading vehicle pursuing a determined course, and occasionally switching abruptly for no obvious reason on to a new bearing, would assume that I knew exactly where I was going.

I knew this too. I was going to Baghdad, but I prayed to my several gods at stated intervals to take me there by the right route. Dark memories of explorers who wandered in a circle until thirst overcame them perturbed me at times and I had visions of the exhausted column with the 25-pounders bouncing along in the rear, streaming into Rutbah again over a wide front, as sunset closed a long and exhausting march. Every now and then, just when I was despairing, the endless piles of stone which had been collected along the course of the proposed Haifa-Baghdad Road would appear on the horizon to reassure me; or we would suddenly, jubilantly, find ourselves running along a maze of tracks across the scrub-strewn desert. At such times it required self-control to keep on a compass bearing, for Grose and Williamson showed a reasonable urge to keep on the widest track, even if it began veering away in the direction of Mosul.

While navigating thus I looked round through the back window of the car to see how the column was following. The Brigadier's utility van and Peter's were lying back fifty or a hundred yards from my car in an arrow-head formation on either side, and seemingly bowling along at a great pace — with the raw, yellow dust funnelling out behind them. The rest of the brigade stretched back in an apparently endless line over the desert for twenty or thirty miles. It was possible, at a rise in the ground, to follow its winding course, like the skeleton of a snake showing the desert through its bones, far back into the distance. And it was while I looked back, at such a moment, that I saw, with surprised eyes, two black tulips of smoke blossom far down the line, and, while the bomb bursts still hovered in the air, I saw the bright white-hot flash of anti-aircraft fire stream upwards across them.

We had been discovered at last. I saw the Brigade Major's utility van peel off behind me and race back to the scene of the disturbance. I went on until the time for our midday halt and Peter caught us up. A truck of the Essex Regiment had been hit, and some men killed. Peter began digging a slit trench beside his utility, for we were stopping two hours in the midday heat. I supposed that Staff College manuals laid it down that slit trenches must be dug at every halt of two hours or more, unless he was expecting all the seventeen unidentified (German) aircraft to arrive from Deraa as soon as the reconnaissance plane had got back with word of our movements.

The heat was appalling. We had halted, by chance, near the earthworks of the Haifa-Baghdad Road, and Grose and I dug a half-hearted depression about six inches deep in the lee of the embankment. The Brigadier did the same. Tea was soon boiling up. The blacker the better. We drank it as thick as soup. Water was scarcer now and it was laid down in Staff College manuals that on the march water was only drunk by order of the leader. But this sort of thing, with a column thirty miles long, was not practicable. The last man on the line would have died of thirst before the order reached him.

So we drank by vehicles, the senior officer keeping an eye on his subordinates to see that they did not drink too much at once. The most refreshing drink in a service water bottle was cold sweetened tea (without milk). I tried this until it fermented from the heat or shaking; and made the inside of the bottle rancid for days. While we were using some of our precious water, which was carried in specially cleansed petrol cans at the back (apart from the drinking water which hung in the canvas bags on the front of the car to cool as we drove along) an R.A.F. tender drove up. From the driver's seat emerged the swarthy, lean face of Cassano.

"It was a Blenheim, on reconnaissance, which dropped the bombs," he told me.

"Not one of ours!" I exclaimed.

"No, I expect it is an Iraqi plane. The bastard sprayed the line with machine-gun bullets from his rear gun, too."

Peter Grant-Lawson's trench was now completed. I thought the discovery of our whereabouts justified a message back to Habforce (which was the base force behind us at H.4.) So I went in search of the Gin Palace — a trade name for the Brigade Signals truck. Before I went, Cassano offered me some water to fill up with.

"Can you spare it?" I asked in astonishment.

"Lord yes. I have a 20-gallon tank in this thing."

We had all we wanted at present, but I told him that I now knew where to come in future. He zigzagged off on a social course, looking in on various vehicles as he returned to his armoured cars which were dipersed on our flank to the north.

We were not visited during the two-hour halt or at any other time during the day. But at a landing ground, where there was a small wired-in enclosure for aircraft necessities, one of our reconnaissance planes, a Gladiator, dropped news on us of Fawzi Kuwuckji's whereabouts.

"Movement seen in area Nuqaib. 50 M.T. (vehicles) and 200 horsemen moving along track eastwards."

This confirmed Glubb, who had of course gone his own way to our appointed rendezvous, west of Ramadi, leaving only the one truck of black-faced legionaries to guide the Advance Guard Household Cavalry, with results already described.

I sought out Brooks in his blue car, and prayed to heaven I was on the right route. He said yes; and that I could either strike left here until I hit the Old Damascus Camel Road ten miles to the north; or persevere through the enclosure roughly following the course of the Haifa-Baghdad road. In so doing I would come to an area of treacherous sand stretching all the way from the Damascus track to the Haifa-Baghdad road, but it should be just passable, if rushed at, where it met the foundations of the new road. There was a stretch of twenty or thirty yards to cross there, nothing more. I decided to chance this.

Peter Grant-Lawson was trying to prove that I was doing more than fifteen miles in the hour; and complaining bitterly (in the heat) that the heavy supply vehicles which had joined us at Rutbah, and which now carried all our water and fuel, could not keep up. The argument became heated. Grose having assured me, almost in tears, that the speedometer had at no time ever bumped over twenty-nine, I assured the Brigade Major that if I was going too fast it must be because his programme was too ambitious. Peter Herbert, the Liaison Officer from Habforce, who had come up to join us on this stretch, was brought in to arbitrate (being of our own regiment), and after a nice calculation as to the exact spot we had reached and the exact moment we had left Rutbah, it was found that we had covered exactly fifteen miles in the hour. So much for speed. As for density . . . .

The Brigadier was also getting redder and hotter as the day wore on, and when I proceeded to drive on, and led the column through the gateway of the barbed-wire enclosure, in order to follow the track through the further opening and so on to the proposed route, I was yelled after not to be a criminal fool and get the whole column caught in a bottle-neck. When I proceeded to turn round and so avoid this imbecile operation I was yelled at to go on, having started; and so the column filed laboriously through, closing in from its widely dispersed front to do so.

This was not my most brilliant achievement, but all round the compound seemed rocky and fortunately no hostile aircraft arrived to make me look foolish. The going became much worse, and the churned-up ground beside the half-constructed permanent way was bumpy and treacherous. Soon a solitary 15-cwt. truck appeared on our left and scudded to a halt in front of me. From it jumped Bobo Roxburghe, his topi shoved back on his shock of dark hair. A spotted red silk handkerchief festooned his neck and a pair of dark brown goggles gave him an even more sinister appearance than usual.

"Thank God it's you!" he cried. "I am trying to catch up with the regiment," he explained. "Can I get along here?" He pointed along the line of the embankment.

"Yes," I said, "but you will come to a patch of treacherous sand, rather red in colour. You want to rush it."

He goggled at me in astonishment and, jumping into his truck, raced on.

This sandy patch, when we did come to it, almost gave me a heart attack. I was, of course, obliged to stop (which upset both the speed and density of the rest of the column), and Peter came tearing up. I had already got out and told Williamson to do the same, in order to lighten the car and Grose was even now taking a flying run at the dangerous patch. Peter Grant-Lawson watched the operation, appalled with horror at the prospect of what might happen to the column if it proved impassable. My car was beginning to flounder in the sand so we rushed at it and with the extra heave it gripped the surface and lurched through. The others followed in and by a miracle all got through. While this was going on an aeroplane arrived, which seemed ill-omened, until it landed on a hard patch of desert and handed a message to the Brigadier from Colonel Roberts at Habbaniya. Then it flew back again. This contact with our objective was reassuring.

We had been driving since dawn and the heat seemed to increase with every mile. Brooks had assured me that eventually we would find the beginning of the 114-kilometre stretch of tarmac which led out into the desert west of Ramadi. All tracks, he said, converged on to it in the end. And he was right. Then I knew that my anxieties as a navigator were over. It would perhaps have been easier to let Brooks go ahead all the way. Instead of which I got the credit for a lucky piece of navigation over the longest stretch of waterless desert. Besides which we had not previously had an opportunity of putting Brooks's quiet confidence to the test, and we should have looked pretty fools if the entire Striking Force had been led off its course behind a pied piper of Hamelin. So now we streamed down on to the thin black ribbon of road and all behind me abandoned their orders to disperse over a wide front; for the lure of a real road was too much for them. The Brigadier drew alongside and said he proposed that the column should not halt until nine o'clock — and took Ian Spence on to lay out the camp for the night. It was dark when we came to the halt and turned off the road on to the various areas of desert allotted to us.

We had driven since dawn and had come nearly 200 miles across all sorts of desert in great heat. We were now within striking distance of the enemy, for twenty-five miles down the road two brigades of them were waiting behind the flood waters of the Euphrates to bar our further advance.

There was to be a brigade conference at 9.30, and I was hoping that Grose and Williamson would have the tea boiling before then. I was wiping down my face in a cupful of water in the half dark when I saw the small figure of Glubb passing, recognisable by the outlines of his keffyeh against the gun-metal sky.

"Hullo Pasha," I said. "The conference is at 9.30 if that is what you are looking for. Would you like some tea?"

He came and squatted down on the ground beside me, Arab fashion with his legs crossed.

I told him that his guides must smell their way across the desert because they had led the advance guard on no recognisable course. Glubb laughed. I asked him where he had been all day. He had been looking for Fawzi, but whether he had met with any success he did not say. It was on the tip of my tongue to warn him that the Brigadier planned to send him off on a wild goose chase before our next advance; but I could not bring myself to be disloyal to Joe and we drank the hot sweet tea luxuriously out of large china mugs (which Grose had stolen, I suppose, from the Naafi canteen at Nathanya).

We were settling down to a friendly exchange of talk when I let drop, foolishly, that I was a Member of Parliament; at which, it seemed to me,

Glubb sheered off, afraid, I think, of seeming to court publicity. If he hoped to avoid it he was likely to be disappointed for, unassuming as he always appeared, his whole background was glamorous and I felt that the Glubb legend was more surely rooted in the hearts of the bedouin than was Lawrence's. Glubb had led them for twenty years (at first under Peak Pasha) and the Desert Patrol was his own creation. His men came from tribes all over the Levant (including Iraq) and were proud to serve under him. His command was more official than Lawrence's, for it had the authority of the established Emirate of Transjordan behind it. I had mentioned Lawrence's name in gatherings of Arabs, perhaps in a village perched high on some crag, accessible only to men on horses, and seen the flicker of recognition which passed around the circle of dark faces at the mention of Lawrence's name. But much of this fame had come after the event from the publicity which it received in books, newspapers and cinemas. Lawrence was a name to conjure with in the Near East, but Abu Hunaik's was accepted as of the Near East itself.

It was difficult to find the office truck in the dark, but eventually we discovered it by a blue shaft of light which gleamed through the flaps from its interior.

We were all tired, angry and impatient at the conference, except Glubb who said nothing — even when the Brigadier assigned to him, as a mark of special favour, the role of reconnaissance to the north while we planned to take the main column south of Lake Habbaniya. Glubb smiled mildly to himself, as I recollect it, knowing that he would be needed before long and preferred to let the Brigadier find this out for himself.

We were growing more cautious about showing lights since the advent of aircraft and with the enemy in the neighbourhood; so we pored over our maps with pocket flash lamps as Joe explained his plans. The message which had been flown out to him from Habbaniya had assured him that he could turn the column off the road with impunity fourteen miles west of Ramadi and strike across desert to the trestle bridge at Mujara. The two Essex Companies were to lead off under Major May and the Household Cavalry on this occasion were to act as rearguard, and would be the last to leave. The 200 heavy vehicles of the R.A.S.C., under Major Newmarsh, were to go in the middle. I was to be at a point fourteen miles west of Ramadi at 7.30 next morning, to start the head of the column on a compass-bearing which would bring it to the Wadi Abu Farouk, where it would turn west until it struck the flood race south of Lake Habbaniya at Mujara.

After the conference the commanders returned to their units while we at headquarters sat down on upturned petrol cans to a meal beside the officers' Mess truck. Brooks was now with us, and I asked him about the route for tomorrow, but he was as familiar with the proposed point of departure as a man accustomed to driving up the Great North Road might expect to be about a heap of stones fourteen miles short of Barnet. So I was thrown back on my own devices.

I drove down the road at seven, to find the Household Cavalry camped just beyond the point of departure. Andrew Ferguson was shaving beside the road and invited me over to share his tea and sardines; which I did, while he concluded his shave. He threatened to have me beheaded for not being properly dressed. Like the Brigadier I wore only a canvas belt with my revolver holster instead of the webbing equipment harness, which preserved a neater appearance. My heavy revolver dragged my shorts down inelegantly at the side. Henry Abel-Smith, the senior Blues officer in the regiment, whom we called Auntie, for his fussiness, came back with me to a point short of kilo 25, fourteen miles west of Ramadi, when I took up my station to direct the head of the column. I calculated the direction roughly by a line on the map, drawn from the point fourteen miles west of Ramadi, and along the line of a wadi (exaggerated on the map) to the Wadi Abu Farouk. Setting my map with its top to the north with the aid of my compass, I squinted through the prism in the direction of the pencilled line and read the mystic figures 140. Auntie asked me, with a twinkle in his eye, if I were going to add or subtract the deviation from magnetic north, to get the same bearing as the map. I glanced at the margin which said magnetic deviation 8° in 1926, liable to a diminution of forty minutes a year, or words to that effect, and so I said stoutly that I proposed to *add* three minutes to the compass-bearing; and was relieved to see astonished approval in the expression of my sometime commanding officer.

I was personally quite unable to see what difference it made, because the column was bound to strike the line of the Wadi Abu Farouk* somewhere, if it could get through at all without a special reconnaissance of the ground, which I doubted. But Colonel Roberts at Habbaniya had said the going was good for all M.T., and what Colonels tell Brigadiers carries weight. It is perfectly true that R.A.F. armoured cars had successfully negotiated this area; but Colonel Roberts had evidently never seen one of our three-tonner supply lorries fully loaded.

---

* Wadi Abu Farouk should, if you want to be a purist, be written 'Abu al Furoukh' — but I daresay that Arabic hairsplitting leaves you cold.   Glubb Pasha.

Major May's smooth face took in the intelligence that he was to proceed on a compass-bearing of 143 degrees, until he came to the Wadi Abu Farouk, then strike west for Mujara; and drive on with his trucks jolting off the road behind him.

How little we realised what the day was to mean, as Henry Abel and I sat light-heartedly on a cairn of stones, watching the vehicles turn off on to the desert. The Brigade Operation Order provided for a dispersal of vehicles on a wide front as a protection against air attack, and the suggestion that on unknown desert the vehicles should follow the leader in single file was not approved.

The point of departure is clearly marked on my memory by a rusty iron plate on a pole, bearing, like the similar signposts along the route, the words:

RAMADI
25 Kilos.

When the Brigade Headquarters vehicles appeared, I entered my car, taking the wheel, and joined the stream. It soon became apparent that the only safe ground was along the shallow declivity where a faint green blush marked the course of the wadi. The ridges on either side looked firm, but they had only a crisp crust, beneath which the sand was soft. We had not been going long when the column halted, inexplicably, as it always seems to those who are not at the front of it. We stood about in the growing heat of the day, wondering what had happened. Soon the heat became intense and, taking advantage of the column's inactivity, I lay back in the prickly plush seat of the car gaspingly trying to rest. Thirst became a menace for the first time, and we knew only too well that water was growing scarce. We had not been able to fill up since Rutbah, and depended for our next supply on reaching Mujara.

The delay seemed to have become an established phenomenon and I encouraged Grose to light up the Primus and make tea. Chris Thursfield of the Wiltshire Yeomanry, who had been acting Brigade Signals Officer during Dick Schuster's absence in the Western Desert, and who had managed to slip along with us unofficially in an assistant capacity so far, came over to share my tea. The heat had completely overwhelmed him. His pleasant square face was a red morass from which the sweat poured; his khaki shirt clung to him as if he had been bathing. He sat down on the running-board inarticulately and merely drank the tea when it was offered to him. Peter Grant-Lawson drove over, wiping the steam off his pebble-eyed glasses and breathing like an engine. He had been watching the distant black dots behind us which marked the Household Cavalry trucks, creeping around to the south, whereby their function of guarding our tail was neglected. So he asked me, kindly enough, for it was too hot to ask anyone to do anything exceptional, to find Andrew and tell him that he was getting out of place. I drove off, when the Primus had been stowed, Williamson cursing because he had just unpacked the back to get at some food.

My course took me over a rise in the ground, and there I saw a sight which made my heart sick. The great supply monsters were everywhere floundering in soft sand. Those which had driven up the crisp ridges were now bedded down to the axles, while their crews laboured in the desperate heat to dig them out. The sand would be scooped away in front of the wheels, and the sand channels, like ten-foot cheese graters, which they carried along the sides of the vehicle, would be shoved under the wheel. All this in weather which made it impossible to touch metal in the shadow where the thermometer reached 118 degrees. In the sun the metal seemed to have become incandescent. Men handled it with rags, grimed handkerchiefs, anything they could lay hold of. Once the sand channels had been thrust under the rear wheels the dripping driver would start the engine and it would roar up with clouds of steam rising from the boiling radiator. The monstrous vehicle would lurch forward only to embed itself deeper into the sand ten yards further on. And the men would have to begin again.

A water truck, carrying some of our precious supply, had to be emptied out on to the sand, while everywhere the loads of petrol cans stood about, their white metal surfaces flashing with a blinding glare, whenever they reflected the sun's rays. I found the Household Cavalry waiting about angrily and told Neil Foster, the adjutant, what Peter wanted. He went cursing to Andrew and I suppose they readjusted their position. Being for the most part light, they could move more freely, although they also had some three-tonners in the squadrons.

News came through to the signals truck after midday that the staff captain 'Corpo', who had been sent ahead, had got across the bridge followed by a 15-cwt. truck at Mujara and had actually arrived in Habbaniya. But as the afternoon wore on and the heat felled us like cattle pole-axed, the chance of getting the main column through began to trickle out like water on the sand. The Brigadier, who had gone forward, came back now despairing.

"It is like Flodden Field up in front," he told us. He seemed a broken man. "There is no hope."

And reluctantly he gave orders that the whole expedition should be drawn out, and return to kilo 25; all of it, that is, which could be extricated. I was sent back to park the vehicles in appropriate areas when they returned. It was like a small boy trying to shepherd a herd of angry elephants into a kraal. The vehicles dragged wearily back over the morning's route, the men anxious only to murder each other, and fall asleep where they chose to stop. Major May of the Essex Regiment complained angrily that there was not room for him because the Household Cavalry were on both sides of the road, and asked him to tell them to get over to the other. I sought out my old regiment and found Gerard Fuller.

"If you want us to move," he shouted, "you go and tell Andrew and see what he says."

Of course you cannot see what a man says and, stimulated by rage and fatigue, Andrew was less inarticulate than usual. "I am staying here, Somerset," he said, "and I don't care what any Brigadier in the British Army says about it." He dismissed all higher authority in a comprehensive wave of the hand.

"That suits me," I replied, and went off to tell May he would have to fit in as best he could. Of course he had already done so. Whenever possible I let units stay where they stopped. Only the patient gunners and the R.A.S.C. column lumbered on up the road 'to turn off a mile up', without protest. I came across Bobo Roxburghe, swaying in the middle of the road. He extended the red silk handkerchief, saturated with eau de cologne. "Take a sniff of that, Somerset," he said huskily, "that will do you good." I followed his advice. "We are going to try again tomorrow, I hope?" he added.

"I hope so," was all I could say.

A conference was called later that night. Now the heat had gone out of the sky; men were slightly refreshed; and when the dust had settled after the disastrous events of the day, it was discovered that only two vehicles had had to be abandoned. The Brigadier had ordered that where a vehicle was left, the crew should be taken on board some other vehicle.

A misunderstanding of this order led to a grim experience for two R.A.S.C. men who remained out in the desert and were subsequently captured by a mounted Iraqi patrol. Thirsty and exhausted though they were, the rebel horsemen stripped them of their clothes and drove them on in the burning sun, with jeers and prods of rifle-butts, until they were tired of the sport. The men stumbled on — back on their tracks towards Rutbah 200 miles away; and would have certainly perished with thirst had they not encountered a supply column which followed us up later.

At the conference the Brigadier faced us with a sorrowful countenance. "We have enough supplies of water," he said, "to stay here one more day. After that we go on or go back." He turned to Glubb.

"I shall want your dusky maidens to help us find an alternative route."

The mere suggestion that we might have to turn back filled us with despair and Dick Schuster (who was the Brigadier's special pet) and I went to him in a deputation afterwards to express our conviction that if only the column were sent in single file along the floor of the wadis, it could get through. At least it was worth trying a single three-tonner first. Joe laid his patriarchal hand on my shoulder and repressed his rage with difficulty. "I know you mean well, Somerset," he said, "but it is not one vehicle that has to get through. It is 500."

CHAPTER 18   *A Bathe in the Euphrates*

Thus it came about that three reconnaissance parties were sent out next day with guides from the Arab Legion to find a way round, while I was sent out into the wide desert on the vague chance of finding water. I discussed the prospects with Glubb, over a map. He pointed to some marshy indications on it. "There is a place here called Abu Jir. There must have been a habitation of some kind once and perhaps a well." I consulted Brooks also, who said that at Awasil, north of the road not far back, there had been at one time some experimental boring of the British Oil Development Co. and a pipe had been laid on from the Euphrates, where it was pumped up. Not only had the place been abandoned for many years, he thought, but the pump at the other end would be in Iraqi hands, for they were in occupation of Ramadi, Hit, Haditha and all the river in between.

So I set out alone next morning, with Grose and my new interpreter Reading, for he would be needed if we came across any local bedouin who might guide us.

"We would be safer," said Reading, "to pretend that we are Iraqi soldiers trying to get back to Ramadi, for they would not speak to us if they thought we were British."

I was surprised at the possibility, but Reading assured me that many Iraqi officers were as fair as I, and we knew that their staff cars and equipment were similar to our own.

"Do you think you can get away with it?" I asked.

"Of course," Reading assured me. It would only be necessary for Grose and myself to sit quietly in the car, while he got out and did the speaking. The bedouin would not know the difference. This opened up possibilities which I had not dreamed of, and I set to thinking. We drove back along the road, to a spot which I had noticed during our approach where two little stone cairns marked the trig point 397, south of which lay the mysterious Abu Jir, seven or eight miles away. We were still on the stretch of tarmac and at intervals along it were crude clay kilns, in which the pitch had been melted during the making of the road. We

218

came in sight of the two little cairns a few hundred yards across the desert south of the kilo 40 signpost. I drove off the road and found a regular track leading up to them. This track descended sharply through a small gorge and, as we turned a bend, I gasped with astonishment.

In front of us stretched a vast lake of dried asphalt, like the floor of some dead crater in the moon. It was bounded on the south by a steep range of hills; but what held our gaze particularly were stretches of greenish water lying like a film over the black pitch. And not far out in the petrified lake, stood the stone ruins of a hut. This was Abu Jir. With rising excitement I drove on down to the edge of the asphalt, and ignoring Reading's lugubrious protests, ventured out along a track which seemed to cross it. Soon enough we were brushing through shallow water.

"It is no use for drinking," Reading said, "it is sulphur water. People come for many miles to bathe in such water."

But two ideas were already in my head. One was that it would do for a bathe (which only yesterday had been an undreamed of ambition) and secondly, the water, while unfit to drink, might quench the thirst of the motor vehicles in our column. The asphalt was spongy in places and made driving over it uneasy, but I reflected that the ruined hovel must have been reached before, and, swishing through the brackish water, I drew up on a hard patch of asphalt beside the ruins. We got out. The sun's rays bounced off the asphalt lake, and the heat was fiery.

Here and there pitch bubbled up black and oily.

"It's from here that they must have taken the tar for the road," Reading observed shrewdly enough.

It was Grose, I think, who found a clear spring of water near by, welling up like crystal in the middle of the black pitch and with a viscous pink substance also showing prettily through it. I decided for a bathe, and we stripped off our khaki shirts, shorts and stockings. Grose and I felt obliged to wear our topis, which amused Reading, whose black hair was used to these extremes of heat, and laughed at the picture we presented, solemnly stepping down into the pool with nothing but our headgear on.

The water was unbelievably cool and I crouched in it, grateful for its refreshing balm, and heedless of the glutinous sensation around my toes, where the asphalt clung to them. Grose produced my towel from the car, which, we were horrified to discover, was beginning to sink slowly into the asphalt. The ground was evidently not as hard as it seemed and we hurriedly moved the car on a few yards. If we got stuck here, we were likely to get left behind, unless Glubb thought of looking for us at Abu Jir in view of my conversation with him on the subject. It soon became apparent that the pitch was going to adhere to us like glue, and there was nothing for it but to try to rub it off with a rag and petrol. This transformed the short flakes of black into a general brown smear which remained indelible for the rest of the campaign. With the aid of this petrol I got the worst of the pitch out, stinging, from between my toes.

While we were dressing again Reading drew my attention to some movement on the escarpment from which we had descended. I ran for my field-glasses and soon picked up the figures of two black-and-white robed bedouin regarding us with equal intentness.

"Come on," I said, "we must catch those fellows before they get away." And so, hurriedly putting on the rest of our clothes, we turned round and drove back the way we had come.

When we topped the escarpment, we could see the figures of the two bedouin, hurrying away northwards on foot beyond the road. I drove after them, and they seemed to be terrified of us, looking furtively back over their shoulders, and fully expecting, I think, to be shot, when we came up with them. They poured out their bona fides to Reading. They were innocent villagers from the Euphrates. They did not meddle in military affairs. Indeed they seemed harmless enough and on foot they could not give intimation of our approach to anyone else. So I left them to walk on and decided to go now in search of the abandoned workings at Awasil.

This was not difficult to find, for there was a large rusted iron sign, at a point where a track left the road, which said simply 'Awasil'. We drove along the curving track until a dark object began to shimmer ahead of us. This developed into a stationary steam-engine such as is used for driving pumps. There were some bare concrete foundations surrounded by the meagre grass, and the line of the disused water-pipe could be easily seen, under the earth, running north-eastwards towards the Euphrates. We climbed about the derelict engine, but of water there was no sign. Away to the west there appeared to be a large square building and I decided to investigate this. But as we neared it, the outlines dwindled to the smallest hovel, such was the inverted distortion of the heat mirage. Then some fabulous black cattle loomed up, with a giant guarding them on a ridge. We drove towards these, only to discover, on approach a frightened bedou with a flock of black goats, grazing on the sparse scrub. Reading got out and addressed him, calling to the man to come near, "Taal, taal." The man approached reluctantly, a rifle slung over his shoulder. "Have you seen any soldiers?" Reading asked him. "We are Iraqis, cut off from Ramadi by the floods."

"Askaris!" The man spat. "I have seen 50,000 British soldiers going along the road in the last two days.

"50,000!" exclaimed Reading.

"More," said the bedou. "But you can get back into Ramadi if you have someone walking in front of the car, to show you the road. The water is not deep."

Reading's first experiment seemed to have been eminently successful. I now decided upon a course of action which was perhaps foolish, but so successful had been this encounter, that I decided to try reaching the Euphrates itself. The enemy could not be holding all of it in strength, and if we chose a lonely spot on its banks, we might find access to fresh water — and another bathe. We had all day for reconnaissance so I took the wheel again and, after studying the map, headed the car for a village on the Euphrates called Abu Tibin. Already the desert was grassier and the hard flat surface now gave way to an intricate maze of foothills, in which we might very easily lose ourselves when returning if we were not careful. There were ridges of considerable height, and it was quite impossible to keep to anything like a straight course or a compass-bearing. Now and again I had to bump the car through the beds of dried-up wadis, but at length we came out above a stretch of flat plain, fringed in the distance by the green foliage along the river. I was, at least, the first of Kingcol to set eyes on the fabled Euphrates. A single line of telegraph posts crossed the plain in the middle distance, and there was the gleam of a track following their course. I set the car downwards to the plain.

Green tufts of scrub grew in large patches in these flats as we neared the river. We crossed the track, but could see no sign of movement in either direction. The telegraph line was the main communication between the Iraqi Brigades in Ramadi and such forces as they might have up the river at Hit and Haditha. I determined to tear them down on the way back. I could discern the black shapes of bedouin tents near the river and decided to approach cautiously. As we neared the river, the desert ground gave way to baked mud flats and it soon became obvious that only a light car such as mine could hope to cross it safely at all. The idea of taking the three-tonners down there to water must, reluctantly, be given up. I picked up a track, leading around the base of knolls, to the village, and we were soon passing the long low black camel-hair tents of the villagers. This was certainly Abu Tibin. I stopped the car. Reading got out and called to a passing bedou, to know whether we could reach the river this way. The man seemed afraid and reluctant to stop. He merely pointed towards the high earth embankment of the river. This was above the level of the surrounding mud flats, which is why they are so often flooded at this time of the year. I took the car as far as it seemed possible to go and left Grose to turn it round, while I got up on to the embankment.

In front of me flowed the wide brown river, surging past, with palm trees and rich foliage on the further bank. I searched the opposite shore, which must have been half a mile away, so wide was the Euphrates, with my binoculars, but could see no sign of life. Further down the river where the track we had crossed and the telegraph line seemed to close in on it, there was a mud building, but the figures walking about it were all robed in black or white like the bedouin. I could see no sign of soldiers. This in itself was an important discovery, for we had believed up till then that the whole course of the river was in enemy hands.

"All clear," I said. "I am going to bathe again."

Once more I retained my pith-helmet, with its thin blue and red regimental colouring peeping above the khaki puggaree. I put my watch in my shoes on the bank and lowered myself into the river. Reading warned me of the speed of the current and advised me to hold on to the roots of the tamarisk scrub which grew on the bank. This I did or I would certainly have been swept away. I felt the cool mud close over my hot sore feet as I stepped in. It was a delicious moment. I believe I was in mortal danger on this as on other occasions of getting bilharzia disease, for the bug lives in most fresh water and rivers in the Near East, with dire results two years later. But two years seemed a century. Neither Reading nor Grose felt inclined to bathe again, and so, when I had dried myself and dressed, we drove off.

Reading volunteered to try out his Iraqi again and went over to one of the bedouin tents, where he remained so long in conversation that I began honking for him. He returned with his proud gait, saying that it would have looked suspicious to leave sooner. He had moreover acquired most valuable information from a black old woman. The Iraq Army had retired through the village a week before, with guns on packs (mountain guns), and had conscripted all the tribesmen of military age in the village, including her own husband and her four sons. She had been in Ramadi to see her son on Saturday, which seemed to indicate that the floods were not such a serious matter. Reading concluded by asking her if she had seen any British soldiers.

"No," she replied fiercely. "But I know what to do if I do," and produced an enormous, long knife. After which we thought it about time to return to our own encampment.

As I drove back, not trusting the car on the soft mud flats to anyone else, I pondered on the best action to take if interrupted by some Iraqi patrol which might have watched our approach, and possibly even have let us pass intentionally. Two revolvers and a rifle would not be adequate armament for a pitched battle, but it was unlikely that any enemy vehicle would be faster than a new Chevrolet staff car, and the obvious course would be to make a dash for it, taking a chance on eluding the stray bullets. However, we were as fortunate on the return as on the approach. We drove across the Haditha track again, but I decided, after all, not to cut the wires, although it was tempting to swarm up the short poles and do so. Such action would immediately betray to the enemy the fact that we had not left the vicinity, and we had no reason to suppose so far that they knew exactly where we were. In this my caution was wasted, for when at length I extracted the car from the intricate foothills and reached the main road, where our vehicles were parked all around, I saw a large black Heinkel circling overhead, and, curiously enough, two of our own Gladiators from Habbaniya gaily flying off without apparently having seen it at all. Every rifle, hotchkiss gun, Lewis gun, machine-gun, anything that could fire was opening up on the marauder, but it circled slowly around, dropping an occasional bomb. I had just got back to Brigade Headquarters and was full of eagerness to report my activities to Peter, but he, in a slit trench, was not attentive. Gwynn Morgan Jones and I, who had both been in England during the Battle of Britain, stood talking on the desert, quite un-aware of the awe which we inspired in those who had never been bombed before, and who were firmly convinced that one Heinkel over a camp several miles in circumference, would certainly blow their own heads off.

I had evidently been fortunate in the timing of my personal reconnaissance to the river for we now received a report from a stray bedou of an armoured car patrol which had set out in that direction from Ramadi an hour ago.

I told Peter about the spring of sulphurous water at Abu Jir and he began organising a system of collecting it, while he asked me to go back there with an R.A.S.C. sergeant to get the latter's opinion on whether the three-tonners could be safely driven up to it without sinking in, provided they did not stay still for long. At least the water could be collected in petrol tins by light trucks and carried to the escarpment.

I was away with the sergeant, who was duly impressed by this discovery, and the R.A.S.C. vehicles were beginning to come up for the water, when one of the reconnaissance parties which had been looking for an alternative route returned in triumph to say that they had discovered a long detour which could be covered in single file by the whole column. This meant that we could go on again next day; and so the sulphur water for the vehicles would not be needed.

The Brigadier had led the successful reconnaissance patrol, accompanied by the Pasha in person, and had gone on by car from Mujara to Habbaniya, whence he was to return by air in one of the tireless Blenheims. He was late getting back and Peter was growing anxious. It was already eight o'clock and dusk was closing in quickly. The Iraqis, according to Belgrave, were astonishingly good at anti-aircraft fire with small arms and had brought down three of our Blenheims over Rutbah this way. A blaze of headlights along the road heralded the return of our leader. He had been landed a few miles down the road near the Household Cavalry, arriving at the same time as the Heinkel.

We slept soundly knowing that we would not have to rise till 5.30 or 6. But Joe was early astir, and stood in the middle of the compound, pawing the ground with his foot like a bull. There was a bird which used to walk about on the desert in the early mornings. It could be heard giving ever and again its plaintive call, reminding me of the curlews on the white beaches of the Western Isles. The Arabic name which Reading gave for the bird was the same as that for dive-bomber. I suppose it was a species of diver. I had difficulty locating the author of the melancholy note, until I saw it through my field-glasses: a tall grey bird on long, thin creamy legs, fretting about on the sand beyond the circle of our vehicles. My memory of the early stages of our march is scarred by the thought of reveille at 3.30, breakfast at 4, move at 4.30. On the other hand our rations were dwindling to the inevitable tinned bully beef and biscuits. I still had some wide slabs of chocolate, bought at Groppi's in Cairo, which hardened up during the cool hours of darkness and became liquid slush inside their waterproof paper wrappings during the day. I spread it as paste on the biscuits, which made them tasty.

The column was to start off on the new trail which led it in a wide loop towards the south-*west*, away from Mujara, in the same order as on the previous attempt. This enormously simplified our departure and as it was to be guided by the Arab Legion truck which had reconnoitred the route, there was no need for me to start it off. This time there were no halts, not even the customary twenty minutes every two hours, for we were determined to get through without taking any chances. We had already been spotted by the Heinkel and a single bomb on the little bridge would force us to turn back for lack of an extra day's fuel. The track was well formed, running along sandy ground where rushes grew in profusion. By the time my part of the column was passing over some of it the heavy vehicles and 25-pounders had scored deep ruts, yet the foundation was solid and, contrary to the disastrous practice before, each vehicle had orders to keep in the trail of the one ahead.

I had been travelling thus for some hours in a cloud of dust from the

226

bouncing guns which were trailed behind beetle-like contraptions called dragons, when a truck-load of Glubb's black bedouin came tearing up the line looking for me. They were shouting, chattering and gesticulating. I drew aside from the column and got out of my car. It was easy enough to see what had happened; there was a grim tear in the radiator of the Chev. truck and holes through the sides of it. And huddled, moaning, on the floor of the truck were two of the Arab Legionaries. One was bleeding from a savage crescent-shaped gash across his mouth and nostril. On the other there was no sign of hurt, for his flowing top garment covered any wound.

I knew that our section of the 166 Field Ambulance was not far down the line and that if we waited it would soon catch us up. Fortunately I had Reading with me and he soon obtained the native sergeant's story. While the Arabs spoke, the whites of their eyes searched the sky in a panic, and they made no bones of their eagerness to get on. If ever men behaved as though the devil were after them, these bedouin did today. They were brave enough, but for the first time they had met a new form of assailant. Just as the tail of the column had been moving off from the camp, four black fighters had roared across the desert drilling the lorries on the ground with bullets and cannon fire. They had disappeared as abruptly as they had come. No doubt the volume of fire directed at the Heinkel had warned them to expect a hot reception.

I saw, with relief, the white circle and red cross on the side of a khaki van, bouncing towards us in the stream of passing vehicles, and waved to it to stop. Doc Arundel's calm, good-looking face appeared and he stepped down. Drawing apart the moaning bedou's clothes, he revealed a neat hole, where the bullet had entered the man's chest, and a slightly larger one in his side, where the bullet had emerged. There was scarcely any sign of blood — just two little holes. Doc Arundel shook his head. The man certainly could not live, and he did in fact die within an hour. I little thought, at this moment, that Doc Arundel would one day be bending over me in similar circumstances. He turned to the bedou with the face wound.

By now the stretcher bearers were ready to take the two men off the truck, and their bedouin comrades, having got rid of them, showed a complete indifference to their fate, leapt back into the truck, and with water still pouring from the gaping radiator roared off, up the line. They would not get far at that rate, but their one obsession was to put as much distance as possible between themselves and the aeroplanes which pursued and haunted their primitive imagination. Reading, who was at least half Arab, had been infected by their panic, and when I turned round Grose informed me that he had jumped into a passing lorry, saying that I had given him permission to go on! Reading, like the bedouin of the Desert Patrol, had proved his coolness and daring at Abu Tibin when confronted with a known danger, but this was his first contact with that third dimensional terror which was, alas, on a later battlefield to drive him out of his senses when he saw me carried away bleeding from five wounds.

While Doc Arundel was dressing the wounds of the bedouin who stank — goodness, how they stank — another lorry drove up with three more casualties from the Household Cavalry. The matter-of-fact way in which they were deposited, as if the baker were delivering loaves on his round, provided an entertaining contrast to the excitement of the Arab legionaries. These wounded men, who had at some time ridden plumed and cuirassed down Constitution Hill, accepted their punishment with a lack of imagination which was wholly admirable. They might have been attending hospital parade to have their teeth seen to. They confirmed in greater detail what the bedouin had said. There had been four planes which had made one run over the camp. They were only a flash, but one man thought they had been marked with French colours, blue, white and red on the tail.

I got back into the car and overhauled the vehicles which had passed me in the interval. A little further on I passed the Arab Legion truck with its engine seized up. It was fortunate, I reflected, that the aeroplanes, which were probably German, had arrived when only the tail of the column was left, and doubly fortunate that the column would have seemed to them to be returning — south-west, in the direction of Nuqaib. This was likely to have baffled them as to our real intention of circling round till we came to Habbaniya. Upon such slender accidents do the fortunes of war depend, for had they found us the day before, immobilised in the soft sand, they could have wrecked the column, and have reported to the newly-arrived German bombers that we were heading in a straight line for the southern end of the great lake.

Mujara was all huts and engineering yards. We rattled over the wooden bridge beneath which roared the broad emerald-green waters of the flood-race coming down from the wide sweep of the lake on our left. It was astonishing to see so much water, after the scrub of the desert we had traversed. On the further side of the bridge was the sturdy figure of a British tommy, with a different kind of topi to ours (he had been equipped in India), but with the familiar Lee-Enfield rifle. There was a company of the K.O.R.R. camped on a knoll beyond the bridge, with Lewis guns on tripods pointing to the sky and a pair of armoured cars, standing on guard. Kingcol was dispersed off the road as it came over the bridge, but I found Peter there and he told me that a despatch-rider of the K.O.R.R. (who had not shown much reverence for our achievement in arriving at all, and were in no way ready for us) was now detailed to lead an advance party to our camping site twenty miles further up the lake, near the cantonment. The Brigadier had gone on to Habbaniya, leaving word that I could do the same, but "Not to talk too much."

There was the beginning of a tarmac road from Majura to Habbaniya, but it soon petered out in new constructional work, and the despatch rider turned us off on to the rough undulating gravel desert which here skirted the lake. We lost sight of this on our left, but an hour's driving brought us out on a hard plateau, where the tarmac road began again. I left the rest of the column to turn off down to the lake, while I sped on, eager to catch my first glimpse of our first objective. At the edge of the plateau I came abruptly upon the cantonment. From the foot of the red sandstone spurs, a level mud aerodrome stretched to the settlement itself, where hangars gave way to a maze of leafy avenues and the red roofs of bungalows. Twenty or thirty aircraft were dispersed about the landing ground. The road descended steeply to join another at right angles. We turned left and in a few yards reached a signpost bearing in clear English capitals, the enchanting legend:

London	Baghdad
2927 miles.	59 miles.

It did not require a third arm to point across the aerodrome to Habbaniya. I drove gleefully towards civilisation and a great determination welled up in me — to secure a hot bath, if I had to tear every building in the cantonment apart to find one.

I had a blueprint plan of the cantonment in my leather wallet, and after passing the sentry at the gate, made straight for Air Force Headquarters. Soon we were driving along smooth metalled roads, between pink-flowing oleanders. It was difficult to realise that I had entered a besieged settlement, as the spearpoint of the relieving force.

Air Force Headquarters was an imposing white building with a central square tower, on the roof of which two tin-helmeted watchers searched the sky with their binoculars. There was a gravel sweep up to the entrance and at the door stood one of the Assyrian Levies: a brown-faced man of truly martial appearance, who wore a pale blue uniform shirt open at the neck and a dark brown felt hat turned up at the side, Australian fashion. He also wore khaki shorts and puttees. His boots were actually polished and the strap of his rifle whitened to a wonder. He was an apparition — a testimony to the stablity of the British Empire, for he had been within an ace of overwhelming extinction. The Iraqi coup had failed by so little and the Iraqis hate the Assyrians; more than they hated the British, did they hate the Assyrians. I asked for the Intelligence Branch. I was shown through into a cool courtyard, where the white verandas were shaded from the sun, and a door was opened into a dim cool set of offices. Here amid wall maps and metal filing-cases was my friend, Pilot Officer Belgrave.

I gave him some account of our journey, of the reconnaissance to Abu Tibin, and of the four aeroplanes which had machine-gunned our column this morning. He led me, smiling, through a door into other offices, where three or four more Air Force Intelligence Officers gathered round me. "Here," he announced, "is a man who has been swimming in the Euphrates." They could hardly have regarded me with more astonishment if I had been Dr Livingstone. For the first time in my life I felt really important — and surprisingly shy. They sent off to London a cable with the intelligence I had brought in. (I was to come across the Air Ministry cable in M.I.2 at the War Office a year later) — 'Euphrates clear of enemy in area Abu Tibin between Hit and Ramadi' — and I asked Belgrave if he could produce a bath.

He led the way in his own car to the Air Force H.Q. Mess. We entered a palace panelled with cedar wood and went through gardens to his rooms in a long bungalow. On the walls hung soft, silky carpets of Shirhaz and Kirmanshah. He had lived long in Iraq and had, he told me, a beautiful young French wife — who was happily evacuated by air to Basra. Like most of the other Air Force Intelligence Officers, he had never piloted a plane in his life, but had been put into a khaki shirt and shorts, with the thin blue stripes of an officer on his shoulder tabs when war came as the only available cloak to intelligence activity.

It was refreshing after the bare boards of the military mind, to step on the carpeted intelligence of a cultured man. The bath next door was as hot as I had dreamed, and after it I joined Belgrave in the Mess, where we sat in soft leather armchairs and drank tea. From the strictly rationed food of the cantonment he spared me a 'Marie' biscuit, and I blessed the moment at H.4 when I had singled him out among the crowd of officers from all over the Levant who had jostled in there to the improvised bar

for a cool drink. We had lunched together and there had seemed
something almost heroic to me about his stepping into the Blenheim
which had been waiting to take him back to the beleaguered
cantonment. But now I could view his indifference against its proper
background. For these people Habbaniya was as much home as London
is to the cockney.

Iraq was, in fact, the first country where the experiment of air
power, as the only and ultimate sanction of strength, had been tried. It
was Winston Churchill's idea when, as Colonial Secretary, he drafted
the treaty with Iraq which was to give them an alliance in exchange for
the British Mandate. Thereafter the ground troops, like the police, were
Iraqi, and the only British force left was the outpost of the Royal Air
Force with its own cantonment at Habbaniya and a battalion of Assyrian
Levies to guard it. When the test came, the Iraqis disposed of 40,000
troops, lavishly equipped by ourselves as allies. But this Air Force
outpost had been able to hold the threat at arm's length until we arrived
to help them. We did not yet know whether the experiment was justified
— for the odds still seemed heavily against us. But we had been
fortunate so far. And as the signpost on the aerodrome reminded us,
Baghdad was now only fifty-nine miles distant.

Before leaving the cantonment, I returned with Belgrave to Air
Force H.Q. where I was met by an officer wearing a strange cap badge.
He was Matthews, the war correspondent, and asked me about our
crossing of the desert. I was too tired to go into details, but I replied
"You can say with confidence, that it is one of the greatest marches in
history, and that it is the first time since the days of Alexander the Great,
that an army has succeeded in crossing the desert from the shores of the
Mediterranean to the banks of the Euphrates." This was quite enough
and it was repeated to millions of listeners the world over next day. The
achievements of men cannot become history until they are told. In
history there can be no deeds without words. That is the trade secret of
history — to write it yourself as you go. I was under no illusions, and
back in the camp on the shores of the lake, I began bringing the War
Diary of Kingcol, for which I was responsible, up to date. Within a few
months it would be safely pigeon-holed in the Records Department of
the War Office.

I find it difficult to recapture the atmosphere of our camp life at Habbaniya. So many of the worries and annoyances which disturbed that period appear trivial in retrospect. There was the total incompetence of my chief cipher clerk, which caused me continual heartburning. He acted quite irrationally and when asked to explain his conduct would stand stiffly to attention and say "Sir." He should have been in the Foot Guards.

There was the notable incident of his receiving and secreting, without a word to anyone, a new code sentence for the inter-service code, upon which, in an emergency, we should have had to depend for communication with the R.A.F. Joe sent for him. I see him now, sitting at a trestle table under the awning of the bulky office truck, and the clerk standing stiffly to attention in front of him, saying, "Sir." Joe spoke to him more in sorrow than in anger. "If we had wanted to get in touch with the Air Force we should have been unable to do so, and it would have been nobody's fault but yours. And I should have had you shot."

"Sir."

"Yes, I would." And I think Joe meant it.

Cipher clerks cannot be changed in a day, for they have to be trained, or this one would have gone long ago. Williamson was coming on well, and after this campaign it would no doubt be possible to get rid of the chief clerk and train a second under Williamson. There had to be two in order to take turn and turn about. At Mafraq, Peter Grant-Lawson had found some of my intelligence papers in the office box, and had made a passing remark to the chief cipher clerk about disposing of them. Whereupon he had set fire to all my information about the German Army as well as the Order of Battle of the Vichy forces in Syria which we were soon to need, and much else besides. I expostulated with him. He replied "Sir." No doubt he had been sent to Brigade Headquarters by the Life Guards on the well-known principle of weeding out the unfit from lower formations when asked for men by higher formations.

During the delay at Habbaniya we returned to something approaching normal life. The column was dispersed all along the foothills which run down from the plateau south of the aerodrome to the shores of the lake. This was suitable for bathing and everybody always seemed to be missing just when they were wanted, and their superiors, being human, shrugged their shoulders and muttered "Bathing." The water was very slightly brackish and was supposed to have laxative qualities. So Peter Grant-Lawson would be seen swimming out industriously until he was beyond the danger point of pollution from the troops, who crowded down to the shore; and would then take three large gulps and return to his devotions.

The Household Cavalry was usually to be found bathing near the Imperial Airways Rest House, a square modern building in brown brick by the water's edge. This had been looted by the Iraqis and a more devastated place it would have been difficult to imagine. It seemed to have been torn wide open with bare hands — every room was knee deep in paper scattered from files and cupboards. (I salvaged enough Imperial Airways paper on which to keep the War Diary for the rest of the campaign.) In one of the upstairs rooms was a woman's green silk high-heeled shoe — which told a poignant tale of hasty flight. I found John Thynne in the water — John who had driven with me one summer's day in England to Baddesley Clinton in Warwickshire. His fine aquiline features and slightly squiffy eye contemplated the water. I asked him to tell me about the four aeroplanes which machine-gunned the column. How were they marked?

"My driver was shot beside me," John said, "and I wasn't looking very closely at the markings myself. All I can tell you is that they were going bloody fast — but I seem to remember a flash of red, white and blue on the tail."

All sorts of apparitions were to be encountered in the green waters of the lake. On one occasion I saw what I mistook for a walrus, only to discover that it was Eric Gooch propelling his great brown moustache towards me. Andrew Ferguson was with him. Eric arose from the shallows in all his majesty. "How is life at Headquarters?" he asked. "Very harrowing," I replied; and told him how I was getting my own back on everybody in the War Diary. Eric laughed. "You will soon be back with us. Well, I have always said there are two books we shall all have on our shelves after this war — yours and Bill Allen's." He was probably right, and I have no doubt that Bill's will be the more entertaining of the two. Ex-Conservative M.P. turned Socialist; turned out, he had finally turned to Moseley and been one of the founders of the

New Party. He seems never to have become a member of the Fascist Party. Indeed, he had reached through trial and error a stage of political detachment in which he could declare that "Like Erasmus I have too much respect for my own intelligence to belong to any party." It was impossible to be outraged with Bill Allen. To his friends in England he sent a doggerel rhyme for Christmas —

> Some of the boys are Ministers
> And some are in different gaols.
> But as for me, sly beggar, I'm
> — Looking at horses' tails.

I had first met him when he came up to our squadron outpost at Juela on the frontier of Northern Palestine and we had talked far into the night. I told him that the one thing left out of his human nature was a conscience. He had a bluish, sallow face and lived, in England, in a small, dark, rambling house surviving in part from Tudor times, on the Atlantic cliffs of Cornwall, which featured in Kingsley's *Westward Ho* under the name of Chapel. He was not with us, for he had gone to Abyssinia, and was now dispensing Maria Theresa silver coin as Paymaster General to the Ethiopian Army!

We were held up, inevitably, at Habbaniya by the floods. These had broken a wide gap in the Causeway which gave access to Falluja. This town was itself in Iraqi hands, and we could not advance eastwards until it was captured. We arrived at Habbaniya just when plans for an attack on Falluja were imminent. The R.A.F. were dropping leaflets on it demanding its surrender under threat of heavy bombardment, while detachments of the K.O.R.R.* and the Assyrian Levies were ferried across the river by night and surrounded the town. The leaflets made little impression, but the bombs which succeeded them did, and, thus assaulted, surprised and surrounded, the place fell into our hands. Several hundred prisoners were taken.

To Peter's envy I spent much time in Habbaniya, not, as he imagined, sipping long cooling drinks in the R.A.F. Mess, but turning over the pages of files in their Intelligence bureau, which was excellent. It had been built up by Jope Slade, until the aeroplane in which he was carrying £60,000 in bullion plunged with him and the treasure into a marsh. He had built up the best library of information about Iraq, Persia and the Caucasus to be found in the Middle East. I worked

*King's Own Royal Rifles.

through it with Belgrave and others. We soon noticed how the stream of German armaments to Persia, by way of Turkey, had been increasing in recent months. The goods went by way of Maidan Ekbese. We examined closely the set-up of the German Fifth Column in Persia, where 4,000 Germans in commercial occupations were organised under Gauleiters and could be mobilised on the telephone. At the most recent manoeuvres the Persian Army had displayed ninety tanks; and we could not rule out the possibility that Germany was going to 'borrow' these from Persia in order to reinforce the Iraqis. Such a move, since we had no armour at all, would have still further diminished our chances of success. It was clear that the Persian situation would have to be dealt with in a forcible manner. As a result of my researches at Habbaniya I was asked to prepare a paper for General George Clark, who was in command of the wider operations on this front.

George Clark was a complete contrast to Joe Kingstone. Joe shared all hardships with the troops and, when water was running low, had kicked Lance-Corporal 'Bloody' Stammers and his bucket of water about fifty yards when he found that gentleman shaving on the way from Rutbah. Joe's stubbly chin and enormous physique had justified such liberties with Lance-Corporal 'Bloody' Stammers's person. One could not imagine George Clark in the same circumstances. A cool brain this, under a rather bald head. It was wise for a General to remain cool in such heat, but his habits did not endear him to the junior officers; and the troops did not know him by sight. So, as soon as Kingcol had crossed the desert, General Clark arrived by air, keeping very cool and went into the most comfortable billets obtainable. These were in Air House, a luxurious white villa, where electric fans stirred the air lazily and the footfalls of booted warriors were deadened upon soft Persian carpets. Joe took me on one occasion into this holy of holies. We encountered Glubb outside, and I was glad to feel that he was in the offing. I sat in a library of a kind that I had not seen since leaving England, while Joe joined the Major-General at his breakfast off a polished mahogany table in the dining-room.

In the centre of all his luxury, like a fly preserved in amber, was Peter Herbert. The amber was still viscous and he sometimes emerged to buzz about, as someone described him, 'like a blue-arsed fly in a tripe shop'. Now he showed me how to get coffee in porcelain cups.

While I was there a message arrived asking me to go down to the aerodrome to meet an aeroplane. I was expecting a Divisional Staff Officer, but the man who emerged from the Bombay Troop Carrier was a lanky young man in the uniform of the United States Army. I was surprised to see another man with a camera pose this youth in the doorway of the aircraft and called out to the photographer that such things were not allowed in the vicinity of the aerodrome. The photographer smiled pityingly and introduced me to 'Captain James Roosevelt'. He was a very charming representative of the President — and I was glad that he had come to Habbaniya.

Another person of importance had arrived soon after us: Air Vice-Marshal John d'Albiac. He had commanded the Air Force in Greece. I was in the R.A.F. Signals Office when he made his first rounds, wearing the broad light blue stripe on the shoulder tabs of his khaki shirt which betokened some personage. He shook hands with all the Air Force officers in the room, but being a mere soldier I was left out of this fraternisation. The Air Force expected great things of Johnny d'Albiac, and we came to rely on him implicitly. "Help yourselves," he told us, "and come back for a second helping."

He was the only Air Force Brass Hat in the Middle East at that time who believed that the role of the Air Force was to assist the Army. All the others were busy fighting their own wars, and were surprised when the British armies, far below them on the ground, melted into retreat. d'Albiac proved for the first time that 100 per cent co-operation was possible

He summoned a conference at which our final plans for the advance on Baghdad were hammered out. He sat at his desk, while George Clark sat, with his legs dangling, on a table across the room. Joe Kingstone and I (with our maps) sat on the floor, behind d'Albiac, with our backs to the wall, while all around the room, sitting on the tables, chairs and floor, crowded the pilots who were to help us. d'Albiac was a short man with a ruddy little button of a face, good natured. He explained the position:

"The Iraqis are all right up to a point, but there comes that moment when they just haven't got the something that is necessary, and they begin to waver. It is at that moment we want to hit them. We have been carrying out some experiments in the workshops here and have fitted organ fluting to the fins of the bombs to make a frightful noise as they come down." (We were beginning to learn the childishness of war from the Germans at last.)

One of his officers explained at this point that they only made a noise if dropped from at least 8,000 feet, which meant carrying them in the Blenheims. There were all sorts of detailed problems for co-operation to be worked out — and all were arranged at this one conference. d'Albiac proposed that the ground troops in Kingcol should all wear white patches on their backs. Neither Joe nor I could see any objection to this and agreed, since it would enable our own aircraft to identify us easily. When an aircraft wanted to drop a message it would fly low first, and then wait for a white sheet to be spread out on the ground by the signal truck so as to indicate where the message should be dropped. (I had a good deal of difficulty in finding a spare sheet in Habbaniya for the purpose.)

It was agreed, after a good deal of discussion, that a main force of bombers should be held in readiness, loaded up with the screaming bombs and called for only if we were in a hole ourselves or were in a position to administer a final *coup de grâce* to our enemy. If this force were required we would use the code word 'Noisy'. For ordinary support two flights of three aircraft were to be standing by, since our advance against Baghdad was to be two-headed. One column, under Andrew Ferguson, and with all Glubb's Desert Patrol, was to be ferried across the Euphrates and reach Baghdad from the north after a wide detour around the Aqqa Quf Floods, while the remainder of the column (750 men), under Joe Kingstone, was to advance direct upon Baghdad down the road from Falluja. Thus both columns might require air support at the same moment. Either could, therefore, call for a 'normal'. The next point was to synchronise the system of map references. The pilots, who covered great distances, all carried maps to the scale of 1 over 1,000,000 and so agreed to use this exclusively ourselves.

In the meantime Squadron Leader Dudgeon had photographed the road all the way from Kahn Nuqta where the tarmac began and where the nearest enemy positions appeared to be. Dudgeon was himself sitting on a table near the door and volunteered the brilliant suggestion that this master photograph chart (now on a strip of cardboard about ten feet long) should be gridded into simple squares, rephotographed and made up into books which all who needed could have. This was agreed to, and Dudgeon worked feverishly all afternoon on the gridding of the chart into large squares A.B.C.D., etc., which in turn were broken up into smaller squares from 1 to 10. The Air Force pilots, who were not used to decimal map references, agreed that we should identify, a place on the photograph by counting sideways first to the right, then upwards, so that a simple map reference for Kahn Nuqta Fort would be A 57, and so on.

This conference actually took place the day before our advance, and

I commend its method as a model for all operations in which more than one service is to be engaged.

In the meantime the Germans had begun to pay us attention at Habbaniya. When I was in an office writing a report on Persia, machine-gun bullets from a raiding Messerschmitt 110 were slapping up against the walls outside in fine style. There is no doubt that the Battle of Britain was an admirable training for air attack, but (as the result proved) deluded one into a false sense of security, for there is in reality nothing similar between haphazard high-level bombing of wide areas and the highly concentrated murderous attacks on a small target of aeroplanes bent on that task. d'Albiac had seen plenty of the latter in Greece and when an air-raid siren sounded while he was showing Joe and me round the aircraft hangars and repair shop (gutted in a previous raid) I scarcely had time to polish my sun glasses before a blur of pale blue and scarlet carried the Air Marshal and my Brigadier into a slit trench. I was to learn wisdom later.

Two Air Force Intelligence Officers were with me at our camp by the lake on another evening when we saw high up against the pale blue of the evening sky, three light green Heinkel bombers flying over, the black cross clearly distinguishable through our binoculars. The bombers went on to the cantonment while we went on down to the lake to bathe. We heard the savage crump of bombs the other side of the plateau, as they dropped their load on the hangars. We saw the planes fly on, growing smaller, while the angry Hurricane kept on duty for the purpose took off and rushed snarling after them. We were standing up to our waists in water, in the slanting sunlight, watching the spectacle. No sooner had the bombers disappeared in the direction of Mosul, with the Hurricane after them, than four Messerschmitt fighters roared past us out of the sun, to send their bullets and cannon shot tearing into the buildings of the cantonment and were off into the distance before we could open our mouths in astonishment. I had never gathered so great an impression of speed as when those four silhouettes ripped past us in a power dive over Lake Habbaniya.

I never could understand why these Messerschmitts did not make a determined attack on our camp. The vehicles were not well concealed, although they were hidden in the rocky nullahs wherever possible. One morning when Fish and I were sitting late over breakfast, under the rush awning where we fed, a nasty mustard yellow Messerschmitt came and looked right into the marmalade pot after spraying the camp, but we were sitting between high banks of sandstone and he could not get a run at us. More of this sort of investigation would, however, have been a nuisance.

A 15 cwt. truck sought me out one day with a pair of beautiful new Vickers machine-guns and thousands of rounds of ammunition. They had been found beside the dead body of an Iraqi soldier on the plateau. The driver told me that he had not wished to tarry in the vicinity of the corpse, but brought me the man's pith helmet. There was a jagged hole in the side of it. I was glad to have the helmet, with its neck flap of khaki cloth, as Andrew Ferguson was always asking me how our troops would be able to distinguish the enemy at a distance. So I had the punctured helmet passed round all the units of Kingcol for inspection. As a trained machine-gunner I was tempted to keep the two Vickers for headquarters' protection, but dutifully sent them on to Ordnance in Habbaniya, who built them up into a surprise barrage with half a dozen other machine-guns which received the next party of Messerschmitts with a lion-like roar.

In the meantime work was going on to close the gap in the Causeway called Hammond's Bund. Joe asked me to accompany him soon after we arrived to see the bund, and I set a compass course across the plateau which soon brought us to the spurs on the eastern side, sloping down to the floods. There, a mile away, was the long black line of the bund, with the broken gap half-way across the floods clearly discernible. We drove down to the road which ran southwards to it from the cantonment, and encountered a worried Engineer officer. "It will take at least forty-eight hours to fill the gap," he said; and when Joe got back to camp he turned the lumpers into navvies and they worked day and night shovelling earth into the gap.

But the more it narrowed, the deeper the flood channel cut and it became apparent, after all the labour, that some other way of crossing the gap would have to be devised. Some black-faced Madrassi Sappers paddled two large iron barges from the cantonment down the river to the beginning of the floods; then steered them, swimming through the channel, to Hammond's Bund, where they were lashed together and topped with boards to make a raft. This was then to be hauled to and fro by the sappers on a hawser. Every day at dawn a Messerschmitt swept along the bund to see what progress we were making with filling the gap. The Messerschmitt would machine-gun the bund as it went along; so it was advisable to be off at these times. But the pilot noticed only the gap, and did not observe that moored to one end of it was the new pontoon ferry. Thus the moment of our advance, when it came, took the enemy by surprise.

The Iraqis, however, were not idle; and in the hour before daylight one morning launched a powerful attack, of which our air reconnaissance had given us no warning, upon Falluja. They had some small tanks and broke into the town where fierce fighting followed, especially with the Assyrian Levies. The battle was not going at all well, and an urgent message arrived from George Clark at four in the morning ordering Joe to go down to Falluja himself and take command of the battle. This was fun for Joe, who seized the opportunity of putting the three good miles of flood water between himself and his staff, and fought the battle as a battalion commander. He only reached the scene just in time; for the Iraqis were employing tactics for taking Falluja, which we learnt later, had been taught by them by General Waterhouse and the British Military Mission, during manoeuvres a year before.

No news came to Brigade Headquarters until the afternoon, when Ian Spence was sent for to bring up a haversack ration and the Brigadier's razor. So I wrote in the War Diary: 'A razor being of more value than an Intelligence Officer, and a haversack ration of more worth than a Brigade Major and a Staff Captain, these (the razor and the ration) were sent for at three o'clock in the afternoon.' ("Bowler hat for Somerset," was Eric Gooch's comment.) Intelligence Officers appear to have been at a discount in this operation, for David Summers, the Household Cavalry I.O., thinking dutifully to visit the single Squadron of the Regiment up at Falluja, got ferried over the bund and tramped the nine miles of winding road through the marshes on foot to Falluja in great heat. On arrival he reported hopefully to Joe, and offered his services. Joe told him unkindly that there was no room (or food) for Intelligence Officers in Falluja, so he had to walk nine miles back again.

The Brigadier returned next day, and slept for several hours. When he awoke we learned some of the story which saved Falluja for us and won himself the immediate award of a bar to his D.S.O.

On arrival at Falluja by launch Joe found that the only British Forces there were the K.O.R.R. and the Assyrian Levies. It was not until the afternoon that he sent for the Essex Companies and C Squadron of the Household Cavalry (who crossed the floods in small boats and then humped all their equipment, including anti-tank rifles, hotchkiss guns and ammunition, for the remaining seven miles on foot). The 237 Battery of 25-pounders were on our side of the plateau, firing across the floods at the enemy approaching Falluja. The situation in the town itself was impossible because our troops were being sniped at from the windows. So Joe summoned the head men of the town and gave them half an hour to get the entire population inside the mosque, after which any civilian seen outside it would be shot.

This had an electrifying effect on the townsfolk and the mosque filled quicker than it had ever done in response to the sing-song call of the muezzin on its tower. Eventually the Iraqis were beaten back, the Assyrians tearing open the tanks with their bare hands, apparently — and Joe returned to resume his duties at Brigade H.Q. The Iraqis when retreating turned from khaki into white under your very eyes — each soldier discarding his martial covering in order to be mistaken for a civilian.

The vehicles in the column were getting desperately short of cooking oil, and, before leaving, I decided to take a foraging party to Mujara, where Brooks said that the bedouin had left unlooted a 10,000 gallon tank of diesel oil used in peacetime for his enormous tractors, which were employed in the construction of the Haifa-Baghdad Road. I set off in my car with a 15-cwt. truck following, loaded with empty petrol cans. We had not gone ten miles before we sighted a Household Cavalry patrol truck which came racing across the sand to have a sniff at us. Further south we saw an abandoned tractor away to our left, and thinking that its tank might be full of oil, we drove over to it. The machine was one of the huge orange coloured monsters of the kind referred to. But its tank was empty and we drove on our way to Mujara.

We found a despondent captain of the K.O.R.R. encamped there and asked him the way to Brooks's engineering shops. We drove over the trestle bridge (still unbombed), across which all our supplies now came in regular convoys from H.4 and Rutbah where the Wiltshire Yeomanry and Warwickshire Yeomanry had been placed to guard our line of communications.

Mujara consisted only of a few mud huts, all now deserted, until we came to one or two small bungalows, in one of which, presumably, Brooks had lived, and finally to the iron repair shops. We wandered about the desolate sheds with their broken machinery. Down an embankment were parked scores of the enormous orange tractors, and in the middle of the yard was the 10,000 gallon tank, standing on brick pillars, of which Brooks had spoken. There was no top to the tap, and no visible hose to fit on to it. The driver of the truck applied a pair of pliers and instantly we were deluged in warm diesel oil. It was some time in the confusion before we could turn the tap off again. The sand was soaked in oil. So now, dripping, cursing and glutinous, we approached the orifice more cautiously, and, starting a trickle, began to fill the empty cans.

The trouble with these cans was that a hole was normally punched in a corner when the petrol was required, and the can discarded for someone else to collect. (The deserts of the Middle East were bright with their glinting in the distance.) So now we corked them up as best we could with cotton waste. We had nearly filled twenty four-gallon cans when a blue saloon car drove up and Brooks himself got out. He was taking a last look around and derived a melancholy satisfaction from the reflection that some of his oil would at least keep the cooking fires of the British Army alight instead of being pilfered by the bedouin or emptied out on the desert sand.

Brooks went about the workshops while we completed our work, but he came out soon to tell us that he had found two 50-gallon drums of paraffin untouched in one of the sheds. This was better far than diesel oil and would have saved us all the mess. So we trundled them up planks on to the back of the lorry. It seemed a pity not to take the cans of oil which we had filled, so we piled these up as well, and set off home. The oil splashed through the cotton stoppings and saturated the haversacks of the men in the truck as we discovered at the end of our journey. So their rations tasted of diesel oil ever afterwards. Our return to a camp, which had no fuel left for cooking, with 180 gallons of such fuel was regarded as a miracle. It was distributed to all the units of Kingcol and rain itself upon the gentle place beneath could not have been more welcome. We found that the diesel oil was quite as serviceable in Primus stoves as paraffin, although it clogged up the jet quicker.

As I look back on our stay by the lake it seems to have lasted for months. Glubb appeared surprisingly at our office truck in a blue and red side-cap. The Brigadier's attitude towards this man of military experience without the military mind had by now changed and he was hailed affectionately "Hallo, Pasha. Come in, Pasha." At one time it was proposed that Kingcol should make a reconnaissance in force to Musayib, and, crossing the Tigris there, come up on Baghdad from the south. Reconnaissances were made as far as the outskirts of Kerbala, but neither Glubb nor I were in favour of fighting in the third holiest City of Iraq and the project was abandoned. Glubb was quick to sense under-currents and his eyebrow went up when Peter, referring to my exploration of the Euphrates bank said, "Perhaps we shall have another 'personal reconnaissance'."

While the Musayib plan was in the air Charles Wood, of the Blues, with an ex-Nairn driver, who went by the attractive name of Long Jack, did go as far as the village of Razaza to see what sort of bridge would have to be put across the dyke there by the Engineers. They were told not to get too close, and at their approach enemy vehicles began to stir, so, after a hurried survey of the dyke, they withdrew. On another occasion Gerard Leigh took a patrol round Lake Habbaniya to the neighbourhood of our original laager west of Ramadi. They had an armoured car with them which got stuck in the sand and eventually fell into Iraqi hands. The patrol was only memorable in that it was attacked by an R.A.F. Gladiator from Habbaniya (where information about the patrol was available), and one Household Cavalryman was shot through the neck and died. After this the patrol wisely opened fire on the Gladiator and it made off. I mention this because it is an incident such as occurs far too often, of lack of co-ordination between air and ground troops. If this could happen under conditions of such ideal co-operation as prevailed at Habbaniya, it is not difficult to imagine the unnecessary tragedies which often occur in other parts.

The way for our advance on Baghdad was now open. Falluja was still in our hands, and the Heath Robinson device for hauling the pontoon across the gap in Hammond's Bund was now completed. Peter Grant-Lawson calculated that one vehicle could cross by the ferry every ten minutes, and the first vehicles to go were to be the 25-pounders in the Southern Column. The rest of this column was to include one Squadron of the Household Cavalry, the two companies of the Essex Regiment, the independent anti-tank troop, three R.A.F. armoured cars and the Field Ambulance Section. The Northern Column was to include most of the Household Cavalry, four 25-pounders, Glubb's Desert Patrol, and the rest of the R.A.F. armoured cars. This column disappeared northwards over the Euphrates during the night, and we were to cross the bund and concentrate inside Falluja for the direct advance on Baghdad.

CHAPTER 21

I was given the unenviable task of getting the column across Hammond's Bund. I received orders to go down to the bund at six o'clock and contact the Colonel in charge of the Engineers, who had been working on the bund.

The red sandstone plateau descended abruptly to the floods, and Hammond's Bund started as an earthy embankment on the land growing gradually steeper as the water lapped its sides, and coming to an end about a hundred yards out. The flood waters swirled steadily past the tops of tall reeds showing here and there in the current. The course of the flood channel from the Euphrates three miles to the north was fringed by thicker growths of reed showing above the water as it grew shallower. The gap itself was not more than seventy-five yards wide and the long line of the bund disappeared into the distance on the further side.

Five men from the Household Cavalry under a corporal had been told to report to me with torches so that I could post them at the critical places along the bund where they should direct the column as it passed along. They were there, but only the corporal had a torch. I had brought two myself, but must now borrow others. On occasions like this the casualness of my own regiment, in which we usually took such a pride, appeared to me in a somewhat different light. I had orders from General Clark's headquarters to report to Colonel Panet of the Royal Engineers.

I found Colonel Panet where the first part of the bund ended. He was a short man, with greying hair and a humorous kind face. He was watching the final preparation of the ferry, where the sappers were laying a pair of heavy ten-foot iron ramps from the end of the bund on to the edge of the pontoon, in order to provide a pair of movable tracks for the vehicles to be run on to the ferry. A similar pair of steel ramps would be lifted on to the ferry from the bund when it reached the further side. I tested the weight of these ramps and was horrified. Not less than six men would be required to lift each, which meant relays of twelve men at work on the ramps each side of the flood gap; for they would have to be lifted

243

on for each vehicle and off again when the ferry was pulled away. Further gangs of twelve native sappers were already waiting on each side of the gap to pull the hawser on which the ferry was drawn. Thirty Household Cavalrymen under an officer were due to report to me for work on the operation and it was clear that nearly all would be required for the ramps.

"You will want one policeman to guide the traffic where the vehicles get on to the bund and send them up to the ferry. Another here," said Colonel Panet. "Let us go across now and walk up the bund so that I can show you the weak spots."

We stepped down into a small dinghy and were pulled across by another thin wire hawser. As soon as we left the embankment the boat was swung violently downstream by the force of the current, and was pulled across in a wide loop. I dipped my hand up to the wrist in the cooling water. We climbed out on the further side and began walking along the narrow bund. On both sides the flooded marshes stretched for miles, and in the hot evening air, wavering in a continuous band above the embankment on the level of our heads, were clouds of gnats. They were so thick that we could almost tear through the band with our hands. We wiped them off our faces.

"I was in Hong Kong recently," said Colonel Panet, "and I think there must have been a brother of yours there — a Lt.-Commander de Chair, who was in command of a destroyer." It was reassuring to meet on this narrow strip of earth, which was to carry our column forward to Baghdad, a man who had been an intimate friend of my own brother in another outpost of the war (soon to fall in diabolical circumstances). So we talked easily, Colonel Panet and I, like old friends. He pointed now and again to some part of the bund where it had begun to sag, and the level of the road had tipped sideways.

"If any vehicle slips half-way down the bank and cannot get back easily, you will have to push it in — that's all. Otherwise it will block the whole stream of traffic." He talked on thus for nearly a mile. "We have laid wire mesh in the worst places," he explained, and pointed ahead to where some sappers were pegging down the recalcitrant wire which showed a reluctance to being uncurled and snapped up into their faces. "That is the last bit."

We had come to a break in the embankment and in front of us was the abutment of a new concrete culvert still under construction. "The road leaves the bund here," he explained, "and winds away through the marshes to Falluja — over there where you can just see the palm trees in the distance. You will want another man here to guide the traffic off the bund."

We turned back and retraced our steps. The sun was low in the sky straight ahead of us, and turned all the floods into beaten silver. We were in no hurry; the head of the column was not due to reach the bund until dusk, since the whole operation must be carried out in darkness, and I had orders to send away any vehicles not across by first light at 4 a.m. They would have to disperse into the desert. Panet had worked hard at the ferry, arriving late in the history of Hammond's Bund and realising the futility of trying to bridge the gap with shovelfuls of earth. Now his work was finished. His contraption would either work or it would not: and upon its working depended our advance. A few miles to the north a similar contrivance was to ferry the other column on to the left bank of the Euphrates whence they would start the long detour which would take them round the floods and bring them down on Baghdad by way of Holy Kadhimain. Panet and I recrossed the flood gap in the little boat. On the western approach we shook hands and bade each other goodbye.

I had by now set about disposing of my corporal and five men: the corporal with his torch at the beginning of the bund, another trooper with a torch at the ferry. The other four I took across the flood with me and stationed two and two in order to relieve each other where Panet had suggested. At one of these places the dip was so severe that in the darkness the road would appear to end altogether, and only a bold driver would persevere without some encouragement. After leaving the bund the drivers must rely upon their own inspiration to follow the track to Falluja in the dark. One of my men was to go down with each vehicle to the beginning of the road through the marshes.

I went back again to the ferry and, crossing it, went over to my own car which was dispersed on the hard sand a hundred yards from the approach of the bund. Grose was there with a meal which he had been preparing on my Primus stove and I ate it gladly enough, knowing that I had a long, tiring night ahead of me. He had also laid out my safari bed by the car, hopefully, so that I would have something to lie down on if the opportunity offered, or at worst when the first stage of the proceedings ceased at four o'clock.

While I was waiting for the column to arrive I walked down to the ferry to make sure that all was in readiness and was surprised to find General Clark standing there in shorts and an open-neck shirt carrying the badges of his Major-General's rank. He was gazing across the flood waters which had so far held up the whole plan of his advance. He was a quiet little man who recoiled when spoken to, but I asked him what he thought of our prospects. The enemy seemed to be very numerous on paper (and the nibs in Habbaniya were betting five to two against our chances). His dark little eyes narrowed as he looked towards the further embankment. "They don't like these 25-pounders," he replied softly. "After twenty-four hours shelling from them, the Iraqis are inclined to retire. I think we shall be all right." I left the silent, bald little General to his meditations by the swirling waters which divided him from his objective. I did not see him depart and I doubt whether anyone else working on the bund realised who the aloof little figure standing there had been.

It was growing dark quickly and I could see the side lights of the approaching column creeping down the edge of the floods from the direction of Habbaniya. I turned Grose and Williamson into traffic policemen for the night also, at the point near my car where the head of the column would have to be stopped and the vehicles fed up to the embankment at a torch signal from the corporal. The 25-pounders, followed by the ammunition limbers were the first to trundle up in the half light. I went with the leading dragon to see what happened. The corporal on the embankment duly directed the driver up the bund, but gave him no indication of what to expect. On arrival at the pontoon I discussed with the young moustachioed engineer lieutenant operating the ferry itself how best to get the 25-pounder on to it. It became apparent that only the dragon would fit on the raft and that the gun would have to follow as a second load. This doubled some of Peter's 'vehicles' to start with, and, once the dragon had gone over, what motive power was to propel the gun itself or ammunition limber up the two steel ramps on to the pontoon when it returned? There was nothing for it but to manhandle the guns and limbers. Fortunately John Wills had arrived with thirty stalwart lumpers.

We arranged that twelve of them should place the ramps at this end, cross over on the ferry with it, resting on the way, repeat the process the other side and return with the empty ferry. It required twenty men to lift the 25-pounder bodily off the bund on to the pontoon. The lumpers heaved and strained to place the first pair of steel ramps and, holding our breaths at the first experiment, we signalled to the dragon to come up slowly. It ran squarely up the ramps and plumped on to the thick planks. The men drew back the ramps and crowded on to the raft, sitting with their legs dangling over the empty steel barges above which it was erected. The first vehicle was on its way and I went over with it to see what happened at the other end. The ramps were similarly placed there and the dragon ran safely down on to the bund.

I returned on the empty pontoon with the twelve men. They were already sweating and cursing, and it was obvious that a separate gang would be needed on each side of the flood if this pressure was to be kept up. We then began on the gun itself. It was a cruel job lifting it in the dark over the yawning gap which separated the edge of the raft from the end of the earth embankment, while twenty men, almost invisible to each other, crowded for a hold; but it was done with a will and sent over. By the time the raft had returned for the next gun nearly an hour had elapsed, and it did, in fact, take three and a half hours, with the men tiring towards the end, to get the guns across. So much for the ten minutes allowed for each 'vehicle'.

I decided to continue my journey with the first gun, offering no guidance to the driver, in order to see what happened. It was now quite dark and I sat in a little boat down by the rushes on the eastern bank waiting until the gun was limbered up, and then climbed into the dragon. I stood up on the seat beside the driver with my head and shoulders through the open roof of it, and watched the pale gleam of the roadway ahead where the side lamps illuminated it. We came to the worst dip and the driver stopped and looked questioningly up at me, but I gave him no encouragement and he plunged downwards. As he did so the dim glare of his sidelights picked up the criss-cross glint of the wire netting in the hollow. The sentries were on the further side of the dip and their frantic efforts by winking of torch to encourage the oncoming vehicles were sufficient to bring any driver to a dead halt in a panic. So I sent the men back to the near side of the dip with a sharp request that they should use their intelligence. We arrived safely at the end of the bund where we were duly directed on to the marsh road. Here I told the sentries that the vehicles were to be halted until six had arrived and then go on in small convoys to avoid mishap.

Fortunately Ian Spence arrived at this juncture in his staff car, having been sent on to Falluja by the Brigadier to make preparations for our arrival, and he arranged to convoy the vehicles as they assembled at the beginning of the marsh road and lead them into Falluja. This was a load off my mind. I asked him how the arrangements at the bund had worked out when he crossed, and he said 'perfectly'. With his help now on the Falluja road, the arrangements ran on smoothly during the night. Shortly before dawn Ian Henderson of the Blues, who had brought up the supply vehicles of C Squadron (which had gone over to Falluja for the battle on foot and remained there ever since), sought me out. It was quite evident that none of his lorries could be got over before daylight, so he took them away on to the plateau. We were just getting the last of the Gunners' supply vehicles over. When daylight came the place was magically deserted. If the marauding Messerschmitt arrived he would find a few men loitering round the end of the bund as if work were starting up for the day. But it did not visit us this morning, which was just as well, for I lay down under my bright white mosquito net near the end of the bund and the target for a fighter would have been irresistible.

It was quite clear that the programme for the crossing of Hammond's Bund would have to be put forward an extra night and I wondered, when I returned wearily to our camp beside the lake, if I had been in any way to blame for the delay. But a personal request was put through to me on the field telephone from General Clark's headquarters to ask whether I could possibly undertake the strain of supervising the crossing on the second night as well (which was flattering) and I agreed.

Peter was upset that the request had not been passed through the usual channels, but I was only too glad to feel that I was being useful for once. The Brigadier was annoyed for a different reason — he did not want his Intelligence Officer tired out before the advance began; but when he saw that I was willing he raised no objection. The truth of the matter was that the romance of Hammond's Bund had appealed to my imagination — carrying as it did upon so slender a thread of wire, all our hopes and ambitions. I knew instinctively that the crossing of Hammond's Bund was the cardinal phase of the campaign, and I was honoured to be given sole control of the operation. I was happy moreover to be alone with my thoughts during the long walks on the bund, with the marsh waters whispering in the reeds — to be away two nights from the trivial, if pleasant, jocularities of the Headquarters' Mess. So I repeated the performance on the second night, when we were able to improve on the arrangements in view of our experience; and the stream of dark silhouettes passed silently over the flood, crept along the bund, dipped to the marsh road and wound their stealthy way into Falluja, all unknown to the enemy.

John Shaw brought the Household Cavalry working party, and I have a recollection of his panting past me on foot in the dark hissing like a locomotive giving off steam.

Once again the Messerschmitt omitted his morning call and once again I slept undisturbed for three hours at the end of the bund after dawn. After the first night's watch a bed and a bath had been provided for me in the afternoon by a friend of Squadron Leader Cassano in one of the operational officers' quarters at Habbaniya. It was the last caress of civilisation which I was to feel for some time, and I was grateful to the unseen officer for it.

All next day was spent in feverish preparation and included the conference I have already described at which our arrangements with the Air Force were finalised. While the photographs of the road from Kahn Nuqta to Baghdad were being made up into book form, I was studying, through an arrangement of prismatic binoculars, with a young Air Force expert just arrived, the evidence in Dudgeon's pictures of Iraqi positions along the line of our advance. There were scores of one-man air-raid shelters on either side of Kahn Nuqta, which indicated a battalion in position, and where the road bridged the Abu Guraib Canal, a network of key-pattern trenches revealed a carefully prepared second line of defence.

The arrangements for crossing the bund were now working smoothly, and as I was myself going ahead to Falluja with the Brigade Fighting Group, John Hampton, the lugubrious young Transport Officer, took over the policing of the traffic for the third and last night. I went across and Dick Schuster was close behind me. He was always the best of company, his sunny spirits seemingly inextinguishable. His father was in the House of Commons which gave us a side footing together during the frequent pauses in the campaign. He was a dark, good-looking young man with a silky moustache. His devotion to his mother (to whom he wrote often) was one of his most endearing characteristics. We chatted idly on the ferry, while our cars went over without us. He was taking Peter's utility van, while Peter accompanied the Brigadier downstream to Falluja in the luxury of a launch.

We found Ian Spence at the end of the bund, a machine of quiet efficiency as usual, belied by his cherubic countenance; and he guided us along the winding track until the feathery outlines of palm fronds against the starlit sky indicated the concealed positions of the 25-pounders in the Palm Grove, and soon we were crossing the imposing iron bridge of Falluja itself. He led us along the wrecked main street of the town, into a side alley and thence to a walled enclosure. Here the vehicles of the Brigade H.Q. fighting group were soon parked, and we crossed a muddy space on foot to reach a low building by the river, near the bridge. We rounded the corner of the veranda and saw, through the wire mosquito netting of the doors, the lamplit scene of the Brigadier and Peter eating a frugal meal. Our valises were soon unstrapped and placed along the veranda. I lay there in the grey half-light where a pale reflection of the night sky in the broad Euphrates at our feet provided a ghostly glimmer. Tomorrow I was going into action for the first time and a warm feeling of anticipation lulled me to sleep.

CHAPTER 22

We were awakened at three and breakfasted at half-past — very punctually, after Joe's comments on the dilatoriness of the Mess wagon (which was going to be left behind in security when we advanced). By four o'clock the vehicles were pulling out of the yard and assembling on a wide open space at the eastern end of the town, where a gap in the barbed wire entanglements showed the way for our advance. In daylight, the damage to the town, after consistent shelling by both sides, was an impressive sight and recalled pictures from youthful memory of the battered towns of Flanders in the Great War. Joe stood by the gap in the wire, his feet in their brown suede desert boots with crêpe-rubber soles, planted wide on the hard ground of the desert. He wore his red-banded cap at this hour of the day, and a greatcoat, for it was still early enough to be chilly. He stood there, reviewing his troops as they poured through the gap in the wire and fanned out into the desert beyond, where the charred wreck of one of our Blenheims provided a dark reminder of the hazards of war. The armoured cars went through first, then C Squadron of the Household Cavalry, followed by the Essex Companies. Then came the Brigade Fighting Group, and I saluted to Joe as my car passed through the wire, Grose's well-tended engine purring happily.

I began to wonder, as the desert sand flashed by under my wheels, whether I could at last be counted a real soldier. I never seemed to get to grips with the enemy. Perhaps I was a poet and saw all, like an Arab through half-closed eyes. Every mirage was for me a citadel to be stormed; every passing camel a symbol of romance. I had written many verses since leaving England and I now scribbled, for no particular reason, in the front of my green covered Intelligence notebook —

'If England die, my verses die,
For everything they say will lie.'

We drove on, discarding our greatcoats in the growing heat. It was

250

only twenty-five miles to Kahn Nuqta where the enemy were known to be and at this pace we would very soon surprise them. There was no road yet, but a maze of tracks following a line of telegraph posts. We were dispersed over a broad front. Presently the vehicles ahead halted; and Peter drove alongside, asking me to take a message back to the rear of the column. I did this and, in returning, overshot the Brigade Headquarters. It was not until I topped a rise and came up with two men of the Essex Regiment lying beside a Bren-gun that I realised I had gone too far. (Peter thought I was trying to be funny.) Joe was already growing impatient and, boarding a passing armoured car of Cassano's, went ahead. I have no doubt that he beat on the gates of the fort at Kahn Nuqta and demanded why they had not already surrendered. The Household Cavalry were now dismounted from their trucks and working round to the north of the fort, which Joe considered a protracted operation. Evidently it achieved the desired result, however, for an Iraqi officer was brought back.

We were now able to move on again. We drove down a slight slope to the fort, a square cream-washed plaster building, which was normally a Police Post. A culvert in the road over a dyke had been blown, but Cheeky Boy had already put two of the ubiquitous 10-ft. reel ramps over it. Our troopers were darting about among the network of ditches with bayonets on their rifles, stirring up Iraqi soldiers who quickly came out to surrender. Already about fifty were inside the courtyard of the Fort, where a single N.C.O. remained on guard over them. I learnt that the enemy had dug wide trenches at intervals along the road before breaking the irrigation dykes and flooding it. The floods apparently submerged the road for a mile, after a short distance. Acting upon this information Cheeky Boy was set to work with his 10-ft. ramps to bridge the trenches under water. The Iraqis had relied upon these hidden obstacles impeding our advance completely and they might well have done so if our vehicles had begun plunging into them, not knowing what to expect.

Meanwhile Brigade Headquarters was moved up the road to a pleasant set of white buildings set about with flowering oleander trees and the rudiments of a garden. It had evidently been the headquarters of the recently ejected Iraqi battalion, and in one room I found a camp bed upon which was laid a brand new pair of Iraqi shorts. These I donned hurriedly as my own had split across the stern in the stress of the morning's activities. More exciting than the shorts was a telephone switchboard in the room and I suggested to Reading that we might try our luck at it. He took the receiver while I lifted all the switches and twirled the handle. Reading almost dropped the receiver in his excitement as an agitated voice at the other end called in Iraqi "Nam-Nam. I've been trying to raise you for two hours. What is the matter?" Reading quickly repeated this, with his hand over the mouthpiece, and I said, "Tell them that we are surrounded by the British; that the British have got tanks, and that the tanks are already across the floods."

Reading spoke to the distant operator in an admirably excited voice, laying horrified stress on the word Bababa — tanks. Consternation followed at the other end, the operator evidently rushing away with his news. I thought it inadvisable to try any more deception, as the enemy might grow suspicious, but I kept Reading on the line to listen in, never dreaming what a rich harvest we were going to reap. I went in to Joe next door where he, Ian, Dick and Peter were having some food, and rummaging about the place. The Brigadier was delighted at my good fortune and for the rest of the morning I kept darting in and out with information, for soon Reading began to pick up snatches of conversation. Evidently the building was normally an irrigation station and was connected by circuit to the telephone system of the whole area.

We next intercepted the distracted voice of the battalion commander whom we had displaced, telling the headquarters of the 3rd Division (just what we wanted to know) that he had 'escaped from Kahn Nuqta with twelve men', and was hiding at a place called, Reading thought, Jisr Milh (the Bridge of Salt). I began sending long signals back to Division at Habbaniya about all this — as it was an opportunity never likely to recur. "Interpreter on telephone to Baghdad spreading alarm and despondency. British with tanks already crossing the floods, etc. Iraqi Battalion Commander with twelve men escaped to Jisr Milh." The Air Force searched their maps for this place and could not find it. No wonder. For a subsequent conversation revealed that it was Qasr Milh (the House of Salt) which might be anywhere.

It was quite obvious that the Iraqis did not know their telephone line was connected to the switchboard at Kahn Nuqta and they babbled on in greater and greater alarm. A patrol was ordered out by the headquarters of the 3rd Division to report on the presence of British tanks, and reported in a great state of agitation later in the morning (we could scarcely believe it) that the British had at least fifty tanks, of which fifteen were already across the floods. A despairing artillery commander, who was indeed shelling us wildly, cried out over the telephone that he was "Engaging a formation of five British tanks" (which could only be Cassano's three armoured cars with their high conning towers, and two tenders). At this, the stern voice of headquarters urged him to stand firm. "For the sake of God (very strong language in Arabic) stand firm." To which the agonised commander replied, "But cannot you hear the firing?" and indeed one of our twenty-five pounders was sending a steady stream of shells at respectable intervals over our heads. So Joe, now suitably impressed by this windfall, dictated a signal himself: 'Intercepted telephone message suggests considerable confusion in Iraq forces. Advance H.Q. 3rd Div. believed Experimental Farm. "Dog." Suggest this suitable for "normal".' Now the ejected battalion commander was on the wire again from the House of Salt asking for reinforcements to 'stablise the retreat' (which was interesting).

"I don't mind about Kahn Nuqta," he said. "What about Baghdad if the British have got tanks?" (He had evidently heard about this too.) "Don't you worry your head about Baghdad," said headquarters, "we have dug a ditch round Baghdad which will stop any tank." (This was even more interesting, especially as we had not even got any tanks!) H.Q. 3rd Division ordered two companies to be detached from the 1st Battalion at Kadhimain and join the ejected battalion commander at Qasr Milh. This they could do, by skirting the floods, for they were working on interior lines.

I sent a signal about this back to Habbaniya also and was amused later when Reading intercepted a conversation between Iraqi 3rd Division H.Q. and the 3rd Battalion at Kadhimain asking what happened about the two companies of the 1st Battalion ordered to join the Colonel at Qasr Milh. "They started out all right," was the reply, "but at the approach of British aircraft they dispersed to bedouin tents" — (villages).

It was not until two o'clock in the afternoon that the line went dead, when I suppose some bright Iraqi had at last discovered that it was on the same circuit. In the meantime the captured telephone had given me a complete X-ray of the forces ahead of us, besides enabling me to launch a wholly imaginary but very powerful tank attack of my own. Peter began at about four o'clock to wonder whether the whole thing had been laid for us as a trap, for resistance to the armoured cars seemed to be stiffening, but Reading's evidence from the telephone was far too circumstantial, and we were relieved to find that the stiffening was only a last burst before the enemy retired to its second line on the Abu Guraib Canal. The first phase of the battle for Baghdad had been won.

Among Reading's other accomplishments that afternoon was some shrewd bargaining with one or two stray bedouin who began to drift in. He sent them off to their villages with orders for chickens and eggs which they brought back to us and for which we paid. This was unheard of luxury and the smell of sizzling chicken soon arose from the bushes near the gate where my car was concealed. A special chicken was saved for the Brigadier, who had gone ahead. Jack Napier, the G.I. at Division, a spry fellow, arrived up from Habbaniya and peered with an amused eye into these sidelights of our campaign which was progressing better than any of them back at Divisional Headquarters had dared to hope. He drove on in order to find Joe, and, as soon as the chicken was finished, we followed. Brigade Headquarters were to be advanced from the Irrigation buildings to a ridge on the further side of the floods.

We soon came to the beginning of these — the road (now tarmac) gradually became submerged until it disappeared into a lake nearly a mile wide. The column of vehicles moved cautiously into the water, the wise men keeping close behind the drivers in front, for there was only a pair of steel ramps somewhere under water to take the wheels over the series of hidden trenches. One 15-cwt. truck which had attempted to bypass the one in front was now three parts submerged, with its crew perching precariously on the pile of greatcoats, haversacks, stores and ammunition in the back. They pulled their knees up dejectedly to their chins as the truck sank further into the mud and the water covered their boots. To add to their discomfiture everyone laughed at them as they went by and the stranded section looked like having to swim for it. I reported their sorry plight when I arrived at H.Q. and an armoured car was sent back, just as the setting sun was going down red over the flooded scene, and extricated the unhappy vehicle.

I found the cars of Brigade Headquarters scattered along a low ridge, the top of which was slightly concave. The Brigadier was sitting on the sandy bank of it, looking back towards the floods. I laid the chicken and eggs before him like a magician, and he was pleased. In return he produced some lime juice from his car. Our drinking arrangements were simple. Toler bought anything he could at such places as Habbaniya — notably whisky and tinned food — and touched us each for £2 at seemingly close intervals to meet the cost. As I did not drink whisky my contribution to the refreshments was always good for a laugh, and Corporal Barnes and Coles at the Mess wagon tried half-heartedly to make it up to me in lime juice. At the moment Toler was back in Habbaniya and the Mess wagon probably still in Falluja. So the Brigadier's lime juice was helpful.

CHAPTER 23

We fed and slept by our vehicles that night and next morning moved down the road another mile to a little caravanserai. It was a deserted wayside coffee house, built of mud; little more than a hovel, and we preferred to stay outside it. Here the Mess wagon found us; the trestle table was fixed up and we began to eat together again. The bridge ahead of us over the Abu Guraib Canal had been blown up by the retiring Iraqis, and Cheeky Boy was sent for. He bobbed up, full of confidence that he would have the canal bridged by nightfall. He asked me to send a signal back to Habbaniya asking for all the F.B.E. they had got (whatever that might mean)* and went ahead to start work. The Brigadier was chuckling to himself at Cheeky Boy's optimism, but liked his spirit.

There was nothing to be done but wait. Beyond the caravanserai was a little stream, with oleanders growing on its bank, and the small signal truck was brought up the road to this point while the 'Gin Palace' was somewhat further back. The truck was used for communication forward to the units of our column and to Andrew's column. The Gin Palace was in touch with Habforce at Habbaniya. Joe wanted to speak with Andrew on the R/Toc. Signals had come in, including a situation report in code from David Summers which was so long that we did not bother to decode it all. He had discovered one fact of importance — the line of communication between the Iraqi Brigades at Ramadi and Baghdad. Andrew's column captured a car carrying influential civilians who told them that the route was Ramadi-Haditha-Baiji, and so down the Tigris to Kadhimain and Baghdad. An Iraqi company was stationed at Baiji. Andrew and Glubb's column was not getting on too well. They had been checked at Taji, where, however, they succeeded in capturing the railway station. An amusing incident was recounted of Iraqi reinforcements arriving by train and, on finding what had happened, rapidly going into reverse and disappearing round a bend in the line.

I had received intelligence of 'tank traps' dug by the Iraqis and covered with matting and earth. I was anxious to warn them of this, but

*Forward Bridging Equipment

255

Peter, whose sense of professional etiquette was offended by the extent to which I had taken the battle into my own hands at Kahn Nuqta, passed a decree in the first year of Joe Kingstone of blessed memory, to the effect that my signals must in future be passed though the Brigade Major, viz., Sir Peter Grant-Lawson. He was now talking on the radio-telephone to Neil Foster. "Tell him about the tank traps," I whispered, but he waved me away without listening to what I had to say, an act for which he repented later in the day, when a message was duly sent.

Eventually Andrew was called to the truck at the other end, and Joe squatted inside our own signal truck, the earphones clamped over his gnome-like head, and spoke darkly to Andrew. "Hullo Gelu, hullo Gelu. Tobu calling. Tobu calling. Can you hear me? Tobu to Gelu over." And so on. "Hullo Andrew. Hullo Andrew. Joe calling. Joe calling. Can you hear me? I can hear you. Strength seven. Tobu to Gelu over." "Hullo Andrew. Joe calling. Have you ever been to India? Have you ever been to India? Have you plenty of pani, repeat pani, for your horses?" (I did not know at that time that pani was the word for water in Hindustani. Andrew's horses had been made in 1937 at the Morris works outside Oxford, but the cavalry metaphor was calculated to bewilder any Iraqis listening in.) Joe was thoroughly enjoying himself. "I am sending you up some oats for your horses" (petrol and oil), "but I want to know whether you have plenty of pani, repeat pani. Tobu to Gelu over."

There was a lot of atmospherics and buzzing at the other end, for Andrew had never been to India and was trying to find someone who had. Eventually he clicked in. Yes, he had plenty of pani and switched over to 'Receive'. Joe resumed, "Tell the young man who lives in my village at home (David Summers) not to be so verbose, repeat verbose, in the evenings. Tobu to Gelu off." The conversation ended, Joe taking off the earphones and climbing out of the truck. He wiped the sweat off his face.

There was a good deal of machine-gun fire going on along the canal where it cut the road about a mile ahead of us; and presently one of the armoured cars came back, with a man standing up in the conning tower, with blood all over his white shirt. Joe spoke to him, and the armoured car then went in search of the field ambulance section which was up on the ridge where a small mud hut showed against the skyline to the north of the road.

The morning was beginning to grow hot, and I was sitting in the driving seat of my car using the steering wheel as a rest upon which I wrote up the War Diary when Grose came up to the window and drew my attention to some aircraft overhead. I got out to have a look. They were not Gladiators. A fighter biplane was skimming low towards us. I grabbed Grose's rifle, while he and Williamson wisely took cover, and began firing at the approaching machine; but it flashed on overhead without hesitating, and (fortunately) without attending to us.

The blue sky seemed to be full of aeroplanes now. There were three of four of our biplane Gladiators, easily distinguishable, for the under side of the wings was painted white on one side and dark on the other. They had come up to escort three of our bombers which had gone over a few minutes before to drop a 'normal' on the trenches at the canal bend. The dogfights were immediately over our heads, and we were all busy watching the spectacle, when one of the enemy aircraft began to fall in flames, the dark smoke trailing upwards, and suddenly a brilliant white parachute opened up against the blue of the sky and began to drop.

I was still holding Grose's rifle and, without thinking, began running in the direction of the falling airman. It was a very hot day, and I have heard myself described by an eye-witness as loping off with my rifle at the trail, my nose pushed well forward under my topi. The aircraft seemed to crash only a short distance away over a rise in the ground. But the distance was deceptive, and I padded on, growing very hot, for nearly two miles over sandy ground, covered with green scrub, until I was brought up unexpectedly at the bank of the Abu Guraib Canal itself.

A moment's reflection would have told me that the enemy were holding the further bank, but there, not a hundred yards beyond the canal, was the smoking wreckage of the machine. Two troopers had also started out after the aeroplane, and reached the canal, panting for breath, at the same time. The faithful Reading was also following me, and now arrived. The troopers gazed like baffled bloodhounds at the water, so I handed my rifle to Reading, and also the wallet from the breast pocket of my shirt, and then plunged into the muddy water of the canal. I had heard of people swimming in full equipment, but had never tried it myself, and I went in, topi, watch, compass, revolver, shoes and all, and felt a somewhat glutinous drag about the shoes, but managed to swim, without difficulty and clambered up the further bank of the canal.

I walked squelching over to the wreckage, which was in a little hollow. Iraqi markings on the tail of the plane, black, red, green and yellow, were clearly visible, and also on the side of the fuselage; but the forward part of the machine was charred and still burning quietly. As I bent over it I was puzzled by an intermittent popping, which I discovered to be the ammunition going off slowly as the fire roasted it. I could not see in which direction it was going off, but thought it prudent to stand back a little. I was disappointed not be able to make a rich haul of papers. I looked around. A few hundred yards further on were the brown huts of a small bedouin village, and not far from these I suddenly caught sight of a man in long trousers, who was obviously the pilot. He was dragging something on the ground — his parachute. I shouted to him in English, "Here, you, come here." He looked up and raised his right arm, in salute, but made no move. So I walked over the intervening ground, waded through a dyke (I was indifferent to a little water by now), and came up to the man.

I still imagined that he was an Iraqi pilot, and was startled when he repeated the Fascist salute and addressed me in Italian. I could not remember enough Italian to cope with this, and tried French, which he understood. I told him to gather up his parachute. He was a tall hulk of a man, and refused at first, saying "Stanco" (Exhausted). However, he gathered up his burden, which was enormous, and staggered under it towards the aircraft, where I wanted him to confirm that there were no papers left. Reading came up now, like a wet spaniel, having carried my wallet on his head, and I told him to take the parachute. The prisoner shied like a horse at the burning wreckage, pointing out that ammunition was still going pop-pop — and that the cockpit, where the papers had been, was burnt out — 'fuoco'. So we went back to the canal. 'What happens,' I reflected, 'if he cannot or will not swim?' On the further bank, by now, some more troops had collected, as well as one or two bedouin, who shouted across to Reading about a bridge only a hundred yards down the canal. As we could see the course of the canal for at least a mile before it bent and there was no sign of a bridge, we ignored this typically Arab suggestion, and plunged in again. The Italian, who was wearing a spectacular wrist-watch, dived in without hesitation and swam so much faster than I that I was afraid he would elude me. I scrambled out after him, determined in my youthful enthusiasm not to have my bone snatched away from me, and trotted off with it, to lay it at the Brigadier's feet. The prisoner was now completely exhausted, stumbling along, saying he was "Stanco". If he had left the Island of Rhodes only the day before, refuelled in Syria, alighted at Mosul, got up at dawn, flown down to Baghdad (250 miles), got into a dogfight and landed by parachute, it was not surprising that he was 'stanco'. It was lucky for him that I had captured him, for alone in the vicinity of the bedouin village, he would soon have been seized (for the bedouin are well armed), and he might have lost more than his wrist-watch.

We must have presented a bedraggled appearance as I marched him up to the signal truck, beside which the Brigadier was standing. My own stockings had fallen to my ankles, and the water still squelched from my shoes. "There is the General," I warned my prisoner. "See you give him a good salute," which indeed he did, and Peter emerged from the shade of the oleanders to offer his rare tribute, "Well done, you."

The Brigadier was interested. We had not hitherto had any inkling of Italian participation in the campaign. Yet now, while the tea was being prepared by Grose, the prisoner began to talk. His machine was a Fiat C.R.42, and a special squadron of them had been sent to Rhodes, in order to take part in the Iraq campaign. Joe came up and told me to give the poor fellow a drink. I pointed out that the tea was nearly ready and retailed the information about the squadron at Rhodes. He had a letter from his wife, and photographs of his family also. Grose said "That's a fine watch he is wearing." He seemed to think it a pity that he should need such a fine watch in a prison camp, but I told Grose that prisoners were fully entitled to keep their personal effects. The parachute was another matter, and this, which included a small seat with a neat grey leather cushion, was now arriving on the shoulders of Reading.

Under the influence of the tea, which my prisoner gulped down, he became even more friendly, when Joe came over again and said that Peter Herbert (the divisional Liaison Officer) was driving back to Habbaniya and had better take the prisoner with him. As Peter Herbert was now leaving, the prisoner was handed over to him, and still complaining that he was 'stanco', driven off.

Ignoring Peter's injunction, I went off to the 'Gin Palace', from which I sent a long signal back to Habbaniya about the arrival of an Italian squadron at Rhodes, the shooting down of a C.R.42 and the capture of the pilot (manfully omitting to state that I had captured him myself). One of our own Gladiators had crashed in the fight, but the pilot was unhurt and came over to join us. I asked him whether an Italian pattern of parachute would be any use to the Royal Air Force, and he said it would be perfectly useless, which was just what I wanted to hear. Grose and Williamson proceeded to strip off the seat and harness for souvenirs, Reading commandeered for his own use the elegant grey leather cushion, which, when placed on an upturned 4-gallon petrol can, made an enviable seat; and I, of course, pinched the white silk parachute as a trophy myself. It had a small pilot parachute attached to it. With startling rapidity a 'Most immediate' operational signal came back to me from Air Force Headquarters at Habbaniya asking 'What aerodrome in Iraq was he operating from?' I replied 'He had burnt the operative half of his map when I reached him.'

When I had changed into a dry shirt and my best gabardine shorts (the only alternative to my wet Iraqi pair) and put on my trooper's black ankle boots, I joined Joe by the stream in the shade. He was studying the long photograph of the road, and trying to gauge from it the width of the canal where the bridge was blown up. His eye, glancing past the card, took in a pair of black trooper's boots sitting on the ground beside him and he looked sideways somewhat startled to see who it was.

"Oh, it's you? Where did you get those boots from? You were lucky to have them with you."

I told him how wide the canal was.

"What do you know about it?" he asked.

"I ought to know. I swam it."

"Did you!" It had not occurred to him (nor to me at first) that it was the same canal lower down.

CHAPTER 24

It was at last beginning to be apparent to the military mind that amateur methods of intelligence, while not conforming to Staff College precepts, and omitting such procedure as sitting still and logging up an intelligence summary all day or making maps with red and blue chalk which only got on to the Brigadier's hands when he handled the maps and made him wild, nevertheless had a method in its madness. Peter could never quite see that, as I was the only Intelligence Officer in the Central Column, if I sat still and waited for intelligence to come in from three non-existent regimental intelligence officers (such as would have existed in a normal brigade) I would wait all day in vain. If I did not get my own intelligence I would not get any. However, now all were smiles, and as we dined at our trestle table in the dusk, Coles whispered in my ear, "There's a big plate up," and I started up saying "Where, where?" thinking for a moment that he had said "There's a big plane up." We all had a tremendous laugh, and Joe thought it a splendid joke. When there was nothing else to tease me about, my fellow officers teased me about my latest piece of lunacy — the information which I had received at Habbaniya on 18th May, that Germany would attack Russia on 15th June.

This was regarded as really funny. "Why should Germany go and do a silly thing like that?" The date was now only a little more than a fortnight distant and the calendar was often consulted for my discomfiture.

During the afternoon I decided to set out in search of the mysterious bridge described by our bedou at the canal, for Cheeky Boy was finding the bridging of it a slower process than he expected. I took Grose and Reading down to the canal bank as far west of the point at which I had swum it as we could get the car. Leaving Grose, armed with his rifle, at the car, Reading and I (both armed with revolvers) walked on down the line of the canal. Turning a bend we could see some sort of iron erection in the middle of the canal and the roofs of a bedouin village showing on the further side. As we approached it the bridge took on a more definite shape — it was a low concrete affair, half-way across which was an irrigation device. There were scores of bedouin sitting about the further bank, and a more murderous looking bunch I have never seen. They were swathed in ammunition and rifles (probably looted from the retreating Iraqis) and many carried long clubs of truly thug-like dimensions, stout rods with a great knob at the end. One man was clearly posted on the bridge as a sentinel, for he lay there insolently with his rifle across his lap.

We walked as nonchalantly as we could across the bridge, which could, I was glad to note, have carried a 30-ton tank, and the bedouin closed round us in a semicircle as we stood at the end of the bridge. The canal banks were above the level of the surrounding land, and it was necessary to know if the lengthy road which seemed to continue from the bridge, past the village and along the course of the canal but below it, was flooded further on or not, and whether it joined the main road beyond the blown bridge. I asked Reading to put these questions, which he did haughtily enough. The men answered sullenly and non-committally; the road went on so and so. They made vague gestures eastwards. It seemed to me that we would get little information out of them and I felt that the interview had gone on quite long enough, but Reading, being a better judge of the bedouin, talked on loftily of the utter rout of the Iraqi Army by the superior British forces which were even now in the neighbourhood, and with that we turned on our heels with dignity and walked away, hoping that they would not shoot us in the back. The square white patches on the back of our shirts must have presented an almost irresistible target. I was excited about the bridge as this seemed likely to provide an alternative crossing to the blown up one. There was a small dyke on our side of the canal, about six feet wide, but this could be bridged with the steel ramps. As we walked back, following the rough track which led from the bridge along sandy ridges, I tore off little pieces of a cable from home and dropped them paper-chase fashion so that I could find the trail again.

About half a mile back we were able to see across the scrub and marshy ground to where Grose with the car stood alone on the canal bank, and waved to him to go back by himself. Arrived back in camp I reported my discovery to the Brigadier, who was doubtful of its value. I suggested that after ramps had been laid across the dyke an armoured car should be sent over it, along the road, to prospect beyond the canal. When, next morning, Cheeky Boy's bridge was still not complete, the Brigadier changed his mind, told me to find Cassano and go down with him and a lorry load of steel ramps (borrowed from Cheeky Boy) to my bridge and see what could be done. I was not to be away for more than an hour, in case I was wanted (which was unlikely). So I sought out Cassano. He was feeling justly angry. For he had been fired at on the bank of the canal at fifteen yards range by a private in the Essex Regiment. "I may look like a Wop," he swore at the man, "but I am not, and you ought to be court-martialled for missing me at fifteen yards."

I went up to the bridging operations, where the pontoon was half finished, and Peter Grant-Lawson was looking at it. He asked me to have his camera sent up to photograph the 'historic' scene. I asked his servant to do this when I passed through H.Q. with my lorry load of steel ramps.

We had a great party down by my bridge. At the approach of the armoured car, protective section truck, a 3-ton lorry and my own car, the bedouin had melted away. It was hot work handling steel ramps and Cassano and I did not do much of it, but a curiously-whiskered R.A.F. officer to whom Joe had taken an instant dislike, who certainly looked (although he was not) alcoholic and was dubbed 'Whiskers' by Joe, proved a tireless heaver of ramps and saved the officer class from derision by standing up to his waist in the dyke while the ramps were handed across. Grose, as usual, made the most practical suggestions. He pointed out that the most stable foundation would be obtained by laying one pair of ramps across the dyke first — they just reached from bank to bank, and then laying two more above each from either bank to meet in the middle. This meant shovelling some earth away.

Eventually a message arrived from Headquarters saying that I was wanted back there, so I left the bridging operations and returned — to find that a bedouin sheikh had arrived and wanted to see me. He had come up in a very smart blue saloon car and was accompanied by two or three relatives and a slave. He was very dark in the face, a small square face, with intelligent eyes under his white keffiyeh and black aqal. I took him over to my car where my camp bed was got out and my small canvas chair erected. Reading introduced my visitor as Sheikh Ali Suhail, and I motioned to him to sit beside me on the camp bed, apologising for the lack of amenities, and his friend sat on the chair. I told them that I could offer no coffee but tea would be prepared. This took an unconscionably long time as the jet of the Primus stove had got enlarged.

To open the conversation I showed them the captured Italian parachute and so great was Ali Suhail's delight at seeing it that I cut off the pilot parachute and gave it to him as a memento. Reading, interpreting, explained that the Sheikh's brother, Hussein Suhail (interned by Raschid Ali at Diwaniya) had received a similar present from General Wavell, a pair of Italian binoculars captured by the British at Sidi Barrani and inscribed by General Wavell on a gold plaque in English and Arabic. I could not emulate this, but I wrote in pencil on the white silk (using the mudguard of Ali Suhail's car as a rest) the date of the pilot's capture and signed it.

The reason for Ali Suhail's visit, after getting past the compliments which he wished to pay to the victorious British who had always been his friends, was that he had captured a Bren-gun from the Iraq Army and wanted to know if he could keep it. My own recollection of this conversation is that I said, with due regret, that all such guns must be handed over to the British Army, but in a convalescent home in Jerusalem months later I met an officer of the battery who had been in the column and to whom the Bren-gun had been handed when Ali Suhail was found with it, and who told me Suhail came back with a piece of white silk bearing my signature, above which was written an order to hand over the Bren-gun! This, the officer said, they accordingly did, assuming that I had good reason for it.

Ali Suhail was full of interesting information. Raschid Ali had bolted from Baghdad. (This was valuable intelligence.) The Germans had sent an Air Mission, but we shot the aircraft containing it down over Baquba and killed the head of the German Air Force in the Balkans, who was leading the mission. He was shot through the jugular vein and buried in Baghdad with military honours. (This story was partially true, as I learnt later. The aeroplane was, however, shot down by the Iraqis themselves on its arrival at Raschid Aerodrome, not by us. This welcome did not encourage very smooth relations between the German Mission and the Iraqi authorities.)

All this information was so valuable that I asked Ali Suhail to excuse me for a moment, while I went over to Joe, who was sitting on the bank of the stream in the shade, where he had been joined by Jack Napier and Sam Maxwell (my neighbour M.P. in Norfolk), who was now commanding a Yeomanry regiment. This was our Divisional Signal Regiment, and Sam had come up with Jack Napier from Divisional H.Q. at Habbaniya to hear the latest news. I stood like a pelican on one leg, while they finished talking and Joe then said, "Well, what do you want, Intelligence?" I told him that Raschid Ali had fled and that the head of the German Air Mission had been shot down. They were excited and asked me where I had got my information. I told them about Suhail, and Jack Napier said they had received a rumour of this at Habbaniya and was grateful for the confirmation. He fell into step beside me as he and Sam went back to their car. He congratulated me on the Italian pilot.

It was interesting to see Sam again, of whom I had only caught a glimpse at Habbaniya for he had arrived there when we were on the point of going forward. They got into the car and drove back along the road towards Kahn Nuqta, Falluja and Habbaniya, while I rejoined Ali Suhail. The tea was ready at last, and Williamson (who wanted some himself) poured it out for the Arabs with a bad grace (fortunately on the opposite side of the car).

As we sat in the sun sipping the tea on my camp bed, the rest of the column was moving on again, for Cheeky Boy's bridge was completed after all, and I remember Charles Wood of the Blues (yet another M.P.) passing in his truck with a smile at the Oriental scene of the Member for S.W. Norfolk squatting cross-legged in a circle of his Arab friends.

Ali Suhail's parting request was for permission to put his men of the Beni Tmimm tribe on to restoring the irrigation system (which had been deliberately flooded by the Iraqis), so that the land would dry up. All his crops and grazing grounds were being spoilt. I gladly gave him permission and, saying goodbye, saw him into his car and then hurried on myself. Before he left, Ali Suhail gave me his visiting card and urged me to visit him in Baghdad after we had conquered it.

Reading told me that the Suhails were a rich family of bedouin with houses in Baghdad. They owned the land between Falluja and Baghdad.

We had left the desert behind us at Kahn Nuqta and entered a region irrigated by dykes and canals, where the hard sandy ground broken by ridges, was covered with thick green scrub, and here and there a line of shrubs and trees. As I drove along the road to the canal, it was necessary to drive at times through shallow stretches of flood water which covered the road in places. The main bridge was a back-broken skeleton, twisted in the muddy water and Cheeky Boy's pontoon crossing was a few yards to the left. The long line of vehicles crept down to it, bumped across, and clambered round to the road again beyond. Here there were signs of cultivation on either side of the road, crops growing. We were not more than twenty miles from the city and our excitement rose as we approached. I wondered how near our foremost men had reached by now.

Soon a road turned off to the left between trees of the eucalyptus variety and long white buildings which I recognised from my map as the Iraq Government's Agricultural Research Station. At the side turning a weather-beaten signpost pointed to Aqqa Quf. We followed the line of trees along the main road until we were halted a mile or so beyond at another group of buildings screened by trees, called the Experimental Farm. We were now only eight miles west of Baghdad and here, apparently, Brigade Headquarters were to be set up. I found the cars lining a grassy ride parallel with the road and screened from it by a thorn hedge. There were plenty of eucalyptus trees and, although they cast a very doubtful shade, they provided good camouflage from the air.

As I had been detained at the caravanserai by my talk with Ali Suhail the Headquarters was well settled in when I arrived — and some of the officers were already sitting in a swept-out room of one of the bungalows, hopefully awaiting the boiling of tea in an improvised kitchen where Corporal Barnes and Coles were bustling about across the corridor. I had expected to find traces of the Iraq 3rd Division headquarters in the Experimental Farm, but either the Iraqis had been very methodical in their withdrawal, leaving no evidence of their occupation, or they had been somewhere else. I almost began to wonder whether their army was a mirage. I decided, therefore, to drive back along the road to the Agricultural Research Station in order to see if I could find traces of the Divisional headquarters there, with possible information to be gleaned from scraps of paper left behind. Peter was not so disturbed at my proposed departure again as I had expected, because he had heard that there was a horse at the Research Station which had been left inside a stable when the Iraq Army withdrew, and felt that the poor animal would probably die of thirst if not turned loose. So, being an ex-Grand National rider, he urged me to find the animal and turn it out.

I took Grose and Reading, leaving Williamson behind, who had to cope alone, in the absence of Corporal Troughton and the office truck (still at Habbaniya) with a mounting tide of signals to be deciphered. We had no difficulty in finding the Research Station again. Broad tracks scored by carts, lorries and tractors turned off the main road into it at three or four places. I chose the central approach and we drove up to a circular patch of ground in front of a long white building. We had little difficulty in forcing an entry and I was surprised to find myself in a library of English books on argricultural practice. Of the Iraq Army there was no sign. Nor had the place been looted, which was an eloquent proof of the fact that the Iraq Army had only left it a few moments before. There were gardens of a wild sort between the buildings of the settlement and a violent clucking towards the eastern end of it spoke of a chicken run. We hurried towards the sound.

As we approached, we caught glimpses of marauding bedouin flitting about among the hedges which screened the chicken runs from us. The place was in a pandemonium. The bedouin had settled like flies on the place. There were scores of them running about seizing the squawking fowls and making off with them hanging upside down, flapping, four and five in each hand. Seeing the arrival of a military car they fled in terror, some dropping their fluttering burdens in their haste to get away, others disappearing through the hedges with their live burdens. A flurry of black garments and the glint of bronze feathers in the sun through a gap in a thorn hedge, then the screeching cackle of the protesting chickens would be the last we saw in any direction. One bunch of hurriedly tied together chickens had been thrown down at the foot of a tree where we pulled up. It was quite evident that unless troops were picketed in here systematically every single fowl would be taken by the bedouin within half an hour of our departure. This was all the more tragic in that they were pedigree fowls, 10,000 of them, in long neat wire runs. We had no troops to spare for such police duties and there was nothing for it but to save what we could from the spoliation of the chicken runs for our own use.

Reading and Grose disappeared through the hedge, and a renewed squawking marked their progress through the runs and hen houses. In the meantime I drove around the settlement, looking into the buildings, in one of which some electrical equipment lay unused, but I could find no sign of army occupation. There was certainly no sign of Peter's thirsty horse.

On my way back to collect Reading and Grose I saw the tangled growth of one of the neglected gardens stir and a lieutenant of the Essex Regiment appeared. I told him about the chickens and urged him to picket some of his men about the place, but he said that was impossible. He had been sent to collect what he could before the bedouin cleaned the place out. When I reached the hedge where I had left Reading and Grose I had to honk loudly before I could draw them out of the recesses of the chicken runs. They emerged staggering under incredible loads. There were very few eggs left, even now, but Reading had collected a dozen or more. In addition to chickens Grose had found a pair of geese and we stuffed the entire screeching menagerie into the confined space of my staff car — twenty birds in all, and, climbing in ourselves, slammed the doors on the feathery turmoil and drove back to camp. I gave orders to Grose and Reading to distribute the birds among the vehicles of Brigade Headquarters, saving a goose and five chickens for the Officers' Mess and Mess servants.

Joe and the rest were already eating lunch. "You've been away for an hour and a half," said Joe, "and I bet you haven't found anything of value."

"I've found a goose and five chickens for the Officers' Mess," I replied.

"Oh," said Joe, "that's different," and no more was said, while an arriving cackle in the kitchen proved the truth of my words. I urged Peter, as Brigade Major, to detail a small party to collect or guard the rest. "There are enough chickens there to feed the whole column for days." But he would not do so. "If you don't get them," I said, "the bedouin will," (which they did before the afternoon was out).

After lunch Joe said he was going up to the front to see what was happening and I urged him to take me with him.

"What would be the use of taking you?" he asked, teasing me as usual.

"You might want your map marked up, or the photographs, or something," I said.

Joe was amused. "Very well," he said. "You come along."

So we set out up the road, my car following his utility van. We passed the parking places of the independent anti-tank troop, and the Field Ambulance Section before leaving the line of trees to our left, and, further on across rough grassland, we could see the roofs of a bedouin village. The scenery became more arid again further on, rising to a bare red sandstone ridge through which the road passed as through a defile. Behind the ridge were drawn up several of the Gunners' supply vehicles. The road ran over a small gully three hundred yards further on, and rose gradually to a knoll upon which were the scattered ruins of three or four mud huts. The roofs were missing, but the walls stood up with an occasional opening in them to mark where a door or a window had been. To our left swept undulating country meshed with the silvery veins of flood water, growing more hazy until a long fringe of dark green vegetation showed us the course of the Tigris. Above the tops of the trees were the domes and minarets of Baghdad, and standing out conspicuously across the marshes to the north was a mosque with two great golden domes glowing in the sun, and four tall minarets capped with gold, which gave the effect of flame-topped torches. That must be the gold-roofed Mosque of Holy Kadhimain. Straight ahead of us, not three miles away, were the red roofs of the Palace of Roses showing above tree tops. We dispersed our cars about the ruined buildings and I followed Joe to the foremost one. There we found Daddy Wright sitting on the ground in the shade while Captain Anderson, who had done so well with his guns at Falluja, sat on the wall of the ruined house staring through his binoculars towards the banks of the Tigris for signs of enemy movement.

Between us and Baghdad stretched three miles of flat open space, green, cultivated ground, intersected by many dykes, and crossed by the curving tarmac road, to the left of which the ground was flooded. I looked through my binoculars first, of course, at the Mosque of Kadhimain. Some said that Kadhimain was at quite a different point of the compass, judging from the map. I did not care about the map. I knew it was Kadhimain. A large species of kingfisher, slow flying, with a black face and neck, but brilliant blue wings, flew through my field of view. It perched on the telegraph wires which lined the road. I could see along this to where Cassano's armoured car was driving as far as it could go. It appeared to have reached some obstacle and was turning round. As it did so the sharp chatter of machine-gun fire came across the open ground. C Squadron of the Household Cavalry were now in front and were dismounting from their trucks just below us and moving down into the dykes to cross the open ground.

Gwynn Morgan Jones, dark, good-looking as ever, came up to Joe, saluted and reported that they were going forward. Joe nodded; he was comparing the photographs of the road with the scene in front of us. He pointed out a thin line of trees in the book, and after looking towards the Palace of Roses, said, "That is the place there. A road runs south in front of the trees. The Iron Bridge here (he indicated the last photograph in the book) must be further round to the left of the road, beyond those trees, where it seems to end." I was the only other person in the column with a book of the air photographs and checked up Joe's statements from my own. Joe was very much better at recognising the lie of the ground from the photographs than I was.

Machine-gun fire was opening up on us now, all along the belt of trees which screened the Palace of Roses, and the Blues and Life Guards were getting well down, to Joe's amusement, in the dykes.

At this moment we became aware of new arrivals at this forward Observation Post. Half a dozen War Correspondents (who had caught me red-handed with the airman's parachute at Kahn Nuqta) had now arrived in a peculiar captured Iraqi vehicle and crept up the sunlit wall of the building to listen in at our informal conference in the shade. Joe let them listen for a time, then he stood up and, turning to them, said sweetly, "You know, if we were fighting the Boche he would massacre us." He had scarcely spoken when a shell burst on the open ground in front of us, causing a mild scurry. Down came another further off. The firing seemed to be coming from the banks of the Tigris away to our left. Evidently the sudden approach of the War Correspondents in force had given away our O.P. Joe lost no time. Anderson was down off the wall and had gone round the back of the building to pick up his field telephone and beat it to a less conspicuous O.P. Joe said, "I am going back to H.Q. to have those armoured cars out of this."

"You don't mind if I stay?" I pressed him. "There is nothing for me to do back there."

"Certainly," he said, "you can stay." And to Peter Herbert, the Divisional Liaison Officer, he said "You stay here for twenty minutes and then report back to me."

The trucks of the Household Cavalry (which they still regarded as led horses) were streaming back down the road to get into concealed ground. Another shell closer than the rest burst right in front of the building and I nipped inside to be behind cover. But the shooting was erratic. The next was far away, bursting with a cloud of grey dust in the green landscape. I emerged again. There was nobody except Daddy Wright still about. I walked round the corner of the building to where Grose, with his tin hat on, stood beside the car with an amusedly anxious expression. Reading was chattering like a baboon. "What are we staying here for?" he asked. "We are not doing any good here."

Grose pointed to the off front mudguard which was scooped neatly into a hollow with a dark streak leading into a spoonlike patch of clear metal. "A shell hit it a moment ago, and richocheted off without exploding."

Daddy Wright was interested. He examined the dent. "That was an 18-pounder," he declared, and, standing by the mudguard looked along the line of the streak it had made. It gave him a line to a point amid the vegetation on the Tigris bank.

Poor Reading. No wonder he was scared stiff. He had been sitting in the back of the car, plucking a chicken, when the shell hit it. Grose said later that he himself had been standing on the further side of the car and had seen the enamel mug which he had placed on the bonnet jump about four feet in the air. "I thought someone was throwing things at me for a joke," he said.

There was no joke about it, and Anderson who had been packing up his equipment near the car described to me in the Convalescent Home at Jerusalem later how the shell had come in with a whine and a wonk and gone off again, God knows where.

I told Grose to take the car back to the dip, where the other vehicles had gone. We were the only people left.

"Are you coming too?" Grose asked.

"No, I'm walking," I said, and Daddy Wright and I started off down the road, while the yellow car disappeared like a streak ahead of us.

I suppose it was a perverted sense of pride which made me feel it necessary to take it all so calmly, but Daddy Wright was walking along quite indifferently, which seemed to be the correct thing to do. I thought wrongly that he had been in the last war.

"You know," he said, "it is a miracle that shell did not go off. A million to one chance," and then added casually enough, "have you ever been under fire before?"

"No," I said.

"You seem to be taking it remarkably calmly," was his comment.

Another shell burst a few yards off the road on our left, and we watched the ground spurt up a hundred yards beyond where the shrapnel landed. "That must be a 4.5 How.," said Daddy Wright. "I think they are firing at us. I suppose we must be rather conspicuous."

I supposed we were, and we were walking rather more slowly than before, each trying not to go faster than the other.

At length we came to the gully, from which Grose's tin-hatted brown face bobbed up. "Are you wanting a car?" he asked.

"No, we haven't far to go," I replied.

"There is a good ditch down on that side of the road," Daddy Wright said to Grose.

"There's a bloody sight better one on this side," was Grose's comment, and retired into it as we moved on. We were heading for the ridge through which the road passed. Daddy Wright said that Anderson had moved the O.P. back to it.

"Why isn't he firing at the river?" I asked.

"I wasn't sure until that shell hit your car that it was the Iraqi guns firing at us. It could have been our own 25-pounders beyond Kadhimain."

"Well, I should open up pretty quick," was all I said.

We reached the ridge and climbed up the back of it and dropped down into a prepared pit, where Anderson and a gunner were already busy with the field telephone. The guns were some way further back.

"Range is about 7,000 yards," Anderson reported.

"All right," said Daddy, "open up." Anderson began giving orders on the telephone; there was a boom behind us, and a long sigh as the first shell soared overhead, then a burst of smoke three miles away against the dark green foliage by the river. The crump followed.

Anderson changed the range and another shell went over. I got out my green-covered intelligence notebook and began noting the ranges at which each shot was fired. I was thoroughly enjoying myself and believed that this recording justified my existence, when Peter Herbert came up the ridge. He had been back to Headquarters.

"Brigadier wants you back at Headquarters," he said.

"Why?" I protested. "There can't be any hurry. I'm never wanted."

"Yes you are," he said, "and you had better hurry."

I was really annoyed, but as Peter appeared to have been sent up again for the express purpose of withdrawing me, I had to say goodbye to Daddy Wright and Anderson, climb down the ridge and walk along the road to rejoin my car.

Back at camp I found Joe and Ian Spence in high spirits. Even Peter Grant-Lawson was in good humour.

"Did you put your tin helmet on?" he asked. "Or did you stick to your topi?"

"I stuck to my topi of course," I replied.

To Joe I said, "What did you want to bring me back for?"

"I want you to take an armoured car," he ordered, "and your own car and go and reconnoitre this aerodrome south of us, and see if it is in enemy hands still."

I strongly suspected that it was a wild goose chase, thought up on the spur of the moment to get me away from the battle.

"All right," I said. I was standing outside the window and saluted half-heartedly.

"Come back here, you," called Joe, "and salute properly."

I saluted properly and went off, hearing Joe's chuckles from inside the room.

Ian Spence came out and I said, rather peevishly, "What have I done wrong?"

"Nothing," he replied, "you're in high favour. That is only Joe's manner."

"Did he say I was to take an armoured car as well as my own? Whatever is the point of an armoured car?"

"That's what he said," replied Ian laughing, and went off on some errand of his own.

I had the feeling that they were all enjoying some joke at my expense, to which I was not a party. I sought out Cassano, who had been withdrawn from the battle at Joe's instructions, and he detailed an R.A.F. sergeant to go with me. I led the way out of the Experimental Farm on to the main road and followed it for a few hundred yards until I came to a turning which I had noticed earlier in the afternoon. We turned down this and I pulled up, signalling to the armoured car to stop. I got out and boarded the armoured car. The sergeant and I stood up in the conning tower, and I beckoned to Grose to follow close behind. I had left Reading in camp to get over his attack of nerves. We had not proceeded far up the road when I saw a white building ahead seemingly at the end of it. The thorn hedges here were very high, and, even standing up in the conning tower of the armoured car, it was difficult to see over them. I could just see, now and then, the bedouin village a few hundred yards away to the left.

I told the driver to slow down as we neared the building. It was a strange place; octagonal in shape and surmounted by a large gilt crown. Evidently it was the summer residence of the Iraqi Kings; a fact to which the neat gravel sweep up to the front door and the attractive flower beds, added testimony. The doors and windows were all tight shut and it wore a deserted air. The road continued round to the right in the direction of some aeroplane hangars, and, reflecting that this was my first mission, I directed the driver to go that way. We quickly came to the hangars and before them was the level ground of a small aerodrome. We got down from the armoured car and peered into the gloom of the hangars. They were quite empty and did not seem to have been used for years. We returned, therefore, to the house, drove up to it and round to the back, where trellises of vines overhung the back door. There were some outbuildings beyond, but these looked equally deserted.

I told the N.C.O. to remain on guard outside while Grose and I explored the interior. We walked around the veranda, which surrounded the eight-sided bungalow, until we came to the front door. This was of plain oak. We leaned against it and the lock gave. Inside were revolving glass doors and we passed through these into a pleasant little sitting-room, furnished entirely in the Western style, with one or two gaudy plaster statues and ordinary sofas, chairs and tables of a luxurious kind. Grose went on down a corridor to the back regions of the house, while I went through a door into a bedroom. The windows were covered with slatted shutters and mosquito-proof wire netting, so that only a dim green light filled the room. There was a heavy scent of perfume in the room, which spoke eloquently of a woman having slept in it recently. There was a wide double bed with a satin bedspread, and the bed made up with beautiful linen sheets. On a modern dressing-table with large triple mirrors was a large jar of face powder with a puff thrust casually into it. There was a new pair of man's hair-brushes. Beyond the room was a bathroom, also in the modern style and beyond that again, a study.

There were no papers, such as I hoped to find, but the place had obviously been lived in very recently. There were evidences in the decorations of an interest in aviation. On the walls hung framed photographs of the late King Ghazi, a young man in white ducks or grey flannels, standing beside a streamlined racing car. King Ghazi had been killed in a motor smash years before. But it was quite evident that some Iraqi general or one of the rebel leaders had been using his little retreat as a place for relaxation from the cares of the campaign within the last few hours; and had left it, not in disorder, as usually happened. That it had not been looted by the ubiquitous and grasping bedouin was a mystery. I wondered if some awe surrounded this royal residence, making them shun it. That very night, however, the bedouin smashed the windows of the place and broke in, apparently overlooking the front door which opened at a push. I learnt this later from an armed Iraqi guard who had been left to watch the place and who must have withdrawn at our approach. He maintained stoutly that he had fired at the marauding bedouin as they left.

Although there was nothing of military importance in the building, its contents were so curious that I thought the crew of the armoured car would like to see round the house and gave them permission to do so before we set off back to the camp. Not a few souvenirs from that building must have found their way back to England in due course. Joe had gone up to the battle again, taking Peter Grant-Lawson with him.

Poor Williamson was still struggling feverishly with the decoding of signals, and was very near to exhaustion. But there was no one else to relieve him at this specialised work and he sat on at it in the front seat of my car, as the dusk drew on, until he was mumbling to himself and his head swayed from side to side, and he finally collapsed from sheer exhaustion of mind on the seat. I had never before seen a man go right out under purely mental strain. It was a noble effort. The information he had decoded told us that Andrew and Glubb were stuck fast north of Kadhimain, where the enemy seemed to be entrenched in strong positions. Moreover Andrew had instructions not to bombard Kadhimain, which the enemy no doubt hoped we would do, for that would give them the leverage of a religious grievance which their usurpation at present lacked.

Far to the south, from the slowly stirring headquarters of the Indian Division forming at Basra, there were the first signs of animate existence. This redoubtable army, which arrived with its tents and its baths, its polo sticks and fishing rods, and was preparing for a two-year campaign on the model of General Maude's, had actually penetrated as far up the lower Euphrates as Nasariya. They went even further and I recorded in the War Diary that 'The Basra Elephant, with its toppling howdah of Staff Officers, penetrated as far as Ur of the Chaldees, but this interesting peep into ancient history does not seem to have affected the course of the present campaign.'

So we were left alone, to seize victory if we could — and Baghdad was very near.

We ate our evening meal in high spirits and Daddy Wright who dropped in, complained to Joe, with a twinkle in his eye, that I had made him walk down a shell-swept road. While we were eating, a flotilla of luxurious civilian cars came up to us from Habbaniya. They bore Iraqi dignitaries whom we had been keeping in cold storage; they came from the Regent Abdul Illah, whose court had been set up just before we left, at the looted Imperial Airways Rest House on the shores of the lake below our camp at Habbaniya. Joe had sent for these emissaries some hours earlier, as he had a feeling that the campaign was approaching a climax.

Nuri Said's son was in one of the cars, with an ex-Iraqi Prime Minister, a bald, bandy-legged little man. The Regent's A.D.C., Major Obeid, in khaki-drill uniform, with the peculiarly bulbous Iraqi Crown on his shoulder tabs, was with them. Each car had an Iraqi driver and, shepherding this flock, was a lean English sportsman in grey flannel trousers and brown suede shoes from the Foreign Office. I took an unreasoning dislike to this wallah. His name was de Gaury — but I was to change my opinion before the night was out.

De Gaury was supercilious and dissatisfied with the reception of his notables, to whom Joe gave short shrift; he was dissatisfied also with the food provided for them after their long drive (of fifty miles). We had no food for them, feeling that they ought to bring their own, and needing what we had got ourselves. The scent of roasting chicken, passing on its way to our own hardened palates did not console de Gaury at all.

He reappeared after a while, interested to hear that I had been in touch with Ali Suhail, for de Gaury bore letters from our notables to potential friends inside the city and they must somehow be smuggled in. Suhail was just the man to do it. De Gaury and the A.D.C. spoke about this in the lamplit room where we had eaten. I told him that Ali Suhail had appeared mysteriously to me across the floods from the direction of Aqqa Quf. He was a portent, but I could not find him again in the daylight, let alone in the dark. Obeid said he knew the way to Suhail's village.

"In the dark?" I asked.

"Yes, yes."

I reminded him that the land in between was flooded. It was of no avail. De Gaury was keen to go.

"Can you give us an armoured car as escort?" he asked the Brigadier.

Joe clamped his great hand down on my knee and said, "Here is your escort." De Gaury looked at me with less affection than he would have done had I been an armoured car. His spirits seemed to droop. However, he was committed to the enterprise and we set off, myself in a state of great scepticism which prolonged exertion and little sleep during the past two days had done nothing to alleviate. I told them that I could lead them as far as the edge of the floods; after that Obeid must find the way. I took Grose and another officer's servant armed with rifles and, of course, Reading.

De Gaury and Obeid followed me out of the camp in a big black saloon car, and we drove with headlights on. I went as far as the battered signpost to Aqqa Quf and turned down that road. We had not gone half a mile (skirting the Agricultural Research Station) before the earth road ended, abruptly, at the bank of a swirling flood. We got out with our torches and I said to de Gaury, "Now what?"

He was not helpful and Obeid was less optimistic at sight of the water.

"Well," I said, "you asked to come. So I am going through this flood, but I am taking the two men with me. You can either come with me or stay here. Please yourselves."

With that I took off my shoes and socks, rolled up my drill slacks (which we wore in the evenings on account of the mosquitoes) and Reading, Grose and the servant took off their boots.

I stepped gingerly down into the dark water and was relieved to find it not deep. I flashed a light on de Gaury who seemed to prefer to remain on the bank with his suede shoes while we did the wading. So we went on. There was grit in the slimy mud under our feet which cut them unpleasantly, and my temper became more violent. We could see the dim outlines of some buildings in the dark ahead of us and Reading began to call, "Taal, taal, we are friends seeking Sheikh Ali Suhail." But there was no response except for a frenzied barking of dogs which broke out. We climbed up on to an earth embankment and walked along it, shining our torches between some trees and into empty huts. Nothing but dogs, shut up and barking fit to smash down the doors. Suddenly I saw a gleam of flashlight, only to discover that it was the reflection of my own in a glass window. We peered through it into an empty room. The population had decamped — as they always seemed to do at the approach of soldiers. Perhaps they were around us in the dark, watching silently. At this rate we could search all night for someone to lead us to Ali Suhail's village, which was certainly many miles further on. So I took Reading and the driver back through the water.

Near the cars I found de Gaury, still in his suede shoes. It was too much for me. I came to the boil. I had only once before lost my temper so badly, and that was when I tried to strangle a man in Milan. Now I told de Gaury just what I thought of a Foreign Office which for years let the political situation in Iraq deteriorate under the eyes of an incompetent nincompoop, and then, when it had lost the country, sent for the Army to get it out of the mess. I was tempted to start on Obeid next for thinking he would know the way in the dark, without having been there for years and with floods everywhere barring the way. But he was the A.D.C. of our Ally the Regent. De Gaury had listened to my tirade without protest in the darkness and merely said, "Let us return now."

I reported to the Brigadier when I got back. He was lying down on a camp bed under a mosquito net and I came up, deliberately shining my torch on my rolled-up slacks and muddy feet. I told him what I thought of de Gaury and he said, "I am afraid you have had a very trying time Somerset. I should try to get some sleep now."

It was after half-past eleven and I went over to my car, where Grose had put out my safari bed, and lay down. On an impulse I got up and went along to the buildings further down the camp and sought out de Gaury. "I am sorry I lost my temper," I said, "only I knew Obeid would never find the way in the dark and I was very tired."

"I know how it feels," he replied. "Don't worry about it."

Then I went back to my car. The Iraqi guns on the Tigris seemed to be opening up into a furious barrage. It might presage a counter-attack in the dark. I did not care.

I may have dozed for half an hour, not more, for it was only a quarter-past midnight by the luminous dial of my wrist-watch when I heard Peter's voice, waking up the Brigadier.

"An odd sort of message has just come in," he was saying. "Two delegates from the Iraqi Army will appear on the Iron Bridge at two o'clock in the morning. Will we send two officers to meet them to discuss terms of armistice?"

"The answer to that is yes," said the Brigadier.

I sat up in the darkness straining my ears, a feeling of excitement refreshing me, and began to dress. The Brigadier sent for Ian Spence and told him to wake de Gaury and our own Iraqi notables. They would be wanted to start in half an hour. As Ian Spence passed me, going down to the other end of the camp, I whispered, "Ian."

"Yes?"

"Fix it with the Brigadier so that I can go too, won't you?"

"I'll try," he said.

I think the Brigadier must have heard me. The night was very still and the barrage had stopped.

"Somerset," he called.

"Yes, General?" I was already dressed by now, and went across to his bed.

"You can go with Ian if you like. You had better warn the Mess waiters and tell them to get some tea ready."

We all assembled in the room we had been using to eat in. The Brigadier wore his red-banded cap and a bush shirt, which came nearly down to his knees; nothing else. He asked Dick Schuster to produce a pole and something white for a flag. Dick came back with a rod marked off in black and white lengths alternately, and the large white sheet which was put out beside the truck when our aeroplanes dropped messages.

The Brigadier stood up and began to tie the sheet on to the upper part of the pole. De Gaury was not enthusiastic about the expedition. He knew the Iraqis too well, and believed the whole thing to be a trap. Our own Iraqis knew their countrymen even better and their deportment revealed a total lack of enthusiasm. Only Ian and I were full of optimism and bubbling over with our good fortune, having already taken a vow that we would be the first British soldiers to enter Baghdad. Joe gave us our instructions — to collect one officer from the Household Cavalry at their C Squadron Headquarters, which was where my car had been hit during the afternoon. We were then to go on as far as the anti-tank ditch, which Cassano had looked into. There we were to erect our white flag. The Iraqi delegates were to show their headlights on the Iron Bridge and if we could see these, we were to respond by switching on our own. We drank tea, and everybody wished us good luck. When all details had been decided we got up to go out, and de Gaury, with a look at me, asked the Brigadier if it were clearly understood that he (de Gaury) would be in charge of the enterprise, as it was a negotiating matter. Joe agreed, and we started out in two cars, Ian's and a civilian one. We did not take an army driver for Ian's, in which he and de Gaury travelled, while I followed with Nuri Said's son and the ex-Premier.

We drove along with sidelights only, until we came to the Household Cavalry Headquarters. Charles Wood was standing beside the road, as we drew up, and we asked if he would like to be the officer to come up to the anti-tank ditch. Charles was amused by the invitation. "No bloody fear," he said, "I've been up there once today, that was enough." (For he had in fact been up to the ditch under heavy fire during the afternoon.) So Ian sent someone to rouse Rupert Hardy, commanding the Squadron, who came up out of the darkness like a hibernating bear, climbed into the car and promptly went to sleep. The Iraqis began asking me if it was safe to go any further forward. "Have you got plenty of troops ahead?" I lied cheerfully, knowing that there was not a sausage ahead of these buildings now, and answered them that the ground in front of us was thick with our troops. So they came on, reluctantly.

We were now moving forward, without escort, into no man's land, where the fighting had been going on all afternoon — during which the R.A.F. had at long last been allowed to drop their eagerly awaited 'noisy'. There was no moon up and darkness closing in on either side of the road brushed past the windows of the cars. After moving slowly forward thus for over two miles, watching the clock in order to time our arrive for 2 a.m., we came to the anti-tank ditch. A huge pile of freshly-excavated earth thrown up from the ditch formed a barrier across the road in the feeble glare of our sidelamps. We got out, and Ian and I took the white flag up the crumbling earth embankment and stuck it on the top.

De Gaury had come up too, and the three of us peered across the vague cavity of the anti-tank ditch into the darkness beyond. If it were a trap, we would soon know, but there was not a sound, not a glimmer beyond. The Iron Bridge would in any event be screened from us by a bend in the road, but we thought we could detect a faint radiance against the night sky in the direction of the bridge. So Ian said, "Turn on the lights," and I ran down to do this, flooding the earthworks in front of the car with a brilliant glare. We left the lights on thus for a minute or two, but no response came from across the ditch. Our own Iraqi delegates now came up, and spoke with de Gaury. The whole thing, they said, was most certainly a trap, and as soon as daylight broke we would all be machine-gunned. Could they not go back now?

"No," said de Gaury. "But you can turn your car round if you like."

"We have already done that," they said, and went down into the darkness and back to it.

Rupert Hardy, who had been fighting all day, remained in Ian's car asleep. The other three of us sat on top of the earth embankment. I turned out the headlights, but every now and then Ian or I would shine our torches hopefully on our white flag. But no answering signal came from the enemy side of the ditch.

We sat thus for an hour, talking in the dark. A feeling of comradeship in adventure now united us to de Gaury; and I discovered later that he had won the Military Cross in the Essex Regiment during the last war.

"I am certain what has happened," I told the other two. "The Iraqis said in their message that they would meet us on the Iron Bridge; and we have been told not to go beyond the anti-tank ditch. They are probably up there, shivering in their shoes, not daring to come forward. At this rate we will never meet. Let me go across the ditch and take the white flag up to the Iron Bridge and see if anything happens then."

"You will do no such thing," said Ian, who was the senior officer of the party. "If anybody goes, I go."

"But you are in charge here," I pointed out, "whereas if anything happens to me it does not matter."

De Gaury thought it about time we consulted our own Iraqi delegates again, but when I went down to find them, their car was gone. I returned to the ditch.

"If this is the morale of the victors," said Ian Spence, "what can the morale of the vanquished be like!"

It was now decided that we should at least cross over the ditch and see what happened on the other side and what Ian later described as a one-man mutiny nearly followed when he ordered me to remain on the embankment while he and de Gaury went ahead. They did not, however, get more than a hundred yards on the further side of the ditch (which could be crossed fairly easily near the left side of the road) before they ran into a barbed-wired entanglement, and came back baffled.

Ian told me to take his car back to the Household Cavalry Squadron

Headquarters, depositing Rupert Hardy there, get on to Brigade Headquarters from their wireless truck and tell the Brigadier what had happened so far. Accordingly I woke Rupert up and got into the driving seat. Back at his Headquarters we found a trooper asleep (inside the signal truck) with the earphones on and cracked him smartly on the knee to wake him up. Rupert then went off to sleep in a horizontal as opposed to a sitting position and I climbed into the truck. We soon got on to Brigade Headquarters. I thought at first that it was Dick Schuster's voice on the other end, but it was Peter's. I told him what had happened and went on to explain my theory about the Iraqis not daring to come beyond the Iron Bridge.

"May I take the flag on to the Iron Bridge?" I asked.

The voice at the other end went away for instructions and returned soon.

"No, you are not to go beyond the anti-tank ditch. You are to watch and wait, but the G.O.C. and A.O.C. have now arrived here and will have further instructions. Hold on."

I waited with the earphones on, my khaki cap on my knees, and talked desultorily to the wireless operator until Peter's voice came through again.

"The Iraqi delegates are now expected at four o'clock. You will wait there till four o'clock. At the approach of daylight you will turn your car round. If you are fired upon you will withdraw, keeping your flag publicly displayed and keeping it under observation if possible. If the delegates appear, showing their headlights, you will turn on your lights. Do you understand? You are not to go forward; you are to watch and wait." (This was just as well, because we discovered afterwards that the road beyond the barbed wire was mined with trip wires, and we should have gone skywards in the dark.)

I drove back with revived excitement. Something was going to happen after all. Ian and de Gaury were equally pleased, and we sat on for nearly three-quarters of an hour, talking merrily until the sky began to lighten.

"Turn the car round," said Ian, and I did so. I now noticed for the first time the sidelights of a car on our own side of the ditch about a mile back along the road. I wondered vaguely whose it could be; possibly an advance section of the Household Cavalry pushed out into no man's land at the approach of daylight.

I returned to the top of the earth mound. The sky was now lightening rapidly and we could see, first, the steep walls of the anti-tank ditch below us, then the barbed wire barricade further up the road which had stopped Ian and de Gaury. On our left lay wide flooded marshes oddly reminiscent of the Norfolk Broads. Suddenly from the right, following unexpectedly the course of the anti-tank ditch itself, came two cars rapidly, with headlights blazing. It was exactly four o'clock.

"Turn on our lights," shouted Ian, and I ran down the embankment to do so. The headlights of our car now shone back towards our own positions, since I had followed the General's instruction to turn the car round, and as soon as I switched them on, the car which had been waiting further back, started to come on, as if it had been waiting for the signal. Of course — it was the General and the A.O.C. But we were not going to let them get in ahead of us now, after we had been waiting there all night to receive the delegates. So I dashed up on to the embankment. "Come on," I cried, but Ian needed no prompting and together we ran down into the dry ditch and climbed up on to the road beyond. De Gaury followed us. The Iraqi cars were already stopping and two officers were getting out. They came towards us in the greying light and de Gaury recognised one of them as an old friend.

"Daghestani!"

"De Gaury!"

They almost embraced one another. Daghestani spoke perfect English and had in fact spent three years at Woolwich. He presented the other officer, "Colonel Aquid."

We were only just in time. The A.O.C.'s blue saloon car had reached our side of the ditch and General Clark in his hurry to be on the scene before Air Vice Marshal d'Albiac, arrived panting across the ditch without his leather-covered stick.

We introduced Colonel Aquid and Captain Daghestani 'whom we have met' to the General and the A.O.C.

General Clark now asked me to go back to the car for his stick, which I did, and was interested to find Glubb and Jack Napier there. Glubb had been with Andrew's column in front of Kadhimain up till yesterday when he had received one of his hunches and returned to Habbaniya just in time to come up with Clark and d'Albiac and so be in at the kill. The three of them had been so inseparable at Habbaniya for a time that they were known as 'The Three Musketeers'.

I took General Clark's stick back across the ditch to him.

"Have you anything to write on?" he asked. I offered him my message pad of army signal forms, and a pencil. He sat down on the grass beside the road and wrote a message to:

H.M. Ambassador, British Embassy, Baghdad.

Your Excellency,

A.O.C. and self have met the delegates. I have ordered advance to stand fast as from 04.00 hrs. I have here in my possession the instructions of my C-in-C Gen. Wavell regarding terms. A.O.C. and I will be grateful if you could see your way to come out here for discussion. We will await your instructions. G. Clark M.G.

This he handed to me with a flourish saying, "By the hand of Major de Chair, Member of Parliament, and Major Spence, Stockbroker." The majority was undeserved, so far as I was concerned, unless it was intended, like the golden spurs of former battlefields, to be a present from the general on the spot.

To Daghestani he said, "I shall keep Colonel Aquid here as a hostage for these officers, while you will take them and Mr de Gaury into the Embassy."

Daghestani led us to his car and the three of us, who had kept vigil together, stepped into it. The car drove off along the edge of the ditch, by the way it had come. We had not gone more than a few yards, however, when we saw Glubb in his yellow keffiyeh strolling along the British side of the great trench. Daghestani ordered the driver to stop the car, jumped out and shouted to Glubb to go somewhere else.

"He is not safe, wandering along the edge of the ditch," he explained as he re-entered the car. "Some of our soldiers would shoot him if they were to recognise him."

It was true that Glubb was hated by the Iraq Army, for to them he was a familiar name, and they had spoken of Andrew's northern column as 'Glubb's army', although he had not a very large number of men in it. Axis broadcasts had only two days previously announced the death of Glubb, for propaganda purposes. So Glubb now wandered off somewhat crestfallen and we resumed our journey. Forgetting that Daghestani was really one of the enemy, so naturally did he speak English, I turned to Ian Spence and said, "Entering Baghdad will make a perfect finish to the War Diary which has to go in at the end of the month." Today was the 31st May. Judging from the grim expression on Ian and de Gaury's faces, I realised that I had dropped a brick, and did not improve it by asking de Gaury to write down for me the names of Daghestani and Colonel Aquid, which he did and handed them to me without comment.

Daghestani now startled us by saying, "We will soon be passing through the defences, so I must ask you to blindfold yourselves." At first we thought he might be jesting, but he was quite serious and so we drew out handkerchiefs and he watched us tie them securely over our own eyes.

It was a curious sensation sitting there in a car, unable to see where we were going; all the more so when we were stopped by sentries at some sort of barricade near the top of an incline. I wondered whether in such circumstances one ought to be strictly scrupulous or, in the interests of our own military advance should the negotiations break down, try to see what one could of the defences. I decided to remain honestly blindfold. Daghestani was speaking through the window in Iraqi, and after a certain amount of scraping, the obstacle was removed and the car went on. After a further ten minutes or so, Daghestani said we could remove the bandages from our eyes, and as we did so, we found ourselves in the outskirts of Baghdad. A triumphal arch in the Babylonian style machicolated at the top and with antique Babylonian sculptured figures in stone, set in niches, stood beside the road at a roundabout. The car sped on, through streets of mustard-coloured buildings with flat roofs and shuttered windows. There were few people about. Here and there an Iraqi soldier, in dark khaki topi and shorts, with face and knees the colour of walnut, and a rifle slung over his shoulder, would look up in surprise at the spectacle of two British officers driving by in a car.

For a month now the British Colony in Baghdad had been shut up within the walls of the Embassy or in an internment camp. Some had taken refuge in the American Consulate. During all this time, a cordon of Iraq police had surrounded the Embassy and at intervals Raschid Ali had made threats to the Ambassador about cutting the throats of the British if any bombs were dropped on Baghdad. It had been an unenviable position — to be at the mercy of the Iraqis — and my mind went back to Nathanya when I had seen the orders given to Kingcol 'to rescue H.M. Ambassador and the British Colony beleagured in the Embassy and to establish itself on the west bank of the Tigris until reinforcements can arrive.' How far we had exceeded our instructions! Baghdad itself was within our grasp, the army suing for Armistice; and here were Ian and I driving in the dawn into the city of the Caliphs.

We drew up before a wooden gate in a wall, and some delay elapsed before we could get it opened from inside. The astonishment of the inmates was remarkable, and a wizened bespectacled Oriental secretary, Vivian Holt, appeared in a dressing-gown. De Gaury knew the ropes here and asked for us to be taken straight up to the Ambassador's room. We entered the building and found ourselves in a circular hall where a tiled fountain played, but were led up some familiarly English stairs and along a corridor that might have belonged to any country house at home, until we came to the Ambassador's room.

Sir Kinnahan Cornwallis lay in bed with a blue cummerbund round his middle. He sat up in bed like one accustomed to focusing his mind on important and unexpected affairs at all hours of the night. Ian clicked his heels, saluted, and handed him the message form, "With General

Clark's compliments."

"If you will give me half an hour to dress," the Ambassador said, "I will be with you. In the meantime I expect they will find you some tea at the canteen, which we have here for the people on night guard."

So we left the Ambassador to dress and went out a different way, on to the flat roofs of the Embassy where men and women were sleeping everywhere. They were beginning to wake as they looked up and saw two army caps passing, a cheer went round. A woman sat up in bed and waved. We went down some stairs into the courtyard and were led through to the garden. Here were more people sleeping — on the lawns, under the porch — everywhere. We were taken behind some hedges to a little canteen. People crowded eagerly around us, scarcely able to believe their eyes — although they had been hoping secretly every day for something of the kind to happen, as the sound of firing drew nearer and nearer to the city.

The buxom Englishwoman behind the canteen could not conceal her tears as she poured me out a cup of tea. "Oh, we have been waiting a long time for this," she said.

And so their ordeal was ended. Among those who came up to us now was a fully-dressed Major General. This was Waterhouse, head of the British Military Mission to Iraq, cut off along with the rest of the Colony when the campaign started; and later on a ceremonial occasion to be called Watermouse by the inspired misprint of one of our signallers. I walked with him on the smooth green lawn, behind which the palm trees grew, and past which the broad Tigris flowed. We walked a little away from Daghestani and Ian Spence as we could not speak freely in front of the Iraqi officer. As we mounted the stone steps in front of the house, I experienced one of those vivid impressions of having lived through the event previously. I seemed to have seen before this end of the white façade of the Colonial House, with its green shutters and creepers and to have heard this voice beside me asking if I had a cousin who used to be in the Sussex Regiment. The impression passed.

Sir Kinnahan Cornwallis emerged from the house, wearing a white topi and white drill suit and was given the front seat in the car beside the driver which I had occupied on the way into the city.

There were more people about now, all the colourful pageantry of an Eastern city — tarbushes, keffiyehs, turbans, robes of every colour; donkeys, mules; and many more soldiers. They looked up at us out of their dark brown eyes as we passed and spat. Once more we were blindfolded, although diplomatic immunity exempted the Ambassador from this. We drove on, coming eventually to the same barrier which had barred our entry. This time, however, there was a violent argument between Daghestani and someone outside. Evidently the idea of an Armistice was not popular at the barrier and Daghestani got out of the car. We were left alone, unable to see, but hearing the talk of angry voices which we could not understand and the clink of rifle bolts. I began to wonder whether, perhaps, the time had come to revise my policy of remaining blind in what seemed to be an increasingly menacing situation. Supposing that Daghastani had no real authority — that it was merely an attempt of the palace party to precipitate an Armistice in the early hours, and that now in the growing day new orders had arrived to the sentinels, cancelling permission to let us pass. Daghestani came back explaining that the officer had not understood the position, but that it was all right now. We heard the barrier shifted with some relief; and the car drove on. When we removed our bandages, the car was running along the edge of the anti-tank ditch again.

And there, towering on the earth embankment above the anti-tank ditch was the real conqueror of Baghdad — Joe Kingstone — in khaki shorts, standing with feet wide apart, the scarlet band of his cap vivid against the blue sky behind him. He was like a vast red-ringed buffer at the terminus of the line to Baghdad.

We got out and, leaving Daghestani with Colonel Aquid on the Iraqi side of the ditch, took the British Ambassador across it to where General Clark and the A.O.C. were waiting in the blue saloon car. Sir Kinnahan climbed in with them.

While they talked about Armistice terms, the rest of us, Joe Kingstone, Jack Napier, Glubb, and, of course, Ian Spence, de Gaury and I sat on the backward slope of the earth mound where we had spent the night; and talked. De Gaury had a little camera, which he had got in Latvia, a real spy affair, no bigger than a cigarette lighter, and took a photograph of us sitting there. Ian was not going to wait any longer, and drove back to camp for a sleep and some breakfast. But I was too excited. Having got thus far I was determined to see it through.

Glubb's views on the Arab peoples were particularly interesting. "We have given them self-government for which they are totally unsuited. They veer naturally towards dictatorship. Democratic institutions are promptly twisted into an engine of intrigue — thus the same bunch crop up after each coup in a different guise, until disposed of by assassination. The same thing used to happen in the South American Republics at one time, so perhaps the falling off in the number of political assassinations and revolutions there augurs well for the eventual stabilisation of Government in the Arab lands." I told him about Waterhouse, and Glubb's views on Military Missions to Arab peoples were even more trenchant. "All we do is to send people to teach them how to fight against us, without any attempt to select men who understand the Arabs to whom they are sent. In future, military missions to Arabs ought to be selected for their understanding of the people they have to deal with rather than their military capacity." We had a very strong card in the young King Feisal, who, de Gaury had elicited from Daghestani, was safe and sound. The boy had so far been brought up with an English nanny, and there was no reason why he should not become a great friend and ally of ours if some thought were devoted to his education.

288

"It is a curious thing that the British and the Arabs get on so much better in their personal relations than the French do. A surprising number of Englishmen have completely identified themselves with the Arabs, sharing their way of living and entering into their point of view. This has made the Arabs, especially the nomad Arabs, feel really affectionate towards us at times."

In this tradition Glubb was merely following precedents set by Lawrence and further back by Doughty. He certainly carried the Lawrence tradition on into the Second World War.

I had felt the friendliness of the Arabs myself in talking to Ali Suhail. There is a common bond also in the unpredictability of both the British and Arab minds, which is foreign to the French or the Turk. The Arab sees everything through half-closed eyes and will be profoundly influenced by the merest incident. The Druzes revolted against the French in 1926 because General Sarrail kept two of their leaders waiting in a corridor. The Turk, on the other hand, makes up his mind as to where his best interest lies and will not be deflected from his course of action thereafter by a mere incident. My stay in the Levant had been short enough, but I was beginning to notice already the different characteristics of the racial blends. In this, of course, Glubb was the master and I only the pupil. I was to learn much, too, from that fascinating Armenian Altounyan, wizened as a walnut, of whom I had so far caught only a glimpse in the Air Force Intelliigence Room at Habbaniya; and who had already been pointed out to me by Belgrave as the author of *Ornament of Honour*.

During my subsequent stay in Baghdad I was to penetrate further into the half shadows of the Arab mind; and Hussein Suhail, after he was released from Diwaniya presented me with the gold aqal worn by sheikhs. My position as Intelligence Officer for the occupying force might have entitled me to affect the Arab headdress and aim at becoming a second Leachman. But I knew no Arabic and without Reading I should have been a Moses in the Wilderness without Aaron. Moreover, I feared the ridicule of my regiment — although I had come across Tony Murray Smith in the dawn light at Rutba surprisingly adorned in a yellow keffiyeh. I was certainly alone among the British troops in being admitted at this period (through my growing friendship with the Suhails) to forbidden Kadhimain and gazed in wonder upon its legendary mosque, with roofs of beaten gold; its mirrored portals, and walls of myriad coloured tiles; and I am glad to think that the three Suhails, one of whom like myself is a Member of Parliament, hold each a

gold star marked with the garter cross in red, which I gave to Hassan
Suhail when he journeyed to visit me after learning from Glubb that I
had been wounded.

I was eventually rewarded for sitting on in the growing heat by the emergence of General Clark from the car, who asked whether I had anything to write on, and then, sitting down, dictated to me the proposed terms of Armistice, the gist of which was as follows (I wrote them in pencil on the back of message forms):

'Whereas representatives of the Iraq army have sought for an Armistice and in view of the fact that H.H. the Regent Abdul Illah is on his way to reign over the country the following terms must be observed by the Iraq army. The mildness of the terms will be noticed because the British army has, in fact, no quarrel with the Iraqi people or their army, but only with the pro-Axis adventurers who were determined to use the army for their own ends:

1. All prisoners of war shall be released forthwith.
2. All enemy (German and/or Italian) service personnel to be interned and their war material retained by the Iraq Government pending further instructions.
3. Ramadi to be vacated by Iraq troops by noon on 1st June.
4. The Iraq Government to facilitate in every way the task of British forces in the war against Germany and Italy.'

This was then shown to Glubb, who pointed out that it did not provide for the cessation of hostilities; so he was hurriedly drawn into the car after General Clark. The door shut on them again and after a further period of deliberation a slightly different version was produced and written out in a fair hand by Jack Napier. One copy was given to the Ambassador who told us, standing in his gleaming white drill suit and white topi, that during the revolt he had been referred to persistently in Axis broadcasts to the Arabs as Cornwallis the Cunning and Cornwallis the Dog; which was the best recommendation he could have. It was now considered safe for him to return with Daghestani and Aquid to lay the terms before the provisional Government. So, after bidding us all goodbye, he returned across the ditch to the Iraqi car and we watched them drive off. Then we returned to our own camp at the Experimental Farm for breakfast.

We sat at a table in the eating room there, and it seemed that everyone who wanted to be remembered in the War Diary had something impressive to say in my hearing.

Air Vice-Marshal d'Albiac pointed out that it should be called the Thirty Days' War, having lasted exactly a month (from 2nd May to 1st June, 1941); and then he and Joe fell into conversation while General Clark explained to me that the campaign had hung on two threads — the two wire hawsers with which the northern and southern columns had been ferried across the flooded waters of the Euphrates. And my mind went back over the events which had carried us so far and so fast. We had achieved something — and had shown something of a genius for improvisation.

As I talked with General Clark, over the best breakfast I have ever eaten, I heard Joe talking about me to d'Albiac. "We have the most extraordinary fellow here," he was telling him, "knows nothing about his job but keeps on producing rabbits out of a hat." And perhaps that is the only way wars are won. Daghestani provides a footnote to this brief page of history. He was questioned by one of our war correspondents after the fall of Baghdad as to why the Iraq Army had given way on the Central Front. "What else could we do?" said Daghastani. "You had fifty tanks there and we only had two old anti-tank guns on that front."

That night we learnt that the terms of Armistice had been accepted by both sides. The Thirty Days' War was ended.

For us it was but another campaign along the eastern marches of our Empire; for them it was a war against the whole distracted might of Britain.

Five days later Kingcol entered Baghdad.

PART III
PALMYRA

LET ME BE a true believer
    If I must believe.
Let me be a true deceiver
    If I must deceive.

Let the day's unnumbered treasure
    Render up its gold.
Let the night's unnumbered leisure
    Yield what it may hold.

When the moon is silver crescent
    Let me make a prayer,
That the beauty of the present
    Stay with me a year.

When the moon is gone for ever
    And the night is dark,
Let us make a pact to sever,
    Stamp upon the spark.

When the bird of evil omen
    Passes through the night
And the silent marching foemen
    Gather into sight,

Many men will know their Master,
    He who made the Plain,
And will float on torrents faster
    Than the fiercest pain.

In that hour of dark discerning,
    In that feeble dawn,
Will I face the brand and burning
    With a noble scorn?

Whose will be the final arrow?
    Whose the tempered sword?
He who spared the smallest sparrow,
    Kill us quickly, Lord.

CHAPTER 28

"I hope it will soon be possible," said Winston Churchill on 15th July, 1941, "to give further accounts to the public than they have yet received of the Syrian fighting, marked as it was by so many picturesque episodes, such as the arrival of His Majesty's Life Guards and Royal Horse Guards, and the Essex Yeomanry, in armoured cars, across many hundreds of miles of desert, to surround and capture the oasis of Palmyra." But the throng of later events in the Middle East provided in themselves enough colour for the successive statements on the war situation which he delivered to the House of Commons.

It is perhaps a pity that the Prime Minister never had time to tell of that 'splendid affair amid the noble ruins', as he called it, or to detail the events which led up to it. In his rich language it would have made a memorable story.

Yet it is doubtful if anyone who did not himself share in the dash of those spirited events could pluck the heart out of the story — for it is largely in the character of the men who led the Column that the interest lies: Joe Kingstone and his fighting group; Cassano, the leader of armoured cars; Glubb with his bedouin guides — these are personalities who will be remembered long after men of greater achievements have been forgotten, for they were, unknowingly, actors who were cast by fortune in a play which must inevitably pass into the literature of the Second World War. Men will ever be interested in the mysterious and the highly coloured. These men played their parts against a curtain so romantic that they could not fail to be spectacular.

I was fortunate to be the official recorder of their doings, but I have told only of what I saw.

Nor can their positive military achievement be ignored. It is not to be measured by the size of the battles nor the numbers of men engaged (for these were small), but rather in the surprise with which it was received.

"If anyone had predicted two months ago," concluded the Prime Minister, "when Iraq was in revolt and our people were hanging on by

295

their eyelids at Habbaniya and our Ambassador was imprisoned in his Embassy at Baghdad, and when all Syria and Iraq began to be overrun by German tourists, and were in the hands of forces controlled indirectly but none the less powerfully by German authority — if anyone had predicted that we should already, by the middle of July, have cleaned up the whole of the Levant and have re-established our authority there for the time being, such a prophet would have been considered most imprudent."

The significance of all this was not, of course lost on General Smuts. Speaking at Bloemfontein, two years later, of this turning point in the war, when Hitler planned to strike at Russia through Syria and Iraq in 1941, concurrently with his attack from the west, he said, "Who prevented this? Greece. Those precious six weeks altered the history of the world. They gave us time to get hold of Syria and save Iraq from rebellion."

Inevitably, towards the close, the narrative becomes more personal; but in doing so it tells a story which has been the bitter experience of unnumbered men in the unprecedented conditions of a three-dimensional war. For such men, going into action under conditions of desert warfare, must read in retrospect as a process of passing through successive bands of diminishing security.

The point of departure will probably lie in some theatre of war remote from enemy interference — Jerusalem or Cairo. From this security they pass into regions where it is wise to look up or over their shoulders; but while going through this band there is no insistent danger, and thought and movement are unimpeded by the enemy; next comes the band through which they pass to get at grips with the enemy and here they are liable to increasing interference; security begins to fall away and suddenly they enter the last band, which they share with the enemy, and here security has vanished altogether; they shoot and are shot at; out of a clear sky they are torn to shreds; they are never left alone; even when wounded they are hounded about; shot at again; wounded again; until at last, mercifully, they are drawn back into the preceding band of semi-security; and from there they bump back hundreds of miles into the next; security flows in over their harassed senses; they are flown back through the penultimate band where the risk of encountering the enemy is slight; and they come to rest in peace — in Cairo or Jerusalem.

The experimental farm west of Baghdad was as still as an English graveyard in high summer. There was no sign of life. Stretched about in the flimsy shade of the eucalyptus trees or in the deserted rooms of the brown brick buildings slept the soldiers who had conquered Baghdad. They were not many. Kingcol, as Joe Kingstone's column was called, had divided at Habbaniya. The northern column had been ferried across the Euphrates and, attempting to come down on Baghdad north of the Aqqa Quf floods, had been halted before the Holy City of Kadhimain. The southern column, commanded by the Brigadier, Joe Kingstone, himself, had pushed straight through Falluja and the floods east of Khan Nuqta, to reach Baghdad. They had forced the far larger Iraq Army back from Khan Nuqta, with the aid of some subtleties; had broken their line on the Abu Guraib Canal; and had fought them to the edge of the newly dug anti-tank ditch west of Baghdad before the enemy sued for Armistice.

It had been a quick but exhausting struggle, and now the conquering British column slept like dead men.

I had gone to sleep after breakfast, when we returned from the anti-tank ditch, jubilant with the Armistice. As I tried then to drowse off to sleep I thought of the great white sheet tied to the black and white signal pole which we had erected above the earth embankment of the anti-tank ditch in the night, and which we had left hanging limp in the growing heat of the morning. It would be a pleasant souvenir of the campaign, and I was entitled to a share of it. I made up my mind to go in search of the flag when I awoke. This was not long after.

Grose, with his wiry dark hair and leathery lean brown face, was moving about getting things out of the back of the car. I had trained him as a machine-gunner and range-taker in the Blues, then asked him to be my soldier servant when I took a draft from Windsor to the Holy Land; and he was now my driver. I often pressed him to try for a Commission. His brother was already a Lieutenant-Commander in the R.N.V.R. But he seemed to prefer his present job.

"Where is Reading?" I asked.

"With the protective section, I think. He won't go near the Brigade Headquarters people now."

"Do you know why not?"

"No. I think he has had a row with them."

"Poor Reading. He is so touchy. Well, find him and tell him I want to take him with me up to the anti-tank ditch again in case there is any unpleasant argument when I try to take the flag down. Can you find some old rag that we can tie up instead? We don't want the Iraqis to think the war is on again. The Armistice isn't signed yet."

Grose went in search of Reading, my Palestinian interpreter, and I dozed off again; and there beside me, it seemed, as if I had summoned a genie, was Reading, tall, proud in spite of his bedraggled khaki shorts. He had been without a change of clothes ever since Edric Nutting dumped him at Rutba. He complained daily about his kit not turning up. He stroked his slight black moustache nervously with the flat of his straight fingers — thinking that I had been looking for him in vain. I struggled up.

"I was sleeping," said Reading.

"I am not surprised," I conceded. "But I want you to come with me now."

Reading was almost too eager to win my favour.

The camp was still sleeping when Grose started up the engine and we drove quietly out on to the road. I felt uncommonly nervous. I don't know why. While the battle was on and during the exciting events of the night which culminated in my being taken blindfold through the defences of the city, I had not felt a qualm. Now the idea of driving out into no man's land while the Armistice was still unsettled, merely in order to gratify a personal vanity, made me think twice. How foolish it would be, after running the comparative risks of the fighting, if I were sniped at by some spiteful or suspicious Iraqi soldier who saw me taking down the white flag!

The reaction from the strain of the past few days and the lack of sleep may have accounted for this ludicrous distortion. Yet I confess that my heart beat faster than usual as we passed the last outpost of the Household Cavalry, where my car had been hit by the 18-pounder yesterday, and drove down the now familiar stretch of winding road to the anti-tank ditch.

On our left were the broad flood waters, almost up to the edge of the road, and far across the marshes glinted the twin gold domes of Holy Kadhimain. The open ground to our right was meshed with dykes until it reached the line of dark green trees which screened all but the red roofs of the Palace of Roses.

As the car approached the earth mound which barred the road I told Grose to drive slowly, and through my field-glasses searched the further bank of the tank obstacle for signs of the enemy. There was not a single soldier visible. The car halted and I told Grose to turn it round before I got out with the grimy white towel which he had produced.

I scrambled nimbly up the mound of earth and was interested to see that the ditch, which a few hours earlier had been dry, was already filling up with the seepage of the flood-water. If the Iraqis had held out another day it would have presented a serious obstacle to us.

I tied the towel to the pole before removing the huge, stiff, white signal sheet which we used normally for indicating to our own aircraft the position of the signal truck when messages were to be dropped.

Having secured my prize I did not delay, and, stalking back to the car, was happy when the door closed on me and we were returning rapidly along the road.

Back in camp I found people active. Tea was being boiled up on primus stoves or spirit lamps beside the trucks and armoured cars. Grose parked my car in its accustomed place beside a tree on the ride and I climbed out with the flag of truce. I folded the flag into three parts and Grose produced some scissors with which I cut along the folds while he held it. Taking from my map case a thick black lead pencil I wrote in bold writing on the corner of each third of the flag —

PART of the FLAG of TRUCE
with which the Emissaries
from BAGHDAD were received
at 04.00 hrs MAY 31st, 1941,
to surrender the city and accept
terms of ARMISTICE.

S. de C.

I then sought out Joe and gave him one of the pieces. He folded it up quietly saying, "Well, I never," and went away to stow it in his utility van. I gave Ian Spence the other bit and his cherubic face lit up. The third I kept for myself; and went back to sleep.

I lay in a ditch, where there was some shade, and did not wake till next day when I looked up, half-awake, to see the black face of Ali Suhail framed in the white linen folds of a keffiyeh, peering at me through the thorn hedge. It was not a dream. Ali was the sheikh of the surrounding Beni Tmimm tribe. I sat up, rubbing my eyes, and beckoned to him to sit on the earthy bank beside me. He looked back over his shoulder mysteriously and then forced his voluminous black robes through the thorn hedge without tearing them. I stood up and shouted for my Palestinian interpreter.

"Reading!" I bellowed, but in all the camp there was no answering call.

I went a little way down the grass ride of the farm which here ran parallel to the tarmac road and was fringed with trees. At a crossing I looked past the brown brick buildings and the army trucks, under which men were sleeping, and shouted myself hoarse. I tried calling my driver's name: "Grose." It had never failed before. No one stirred. The sun beat down and the heat was like a lid to the silence.

I came back to the shaded bank where Ali Suhail was sitting imperturbably and squatted down beside him in my drill shorts and open-necked bush shirt. I wiped the sweat round my neck.

"Qwois," I said.

"Qwois," said the sheikh.

There was an interval of silence. Then I indicated the trees and the shade.

"Qwois," I said.

Ali Suhail agreed: "Qwois."

We smiled at each other.

In vain I tried to recall the Arabic phrases which I had learnt. "How much does it cost?" "That is far too much."

No. It was no use. I had come to rely entirely on Reading. He could translate the very inflections of my voice into Arabic; but he was somewhere in that camp asleep. I cursed inwardly.

Ali Suhail tapped his wrist watch. "Baghdad?" he queried.

I smiled. "Baghdad," I replied.

He indicated the hands of the watch more distinctly, his brown finger pointing first to 1, then to 2, and finally coming to rest at the figure 3.

"Baghdad qwois?" he asked.

I frowned. "Baghdad 1 o'clock? 2 o'clock? 3 o'clock? Splendid?"

He wanted to know when it would be safe for him to go in.

The road was cut by the great anti-tank ditch where Ian Spence and I had spent a night with de Gaury waiting with our white flag for the Iraqi officers to materialise out of the dark. But a side road which led into the city by a roundabout way was being cleared of the barbed wire obstructions further south. It should be passable in an hour's time.

I laid my own blunt finger on his watch at three o'clock.

"Baghdad," I said firmly. "Qwois."

Ali Suhail smiled delightedly, stood up and tiptoed to the hedge. He beckoned to someone beyond. The bushes parted and a small Arab boy appeared with a load of ripe yellow melons. Ali took them from the boy one by one and laid them at my feet.

I put more feeling into my, "Qwois." He made ready to depart so I accompanied him across the ditch to the hedge and, peering through it, saw his blue saloon car drawn up at the side of the road. There was an Arab driver and another bedouin in the back. They were both armed with rifles and swathed in bandoliers of cartridges.

I shook Ali Suhail by the hand. He went over to his car and pointed down the road to the left.

"Baghdad," he said and got in. The blue car flashed forward, glinting in the sun, and I returned to my ditch to sleep. But first I stowed the melons in the back of my yellow staff car. If others were to awake while I was asleep the fruit would quickly dwindle.

It was the third time in three days that I had seen Ali Suhail. First of all he had come to me at the mud-walled caravanserai called Monasir, east of Khan Nuqta, asking for permission to keep the Bren-gun which his men had taken from the retreating Iraq Army. He had given me news of the rebel leader's flight from the capital. Raschid Ali al Gaylani had (he thought) fled to Turkey.

Quickly upon the heels of the Armistice — for no doubt the eyes of the Beni Tmimm tribe had watched us parley at the anti-tank ditch after dawn — he had come a second time to our encampment. I had dragged Joe protesting from the shade of the building which we used as a Mess, and had told Reading to explain to the sheikh and his cousins that the giant with the powerful red face, standing before them in shorts, shirt and red-banded cap, was none other than General Kingstone.

"A very great conqueror," I said.

The Arabs were tremendously impressed. Joe played up well, while Peter Grant-Lawson, the Brigade Major, photographed the meeting and the Arabs went back to their bedouin tents at Aqqa Quf (not far across the floods), and Joe went back to sleep.

The ruined temple of Aqqa Quf stood up in the middle of the floods — a massive pile of cream-coloured masonry a hundred feet high.

"Here, Intelligence," Joe had said to me when we camped, "what is that?"

I had, of course, to ask Reading, who explained that it was formerly a temple.

I spent the following day in completing the War Diary of the Advance Striking Force. Joe asked to see what I had written. I prudently showed him only the typed part which carried it to our arrival in Habbaniya. He commented only on the long-legged Life Guards tramping round me in a ceaseless circle.

"Now, don't you write too much rubbish," he said: "the lumpers have always had long legs and tramped round in ceaseless circles." But I had the feeling that having lodged this formal protest against too much flourish, he did not wish to pry deeply into the record. Peter had continuously harassed me to keep it up to date, but for similar reasons I was anxious to get it despatched without his censorship. He went through the file of operational telegrams, selecting those which I was to include with the War Diary. As his selection omitted all those signals which referred to my own activities, I took the liberty of including two of these about the imaginary tank attack which I had launched by telephone against the Iraqi 3rd Division, and the Brigadier's own signal about it.

As I sat writing against the driving wheel of my car in the shade, and Grose sat on the earth bank near by copying out in a fair hand the part which, in the stress of the campaign, I had omitted to do with a carbon copy, I thought of a sonnet. It was as if my mind which had been simmering all through the fight now came to the boil and began giving off steam. The lid was jumping and I wrote some lines in red pencil on the back of an Imperial Airways time sheet — salvaged from the looted rest-house beside Lake Habbaniya.

The sonnet provided its own title, 'The Golden Carpet', and I wrote this for effect in yellow chinagraph pencil at the top and signed it with the date, 2nd June, 1941.

When I had completed the War Diary and ruled it about with blue and red pencil to give it some semblance of formal shape (for I had long since run out of the printed forms), I put it all in an envelope and consigned it to Corporal-Major Dicker ('Kicker'), who was still back at Habbaniya with the office truck. Once this was out of the way I could face Peter with the same jauntiness as that felt by a burglar who has got the sparklers off to the fence before the police-inspector stops him in the street. Fortunately Peter was sickening for sandfly fever so beyond an automatic prodding on the general subject of War Diaries having to be sent in at the end of the month, I did not hear any more about it.

The rest of Brigade Headquarters had now begun to look into the little summer palace by King Ghazi's aerodrome. Ian and Joe professed to having seen a standard of the Iraqi Second Division lying on the grass near the outbuildings, but they may have been pulling my leg. I went back and searched, while Peter Herbert, the divisional liaison officer, was peering about inside the house and borrowing for our use a flit-gun to spray the flies where we ate.

Peter Herbert was always trying to bludgeon people into doing work for him, and considered it my responsibility to take Reading off to the nearby bedouin village in search of eggs. I went, not because I had any wish to gratify Peter's idle whims (for I had already lost my temper very violently with him at Monasir when he asked me to find the Brigadier's card-photograph of the Baghdad road and I had left him to find it himself), but I went now, for I hoped to intimidate the villagers into disgorging the Iraqi standard, if one of them had picked it up. But they stood in the doorways of their huts, dark-faced and swathed in black cloth, when Reading called to them; and they one and all professed ignorance of the missing standard. They sold us some eggs.

I went over to Joe after breakfast where he was standing in the early morning sunshine outside the window where we messed, his red-banded cap looking very cheerful. I saluted and he shied in alarm.

"I should like ten days' leave," I said. "I haven't had any leave since I arrived out from England. Every time I have been going to get leave I have been appointed to a new job or sent on a course or a campaign or something. It looks as if we are going to be here for at least ten days and I should like to go back to Palestine."

"*Would* you?" he said. "Well, I haven't had any leave since I have been out here either. So you can't have any." But he spoke very kindly and appeared to ruminate. "What makes you think we are going to be here at least ten days?" There was a twinkle in his eye.

"Well," I said, "while I was lying with my eyes closed on the bank beside the road at the anti-tank ditch, when we were waiting for Glubb and Clark to come out of the car, I heard Jack Napier telling you that the next move for us was obviously to go back across the desert and capture Damascus. That means a little time to refit and the campaign has not even started."

Joe was amused at this method of picking up intelligence, and the lot of Intelligence Officers would be eased if their Commanders took them into their confidence earlier than they sometimes do. (I had already sent back to Edric for a duplicate of the Syrian Order of Battle which the senior Cipher Clerk in his madness had burnt with my other papers at Mafraq.)

I got no change out of Joe, except a chuckle, as far as leave was concerned. Joe was getting ready to depart, taking Ian with him, to the Embassy in Baghdad, as soon as the road was clear.

Peter asked me to call the other ranks of Headquarters together and say a word (in Toler's absence) on their smartening themselves up before appearing in Baghdad. I had the whole lot up in a thin brown line before the trees of the Grass Ride. They looked a scruffy crowd. Their arms hung loosely like gorillas. The cooks were greasy from the pot. I startled them into rigidity with a display of militarism unusual in me. "Squad," I shouted; "Squad, 'shun!" They snapped into shape. "Stand at ease. Stand easy.

"You are about to enter a great Oriental city," I told them, "as the first representatives of the British Army. Out in the desert you went without water and it may even have been a virtue to go unshaved. The campaign is over. I do not know how soon we will enter Baghdad, but when we do you must look a lot smarter than you do now. Squad, Squad, 'shun! Dismiss." They clicked smartly round and saluted me, then broke away.

Joe and the others sitting within earshot were incredulous. "What is your military history?" asked Ian, amused.

I told him, "Very brief."

Reading came to me. "Why do our troops not go into Baghdad?" he asked. "Already there may be looting. I know. There will be many people killed if our troops do not enter."

This was my own view and the ways of the Foreign Office were beyond my comprehension. From the hour of the Cease Fire their word had prevailed. Having fought our way, step by step to the threshold of the city, we must now cool our heels outside. It would, apparently, be lowering the dignity of our ally, the Regent, if he were seen to be supported on arrival by British bayonets. It was apparently believed in Whitehall to be beyond the imagination of the wily Baghdadis to see that his return was brought about by the victory of British arms. "Were there not Iraqi troops enough in the city, now loyal of course to the new Government, to keep order?"

So we waited and, as darkness settled like a mantle over the domes and minarets across the river, the shooting began. We did not hear it, but to the Brigadier's ears, sleeping in the white colonial house of the British Embassy, came the growing crescendo of rifle and machine-gun fire. Baghdad was given up to the looters. All who dared to defend their own belongings were killed; while eight miles to the west waited the eager British force which could have prevented all this. Ah, yes, but the prestige of our Regent would have suffered!

It was argued afterwards in the Chancery of Baghdad that the Iraqis would have gone on fighting rather than agree to an Armistice on the basis of our immediate entry. Again, it was argued that our arrival would have precipitated street fighting with the brigade which we had pushed back into the town. Yet why, I asked, if they crumpled up on the outskirts, should they have stiffened in the middle?

Diplomacy is the continuation of war by other means, but it should not begin too soon.

Genius is a grasp of the essential; and, after victory, the essential is to keep control of the situation.

Without Joe and Ian, the Brigade Headquarters felt incomplete, although Corpo, the Staff Captain, had arrived up from Habbaniya. He said that back there one gathered that I had taken complete charge of the battle with my telephone; a jest which had enough truth in it to draw Peter Grant-Lawson's brows together above those thick-lensed glasses through which his eyes always glared at me like baffled fish in an aquarium.

Now Ian returned to the camp saying that Joe wanted me to go into the Embassy at Baghdad as his personal liaison officer until such time as the rest of the column were allowed to enter the city. This was Joe's quiet way of giving me a little leave. There was a wireless truck of ours in the garden of the Embassy now, and Joe would give me a list of codes to be used in the event of my having to send for help. I would find Joe there and he would give me his own instructions before returning to the camp himself.

This was unbelievably good fortune; it was a break for Grose too, who deserved some reward. I was only sorry that Williamson would have to remain decoding signals, and that Reading, our only interpreter, would also be required in the camp. There was the problem of sorting out the rations which were stowed in the back of the car for the four of us. There was a lot more sugar than when we had set out from Palestine and I had noticed a remarkable lightening of this problem after our forward elements entered the battered town of Falluja on the Euphrates.

I presented ripe melons far and wide; and stayed not upon the order of my going. I feared that the mirage might fade.

CHAPTER 29

I never saw a city so quiet as Baghdad when I entered it for the second time. The overnight shooting on the further bank of the river accounted for this. No one dared emerge into the streets, even in this part of the city. We drove into the Embassy by the main gates, where an Iraqi police guard was posted. I had an uneasy feeling that the enemy were beginning to think they had been fooled and that, after a day and a night had passed without the appearance of the formidable army which had driven their comrades back upon them, they were watching us, lynx-like, out of their dark brown eyes, and that any moment the trap might close again on the British colony.

I found the Brigadier, and he took me to the little 15 cwt. signal truck, with its three men, parked on a small lawn behind a tall hedge near the canteen. He gave me a slip of paper on which he had written three codes, should the Ambassador want me to send for help: 'Brigadier come,' (which would bring Joe alone); 'Cassano come,' (which meant the armoured cars); or 'All come,' (which meant the whole shooting match).

Joe introduced me to the Counsellor: "The most important fellow here," he added diplomatically, and Adrian Holman preened himself delightedly. He was a dapper gentleman and would have found me a room in the Ambassador's residence if Joe had not said that any corner would be good enough for me. So I was handed over to Vivian Holt, the Oriental-looking Oriental Secretary whom we had roused startled in the dawn of the Armistice, and he nobly provided me with a bed and made me free of his bathroom, beyond which he himself slept on a small balcony for coolness. I believe this was a great sacrifice for Vivian Holt, who loved to enjoy his comforts undisturbed, and had now for a whole month sacrificed his room to a succession of beleaguered British residents of Baghdad. His room opened out on to the roof, where a balustrade protected the sleepers from rolling down into the courtyard of the Chancery.

Adrian Holman conveyed Sir Kinahan Cornwallis's invitation to dinner in the private part of the Embassy. He also undertook to have a cable sent home for me from the Embassy, saying that I was enjoying myself after a romantic campaign.

With the return of peace, dignity came into its own again and General Waterhouse resumed his duties as head of the Military Mission to Iraq, with an office in the Chancery. We had hoped that Daghestani would be allowed to act as liaison officer between Kingcol and the Iraq Army, for we had taken a warm liking to him after the meeting at the anti-tank ditch under flag of truce. Moreoever he had been to 'the Shop'. Perhaps the Difaa thought him dangerously pro-British. At all events it was another officer, Nuri Jamail, who presented himself to the Embassy on the evening I arrived, and was introduced to me by General Waterhouse. He was a somewhat heavy-faced youth, with the walnut complexion typical of the Iraqi soldier; but he was very civil and had, in fact, done a gunnery course at Larkhill in Wiltshire. He was to be at my disposal for information and military liaison and we arranged that he should call on me early next morning so as to put me 'in the picture'.

I found my way up to the room which Vivian Holt had placed at my disposal and enjoyed the luxury of a bath for the first time since Habbaniya. I lay on the iron bedstead. Evidently I was not the only guest with access to the room, for there were several officers' chests marked 'Colonel Skinner, 19th Lancers' in white script. I had fished a fresh leather-bound diary out of my car — the previous volume having been completed up to our departure from the Mediterranean shore at Nathanya, and sent back, hurriedly sealed, from H.4 with a War Cameraman called Tozer to safe custody in Jerusalem. I had been lectured in Cairo upon the dangers of taking diaries into battle or of keeping them when there. Now, however, I felt it safe to resume. I had enough kit with me, thanks to the luxury of a staff car, to change into gabardine drill for the Ambassadorial board.

It was an astounding experience after the rigours of desert warfare, to find myself sipping a cool drink in an English drawing-room, where oil paintings, gilt furniture and soft carpets carried British diplomacy back to the Garden of Eden (which some believe to have been hereabouts). There were other guests — all men, so far as I can remember, or, if there were women, they made no impression. I have been told that Freya Stark was in the Embassy when I arrived, but, if so, she remained as indistinct as the shadows. (I remember two very spectacular Polish blondes sitting disconsolately near the fountain in the hall, waiting for somebody to befriend them.)

The Ambassador's dinner table was of shining mahogany, in which the brightly polished silver and the shaded candles were rosily reflected. It was a glowing, heart-warming scene. There was a cadaverous man called Bailey, with sunken eyes, who had been caught by the Iraqis distributing propaganda pamphlets from a launch after the outbreak of hostilities. Him they had chained in prison. I looked into his grey face. How little we can see of the minds of other men; how difficult to share their feelings. We go through some experience which others think they understand when they have expressed their sympathy. A great weariness of spirit comes over us at the mere thought of trying to convey an impression of it; yet we feel impelled to speak of our experience, if only in self-defence, fearing that we must in some way fall short of our fellows' expectations, that some allowance will be made for us when it is known what we have suffered. Afterwards we wish we had never spoken at all. How aptly the German commentator expressed it when he said, "One day the German infantryman who has been here at Orel will go home; and they will ask him all about it; and he will say 'Ja, ja'; and not another word will you get out of him, for it would be quite impossible for him to convey anything of this hell." Perhaps I, alone, at that dinner table was gifted with enough foresight not to prod Bailey's still tender memory. At first we babble, then we try to forget, and long after we can remember without pain and without regret. It is as if we reread a familiar story which holds some peculiar significance for us. Perhaps Bailey was anxious to talk; he did not seem to resent questions.

Sitting opposite me was Holman, very spruce in a dinner jacket, with a small dark moustache; very much the Counsellor. The talk turned, as it so often does in remote Embassies, to England and he asked where I lived. It was a pleasant surprise to both of us to learn that the woman from whom my wife and I had bought our London home was now remarried — to Adrian Holman. She was in Basra with the other wives who had been flown out of Baghdad by way of Habbaniya.

The Embassy could not do enough for us, but I was for a while the only representative of Kingcol whom they could entertain, and the Ambassador very kindly invited me to dine again before I left.

After dinner he asked me to join him in a four of bridge. He was a tall man, hard, stringy as a dried bean, with greying hair and a truly imposing nose. His eye was as keen as a vulture's. The Foreign Office had put the right man in the right place about five years too late; but although he had only arrived in the nick of time to be locked up inside his own Embassy by the Iraqis, his character, which had the edge and hardness and flexibility of a Toledo sword, may well have saved the lives, while maintaining the dignity, of the British subjects who were for a month at the mercy of an unscrupulous enemy.

The library to which we repaired that evening provided me with a shock, for it contained an air-conditioning plant in a walnut cabinet, which lowered the temperature abruptly from the hundreds to the seventies. "It is impossible to keep a cool head and work steadily without it," Sir Kinahan Cornwallis said. He told me that 2,000 people, mostly Jews, were believed to have been killed in the one night's looting, a figure which was subsequently reduced to 700 when more information became available.

Personality is an indefinable thing; yet it bites into the memory like sunlight on to a photographic plate. I can remember the Ambassador as clearly as if the hand we played were last week. Adrian Holman, playing opposite him, I can remember too; but who my partner facing me was I cannot recall. I am not a good bridge player. Poker, yes. When I arrived in Palestine the hardened warriors in my regiment unquestionably believed that another chicken had arrived for plucking, and were vaguely disturbed to find themselves paying my Mess bills for the duration of my brief stay with them, before I was taken by Joe King-stone from their midst to be his Intelligence Officer. So, if I am to be judged in Baghdad by my performance at bridge, no doubt I have faded, as my partner faded, from the recollection of the scene. I have a sort of feeling now that my partner must have been General Waterhouse, for he would scarcely have been left out of the Ambassador's game.

After the coldness of the library, where it was really necessary to wear a coat in order not to catch cold, the heat in the passage outside leading to the courtyard was extreme. Yet I slept reasonably well when I got up to bed.

I had hardly begun my breakfast in the canteen, the first morning when Nuri Jamail arrived, so I invited him to join me. He had already eaten, but consented, with some embarrassment, to sit beside me while I fed. Indeed, so great was his confusion that he babbled answers to all my casual questions: and from this one-sided conversation I was able to learn all that had passed on the Iraqi side of the campaign.

It was the Royal Air Force bombing in the early stages around Habbaniya that had caused most of their casualties. The Germans, he told me, during their bombing of Habbaniya were working to a detailed plan of the Cantonment, which they had got, he thought, from an

Italian aviator who helped in its construction and had now gone to train
Italian pilots. The Germans had never had more than a dozen Heinkels
and half a dozen Messerschmitts, and the Italians perhaps one squadron
of fighters. The Germans had found that the aviation spirit promised
them by Raschid Ali was not the right octane content for their
Messerschmitts and had been obliged to send for a chemical expert who
imported a Heath Robinson device for refining it at Mosul. This had, of
course, completely upset German calculations. I gathered that relations
between the Iraqis and the Germans had been very strained. The
Germans had not wanted the Iraqis to revolt so soon in the war; but
Raschid Ali had watched with growing alarm, shortly after his *coup d'
état,* the landing of considerable British forces from India at Basra. He
had been afraid to wait any longer and so he had struck, prematurely.

Nuri was quite frank with me about the attitude of the Iraq Army to
the British. They accepted the Armistice with reluctance and remained
violently anti-British and largely pro-German. It was an amazing
conversation, which could only have taken place so soon after the
cessation of hostilities. Later, relations between the Iraqis and ourselves became more wary, as they began to discern our material
weakness and to plan secretly for a resumption of hostilities under more
favourable conditions.

As soon as Nuri Jamail had departed, I wrote out a report of all he
had said, for he had in no way asked me to treat it in confidence, and
Vivian Holt agreed to have this typed for me. Unhappy man, he was
fated to go through life with a look of acute dyspepsia on his face. Yet it
was not as if he had worried himself into his grave over the situation in
Iraq. The reports from our Embassy immediately preceding the revolt
have passed into the archives of Military Intelligence as classic
misreadings of the situation by our accredited representatives.

The report was typed in time for me to give a copy to Colonel
Elphinstone, a dry-looking little stick of a man who yet had a kindly
heart and a wide knowledge (perhaps too retrospective) of the Levant.
He had arrived by air from Habbaniya and was returning almost as
soon. Another copy, with a covering letter to Habforce at Habbaniya, I
entrusted to the lean, hard-riding cavalry Colonel Skinner, who wore a
jaunty type of bush jacket, that hung outside the shorts, and was open at
the neck, with short sleeves. I had not seen one before, but they were
common in the Indian Army, I believe, and Joe and Ian soon set about
having them copied in Baghdad.

I had scarcely completed the report and was looking for Vivian Holt to get it typed when Joe arrived. A signal had come through to the truck from Brigade H.Q. saying that arrangements were being made for anyone who wanted to send a cable home to send it in to me for despatch in the town; and, when these arrived, Joe said, "Come on. Let's take a chukka round the town," and led the way down the drive in his utility van, with his driver sitting, as usual, behind him, while Grose drove my yellow staff car.

We turned half left outside the gates, where the police guard eyed us dubiously, and drove to the Feisal Statue, a magnificent equestrian bronze, where a wide street runs up to the Maude Bridge. This broad, low, graceful span carried us over the quarter-mile wide fast-flowing brown waters of the Tigris until we came to Raschid Street, the main street of the city which runs parallel with the river on the east bank.

Here everything was disorder. The steel shutters of the shop windows were wrenched away or hacked open with axes. The dim interiors of the looted shops were bare of merchandise. There was no one to be seen. Baghdad might have been a city of the dead.

Turning right in Raschid Street we came to the General Post Office, where a clock hung out over the pavement on the left side of the street. We drew up beside the kerb and went inside, leaving our drivers to guard the cars. The Post Office would not have been out of place in any small provincial town at home. A single clerk wearing European clothes gave us cable forms, with some signs of embarrassment, and Joe and I began to lick our pencils meditatively.

First of all I copied out the cables for Peter Grant-Lawson, Corpo, Ian Spence and Dick Schuster. Dick's was to his mother — I remembered the address long afterwards because of its robust Anglo-Saxon — Great Tew, Oxon — and told her everything. 'Long hot hack to meet. Easy kill. Don't know where we draw next.' Having sent these I began on a night lettergram of my own, and I decided, as a brief cable had already gone from the Embassy, to see how much the censorship would swallow so soon after the reopening of communications with Baghdad, and wrote, 'Have been having time of my life, picturesque campaign, captured Italian pilot on enemy side of canal, 18-pounder glanced off my mudguard without exploding, entered Baghdad blindfold after receiving Iraqi delegates with flag of truce.' Joe saw me pencilling away and no doubt throught I was writing a personal communiqué. He sidled over to the counter and said, "Come on. Let me see what you *have* written." He was much entertained, but I explained, "It is only for my wife and children. They will be thrilled by all that sort.

of thing."

"You will probably get shot for it," Joe chuckled.

He left me to send it and wandered out of the Post Office in search of lime juice and whisky. When I emerged into the glare of the street I found his utility van still there, and with the driver beside, wondering where his brigadier had got to. "He shouldn't go off like that by himself."

Possibly it was unwise, but Joe and I carried our revolvers in canvas holsters attached to the belt of our webbing equipment, while the drivers were armed with rifles.

I found Joe in the Claridge Hotel concluding with the proprietor a deal in bottles of lime juice and whisky. I contributed some of the cash and we walked on to the Semiramis Hotel. This was a long low building of cream plaster with pseudo-Egyptian designs round the door. We found the proprietor. (Everyone with whom we spoke seemed to be holding his breath — since the riot.) He was a shrewd Baghdadi and had known how to keep in with the looters. He had a lot of provisions which he was glad to sell us.

So far we were only buying for the Officers' Mess, but Joe was turning over in his mind ways of victualling his whole force which had lived on bully beef, biscuits and tea for three weeks. He meant to secure promptly some portion of the luxury of this great eastern city for them. If he waited for the ordinary army commissariat to function, we should be gone again before the men of Kingcol had tasted so much as a fig.

We walked back to our cars and recrossed the river by the big green bridge. To right and left curved the City of the Caliphs, a crescent town, where an occasional minaret broke the skyline of the water front; but not beautiful at close quarters. It was an overgrown Arab village, an enlarged version of Nablus; yet in its crowded alley-ways and behind its mud-coloured exterior glowed the mystery of Oriental carpets and the dark doings of cruel men.

We found the Rest Camp, where our troops were to be quartered, next to a yellow brick church of the Scottish Mission. The camp was surrounded by barbed wire. Within its compass were a number of palm trees, which offered an inviting shade, and some neat rectangular brick buildings with flat roofs and verandas leading into bare, swept-out rooms. The camp had apparently been used to intern the British who had not found refuge in the Embassy. Indeed, it savoured ominously of the mouse-trap. Once inside we should be easy meat for the 40,000 Iraqi troops whom we had fought to a miraculous

Armistice. This danger was all the greater since a fresh brigade from Kirkuk had been rushed down to quell the rioters; which it had only done by opening fire on the mob. Nevertheless there was a sense of incompletion about our conquest so long as we were kept at arm's length outside the city by diplomatic niceties.

Joe's enquiries at the Embassy for a man who could buy up half the provisions in Baghdad without letting us be robbed in the process led him to a retired Colonel Dwyer, who had at one time been an Army Supply Officer in these parts. I was despatched to his house, which I found with some difficulty in a side street leading down to the water's edge on the west bank. The house, like others in this quarter which seemed to be a residential part for Europeans, was in the Florentine style, with wooden shutters and some carving on the weather-beaten oak door. It was opened furtively by a daughter who said that the Colonel was round at the Embassy, so I went back there and found him for Joe.

"I must take you into my confidence," Joe told him. "I have only got 750 chaps out there, all told." The Colonel's eyebrows nearly disappeared into his thin hair. 'And I don't want any of these Iraqis to know it. Do you think you can buy up enough stores for that lot from different people without their knowing how many are being fed?"

"There would be no difficulty about the buying," said the Colonel. "The trouble would be delivering the goods."

"We can arrange to collect them," Joe said. "If you will have the merchants dump their loads at the Iron Bridge I can send my lorries in to collect the stuff there."

"All right," said Dwyer. "Now what will you want? Butter and sugar, I suppose. Meat and fresh vegetables." And there was no more fuss about it. By a curious coincidence most of the buying was done by Colonel Dwyer from the proprietor of the Semiramis Hotel whom we had already met; and all that the Army Supply Officer, who eventually arrived from Jerusalem to regularise the position, had to do, was hand over the taxpayers' money. Napoleon, pointing to the fertile plains of Lombardy from the Ligurian Hills, could not have offered his ragged army richer fare than we obtained; and obtained it, moreoever, not by loot but by a transaction which smoothed relations between the occupying force and the merchants of the conquered city.

Joe returned to the Experimental Farm and I got some tea at the Embassy canteen, where a number of people who had left the grounds at the first mention of the Armistice had hurriedly reappeared when the looting broke out. Everyone had tales of houses stripped of furniture, plate, linen; the collections of a lifetime gone.

After tea, while I was getting things out of my car, now parked conveniently beside the signal truck on the lawn, a swarm of war correspondents descended upon me. They had been landed by air from Jerusalem in time to witness the ceremonial entry of British troops into Baghdad — so far the only city of renown captured by ourselves during the opening hazards of the Second World War. My Italian parachute and a dented mudguard were not much to get on with, but in the absence of anything else they were photographed from all angles, and I was posed in an attitude of concentrated surprise holding swathes of white silk; while Grose stood by, grinning happily at the recollection of our adventures in the campaign. By a curious coincidence this picture was published in the *Palestine Post* the day after I arrived wounded in hospital at Jerusalem and earned me an inflated reputation for an episode which by then seemed ludicrously safe in retrospect. This wretched Italian airman seemed destined to dog my footsteps right back to the shadows of Westminster, where the wraith grew gradually dustier and finally disappeared.

I decided to do another 'chukka' next day round the town on my own, and, taking Grose, drove over the Maude Bridge again into Raschid Street. The scene was very different today. The streets were thronged with Iraqis who stared first in astonishment, then in sullen resentment, and soon with rising anger at a British car. When I got out to enter a shop I was elbowed with ostentatious indifference towards the gutter. It was difficult to keep my temper. If this sort of thing were going to happen often, it would be impossible to avoid precipitating a scene. It was evident that the Iraqis, who had been led to fear the invasion of a mighty army, looked with contempt upon a single khaki car. If this is the

314

whole British Army, their hating eyes declared, we know how to deal with it. I went into a shop in search of some sock suspenders (I had been reduced to string for holding up my buff stockings) and had to pay an exorbitant price to a cynical merchant in front of some obviously contemptuous Iraqis. Under these conditions my revolver was dead weight. The press was everywhere too tight and the crowd would have lynched me as soon as look at me. I found Grose, too, in a very ruffled mood, although looking as casual as he could beside the car, when I rejoined him where he stood smoking a cigarette (which he stamped on with his boot at my approach). The crowd spat in the gutter as we pulled away from the kerb.

I resented the idea of being chivvied out of a city which we were supposed to have conquered, and although it was tempting to withdraw hurriedly to the peaceful enclosure of the British Embassy, I decided to visit the leading carpet shop in Baghdad. I had found in the street of the Khalil Mosque in Cairo an Isphahan carpet of the sixteenth century; so rare as to be considered unobtainable nowadays. But where, I thought, was I more likely to find another than in Baghdad? I had been told of the shop — it was in a side street turning off the approach to the bridge on this side of the river. I found the door closed, but after some knocking it was opened cautiously, and the proprietor let me in. He was a youngish man, and he sat dazed on a chair in the middle of his shop accompanied by an assistant. Nothing but his ledgers had been left to him and these were all strewn about the floor of the inner office. There was a porcelain plate also, of a misty blue design, which had been broken when it was wrenched off the wall. Of the carpets for which his shop was celebrated not one remained: not a rug; not a prayer mat.

"We are lucky to have been left alive," the owner said. He spoke English fairly well. "I am sorry that I have nothing to offer you. Perhaps if you come again one day . . . . "

I left him, appalled.

Mob violence is something to which we are not accustomed in England. I have seen law and order vanish in the wake of military force — first among the bedouin who despoiled the pedigree chicken runs at the Research Station; now in Baghdad itself. Anarchy wears an ugly face; or is civilisation only the painted mask which we hold before it?

I drove thoughtfully back to the British Embassy.

I found a surprise waiting for me; two letters from my wife. They were, like all letters which fetched up in the Near East, a haphazard selection from a faithful sequence despatched against the ordered background of life in England. Ah, well, separation is the saddest thong of war: which the Army Post Office seems to wield with savage glee.

One of the war correspondents sought me out near the wireless truck and told me of an interesting group of people whom he had met, who had been devoting themselves, in the best Phillips Oppenheim manner, to some amateur intelligence. They had been interned by the Iraqis during the campaign, but were now out and about, a little shaken, but with their enthusiasm in no way diminished. They had a flat on the east bank of the river in a cul-de-sac near the Zia Hotel and had taken the precaution of fitting an armour plated door to it, to which they would be happy to give me a key should I at any time find myself in that part of the city and in need of sudden refuge.

This evidence of my notoriety was surprising, and I readily agreed to be introduced to a member of this mysterious gang.

Within a short time the correspondent reappeared with a weedy-looking doctor in the middle thirties wearing a dirty white drill suit. He was obviously in a highly strung condition. He made certain violent allegations against some of our official representatives, one of whom, he assured me, was laughed at throughout the Orient as well-known sexual pervert, and declared that the other had failed to keep a rendezvous on the night of Raschid Ali's rebellion, leaving him and his companion to be caught and imprisoned by the Iraqis. By this time I had acquired a sober incredulity in listening to people, which enabled me to preserve an interest in their own activities while professing to keep an open mind on their assertions.

There might or might not be any truth in the doctor's assertion that he and his friends had been left to take the rap by respected officers who paraded before me their importance and standing with the Arabs. I meant to leave no source of information untapped.

The doctor had, he told me, a small house near an important engineering works, and, since he assured me that these works were capable of repairing anything from an 18-pounder breech block to a locomotive, I thought of our own damaged 25-pounder, and offered to drive the doctor out to his house. Joe passed, lightfooted as an African elephant, which can move swiftly through the jungle without breaking a twig. He was going down the drive, I do not know where, but he gave me no more than a glance out of the corner of his eye when he saw me sitting on a trestle table opposite the signal truck, deep in conversation with the doctor in white drill. Joe did not, like Peter Grant-Lawson, prod and pry into my intelligence activities. He left people to get on with their own jobs in their own way, and teased them only by the results.

I got into my car, taking Grose to drive it, and went west until we were on the outskirts of the city; then we followed a mud road, where it divided, and were soon bumping across a railway line and skirting the corrugated iron palisading of the engineering yards which the doctor had mentioned. There were trees growing on the right of the road and some rough grass. Turning down a lane we came to a little two-storeyed white cottage, with a pleasant garden behind it. The front door was open, but it was evident, as soon as we stepped inside, that the place had not been looted. It had even been dusted by the doctor's Iraqi servant, who combined the duties of cook-housemaid and gardener, and whom he was delighted to find in response to a shout. There were shelves of books, coloured reproductions of famous oil paintings, a wireless set and a gramophone. In the scullery were enough crockery and provisions for the doctor to prepare some tea, of which I suggested giving Grose a cup.

The doctor was relieved to find his belongings intact. This he attributed to the cottage's remoteness from the centre of the city and the fact that he was in peacetime an employee of the Iraqi Government.

He told me that I could make use of the cottage any time I liked, and gave instructions to his servant accordingly. He himself was living at present in the flat near the Zia Hotel, which I had not yet visited. On the drive back to the Embassy the doctor, who was still in a very nervy state, told me how he had shot an Iraqi who was shadowing him on this very road, and buried the body in a ditch, shortly before the rebellion. As I had been Intelligence Officer to the Striking Force, which for the past three weeks had been engaged in killing as many Iraqi soldiers as possible, there did not seem to me to be anything odd in this pronouncement. A few days later, however, I found one of the officers, to whom the doctor had referred in such pointed terms, discussing with Adrian Holman the need for getting him to the Air Force Hospital in Habbaniya, where he could be kept under observation, as he was going about telling everybody that he was in the British Secret Service and had shot an Iraqi. Since I was only supposed to know him as a doctor who had been employed by the Iraqi Government, and he himself had asked me not to reveal that he was having any dealings with me as an Intelligence Officer, I expressed only a casual interest, and agreed that when I met him he had certainly seemed in an excited condition. I had yet to meet his partner in amateur research.

The war correspondents, with whom I enjoyed the friendliest relations and to whom I gave advance information whenever possible, were eager to know when the ceremonial entry of Kingcol into Baghdad was going to take place. This I was very keen to tell them, as it seemed to me of the first importance to capitalise the propaganda value of this romantic and, in many ways, spectacular achievement. I was about to ask Joe whether this information could be given when he himself tackled me. "You haven't told those fellows when we are coming in, I hope?"

"No," I replied. "But surely it would be a good thing for them to film the entry of our troops."

"No," he said firmly.

Possibly he was afraid that, if they knew and were waiting with cameras in readiness, a hostile crowd would begin to collect, and that the arrival of our troops might then precipitate a riot: but I really think that it was no more than the inherent aversion to publicity of the professional British soldier.

I wondered if it were an occasion for putting the telescope to the blind eye and was tempted to tell my war correspondent friends that it would be healthy for them to take an early walk at about 5 o'clock next morning near the Feisal Statue. But the responsibility for the safety of our troops did not rest on my shoulders, and I felt that Joe had enough burdens. I probably also feared his wrath: at all events I remained dumb and got up silently at 4 o'clock next morning when Grose came to wake me. He had prepared some tea and brought it up to me. I was sleeping on the roof, near the parapet which overlooked the garden, so that the signallers could wake me with a shout if I was wanted urgently at the signal truck during the night.

Before he returned to camp, Joe had left a note for me, written in pencil on the back of a pink army signal form.

> Somerset.
> (1) I am returning to Bde. H.Q.
> (2) You will stay here overnight and will meet me (or wait) at Iron Bridge at 05.15 tomorrow.
> (3) WT set will stay here until further orders.
>
> J.K.

I dressed in shorts and bush shirt, put on my army cap, and tiptoed across the roof and down the stairs, fearful of waking up the people who were sleeping about the roof. Grose silently rolled up my bedding and the mosquito-net, then followed me down to the car. We drove out of the gates, before even the wary war correspondents had noticed our departure.

My orders were to meet the head of the column, which would consist of Cassano's armoured cars, at the Iron Bridge over the Wash-Wash channel and direct him to the roundabout, after which Corpo would have arrived and would go up to the Feisal Statue, and direct them down to the Rest Camp.

As I crossed the bare space of the roundabout, where the lofty Babylonian Gateway stood in vacant ceremony, I noticed that there were Iraq Mounted Police everywhere about, sitting easily in their saddles. The Defence Ministry were evidently prepared to 'play'. I went on to the Iron Bridge and waited at the near end of it. Five o'clock passed and there was no sign of the armoured cars. An Iraq Army guard was encamped at the further approach, and I began to wonder whether we had been lured into a trap; but presently I saw the first of the grey conning-towers creeping up the further ramp and enter upon the bridge span. Cassano's dark hair and Mephistophelean eyebrows leant towards me from the conning tower.

"The bastards haven't repaired the road over the anti-tank ditch yet," he explained, "and we have been going round in circles. Where do we go from here?"

"Is the rest of the column following?" I asked.

He raised himself on his forearms, so that the half of him in greasy white overalls appeared, and looked back.

"There seem to be a hell of a lot of things behind us."

I told him to go on, past an aerodrome on his left, and a road on his right, leading to the Wash-Wash camp, where an entire Iraqi brigade was quartered, and he would come to the roundabout.

"After that you go on up the street with flower beds down its middle, until you come to a whopping great bronze statue of King Feisal on his horse; turn right and you will come to a yellow brick church. The camp is just beyond that. You can't miss the barbed wire."

"We shall probably find ourselves in the bag," said Cassano gloomily. "It is all too quiet for my liking."

He turned in the opening of his conning tower, signalled with his arm to the two armoured cars following, and slipped down out of sight.

Soon Joe arrived in his utility van. I followed him as far as the roundabout and he went half-way up the street to take the salute of the column as it rolled past. Ian, who was following him, and was acting Brigade Major in Peter's absence with sand-fly fever, went on to the camp to make arrangements, while Corpo, in another staff car, I

320

directed to the Feisal statue. I remained standing beside the Great
Ceremonial Arch with its antique, long-bearded statue of King Sargon
in stone. I watched the faces of the Iraq police on their grey chargers.
They were smartly turned out, and the polish on their saddlery would
have satisfied a Corporal of Horse in my own regiment. Their eyebrows
went up a little at the armoured cars. Perhaps they were expecting some
of the famous fifty tanks. Their expressions remained contemptuous.

My job at the roundabout was that of a traffic policeman; to prevent
the vehicles turning off down one of the wrong turnings. I had placed
my car, therefore, at the beginning of the correct road, and as the
vehicles plumped over the level crossing and nosed their way into the
circle, they would stare this way and that, then seeing me, gather speed
and go by, giving me a wave if they happened to know me. Thus the
stream of vehicles belonging to the composite squadron of Blues and
Life Guards (the only squadron of my regiment in this column) passed
by me. With its supply vehicles, a modern army equipped for fighting at
long range across the desert contains an imposing number of vehicles;
and, as the stream came on and on, this squadron followed by two
companies of the Essex Regiment, and a seemingly endless line of
R.A.S.C. supply lorries, the contempt on the faces of the Iraqi police
began to give way to surprise. Then came the two Bren-carriers which
had covered the whole seven hundred miles of our journeyings,
although never, as events turned out, used in action; and lastly came the
murderous snouts of the 25-pounders, rattling by in the tow of the
hump-backed 'dragons', and followed by the ammunition limbers.
Then at last I saw awe on the faces of the men we had beaten, and
they exchanged understanding looks with each other under their heavy
black brows.

It took over two hours for Kingcol to file through the roundabout,
and I thought sadly of the cinema audiences of America (not yet at war),
of the Argentine, Chile, Brazil, Portugal and Spain, who might have
watched with the same dawning look of wonder this evidence of British
striking power at the end of an historic march. For it is no ordinary army
that can cross a waterless desert for the first time in history, and deliver
at the end of seven hundred miles of desert going a punch which sends a
well-equipped army of four divisions reeling into Armistice. Kingcol,
and Kingcol alone, had done this; while, far down the lower reaches of
the Tigris and the Euphrates, a division of the Indian Army was
laboriously preparing for a long campaign. But the cinema audiences of
Britain and the world must get only a pale rehash of it after the event.

Indeed, Joe went so far as to permit them to film men polishing their rifles and tending their guns, while I was told to take a section of lumpers up to the Embassy, where they filed along the parapet which overlooks the Tigris, and looked as murderous as only an army of twelve men can. In lieu of armoured cars and 25-pounders passing the Sargon Gate of Khorsabad, the cinema recorded only the homely scene of my offering Corporal Major Barrat a cigarette (from a tin which was not mine) against the romantic skyline of the eastern bank which shows across the river from the British Embassy. 'After the fall of Baghdad.' 'The British Army is coming. Hush, hush, my child. Turn down the wick and shed a feeble glow.' I believe that the photographers with commendable realism depicted two British officers, blindfolded, entering Baghdad. I do not know whom these posthumous bandages concealed, but they were certainly not Ian Spence and myself, whom the scene was reconstructed to represent.

After the freedom and luxury of a British Embassy the return to camp life was circumscribing. But I could not complain; indeed I was deeply indebted to Joe for his thoughtfulness. Moreoever, with Ian Spence acting Brigade Major in Peter's absence at hospital, I was not badgered.

We had been warned to expect a ceremonial visit from the General commanding the Iraqi garrison as soon as we had moved in, so Joe told me to have the whole guard turned out in his honour. The party of Iraqi staff officers arrived in cars at 10 o'clock and the guard presented arms with a flourish which would have done credit to their appearance on the barrack square at Windsor. The General was tremendously pleased, and Joe gave me a wink which made it difficult for me to control my features.

The Iraqi General was a bulky man with grizzled hair, whose buff linen uniform sat lightly on him, and who struck me as a very able commander. His was the brigade which had been brought down from Kirkuk to quell the rioters, and I was glad that he had remained on guard over the oilfields during the campaign. We invited the Iraqis into our Mess and they sat at the long trestle table with us, while tea was brought in for the party. Nuri Jamail sat next to me and did most of the interpreting, although Reading was also there to help.

Two hours later we returned the compliment, driving in a line of staff cars to the Wash-Wash camp. The Brigadier's van led, followed by Ian Spence. I brought up the rear and, as we pulled alongside the lofty barrack building of clay walls, the Iraqi sentries saluted us.

We went up some stone steps into a dim, cool room, where the walls were of peeling plaster. We passed into an inner room where tea and sweet, coloured biscuits were served to us on dainty porcelain. The conversation was amicable, but avoided the recent fighting, and, after a short stay during which I had two cups of tea, we went back to our own camp.

There the first building was given up to a guard-house and Brigade Headquarter offices; the next to our Mess, and the third to our sleeping quarters. Joe had a room to himself, but the rest of us doubled up; and, although as a rule I hate having to share a room with anyone, I was fortunate in having to share with Dick Schuster. I had my suitcase and valise dumped in there, but slept outside on the mud compound where it was cooler, although Dick did not seem to find the room with its fly-proofed door and window oppressive.

Brigade routine returned to normal for the first time since Habbaniya. The office truck with its heavy canvas awnings was parked at the end of the administrative building. One officer slept each night outside the offices on duty. The allocation of office space was cramping. I was expected by Peter (when he returned) to share a narrow room with the Brigadier and himself. No doubt he wanted to be able to keep an eye on my doings, but I knew from experience that, where the Brigadier was concerned, a little of me went a long way, so it would have been quite impossible for me to scratch away at my maps and reports while the Brigadier was trying to work. So I took to sitting in the office truck, where I looked very studious, when Joe passed, but was most of the time memorising Russian proverbs in the firm conviction that we would soon be going through Persia to the foothills of the Caucasus.

Regular mails began to reach us again. Fragments of literary experiment turned up unexpectedly in Baghdad. The typescript of *The Teetotalitarian State*, on which I had been working when war broke out, had been returned to the Cavalry Barracks at Windsor and thence sent on to the Middle East. A letter from my literary agent, in a pulpy envelope rubber-stamped 'Salvaged from the sea', informed me that the only manuscript of my novel on Oliver Cromwell's experiences as a back bench member of Parliament, for a Fen-land constituency in the Eastern Counties when he was twenty-seven, had been destroyed in the fire which blitzed a publishing house. That meant one novel less in the world. Perhaps it was just as well: but the fate of both manuscript and letter was a vivid reminder of the dark background of war against which our own sunny campaigns were staged.

It was almost as difficult to be away from Brigade Headquarters without having to justify every second's absence to Peter Grant-Lawson as it had been at Habbaniya. However, I did not let this worry me very much, and Peter breathed heavily in contempt of my 'fly-by-night' methods of intelligence, when I ought, in his opinion, to be keeping an intelligence summary (of life in camp?); and marking up maps (of which campaign?)

Our army signal truck was still in the Embassy grounds, and I had arranged with the doctor that, if he wanted to see me, he would leave a message with the operator: 'The doctor will be calling at . . . ' such and such a time, when he would be at the Embassy. I had not yet availed myself of his invitation to visit the flat near the Zia Hotel, for I had been very busy; but I now got a signal: 'The doctor will be calling at six o'clock,' and drove up to the Embassy. He was accompanied by his friend, a most surprising young man called G.D. — who wore a khaki shirt, riding breeches and black jackboots, in a temperature which made a shirt and shorts uncomfortable enough. He looked for all the world like a member of the Hitler Jugend; and it was clear to me that he enjoyed dramatising himself. He told me how he and the doctor had seen lorry-loads of ammunition passing through Baghdad on the way up to Habbaniya before the Iraqis opened fire on the cantonment, but had not been able to communicate the warning in time. They had, however, succeeded in removing the fuse-caps from a number of the shells, thus immunising them. I wondered if I owed to him the fact that the 18-pounder which hit my car west of Baghdad had failed to explode. He was now going off by aeroplane to Habbaniya to report his experiences and would like me to use his organisation while he was away. He had an Indian clerk, with a typewriter, who had, he said, an amazing flair for picking up information, and knew the names of all the German, Italian and Russian agents in Baghdad.

This was an assertion not to be overlooked, and I promised to seek out the Indian at an early opportunity. My idea was that in Baghdad, where the German intrigues for the Near Orient had found a focal point, the clue to their plan of world conquest might well be found while the trail was still hot. It was less than a week since the German Air Mission had left, when Raschid Ali bolted. G.D. departed on his errand, to which he managed to convey an air of mystery — although others were flying to and from Habbaniya every day — and the doctor returned to the flat, which of course they occupied openly as normal civilians. I did not, however, wish to be seen visiting it, as I was known to be the Intelligence Officer to the Occupying Force.

A convenient opportunity presented itself with the invitation of some engineers of the Raffadan Oil Company, who were returning to Khanaquin and who called to see Dick about opening up signal communication with us in the event of danger. They asked me to come for a drink to the Zia Hotel. I found it down a narrow alley off Raschid Street. The hotel was on the river front, very nearly opposite the point where our own camp was situated beyond the east bank. The engineers were stimulating fellows and they introduced me to a retired naval commander in the Iraq Petroleum Company who had been in the country for many years. I asked him if he could give me detailed information of the water supplies, and pumping capacity available on the Tripoli pipe line. (If we were going into Syria this would be important.) He said that he could not reveal these facts without authorisation from the Embassy, but, if I would get the Commercial Attaché to sign a paper, the company would naturally give me any information they possessed. I told him that this could be very easily fixed with the Embassy and we arranged to meet at the company's offices next day.

In the meantime his friends pressed me to stay on for dinner, and I was learning so much from them that I agreed to do so (Peter notwithstanding). I felt, moreover, that, if the Iraqis knew that I had been dining in the hotel, they would be less likely to connect me with the flat next door. As it was now dusk I excused myself for half an hour, on the pretext of an errand in the city, and, slipping out of the hotel, went up the flight of steps which had been described to me, and unlocked the iron door with a Yale key.

Once inside I found myself at the foot of some wooden stairs and called up to know if anyone were about. The Indian of whom I had heard appeared at the top of the banisters, somewhat alarmed, but I explained that Mr. G.D. had left his key with me and told me to make use of the place. According to G.D. there were enough provisions in the flat to stand a siege. The Indian was relieved when he heard my name. He was dressed like a European and I did not like the look of him; a crafty fellow. However, I went up the stairs and we entered a corridor out of which several rooms opened, and which led straight through to a balcony overhanging the river.

In a sitting-room on the left was a table laid for tea and a young schoolmaster, called W —, who taught normally in the Iraq Government School at —, but who had been shut up on the outbreak of hostilities. Like the others I had seen, he was still considerably shaken by the experience. He was now, it seemed, working with G.D. and the Doctor, and I had, in fact, heard one of them mention him. The Doctor was out somewhere, but W — pressed me to have some tea, which I did. I did not, however, know how much he was in G.D.'s confidence, and so asked the Indian to show me over the flat, in case I should have occasion to make use of it at any time. The balcony was, in fact, an extension of the one belonging to the Zia Hotel, and was divided from it only by a partition. I reflected that, in the event of trouble, it would be easy enough to identify the flat from the river and gain access to it, by boat, if necessary. I now told the Indian that I was anxious to have names of any enemy agents, and he was full of self-confidence as to the importance of his contacts in this connection. He promised to prepare for me an exact list within a day or two. Having obtained this promise I had nothing further to gain, and, after expressing myself duly impressed by the flat, which was even fitted up with some folding iron Army bedsteads, in case several people were trapped in it, I was seen down the stairs by W — and the Indian, and slipped unobtrusively back into the hotel.

It was a pleasant evening, dining there, and sipping our coffee on the veranda afterwards, as darkness fell with a rich blueness over the broad river and the twinkling lights began to come out along the further bank. I learnt, with interest, that the petrol wagons of the Anglo-Iranian Oil Company travelled freely into Persia right up through Tabriz to the Russian frontier. I asked them whether they thought I could be disguised as an assistant and thus be smuggled into Persia to do the round. They did not think so, but suggested my seeing the Manager of the company.

While Rupert Hardy's column was racing across Iraq to show the Union Jack in the oilfields of Kirkuk, another squadron of the Household Cavalry, under Eric Gooch, known as Gocol, was sent up to Mosul for the same purpose. This squadron was part of the northern column which had been blocked in its attempt to outflank Baghdad at Kadhimain, and had returned, somewhat crestfallen, after the Armistice, to Habbaniya, without having been allowed a glimpse of Baghdad. They thought evilly of our good fortune.

Harcol and Gocol were no sooner in position than an exciting signal passed through our headquarters to them, saying that Raschid Ali, who had fled to Persia by way of Qasr-i-Shirin before the Armistice, was now trying to get back across Iraq to join the Axis Powers. He was believed to be travelling in a grey saloon car by way of the Rowanduz Gorge, which would lead him straight into Eric Gooch's arms. We waited hourly for news of the grey car or its capture, but the wily Gaylani was not to be caught as easily as all that, and we next heard of him being fêted by Hitler in Berlin.

CHAPTER 32

While waiting for the report of the Indian to come in, I was anxious to re-establish contact with Ali Suhail. He had given me his Arabic visiting card at Monasir, and written in ink with his fountain pen a telephone number on the back of it. Reading said that Ali Suhail's house was actually in Kadhimain where the holy shrine of the Shia Sect, with its famous golden domes, was situated. Kadhimain was forbidden to us at present, under orders from General Waterhouse, for fear of religious feeling there, which might be excited so soon after the campaign. A political officer, called Captain Jeffries, with the Indian Army at Basra had gone into the Sukh at Nasariya with an Iraq police escort; both he and the escort were beaten to death. So I asked Reading to telephone to Ali Suhail's house; and the sheikh invited me to lunch. Peter was furious at my wishing to absent myself at all, and asked pointedly if the house were in Baghdad. I said it was in the northern part of the city (if we can regard Kadhimain as a suburb) and so turned the conversation to a captured Iraqi rifle, which Ali Suhail had handed over, and which, he said, the Brigade Major had promised to return after the campaign. Peter denied having promised anything of the kind, and said, "My policy is never to put a weapon in the hands of a black man." It transpired that Ian Spence had promised Ali Suhail the rifle while I was away at the Embassy as liaison officer. Therefore I took the rifle and set out in my car with Grose and Reading.

We drove over the Maude Bridge and, turning left, passed through a part of Baghdad which I did not know. We must have driven for two miles, passing the Defence Ministry, called Difaa, and so on to a less populated part of the city where the residences of wealthy Baghdadis were screened by cool green gardens, until we came to a pontoon bridge over the river. Here we were stopped by Iraqi guards, but they did not detain us, although we had a to wait for a vehicle crossing from the other side, as there was only a single track across the plank bridge. This crossing, supported on barges, had been in existence for some years, but was not marked on our ancient military maps.

327

On the farther side of the bridge (where Kadhimain began) we found a slave of Ali Suhail's, in keffiyeh and gown, armed with a rifle, waiting to escort us to his master's house. This was a surprise, and, to me, a disappointment for, like other buildings of the wealthy Iraqis here, it might have been copied faithfully from any villa in Kingston or East Sheen. The Western ideal of the Oriental in these surroundings was shattering. We pulled up in a narrow road in front of the house, where Ali Suhail was waiting to welcome me. I got out, flourishing the rifle which I had brought for him and his black face shone with white teeth. We passed on foot through a small gate in the front garden, down some steps into a hallway (where I almost expected to see a hatstand — if the Muslim did not abhor such headcovering) and were shown into a small parlour. This was the East Sheen equivalent of an Eastern audience room, for, ranged against the walls, were patterned armchairs. Ali Suhail sat beside me; while coffee was served on little tables before us. I laid my topi and leather-covered knotty cane on the table. I had come unarmed purposely, but Reading, still wearing his only pair of khaki shorts and shirt, had a service revolver in a canvas holster in his belt, and Grose (who ranked as my slave) waited outside with a rifle.

Ali Suhail and I exchanged compliments through Reading. I said that to be welcomed into his house was indeed an honour; to which he replied that to have me under his roof was an even greater distinction. He had, he said, invited both his brothers to meet me, Sheikh Hussein and Sheikh Hassan, both of whom had been detained at Diwaniya by Rashid Ali for their known British sentiments.

Hussein Suhail was the first of the brothers to arrive; a regal personality with a lean brown face, hawk nose, and thin black beard. He wore a brown robe with gold embroidery and a delicately patterned white linen keffiyeh fastened to his head by the double ropes of a gold braid aqal, such as only important sheikhs wear. He was a sick man, but carried proudly, slung over his shoulder, the presentation binoculars which General Wavell had sent him. They had been captured from an Italian officer at Sidi Barrani, and on the top of the leather case Wavell had put a gold plaque, on which the gift was inscribed in English and Arabic. He said that the binoculars had been described as his 'death-warrant' during the rebellion of Raschid Ali, but he and his brother had, in fact, been detained with every mark of consideration. They had been taken away from Baghdad for fear that their influence in the capital was too great. "But," laughed Hussein, "our influence was not small in Diwaniya."

Sheikh Hassan, who next arrived, was a man of much more robust build, and displayed a Western note in a tailor-made cream jacket over his ample cream robe. His face was square, with a broad black beard closely shaped to his chin. He was much more massive than either of his brothers, and conveyed, indeed, an impression of great power. He had the same twinkle in his dark eyes as Ali. We exchanged greetings as fellow Members of Parliament. He gave me a photograph of himself, which he signed on the back, and, not to be out-done by this, I found the spare copy of a photo fixed to my army identity card and returned the compliment.

We then went into lunch and, here again, the shock of sitting up to a table and eating from plates on a table-cloth with knives and forks overwhelmed me. We were served with boiled fowl and rice, seasoned with gherkins. Reading, of course, was admitted to the board, and I noticed that the three sheikhs treated him very much as an equal, exchanging jokes, which confirmed my conviction that Reading was a very high-caste Arab himself.

As lunch proceeded, Hussein Suhail told me something of great interest: until yesterday the Iraq Army had been planning to resume the war against the British, and before the Armistice had removed all their heavy ordnance to Shahanaban, about forty-five miles north-east of Baghdad. There they had been reorganising; but now they had abandoned the idea and this morning their warlike stores had been moving back into Baghdad. We talked mostly of Churchill, about whom they could not hear enough anecdotes. He was obviously a figure which appealed to the Arab mind; his strength, his courage and his sense of humour; his robust indifference to puritan standards of conduct; all this endeared him to the Arab. I could not profess a close acquaintance with the wartime leader of the British Empire, but I told them how he had entered the House of Commons when I (aged twenty-four) was about to make my maiden speech and had sat beside me. I was in fact sitting in his accustomed place (which amused the brothers Suhail almost as much as it had amused the House of Commons) and I had made to give way to the great parliamentarian. But Winston had said, "Are you going to make your maiden speech?" On my replying that such was my hope and intention, he had pressed me back into the corner seat below the gangway and taken the next place.

His description of Parliament enchanted the Suhails.

The conversation next turned in an unexpected direction. A warrant for Ali's arrest had been issued by the Difaa.

"Why?" I asked.

"For helping the British," explained Hussein.

I thought this was monstrous, but there might be other reasons. I suggested that he should seek the protection of the Regent, whose A.D.C. had led us to seek Ali Suhail's help in the matter of smuggling letters into Baghdad.

I was naturally anxious, while I was in Kadhimain to see the mosque; but put the request through Reading with some diffidence, knowing that I might be treading on delicate ground. The brothers exchanged questioning glances, and Hassan said that it would be difficult for one of them to be seen in the vicinity of the mosque with an Englishman.

"If you had come by night we could have disguised you," Ali interposed with a laugh and a shrug of his shoulders, but they would ask Lieutenant Baghat if it could be arranged. Ali Suhail it was, I think, who went out to telephone, and returned to say that Lieutenant Baghat, who was Commissioner of Police for Kadhimain, would come round in person to escort me. This was surprising, since it was Baghat who had the order for Ali's arrest.

We waited in the ante-room and our compliments became even more flowery than before lunch, until Baghat was announced. He was a young man in the khaki drill uniform of the Iraq Police, armed with a big pistol. The three sheikhs came with us out into the road and showed the liveliest curiosity in the 18-pounder dent on the off-side mudguard of my car. I bade my goodbyes and Lieutenant Baghat came in my car. He spoke very good English.

I asked whether it were true that Ali Suhail was to be arrested.

His reply was, "Yes. I have an order to arrest him."

"What for?"

"Because he helped the British during the campaign, I expect. Also there were a lot of arms hidden in his village and he would not hand them over."

"But will the Regent allow the Difaa to arrest a man who has helped us?"

Baghat shrugged his shoulders. "Why not? The Suhails are rich. The Government will fine them. That is all. The Government needs the money. The Suhails will pay the fine. Then Ali Suhail will be released." He dismissed the matter as if it were very simple; an everyday occurrence. Evidently the affair was not more disturbing than when a wealthy Englishman receives a new assessment for super-tax. He complains; of course he complains; but the Government does not even have to frame up a charge of helping the enemy.

We drove into the centre of Kadhimain and came abruptly to the entrance of the mosque where its walls, meeting the Street of the Bazaar at right angles, formed a dead end. In the corner a narrow alley divided the houses from the high wall of the mosque. The great archway of the entrance was made of glazed and coloured tiles, thousands of them, and through it I could see a still courtyard where the sun beat down on the flagstones, and facing me was the entrance to the shrine itself — a soaring edifice of blue and white tiled pillars surmounted by a fantastic arrangement of concave mirrors, gleaming metallic in the shadow of overhanging eaves.

Baghat explained that no infidel could set foot inside the mosque itself, but he would arrange for someone with a house overlooking the courtyard to let me up on to the roof. In the meantime he led the way a few doors down towards the Sukh to the door of a house used as a police post. As we went, Reading pointed to the great chains hanging across the gateway of the mosque. "Remind me to tell you the meaning of those afterwards," he whispered.

The police post was not clean. A lavatory door stood wide open advertising its insanitary existence. Baghat closed it delicately with the back of his foot while drawing my attention aside. He gave orders in Arabic to an Iraqi policeman to go and see the owner of a certain house, and invited me to fill in the time, while we were waiting, by walking through the bazaar. This was a lofty arcade, roofed with corrugated iron, upon which the sun beat mercilessly. But the atmosphere in the Sukh was reasonably cool. On either side were booths and shops. Fruit was being sold off carts; and donkeys passed to and fro along the shaded street. Above the shops were overhanging windows, where the rooms of pilgrims' caravanserais accommodated the thousands of worshippers who come yearly to visit the second holiest shrine of the Shia sect in Iraq. Most of the devotees, he told me, came from Persia. At the end of the bazaar we came unexpectedly upon two empty trams standing disconsolately at their terminus. This was rather disillusioning until I learnt that they were drawn by horses from Baghdad to bring the pilgrims out to Kadhimain.

We made our way back through the bazaar and Baghat bought one of the quaintly-fashioned wooden smoking-pipes, with brass-lined bowl which are a feature of the place. He presented it to me as a reminder of the visit (and it is indeed one of my treasured mementoes of the

Near East).

The Iraqi policeman had now returned and told us that all arrangements had been made. We went down the narrow alley and I was entranced to find it overhung with timber-framed windows for all the world like a Tudor street in Cheshire. There was only just room to walk between these and the high brick rampart, brown with age, of the mosque. This imposing wall had been erected as an offering by a wealthy devotee of the Sect in years gone by. We turned and twisted down various alleyways, passing bookshops with fascinating Arabic manuscripts from the Koran which, Reading assured me, were not for sale to a Christian like myself; and so we came to a tall house of crumbling plaster. We went straight through the door and climbed some dark winding stairs until we came out abruptly on a flat roof and almost toppled over into the great courtyard of the mosque below us. There, on a level with my gaze, were the two enormous domes, of dull, burnished gold cut sharp against the blue sky. Reading said, "The gold is a sixteenth of an inch thick."

The four principal gold-capped minarets stood in a separate courtyard before the domed shrines were reached. From this height the stone-paved courtyards, which were much in shadow, seemed wonderfully quiet and peaceful. No one walked in them, whereas at my feet a crowded Oriental city jostled against the outside walls of the mosque.

Hussein Suhail had told me that the Iraq Army, during the battle, had used one of the minarets of the mosque as an observation post for the guns, and a very good one it must have been. From such a vantage point their binoculars could easily have seen us moving about the forward observation post west of Baghdad; while at the same time keeping an eye on the northern column advancing upon Kadhimain itself. I peered down into the courtyards. Baghat told me that there were seven gates in the surrounding wall. He said, "If only you had come at night and could have been disguised." We climbed down the winding dark stairs again and went back to the car. I was rather worried at having left Grose, a British soldier, all alone in the Holy City of Kadhimain, where feeling was supposed to be so much more inflammable than in Baghdad itself. When we rounded the corner of the last alley I saw Grose exchanging cigarettes with an interested crowd, which dispersed quietly at our approach. The inhabitants of the Holy City could not have been more friendly; and this was not altogether surprising, for the people of Kadhimain are mostly hostile to the Gaylani family and had no reason, therefore, to hate the overthrowers of Raschid Ali.

We got back into the car after one last cool glimpse through the tiled gateway into the bare courtyard of the mosque, and drove off. Baghat wanted to show me his police station, and it passed through my mind that a man who accepted the arrest of Ali Suhail for being too pro-British might think it an excellent joke to shut us up in one of the cells. But it was merely professional pride. The police station was a quadrangle of yellow plaster and we walked under an arch on the street side of it. Here in the shadow were coloured illustrations of the markings of British and Iraqi aircraft for identification. Inside the cell crouched the sordid prisoners of an Eastern city, beggars in rags and one-eyed crooks. Baghat took me up to his office, which was quite Western except for the Arabic script on the wall map. He came down to the entrance to see me off. We had to cross the Tigris by way of the pontoon bridge again, and were soon back in the centre of Baghdad.

Reading had relations in the city and had asked my permission to visit them. I told him to be back in camp by eleven o'clock. I also had an errand in the city. Freese Pennyfather, the Third Secretary at the Embassy, was enthusiastic about the delicate miniature Persian paintings by Imami, on mother-of-pearl or ivory, which are made into bracelets and are to be bought in Baghdad. There are also many imitations of Imami, but I was told of a casket painted all over with hunting scenes by Imami himself, now an old man in Persia. It was in the shop of a man called Kashi, down a side turning from Raschid Street. I stopped the car and went down the narrow passage to the shop. I told Grose to drop Reading at his end of the town and come straight back for me.

Kashi's shop was full of fascinating wares; it had not been looted. But when I spoke of the casket he looked this way and that. It was not in the shop. He kept it at home. If I liked to return on such and such a day. I explained that I would not have much time and asked if we could not go and see it. He agreed and, locking up the shop, came with me into the street. Grose had returned and we got into the car. Kashi directed us south through the town, and we turned off into a quarter which I had not yet visited. Here we had to leave the car and proceed on foot through a labyrinth of side streets, which grew dirtier and dirtier until we were in byways of dirt, where soapsuds and filth drained over the footway. We came at last to Kashi's house. He opened the door furtively and slipped me in. He showed me into a small parlour and spoke hurriedly to a woman beyond. In an instant he rejoined me with a large square parcel of old brown paper. He unwrapped this and showed me the casket. The ground work was of gold and on it were many cleverly depicted scenes — here a man riding a horse down a deep ravine, where a mountain torrent swirled, there a flight of birds. But it did not appeal to me. I had seen the same kind of thing too often in West End shops in London. I think he was asking twenty pounds for it.

I apologised for taking him so far away from his shop, but he was, like most Orientals, indifferent to wasted time, and after concealing it once more from prying eyes led me back to the car. On the way back to camp I visited the Street of the Silversmiths, and bought a bracelet with nine Persian miniatures on mother-of-pearl linked together by silver.

I let Grose drive on to camp so that he should be in time for the troops' tea-up and walked home by way of the Embassy. As I was crossing the Maude Bridge on foot an army truck belonging to the Essex Regiment drew up beside me. I recognised Major May's smooth face and smooth dark hair in the front seat.

"Want a lift?" he asked.

I thanked him, but said I preferred to walk. He seemed surprised to see a British soldier walking about alone in Baghdad, and drove on with a wave of the hand and a reproving shake of the head.

I did not tell anybody at dinner that I had visited the Holy City. It would only have precipitated a controversy with Peter, but they thought I was drunk. I was: with secret glee. There were guests, the Ambassador, Sir Kinahan Cornwallis; Adrian Holman; and General Waterhouse. Dick and I sat, very junior, among the lower salt and gurgled when a message was handed to him (as Signal Officer) for 'Watermouse'. We corrected it and straightened our faces before passing it in among the nobs.

After dinner the General's car was summoned, and Dick and I shouldered the spades which stood (for some reason or other) outside the flyproof door of the Mess. My foot drill on the Square at Knightsbridge had been so brief and was so remote that I could not for the life of me bring my spade to the 'present'. Joe and Peter looked on in astonishment.

"Come on, come on," Joe said, "you must know how to do it."

"I know how to do the other thing," I said, and gave a fine display of coming to attention from the 'at-ease' position and shouldering my spade.

"The other thing!" snorted Joe and walked away laughing.

This all added to the hilarity of the evening and, when we repaired to sleep, I was unable to find my camp safari bed with its neat square sand-fly mosquito net — Corpo and Dick had pushed it up on to the sloping roof of the veranda. When I discovered this, I swung myself up by the arms, so exuberant did I feel, and went to bed there without more ado. This was one up on the others and we exchanged comments on the practical joke from above and below. It was an amusing speculation whether Grose would wake me with a cup of tea as usual. He did. I heard afterwards that his surprise at the total disappearance of his officer, bed, bedding and all, was considerable, and he went round and round the building with a cup of tea in his hand. Then looking up he accepted the situation without further argument and went off to find a ladder.

Our stay in Baghdad was drawing to a close. It was not likely that Kingcol, tried in desert travel and foray, would long remain at ease. We were merely holding the door open for the Indian Division, and an army of Staff Officers descended upon us one day for lunch, before going out with Joe to inspect camp sites north of Baghdad. By night their advanced elements, armoured cars, Air Force ground staff and so forth, were poured through the railway station to strategic points on the way to Kirkuk and Mosul.

Peter asked me to go and see whether the road had been filled in where the famous anti-tank ditch had cut it; and so I drove off with Grose. Reading had not returned from his night's marauding and I meant to have a sharp word with him when he did. We found the road repaired and several bedouin roadmen loafing about. The barbed wire road blocks were pushed to one side, the anti-tank ditch was now full of water and would have served as a passable canal.

On the way back to camp I noticed the turning to the Palace of Roses, and, recalling the injustice done to my friend Ali Suhail, decided to seek out Major Obeid and ask for the Regent's intervention. When I told Grose to turn the car and explained that I was going into the Royal Palace, he said, "One certainly gets about a lot, driving you."

We were challenged at the lodge, but allowed to proceed along the gravel drive between privet hedges to the palace. It was a white Western building like any twentieth century country house in England, set about with well-tended lawns and rose gardens. I was shown into an office and soon Major Obeid appeared. He had pressed me, when we last met before the Armistice, to visit him in Baghdad and was pleased that I had not forgotten the invitation. I explained that I had also come in connection with Suhail's threatened arrest. He promised that the Regent would look into the matter (and I was glad to learn from Major Obeid when he visited me in Jerusalem later that the order for Ali's arrest had been cancelled). I asked the A.D.C. why Ali Suhail should be arrested and was staggered when he too said, "Probably because he was too pro-British."

Major Obeid said he was certain that the Regent would wish to see

336

me before I left and went out into the garden in search of him. I waited in the cool shade of the porch at the top of the front steps. The Regent, Abdul Illah, emerged from the rose garden and Major Obeid introduced me to him. He was younger than I had expected and wore a spotless white drill suit, well tailored. He wore no hat over his neatly brushed black hair. He presented in face and bearing the picture of an intelligent Arab spending a year at Oxford or Cambridge.

I showed him the dent of the unexploded Iraqi shell on the mud-guard of my car, and noticed the unguarded gleam of pleasure in his eye. It seemed to say, 'That was one of ours' — for all that we had been fighting his battle! He thought that the young King would be interested by this battle scar and Obeid went into the house to find the boy, and I told the Regent about Suhail and how he had helped me in the campaign.

Obeid reappeared presently with Feisal, who was also accompanied by a grey-haired English nanny in a white starchy uniform. Obeid had armed himself with a Leica camera and posed us in a group beside the tin scar.

The boy King was dark skinned, with lively curious eyes and unruly black hair. He wore white shorts and a shirt. He too looked cheerfully at the mudguard and then paid his attention to the spare wheel which most of us in Kingcol strapped to the bumper bar in front of the radiator.

"Why do you keep the spare wheel in front of the car?" he asked.

"To make more room for food at the back."

I could not question the English nanny in front of the others as to her adventures with the boy King during the campaign, but she did tell me that they had been hustled out of the capital just before the end and taken up north.* She was so like any other English nanny that we might all have been standing in an English garden, if I had not been wearing a topi, which these Iraqis do not need. My fair hair did not acclimatise itself easily to such exposure. It was evident that the nanny, like all her tribe, had done her best to spruce up the boy for the benefit of a visitor, for I cannot imagine so lively a child going about spotless every morning in a garden full of earth.

I said goodbye to Feisal and his uncle, shaking them both by the hand, and we drove away. I had barely reached the main road leading from the anti-tank ditch and turned back towards the rest camp, when the Brigadier's car passed me (with himself at the wheel as usual), and I

---

* I learnt subsequently that King Feisal had been kept safely on a British cruiser in the Persian Gulf.

338

saluted with a slightly guilty conscience and the inner satisfaction of knowing that my visit had been accomplished without the palaver of going through the 'usual channels' (the Embassy).

No doubt Peter would have obstructed any such visit, and I did not allude to it on my return to camp, where I simply related that the road over the ditch was in order.

The Indian's report was now ready and was creditably typed out in purple ink, with an impressive reference number at the top. The list of enemy or foreign agents was intriguing. Madame So-and-So consorts with Signor — , formerly of the Italian Legation. They meet at the — Café. Or Somebody Else is acting as go-between two foreigners. There were four or five pages of suspects which no doubt represented many hours of patient observation. Among the foreign agents I noticed the name of the notorious David Hall, the former spy for Italy in Abyssinia.

"Is he in Baghdad now?" I asked.

"Certainly," the Indian said. "He is very active."

I went off to the Embassy and sought out Vivian Holt. "Why isn't David Hall arrested?" I asked.

The Oriental Secretary looked at me pityingly through his spectacles and his desiccated face appeared even more discouraged than usual.

"What can you prove against him?" he asked. "He lives here as a respected citizen, wearing the order of the Setting Star or whatever it was, presented to him by our ally the Emperor Haile Selassie."

"There may not be evidence of his activities here in Iraq," I agreed, "but it is quite clear that he is an Axis agent."

"Well, you will have a job to prove it," was all the consolation I got out of Holt, and turned the conversation to safer topics. It appeared that one of Raschid Ali's family, the numerous Gaylanis, had been up at Balliol with me — Jussuf Gaylani. I remembered passing the ball to him at rugger. Now he was Occidental Secretary (Vivian Holt's opposite number) at the Iraq Ministry of Foreign Affairs.

"You might go and see him," Holt suggested. "It would look well in one of your reports — a talk with the Occidental Secretary."

I went out of his office, reflecting that the task of an occupying army in a country which has been handed over to its own rulers and where all is diplomatic nicety was not easy or straightforward. If I could not act in the matter of David Hall, what action could be taken through the usual channels over the other suspects?

I did not leave Vivian Holt's office empty handed for he noticed my interest in a paper-bound copy of Giselher Wirsing's *Engländer, Juden,*

Araber in Palästina — and told me that I was more than welcome to it.

One thing of interest which the Indian had said was that again and again in his researches he had come across evidence that Russian troops were about to move into Persia. At this time (in the first fortnight of June, 1941) I was hourly expecting Germany to invade the Soviet Union — and the two reports seemed to clash. It must be remembered that at this time most people ridiculed the suggestion that Germany should blunder into Russia and I was especially teased for this prophecy. Russia's part in the war was still enigmatic, and, with the arrival of British forces on the Iraq frontier of Persia, it was by no means impossible that the Soviet Government (in spite of or because of its pact with Nazi Germany) should occupy the northern part of Persia in the fear that we would do so ourselves. In the event we both marched in, as allies, and divided the protection of the country from Nazi ambitions between us.

I walked down the dim passage, which led out into the garden past a pile of sandbags, and was startled to find G.D. back from Habbaniya. At first I thought that he had been taken on by the Air Force as a pilot officer, for the tabs of his plain khaki shirt were adorned with two brand new pale blue stripes of Air Force rank. But he was still wearing his riding breeches and black jackboots, so I was relieved when he said (as my gaze rested on the kingfisher blueness of the badges of rank), "Oh, I just slipped those on to get through the lines."

This would have been dramatic enough if there had been any Iraqi lines left to get through, but I did not rob him of his glamour, especially as he went on to tell me that he was just off to Syria. I told him of the Indian's suspicions about an impending Russian coup in Persia, and asked him if he could sift out, through his interesting contacts, the apparent inconsistency between this and the expected German attack on Russia. He promised to give the matter instant attention, and marched off down the drive — not quite at the goose step. He sought me out in the camp later — to Peter's profound suspicion — and, if his hope was not to be identified in Iraqi eyes with the British Army, he certainly went a queer way about it. He said that a wide check-up of the agents confirmed the fact that Germany would attack Russia within a week, although there was certainly some ground for the Indian's belief about a Russian invasion of Persia too.

I gave him back the keys which he had lent me in his absence and said that my other preoccupations and the quiet turn of events had made it unnecessary to seek refuge behind his armour-plated door; but I was grateful for his thought, and the possession of two keys to a strange abode in the city of Haroun-al-Raschid had added something to the imagery of my stay in the city. A Brigade Intelligence Officer's job is, of course, a humdrum affair in the ordinary way. He is not a spy; and does little more than sort out the evidence of spies and translate it into red and blue hieroglyphics on the talc which is put over operational maps. No doubt Peter was right in thinking that my job was to sit with folded hands at his feet, waiting for manna to drop from heaven into my lap; but we are only young once; our blood is not for ever quick-silvered; and in war we can only dash about while our legs are intact.

When I look back on the twelve days I spent in Baghdad there seem to have been more doings than can be accounted for in the short time. I remember going to see the native employees working for the contractor in our camp, when they were being paid. I went partly because my Indian informant said that three of them were enemy agents, and partly because the officer supervising the payments was he who was alleged to have left the doctor in the lurch. I wanted to study his face.

Perhaps my own over-expressive countenance was becoming something of a substitute for the inscrutability of the Oriental.

On another occasion Sir Kinahan Cornwallis, the Ambassador, came to thank Kingcol officially on behalf of the British Government and the British Colony for our capture of the city and rescue of the European population. The incident is memorable in that, standing in his white drill suit and topi, the Ambassador was able to address the whole of Kingcol, facing him in three sides of a hollow square, without raising his voice. We were very few. We tried to make a brave show for the occasion.

"See that your Engineers are smartened up," Joe had said to Cheeky Boy.

"They will be as smart as anybody else present," Oldham replied stoutly, his impudent podgy face alight with Canadian self-assurance.

On another day there was a flag-hauling ceremony at the Embassy, but as I was Duty Officer I could not go and so missed the rare treat of hearing Joe Kingstone make a speech. But I heard that he deported himself formidably — and of course General Clark flew up from Habbaniya for the ceremony, as the Press photographs of the occasion revealed.

One hot afternoon Joe Kingstone drove Dick Schuster and myself out to the Alwiyah Sports Club, now slowly reopening, for a bathe and a cooling drink. We were also made free of the pleasant swimming pool of the Railway Club, set in a secluded garden near the camp, and I often slipped off there quietly by myself in the evenings. But I can only fix precise dates to the more significant happenings. My visit to Kadhimain was on 11th June, and, after I had been to the Palace of Roses next day, I received a visit from Hussein Suhail. He had taken my advice to heart and sought an audience with the Regent himself on his brother's behalf. Reading had now returned to camp. In answer to my protests at his overstaying his leave, he pointed out that he was a civilian interpreter. This was true, but I said that we might have to move at any moment and I must be sure he was in the camp at a reasonable hour after dark. He interpreted now for Hussein Suhail, who seemed unusually furtive. The sheikh wore his brown and gold robe with the headcloth and golden ropes, which accorded oddly, I thought, with a pair of Western brown walking shoes.

We sat in the Brigadier's office (which I, of course, shared) and I surrounded myself with the most imposing maps I could grab, including Peter's folding canvas map-case which I opened. At this juncture Peter darted in, scowled at my borrowing his map without asking him, scowled at the white-robed sheikh and with a hurried, "Excuse me" grabbed something he was looking for and darted out again. These high-speed British manners would have offended a sheikh if they did not think us all mad. I apologised for the interruption and for the Brigade Major's preoccupation, which, I said, was occasioned by the arrival of two British divisions which were going into camp north of Kadhimain. This was a slight exaggeration (for two divisons read one Indian brigade), but in the East we lived on our imaginations. Hussein Suhail wanted me to know that, when the Iraq Army had retired across the Abu Guraib Canal, after blowing up the bridge, they had dumped quantities of abandoned arms and ammunition in the canal. I was puzzled that he should bring this information to me instead of quietly fishing it up for the Beni Tmimm tribe, but he explained that there was a British Army picket at the canal, one of whose members had been seen to emerge from a swim in it, festooned in belts of machine-gun ammunition. It called up a picture of some British Tommy arising like Venus from the foam with coral necklaces. Hussein Suhail said that he would like to meet me at the canal with some swimmers of the Beni Tmimm tribe, when we could probe the matter for ourselves. My presence would, he pointed out, satisfy the British picket.

I knew that we were soon leaving, so I told him that Reading would telephone a time for the rendezvous. Hussein then expressed the hope that we would soon attack Syria and get rid of the French. After some general exchange of compliments and some photography by Grose, the sheikh said goodbye; and left me with the wish that we should soon meet in Beirut, which he visited every year.

I was invited to lunch next day at the Embassy, where Sir Kinahan had been joined by his wife, next to whom I was seated. She had heard a lot about the war diary of Kingcol which I kept, and was most anxious to see it, knowing that her husband must play a prominent part in the story of the dramatic climax. She was very disappointed when I told her that it had been sent in at the end of the month. I could not have shown it to her; but she need have had no anxieties. I am not easily impressed, but I had given this Ambassador his due — he was the best representative we could have had. Lady Cornwallis was a cheerful, thin, strong person, with greying hair, and later I had the pleasure of taking her and her daughter, a facismile of the Ambassador, round a pottery in Jerusalem when they were on leave there.

Back in camp I learnt that we had orders to move at last. I suppose the Army thought we had been resting; but Baghdad is no place to rest in, and we all felt far less fit than at the beginning of the campaign, in spite of the afternoon siestas we allowed ourselves in camp. In my absence Hussein Suhail had been to see me again, this time bearing presents — a new gold aqal such as sheikhs wear, with a beautifully embroidered keffiyeh for me, and a similar headdress for Reading — not new, or quite so imposing, but an undoubted honour. In the meantime I had told Reading that he could go off to see his relatives, or whatever they were, but that he must be back by nine o'clock.

Reading's civilian kit had at last arrived, and the transformation in the man was astounding. From the gaunt and rather bedraggled private, with his oft-washed linen khaki shirt and shorts, he changed into the debonair civilian in gleaming white drill jacket and well-pressed grey flannel trousers. No film star could have looked more the man of the world at large in the Orient than Reading with his small black moustache and aristocratic features. Grose, who drove him into the city, told me sheepishly he was certain Reading meant to stay away all night again. (Grose had a fair inkling that we were leaving in the morning.) So I sent him back to the house to find Reading, if possible, and tell him that he must return on time. It was a wild goose chase.

When Reading did appear next morning, I was furious with him, explaining that the column might have had to leave in the night without its interpreter. Reading dissolved into tears. He might never see his relatives again — and so on. It was no use treating him like a soldier — so

I turned away.

Joe gave me my orders for the day, which were considerate and, I think, purposely elastic. I was to go out to the new Indian Brigade, which was settling in beyond Kadhimain. (Was there a hint that, if I wanted to see the Holy Mosque before we finally left Baghdad, I might thus have a reasonable excuse?) The rest of the column would be moving direct back to Habbaniya, and I could report to him at the Rest House by the lake when I got there. Joe did not know that I had already visited Kadhimain, but this arrangement allowed me a splendid opportunity to meet Hussein Suhail at the Abu Guraib Canal, which was on the way, and search for the ammunition. I set Reading to telephone Ali Suhail's house and state the hour at which I would reach the blown-up bridge.

Grose was already packed up. We drove out of camp independently of the others, and were soon going over the railway line on the dusty road which follows the west bank of the Tigris and passes within a mile or two of Kadhimain. As we drove over the level crossing, I told Reading of Hussein Suhail's gift to him. I was driving the car at the time and spoke over my shoulder. With his absence of the night before in mind, I added, "I am glad he gave you one too; although you don't deserve it." At this Reading burst into floods of tears and wailed, "You may be very clever and very brilliant and very brave, but you are very difficult to work for." I was horrified, for I realised that he had taken my remark to mean that he was not worthy to wear a sheikh's aqal, but he was now in no condition to be reassured by my explanation that I was referring only to his disobedience. He cheered up after I had poured oil on his troubled spirit for some minutes, and urged me to wear the aqal headdress in future. He told me how he had worked with another British Army Intelligence Officer in the Palestine Rebellion who had always gone about in a keffiyeh. Now that a sheikh had given me one, it would be proper for me to wear it. I had visions of Reading and myself robed in white sitting on the floor of some Damascus house; but it was not convincing.

The road was passing across low marshy ground now, and we could see the mosque away to our right and a dense grove of palm trees beyond the town. The railway line was near the road here and we passed the little empty railway station which seemed to be standing cheerfully in spite of all the 25-pounder shells which our northern column said they had fired at it. I was anxious to be on my way to the secret rendezvous with Hussein Suhail, so I left him to tell the tense days of the British Colony in Baghdad before the arrival of Kingcol.

It was interesting to pass back along the road over which we had fought. The Experimental Farm looked quite deserted now behind its screen of trees. At the Abu Guraib Canal I found a number of Iraqi roadmen about, but no sign of the British picket, which had no doubt been lifted this morning as the rest of the column returned westwards. Reading asked if anyone had been at the canal looking for me, and was told that a saloon car had hovered about some minutes before and then gone on towards Khan Nuqta. This must certainly be Suhail, but he would no doubt have turned off beyond the caravanserai to Ali's village at Aqqa Quf. I decided to seek him out there. To find the way, we would need a guide, and stopped at the little caravanserai, which was once again used for giving coffee to thirsty travellers. There we found a nephew of Ali Suhail and took him with us (the innkeeper firmly believing that we were kidnapping him). The man stuffed himself and his garments into the car, beside Reading at the back, and directed us off the road a little further on. We followed a track which carried us, with difficulty, over a series of small smashed culverts, which had undoubtedly been destroyed on Ali Suhail's order, to make his village inaccessible to either Army during the fighting.

We twisted and doubled about for two or three miles, until we came in sight of a cluster of mud-walled houses and long low black camel-hair tents. There were horses and cattle grazing about. We were a long way from help and no one would know where to find us if I had misjudged the friendliness of the Suhail family — although no Arab would do anyone a hurt while he was actually a guest. I got out, telling Grose to keep an eye on the car. There was no sign of the saloon car we had heard about, but a slave of Ali's appeared and told us that the sheikhs were at another place near by. The nephew ordered a bedu to mount an indifferent horse and he cantered off to warn them of our arrival.

Meanwhile we sat down on carpets beneath the black tent reserved for visitors, and a man put coffee beans into a brass jar and began beating it with a brass pestle which caused a lovely chime. In this way the

344

bedouin were warned that guests had arrived and that coffee was being brewed. They came drifting in and crouched round the farther end of the tent, watching us with sharp unwinking eyes. Another slave poked the smouldering ashes and thrust great bronze pots with toucan-billed spouts over the burning embers to boil.

The blue saloon car now arrived, followed at a distance by the persevering rider. The two brothers were Ali and Hussein, who advanced full of smiles and apologies for not having been here to welcome us. They came into the tent, sweeping up their robes to seat themselves, and asking us to do the same. Grose was brought in to join the circle, where we sat cross-legged on the ground. The coffee was now ready, and it was poured into tiny porcelain cups without handles and flavoured with a special spice from the Hejaz. We sipped appreciatively. A superb red Arab mare was grazing close to the tent and I admired it. Ali Suhail immediately offered it to me as a gift; a polite gesture which I declined with equal courtesy, pointing out that there was no room for it in my car; a jest which they seemed to appreciate. I thanked Hussein for his beautiful gifts to Reading and myself, and he asked why I was not wearing the aqal. Ali also was anxious to bestow some gift upon me, and, noticing that my quizzical gaze rested on a Bren-gun cleaning rod which his son was holding, he immediately insisted that I accept this as a present. I accepted it with due ceremony, and Reading took charge of it. So far as Ali was concerned this gesture of his was calculated to avert any embarrassing inquiry from me as to how it had come into his possession. I asked about the massive ruins of the temple which loomed above the floods, but they could tell me nothing more than I already knew: that the ruins were very old.

After we had drunk several cups of coffee we went outside the tent, where Ali Suhail was very anxious for a photograph to include all his relatives and slaves crowded into the picture; and Hussein produced his celebrated binoculars, the present which Wavell had sent him in return for a jewelled sword. I had to tell Hussein that, as soon as I returned to Palestine, I hoped to be able to send him and his brothers some memento by which they should remember me; a prospect which pleased them. What Ali would have liked best would undoubtedly have been a service revolver, for he collected all sorts of arms, and he contrasted the automatic he was wearing unfavourably with Reading's (far too heavy) army pistol. I was not wearing my own.

We climbed back into the cars, a number of bedouin standing on the running boards, and regained the road. I noticed a bright green car, full of Iraqis, pulled up a little beyond this point, and it turned to follow us at a discreet distance. When we reached the bridge the green car had necessarily to go on unless it wished to make plain its task of shadowing us, but the occupants gave us a sharp look as they went by and crossed over the pontoon bridge, before continuing along the road to Baghdad.

As soon as the green car had disappeared, the Beni Tmimm stripped off their robes and plunged their black and shining bodies into the smooth brown waters of the canal. They dived under the surface and reappeared in unexpected places.

"It would be wise," said Hussein, "to say that we are helping you to look for part of a lorry that fell into the canal."

Now one of the swimmers bobbed up from the muddy bed of the canal and held up a rusted Bren-gun magazine. This was getting warm. Soon another tribesman brought up a live anti-tank shell, of foreign make. I examined it. Now the finds became more frequent — a number of live .303 cartridges being found. The men clung to the twisted wreckage of the bridge, every now and then panting for breath; then dived again. The current was fairly fast. The roadmen on the far side of the bridge were curious as to what was going on, but Reading told them about the missing part of the lorry.

At first we had been hopeful of great finds, but, either the guns and ammunition had sunk deep into the oozy mud or had already been recovered by others — possibly even by the Suhails when they discovered, earlier, that our picket had gone. At all events, the glittering prizes eluded us, and we decided to give up the search. It was my last meeting with these two brothers, standing there on the bank of the muddy canal, with their fine robes fluttering out in the breeze which rippled the water — while not far away across the half cultivated scrub were the black outlines of a bedouin encampment. We said farewell in the bright morning sunlight and went our several ways — they to Baghdad — I to Falluja, Habbaniya, Ramadi and the Old Damascus Road which leads across the desert into Syria.

CHAPTER 35

At Khan Nuqta the tarmac road ended and a maze of tracks passed out over the hard desert, where a line of telephone posts guided us without difficulty to Falluja. Half-way there we drew up beside the burnt-out wreckage of a Gladiator — a charred black frame with broken spine, sprawled on the hard yellow grit of the desert, where it had fallen for ever from the harsh blue heaven. We were examining it when Peter Herbert, the Divisional Liaison Officer, busy as ever on some errand which took him away from work, drove up. We exchanged news of our friends and went in opposite directions; our cars like yellow beetles scudding busily across the wide Iraqi desert, until they disappeared from each other in dots and puffs of dust. How puzzling our activities would appear to an Olympian deity!

The road between Falluja and Habbaniya, which had been under water when Kingcol had to be ferried across the gap in Hammond's Bund three miles to the south, was now passable to one-way traffic. The day was divided into periods of two hours for east-bound and west-bound traffic, alternately, and I had been warned to go through between 11 and 1. In places the tarmac foundation, disintegrated from immersion, was patched up with criss-cross wire netting, laid by our persevering Engineers. Ditched beside the road was a line of Iraqi vehicles, holed by our bullets, where the Royal Air Force from Habbaniya had caught them jammed head to tail when the Iraqis had surrounded the cantonment and opened fire.

I found the headquarters of Kingcol in the Imperial Airways Rest House, beside the vast smooth grey-green waters of Lake Habbaniya. The building was in very different condition from when I had last seen it — looted and littered knee deep in papers torn by the Iraqi Army from the desks and files. My own regiment, the Household Cavalry, had been comfortably ensconced there until this morning, when Joe had found the greatest pleasure in turning them out on to the bare desert where the sandstone plateau descends in narrow gullies towards the lake.

A stretch of tarmac road led down from the plateau to the Rest

347

House, and the various units of Kingcol were turned off it at different places on to the desert. In parts the sand was treacherous. I remembered the patch not two hundred yards south of the Rest House where my car had embedded itself on the way to visit Cassano's armoured cars during our previous stay by the lake. So soft had been the sand that Grose's persevering experiments alone had overruled the transport officer's decision to abandon the vehicle as unrecoverable.

On another occasion I had chased my copy of an operation order for nearly two miles before I caught it, in gusts of wind which carried it with the driving sand ever beyond my grasp. As I had raced up each sand dune, I had seen the pink foolscap twirling over the next — to fall at last, I had feared, into the hands of some intelligent bedouin far across the desert who would have sold it to Iraqi Headquarters. Now all these anxieties had turned westwards, and our eyes were fixed on Syria.

I made an early visit to Habbaniya. Since my last stay, the Army had so far eclipsed the brilliant light of the Air Force Intelligence Headquarters as to cloud its face with a combined Intelligence centre, where both Services concealed from each other their most interesting and secret thoughts. Thus did we darken counsel without knowledge and, although I had the run of my old friends' offices, military etiquette drew me into the field of force among the iron filings. Here I was not met with the awe which my adventures seemed to win me in Air Force circles. Edric had not supplied any of my signalled requirements for more printed forms for War Diary and Intelligence summary; he had not sent me a portable typewriter, and complained bitterly that his was not a stationery office. He had not even sent me the Syrian Order of Battle: and it seemed to me that the supply of maps for our column on its next move had been completely overlooked. I was very caustic. This Hab force (Habbaniya Force) had expanded itself in the best military traditions, and above Edric was now a Captain of the Indian Army, with a glittering eye and waxed moustache, to whom I took a particular dislike. They could not, however, deny me the means of intelligent existence, and were reluctantly forced to admit that the people who needed maps and plans were the people who were going to do the fighting. So I walked off with all the best diagrams of enemy defences; Edric's list of fighting units in Syria; and the only copy of a military handbook on Syria, which should have been in the hands of every officer in the column.

The Royal Air Force carried air reconnaissance to artistic lengths and their target maps were a joy to behold — engraved in fine shades of chrome and brown on a rough cream card. Every important building was numbered with a key at the bottom. These cards would not have been out of place when framed on the walls of a drawing-room. They erred only in minor ways — for instance, the Bordel Militaire de la Campagne, outside Palmyra, was listed as a powder magazine and the vicious attempts of our pilots to bomb it were attributed by the French I learnt later, to jealousy or puritanical instincts. They gave me five copies of the Palmyra card and some of Homs.

Our plan of campaign was taking shape. Kingcol was now to be reformed as the 4th Cavalry Brigade, thus losing the two companies of the Essex Regiment and receiving the Wiltshires and Warwickshires, who had been guarding our line of supply. We continued to think of it as Kingcol, for the brain and face were the same. All we were doing was to lose our shoes and take on a stout pair of boots. The Household Cavalry was to advance up the Euphrates, by way of Abu Kemal, where Eion Merry's squadron was already exchanging shots with the French garrison and our old enemy of the desert Fawzi Kuwuckji. They were to advance noisily, sending back bogus wireless messages for tank tracks and so forth to delude the enemy into expecting an armoured attack on Deir Ez Zor. Even the B.B.C. co-operated, perhaps unwittingly, with talk of an armoured division moving up the Euphrates from Iraq.

A strict wireless silence was to be imposed on the rest of the Brigade, and we were to retire silently to Rutba and H.3.

There we would be joined by Glubb again, and on the appointed day, 21st June, we would race northwards across the intervening 150 miles of desert to surround and occupy the historic desert fortress of Palmyra, while the phantom Household Cavalry Armoured Divison would dissolve into thin air and converge on Palmyra from the east. It was a cunning plan, which confirmed my opinion of General Clark's cool brain and would have been all right if the air support which we enjoyed in Iraq had followed us into Syria.

I found the Headquarters Officers' Mess in a room on the ground floor near the side steps. Here we sat back, dazed with the heat, and implored Coles and Corporal Borman (inadvertently referred to as Corporal Barnes in *The Golden Carpet*) to be more generous with the lime juice. I had been allotted a bedroom upstairs, and my little safari bed, which only just cleared the floor boards, was tucked into the corner. There was no electric light or running water, but the shelter was luxury.

David Summers, the Household Cavalry I.O., had been up with

Eion Merry at Abu Kemal, and now returned with a thrilling tale of an encounter between the Blues squadron and Fawzi Kuwuckji, which had ended with honours even and Fawzi asking to discuss an armistice, under which he would come over to our side and swear allegiance to the Regent Abdul Illah. This would have been an honourable gain of far-reaching consequences in the Arab world, for Fawzi was not merely the general who had led the Palestine Rebellion, but was the most successful and elusive of our opponents. He had realised the potency of guerrilla warfare in the desert; for every man who is attacked, a thousand stop in fear of attack. Andrew Ferguson brought David up to tell his tale to Joe, while Peter and the rest of us sat round the table. The account of trucks being recovered under fire left Peter cold, and he observed that the only important part of the report was the last. The idea of recruiting Fawzi Kuwuckji appealed to me, and I asked Joe if I could go up to Abu Kemal to parley with him.

"You can go by all means," Joe said, with a wicked smile, "but you cannot take Reading with you. We may want him." My spirits were dashed, for without Reading I could only stare speechlessly at the Arab general. So the opportunity was lost. Fawzi came in to parley with Eion Merry, who was not called 'Old Misery' by the troops for nothing, and stared crossly at the rebel leader, not knowing whether to treat him as a prisoner of war or an honoured guest. The occasion was not auspicious — Fawzi withdrew and melted into the night with his roving band. Next time he reappeared it was to seize the tail of the Household Cavalry's column as it was crossing the desert to Palmyra.

We had left Baghdad on Friday, 13th June, and the powers at Habbaniya mocked fate by killing Kingcol on this ominous day, to recreate the 4th Cavalry Brigade. I wrote a funeral oration, which was duplicated with difficulty on our expiring Roneo machine. Of the twenty-five copies printed, only five were readable and, as these were controversial, I did not show them in the neighbourhood, but sent them off to Force Headquarters, as ordered, and a spare copy to my old instructor in the dark arts — Brigadier Shearer, who was Director of Military Intelligence for the Middle East in Cairo.

While I was writing, a silver flying boat came skimming down on the glassy water of the lake in front of my window. It was bound for Lake Tiberias and the old nostalgia for Palestine came over me. I still felt entitled to some leave and sought out Peter in the eating room. "The Airways flying boat has just come in," I told him. "Do you think it would be any use my asking Joe (who was in Habbaniya for the morning) if I could have a few days' leave?"

Peter smiled artfully. "If you can get me a promise from the A.O.C. that he will have you flown back any time we require, you are welcome to go.' He never expected me to put his joke to the test, but I went to the field telephone and looked up the number of the 'Senior Air Staff Officer' and dialled this number. An ominously military voice answered me — but, like wanton boys who play on bladders, I drifted airily to my doom.

"Who is that?" rapped the voice.

"This is de Chair."

"Who?"

"de Chair, the I.O. to Kingcol."

"Well? What do you want?" (I might have realised that this was unusually uncivil for a Senior Air Staff Officer.)

"It was really a personal matter," I faltered. "I wanted to speak to Air Vice-Marshal d'Albiac," (who was a good sport). "Do you happen to know if he is back from Basra yet?"

"Yes. He is sitting in the room here listening to the wireless with General Clark. What do you want to ask him?"

"Well," (my courage almost failed me), "nobody here seems to know anything about what is going on in the Syrian campaign, and I wanted to fly back to Palestine and find out. There is a flying boat on the lake now, leaving in twenty minutes and the Brigade Major says that there would be no objection to my going if I could get a personal assurance from the A.O.C. of being flown back at short notice."

The voice froze; then turned away from the microphone. "It's de Chair," I heard the voice saying acidly, "wants to fly off to Palestine to find out how the French are fighting, if we can fly him back."

The voice now assumed menacing shape. "This is Napier (the G.I.) and Brigadier Kingstone is in here. He is returning to camp with news of the plan of operations which will, I am sure, make it extremely improbable that he would give you leave at this moment," and rang off.

No. It was not a good effort. How was I to have known that the office formerly occupied by the Senior Air Staff Officer was the one which had been taken on by General Clark for his personal use? Whom the gods wish to destroy . . . .

Joe returned in time for lunch and I sat next to him, whistling to myself. He put his head in his hands.

"Somerset," he said sadly, "why do you do these things?"

"It was a joke between Peter and me," I said more jauntily than I felt, "I thought it was worth trying to get an aeroplane. I could find out all sorts of things about how the campaign is going."

"They ask me why I keep you here," Joe resumed mournfully, "and I told them that only the other day you said Russia was going to attack Persia. It is beyond explanation." He went heavily upstairs for an afternoon siesta.

Ian took me aside. "Joe is terribly hurt," he said, "because he thinks you were trying to ask George Clark for leave, over his head."

"Good lord!" I was appalled. This was even worse. I hovered about the balcony until Joe emerged through the flyproof swing door of his room two hours later.

"General," I said, "Ian tells me that you think I was asking George Clark for leave over your head. Of course I would not dream of such a thing. I only wanted to find out if an aeroplane would fly me back, and looked up the number of the Senior Air Staff Officer. I had no idea it was Clark's office."

Joe nodded sadly and went down to tea. I had the impression that Joe had just been interceding on my behalf, for some reason, at the very moment when my voice came like a *deus ex machina* over the telephone, to shatter the glassy reflection of my good character which he was building up. There was something behind his disappointment which I could not understand.

Of course, the incident got about, magnified. Opinion tended to be breathless with wonder that anyone should have the courage to telephone the General Officer Commanding and the Air Officer Commanding and ask in one breath for leave and an aeroplane to enjoy it. The V.C. was not considered too high an award for such gallantry. I went down to where the officers of my own regiment, sitting on upturned petrol tins, were eating their evening meal from a trestle table on the sand. Andrew Ferguson sat at the head of the table. He gazed at me with his mouth open, trying to form words. His pale oval face under his dark hair, was as philosophic as usual. The words came at last, "S-Somerset?"

"Yes, Colonel?"

"Have you got a woman in Jerusalem?"

"No," I answered stoutly.*

"Well, then, I give you t-top marks."

This was consoling and I joined the table, next to Nicholls, the

---

*She did not live in Jerusalem.

cartooning quartermaster, for I wanted an advance pay book, without which the Army would not disgorge money in the desert. He said that if I came round before we left in the morning he would have mine ready.

Ian Spence, with round cheerful face, smiled upon me too. "You know," he said, "I believe you are one of the people who can get away with anything." And I must say that I never heard any more about that aeroplane, except by way of good-natured jest.

After dinner Joe returned to my German invasion of Russia. I had promised it for 15th June and it was nearly midnight on that day. He laid his watch on the table. "No news yet?" he said looking at me.

"We might not hear about it for days," I defended myself.

Joe laughed. "Well, I must say, Somerset, you are the best-natured of men. I bait you without ceasing, and you never take umbrage."

Kingcol (for I shall call it that to the end) was due to leave soon after dawn, and I walked over to the Household Cavalry lines before starting, to get my pay book. The place was like a dormitory. Everywhere the men lay asleep, as if a spell were on them. The Roman sentinels of Pompeii could not have been laid in more permanent attitudes of immobility. I stepped over the bodies, looking for the 'office' clerks. At last I identified a sleeping face and roused it. The owner stirred and found the key of a padlock, with which he unlocked the shed where regimental papers were being kept. He said that 'Mr Nicholls' had told him I could have 'Major Wignall's' pay book. Boy Wignall, with a doubtful inside, was last heard of in hospital at Alexandria. (If only his pay book had entitled me to draw on his account!) I pushed the folded buff pay book, which resembled a cheque book in shape, into one of the breast pockets of my bush shirt, hitched my Sam Browne (worn in the interlude between campaigns) into place; and, raising a hand to my cap in answer to the sleepy salute of the Corporal of Horse, went back to Headquarters.

The vehicles were beginning to draw out on to the road, and I was to lead the Brigade Headquarters group. I got into my car beside Grose, with Williamson and Reading in the back, and drove up to the head of the column. At a signal from Peter, I started off up the winding hill to the plateau, turned left for a few hundred yards, and then descended abruptly to the road which skirts the aerodrome. Here I turned left and drew in to the right-hand side. All across the aerodrome, head on to the famous London-Baghdad signpost, were arrayed the grey Air Force armoured cars of Cassano's squadron. They were old friends, dusty, bullet-scarred, with great spare wheels jammed up against the sides of the long square-ended bonnets and the men, in greasy white overalls, lolling out of the conning towers. The Lewis guns were pointed to the sky, but the machine-guns and anti-tank rifles pointed sharply in the direction they were going.

Peter's utility van, open at the back where luggage bulged, slid past me to give instructions to Cassano, and in a moment the armoured cars were turning right in file on the main highway bound for Rutba. They had to squeeze past the long line of vehicles belonging to the Essex Regiment which, although now directly under the wing of the parent Habforce itself, seemed to be moving along the same road so early in the morning. I fell into place behind the armoured cars, and waved the column behind me to follow on.

Soon we began passing truck after truck of Indian soldiers, who must have been travelling all night, for they slept with the white dust on their brown arms and faces, which were turned upwards, pale-turbanned, to the rising sun.

Gradually we drew clear of all these fellow warriors, and were passing over the repaired and many-arched culvert which the Iraqi engineers had blown up between Habbaniya and Ramadi.

The flood waters of the Euphrates had gone down, leaving the land wet in patches, and, under the culvert which we crossed, were fed the waters which filled Lake Habbaniya.

I was intent to see Ramadi, which had always been hidden from me behind its floods and soldiers. I found it a small town much shaded by palm trees. There was a fort, on the left of the single main street, which showed no sign of the vigorous pounding which the Air Force were believed to have given it. The streets were not even littered with the leaflets which had demanded, in vain, the surrender of Ramadi 'lest the fate of Falluja overtake it'. There was a dense green palm grove west and south of the town, where most of the two Iraqi brigades had no doubt been hidden.

Beyond Ramadi the thin, poor tarmac road drew itself forlornly out into the bare gravel desert. Soon we began passing the familiar road signs: Kilo 25, beyond the cairn of stones where Henry Abel and I had watched the column lumber off, on its disastrous attempt to reach the trestle bridge over the flood-race at the southern end of the lake.

Joe was in a rising temper, his face redder than ever. He would drive past signalling obscurely with his free hand, the other being on the driving wheel even at the start of this long day. At first I took his signal to mean 'Go on,' and he chased me, shouting, "Here, where do you think you are getting to?" So I halted, and signalled to the column behind me to do likewise. Joe gave me instructions about Rutba. I saluted and got back into my car, noticing that the sun was getting too hot for an army cap. I put on my topi and told Grose to drive on. Next time the Brigadier passed, he was waving even more frantically and pulled up off the road to the left. So I stopped the column hurriedly, especially as it was just about twenty minutes short of the hour when our two-hourly halt was due. This time I was cursed for stopping the whole column when Joe was only pulling out to have a shot at a gazelle, which he had seen on the horizon. His signal should have read (to an arm-reader) 'Go on. For Christ's sake don't stop. I am only going to have a pot at that gazelle over there.'

I climbed back into my car cursing, for the heat was getting on top of us, and beat down on the metal roofs of our cars with a ferocious glare.

Grose muttered, "Well, I do think the General is being unfair to you today, sir. I certainly thought he meant you to stop."

So we drove on.

By now we were out in the open desert, following the several camel tracks which threaded and twined in a broad pattern westwards. When we halted for the two-hour pause at midday, the heat of Iraq was waiting in ambush like a lion, and devoured us. To remove my smoked sun-glasses even for a second was blinding. We would do better, as an Army, to dress as the nomads of this waterless desert have done since before the days of Alexander the Great, and wear white linen headdresses which can be scalloped under the eyes to shield them from the desert glare. But we pushed Britannically into the barren heart of Asia.

While I was standing beside my car, and Grose and Williamson tended the primus stove and kettle, I watched Joe unloading himself from his utility. He walked about the desert for a while, light-footed, getting rid of his temper. Then he called to me in a soft voice, "Somerset," and I walked towards him.

"Look at this little fellow." He pointed to a tiny kangaroo rat, which hopped, frightened, on long thin hind legs across the desert at his feet, and finally darted into a hole under a tuft of scrub. It was Joe's way of making amends for the violence of his temper on the way; and my own anger died at once. We talked a little and I went back to my car, where the snaky spout of the kettle was adding its defiant hiss to the heat.

Dick Schuster, lean, fine-featured, with his dark silky moustache and humorous dark eyes, came seeking food. He was ill-equipped or tired of hard tack. I showed him my molten chocolate from Groppi's, in its waterproof paper, and spread a sandwich of it between two army biscuits for him. He munched gratefully, sitting beside me on the shadier side of the running board of my car. It was really hot.

The halt rested us only from the ceaseless jolting of the desert, where I, however, enjoyed the luxury of good springing, even if the plush seat fretted the sticky inside of my bare knees. I felt for the troops, bouncing behind in light open trucks, open to the furnace of the sun, with their officers, dusty to the rims of their goggles, sitting with boots to the hot engines beside their drivers. They had grown hardy with much travel; although the farthest flung, Harcol and Gocol, who had been to Kirkuk and Mosul, remained with the regiment at Habbaniya for the Abu Kemal diversion.

After the two-hour halt, we went on again. The route was easier to follow going westwards. We were now on the broad-tracked ribbon of the Old Damascus Road, and the Ramadi signposts showed up, like blobs in the shimmering heat ahead of us, every five kilometres. They were iron plates on posts stuck in the sand. Half-way through the afternoon, a part of the column from the rear which had got separated from us loomed up on the horizon to the south, a giant convoy in the mirage, reflected in a non-existent lake. They converged upon us, dwindling in shape, and merged finally into the tail of our own column.

At twenty to four I halted the column, with the snout of my car well forward of the rearmost armoured cars, who stopped and started whenever they felt so inclined. We were quite near the wired-in enclosure and landing ground, through which I had led the reluctant column on our outward journey. I realised now the meaning of Brook's remark that, at this point, two routes were then open to me — the Old Damascus Road, along which I had now returned, or the course of the new Haifa-Baghdad Road, which was under construction.

As the afternoon wore on, I gave up trying to keep touch or station with the armoured cars; and there was, in any case, no menace for us in the now friendly and familiar desert remaining between here and Rutba. Our one possible enemy was the guerrilla leader Fawzi, who might have come raiding our soft-skinned column from the north, but we believed him to be preoccupied with Eion Merry north-west of Abu Kemal. Thus we crossed the foundation of the unfinished Haifa-Baghdad Road, as dark approached, and I led the Brigade in a wide sweep across the plain, where a rugged range of sandstone hills formed a rampart to the south between us and Arabia Deserta.

By now Rutba was in sight, and the vehicles took each their own ground and poured in over the plain to the familiar camping grounds beyond the town. That night we pitched our fighting caravanserai of cars on the very ground where we had slept before.

We felt a lightening of our spirits in the cooler atmosphere of this desert plateau. We had climbed out of the fetid palm-fringed valley of the Tigris and sniffed the desert air. There was the sting of adventure in the wind again.

We spent only one night at Rutba, leaving the Warwicks in the town undisturbed, and pushed on to H.₃ next day. Most of the officers in Headquarters went ahead, while I was left to bring on the Brigade group as usual, and amused myself shooting at the abandoned petrol cans which we passed in the desert. I would get Grose to drive as close in to them as possible while I leant my arm out of the right front window and fired my revolver. I used up a dozen cartridges before I succeeded in hitting one of the bright four gallon metal tins. After that I got my eye in and could send each tin bouncing with a clang as the .38 lead bullet crashed into it.

The route to H.₃, winding south and up a gorge, often close to the preparations of the Baghdad-Haifa Road, was too easy. When H.₃ was in sight, the column behind me stopped for some reason without my having halted. Old Toler, the Camp Commandant, was back there, probably fussing about something, so I left him to fuss and went on through the gate in the wire enclosure of the I.P.C.* station. The car bowled across the compound and turned into the fort, where Joe and Peter were working for the morning in rooms which opened into the courtyard. Our headquarters, however, were to be in the bungalows, where we had first met with Cassano on the way to Rutba, and where I had obtained my first sparkling goblet of cold water in Iraq.

These bungalows were white, with some sorts of garden and paths between them and were luxuriously fitted up with baths and basins. Water, however, must be rigidly conserved.

Corpo had allotted the rooms. Dick and I were to share as before. There was a table in the window, and I somewhat ruffled Dick by spreading a huge map of Syria over it, under talc, and marking it up with French positions. However, I apologised for a job which was best got over quickly and made room for his own signal papers too.

The room opened into a narrow passage, which led to a charming sitting-room with a cedarwood table and dining chairs. There were two comfortable armchairs as well. I erected my map of the Syrian Order of

*Iraq Petroleum Company.

Battle on the sideboard for all to study; but baffled any marauding Fifth
Columnists by putting a large blue circle, in chinagraph chalk, round
the Krak des Chevaliers and labelled that 'Primary Objective'. Baalbeck
I framed in a square and added 'Secondary Objective'. Our real
objective, Palmyra, was only indicated, like other towns, by units of the
Foreign Legion, Artillery and the Desert Camel Corps which were
garrisoned there. But I had brought with me from Palestine a guide
book to the Levant, which told us something of the quaint history of this
once famous city, with its lofty marble ruins far out in the desert. It had
been ruled over by the celebrated Queen Zenobia in Roman times; and
in more recent years a notorious countess* had lived there, until she was
sentenced to death by an Arab court in Mecca. Only the intervention of
Peake Pasha, who dashed across the desert in an aeroplane, had saved
her on the scaffold. Her son now ran a white plaster hotel, just south of
the town. Beyond this our knowledge of Palmyra was limited, until
Glubb arrived.

"Hullo, hullo Pasha," exclaimed Joe, and we made a place for the
leader of the Desert Patrol. Glubb was not wearing his usual yellow
keffiyeh and aqal, but an army side cap, such as most of us wore on
informal occasions. Possibly he did this out of deference to the
Brigadier. Without his bedu headdress Glubb emerged as a short man of
about forty years, with close-cut sandy hair, light eyes, and a sandy
moustache. His chin was ineffective, possibly from the bullet wound
which gave him his name among the Arabs — Abu Hunaik. He was
quiet, modest, with a known store of desert experience which no one else
in the Middle East possessed. He never wore bedouin clothes, but
always the buff drill uniform of the Emir Abdullah's Arab Legion, of
which he was Commander-in-Chief. However, the Arab headdress was
usual on him.

It is difficult to place Glubb in perspective. Lawrence played a
different and more exciting role, for he identified himself at a turning-
point of time with Arab aspirations, in an Arab revolt which changed the
face of the Near Orient. Glubb slipped quietly into the sandals of Peake
Pasha who had built up the Arab Legion for our ally in the protectorate
of Transjordan. Glubb Pasha, as he was titled, organised the Iraq
Desert Police, giving them mobility in open trucks armed with Lewis
guns (which were eventually turned against us). More important still
was his own Desert Patrol, a band of devoted bedouin, dark faced, with

*Comptesse d'Andurain

long black shiny hair, wrapped about in buff robes and pantaloons, wearing pink gingham headdress with the Emir's silver crown on the forehead and swathed in bandoliers of ammunition. They volunteered from all over the Levant and were Glubb's men. We called them Glubb's girls on account of their flowing robes. The desert was their native heath and they roamed about it, running in circles round us like destroyers guiding a convoy of big ships; often disappearing over our hard horizons, only to reappear unexpectedly from some other direction.

Glubb was an old friend of ours now, and it was noticeable that his personality did not jar the military mind.

"Where have you been?" Joe asked, for the last we had seen of him was in the bright early morning of the Armistice, when Clark, d'Albiac and he (the Three Musketeers) had come up to the anti-tank ditch where Ian Spence and I had received the Iraqi delegates.

"I have been in Amman," Glubb explained, sitting down to our square table. "We have been relaxing."

"Lucky for you," was Joe's comment. Nearly all the Desert Patrol had their houses and families in Amman and could refresh themselves there between campaigns, while we sweltered in a 'rest' camp at Baghdad. Glubb himself had a wife in Amman, reputed to be a quiet creature who ministered to his unexacting needs.

Some asked what difference Glubb's little patrol made in our enterprise. I could have answered that it shot through all our doings an underglow of colour. What I chiefly emphasised was that the mere presence of Glubb's Desert Patrol was a talisman among the bedouin, who would otherwise have molested our straggling supply columns, thin-drawn across the blinding desert, and have raided our solitary outposts along the route. In the event, we had no trouble from the tribes, who remained amicable with so many cousins under our flag, while the town dwellers of Iraq were loathing us with deadly passion. Glubb's role was therefore somewhat negative, but none the less useful, and each of his men was a walking guide book to the desert.

"I have some information for you," he told me, but did not enlarge on it in front of the others.

He sought me out after lunch, in the office which I shared with Joe and Peter at the further end of the next bungalow. I was alone with my maps. Glubb pulled up a chair and we went over the ground between H.3 and Palmyra.

"I have just heard from my men," he said, "that the fort at Palmyra is very big, 'larger than the one at Rutba' is how they describe it."

"Then it must be pretty big," I reflected.

"One of my men comes from Palmyra," Glubb explained. "He says that the French sergeant-major at the fort sleeps out in the town because he has a wife there."

We turned our attention south-west to Saba Biya (Seven Wells).

"The fort there stands very high up and commands the surrounding country for miles. It is the French fort Dusquesne."

I noticed from my own information that a company of the Light Desert Camel Corps (now three parts motorised) was stationed there. I was grateful to Glubb for these glimpses of what lay beyond the desert frontier. He had not got the military mind, which is incapable of unbending more than two pips in rank outside its own unit. I thanked him very warmly. He wandered off to the blue saloon car in which he normally travelled, and drove back to his cluster of armed trucks, somewhere outside the camp on the desert.

We obtained some equally valuable knowledge about the route ahead of us from an ex-Nairn driver, who had travelled the desert tracks in peacetime. He had been put into uniform as a second-lieutenant, and quite dominated the gathering by his intimate knowledge of the ground. I wish I could recollect his name. I remember our wondering who this rumoured subaltern could be, whom Force Headquarters was sending up to advise us.

Joe was particularly insistent in his questions about the great salt-pan south of Palmyra. After the disastrous experiment west of Lake Habbaniya, the Brigadier was like a rider who has had a bad fall and wants to know more about the far side of the fences next time. The Nairn driver said that the salt-pan was just traversable for light touring cars, if the track across the middle of it were followed; but it would be folly to take heavy vehicles over it. This was quite enough for Joe, who arranged forthwith for all units to bypass the salt-pan. Our informant had not been through Palmyra for many years, but he remembered it as a large Arab town, with the French General Headquarters of it somewhere in the middle. The great fort was on the outskirts, with the aerodrome in front of it. The celebrated Roman ruins lay to the south-west of the town, and there was a Roman castle on a high hill to the north, a prominent feature, visible for miles. The oil pipe line from Kirkuk, dividing from the Haifa line at Baiji, passed through Palmyra on its way to Tripoli. Thus the I.P.C. control-settlements along it were numbered T.1, T.2, T.3, just as the place where we were sitting was called H.3, on the Haifa pipe-line. The occupation of T.1, T.2, and T.3, with their ample supplies of water (as I had learnt from the head office in Baghdad), would be vital to any plan for encircling Palmyra itself. T.₃ lay thirty-five miles due east of the old Roman fortress.

Our preparations for the advance were nearly complete. General Clark, who had flown back to Jerusalem, where Force Headquarters were conveniently situated above the bar of the King David Hotel, now arrived at H.₃ with the latest information about the wider plan of Jumbo Wilson's operation against Syria. The Australians, who had gone up the coast road, outflanking a veritable Gibraltar in the hills at Ras Naqura, had had to force a nasty passage over the Damour and Litani rivers. A British and Indian force was held close to the Palestine frontier at Mergayoum, while yet another push was overrunning the well-gilded Druzes with the intention of reaching Damascus and the Mezze aerodrome, without which (according to those remote from danger) we could not be supplied with fighter support.

We gazed, bewildered, at the hard even surface of the desert around us, and at the landing ground and hangars opposite the gate of H.₃ itself, where General Clark was landed, and doubted the veracity of Generals. A Brigade conference was held in our little sitting-room; whither came all our old and new friends: Daddy Wright, short-legged and calm; Guy Jackson, a bulky Major who commanded the two squadrons of Warwicks from Rutba; Colonel Bill Williams of the Wiltshires, a thin twitching man with wiry moustache; Cheeky Boy Oldham of the field troop of Engineers; Cassano of armoured car fame; and Colonel Sparrow, a well-intentioned man, who was Doc Arundel's superior and head of the Field Ambulance. Joe unfolded his plan with simplicity, and some savagery when the Warwicks' Major (un-used to his command) tried to argue about the hour of starting. To Cassano Joe turned as to an old and well-tried ally.

"You, Cassano, will guard the flank and, if there is trouble, you will go at once toward the sound of the guns."

Glubb agreed to carry out wide sweeping scout patrols west and east of the advance, and to lend a few truck loads of bedouin to the main column. Three of the armoured cars under Cassano himself were to go with the Wilts, who were to be advance guard of our advance. They were to cross the frontier by night and approach Palmyra about seven o'clock, three hours after first light. (The distance I had worked out with Joe on the map; but the timing, which baffled me, was his own.) The Warwick companies were to go next, followed by the rest of the Brigade group, with three more R.A.F. armoured cars as protection on the move. The plan was too simple. The Wilts were to enter Palmyra at seven, the Brigade at ten and the Division, close on our heels, with the whole Essex Regiment now under its command, was to move in at two, by which time we were to be well on our way westward to Homs. It was lovely; all to be done on Day One, like a jubilee procession.

"What air support do we get?" I asked.

"None," said Joe without enthusiasm.

We joked about the impatience of Division. "Suppose we just stand aside," we chuckled, "and let them whizz through?"

After the conference was finished and the commanders had returned, loaded with the rolls of maps which I heaped upon them, to unfold the plan to their units, Cassano remained in our Mess. His sharp, Lucifer features revealed a satanic doubt.

"I don't like this 'no air support'," he said. "I know something about those French aircraft. The Potez 63 is a bloody good bomber. They have 400 aircraft in Syria."

However, he was not lightly put out of countenance and went into reminiscences of English village cricket, performing imaginary strokes in the confined space, and reciting by heart the whole passage from his favourite book, *England, their England*, about the village cricket match. Cassano might have been an actor as he peeled off imaginary sweaters, handed them to the village umpire, took his stance at the crease, and looked round bewildered for the missing bowler, who suddenly hove in sight, cresting the rise beyond the further wicket. Cassano was a permanent and honorary member of our Mess now; and was intrigued by reports of a case loaded with 2-inch mortars which was addressed to the Household Cavalry. As the lumpers were still far away, Joe, who suspected that the heavy case probably contained bottles of champagne, told Cassano he could open it up and help himself. Cassano was pathetically grateful. He had been all round the units of the Brigade trying to swap anti-tank rifles (soon to be officially described as The Boy's anti-tank pistol) for 2-inch mortars.

Reading was not happy. Some chink in the curtain of his Oriental mind warned him what was coming. He walked over to me on the bare earth garden outside the bungalow, where a few untended rose trees still clung mysteriously to life from some hidden moisture in the soil.

"I wondered, sir," he began, "if you could help me to get a commission. In the Palestine Army, you know."

This was a surprising departure for Reading, who had hitherto clung to his civilian status as in interpreter.

"I will always follow you," he added hastily, for fear that I should mistake his intentions, "but, suppose anything were to happen to you, I should like to go to Palestine and train to become an officer."

"I am afraid there are no transfers allowed now," I explained. "We shall be off soon, and you may be needed any day."

"I should like to go to Palestine," he repeated dully.

He sent his pay regularly to an address in Haifa. I had to censor his letters. One of them was to his relations in Iraq, thanking them for their hospitality. It was in Arabic. I had to make him promise that it countained nothing about our movements.

We were just sitting down to tea when a smart young Australian lieutenant arrived. He had been sent up with an anti-tank troop of 2-pounders to join us in place of the competent Barraclough. The Australians had a better reputation in the Middle East as fighters, especially in attack, than as organisers or disciplinarians. But this one put us all to shame, for the closeness of his hair-cut, the brightness of his face, the neatness of his ankle puttees over his black boots, the cool efficiency of his whole bearing. Joe was duly impressed and asked him to stay for tea.

"No, General, if you don't mind, I'd like to go back and see my chaps settled in," and, although he had travelled far (without visible signs of wear or tear) he went back to his troop.

We were beginning to get a little light-headed — possibly like men who become dizzy on the edge of a precipice. Dick violated all the rules by filling the bath with cold water and getting in. Horrified as I was, I was not going to see it run to waste, and had one after him. Mild reproaches began to greet Dick when he appeared in the sitting-room; but he dashed back into the bathroom and sounds of another imaginary bath, much banging about and the hissing of a man drying himself down luxuriously, assailed our ears, until even the Brigadier was laughing. Nobody could be annoyed with Dick.

Most of the officers slept indoors in spite of the heat. I preferred to have my bed set up outside the window on the hard earth. I am not a gregarious animal. It was luxurious, after the night heat of the Tigris to be wakened by the chill of the desert in the dark hours of the morning and draw my white sheepskin coat and travelling rug over me. I slept well and began to feel refreshed.

In the afternoon we all siesta'd. My white sand-fly net may have been conspicuous from the air, but without it the ordinary flies prevented any rest at all.

Joe and Ian returned from a chukka round the desert with a shot gazelle, and I, who remembered some achievement at markmanship in the Cadet Corps in Australia, thought of bringing in more of this savoury meat, such as we loved. Joe's gazelle had been shot in the hills between H.₃ and Rutba, and an opportunity of going there was thrust on me by Peter, who told me to take the Warwicks' maps over to them. My alacrity baffled Peter, and I heard him and Joe with their heads together, afterwards, saying that I must be up to something.

I started out with Grose — and Williamson, whom I took for the sake of an outing and since the new cipher clerk, Baillieu, from the Life Guards, was well settled down under him. We drove for some miles, keeping a sharp look out for gazelle, and suddenly Williamson, whose sharp eyes had been trained to pick out Waziris on the North-West Frontier, shouted "There's one," and Grose pulled up. The gazelle was standing half a mile away, with head up, staring at us. The low earth embankment of the proposed road foundation lay in between. She was near a telephone post. I got out stealthily and rested my rifle on the blistering metal of the back of the car, where it sloped down to the rear bumper bar. I thought it a sitting shot, but there was a haze of heat low on the ground which made the target difficult to focus. I put the sights up to 600 on Grose's rifle, took aim and pressed the trigger. The poor little beast went down on one knee, then got up and hopped a few yards. I must shoot it again, but this time my grip was less steady and the rifle banged and jumped in my shoulder when I pressed the trigger. I handed the rifle to Grose and Williamson in turn, but they were no more successful. The gazelle began to run round in a circle, and with a sickening heart I saw that one of her forelegs was flapping helplessly. I had broken it. Now she was hopping away on three legs. I would never hit her. So I began to run, thinking that the best plan was to head her off, lame as she was, and drive her back towards the car. I ran in a wide circle, as fast as I could, panting in the heat. She stopped, bewildered, staring at me. I must finish this off. I dropped on one knee and took aim again. I did not hit her, but saw the bullet spurt up the yellow dust behind her. She lay down, probably in pain; then, as I circled closer, she lurched up and began to run again. She did not go far; but stood there, wild-eyed, with sides panting. This was agony and I fired again; my bullets went wilder and wilder until I pressed the trigger and nothing happened. A feeling of desperation came over me. I must finish off this poor wounded animal who would otherwise go hungry about the desert until she died a slow and painful death. So I ran nearer, heading her back towards Grose and Williamson at the car. The gazelle hopped nimbly on her three legs for short spurts, only to collapse and then start up again as I overtook her. Finally she reached the earthy embankment of the unfinished road and stood on it, peering round in a bewildered way. I walked up stealthily, taking my revolver out of its canvas holster. I took careful aim, not more than twenty yards away, hoping to kill her behind the pricked ear. The bullet thudded into the ground beyond in a cloud of dust. She just stood there, dazed, and did not try to escape. I fired once more and may have hit her or grazed her; she went down on her only fore knee. I rushed upon her and saw that she was still alive, her liquid brown eyes staring up at me. I must kill her; and using the rifle as a club began to beat the back of her skull in desperation. At last she died.

It takes a lot to kill a living thing. I felt terribly upset by this experience, but tried to conceal my feelings from Grose and Williamson, who merely rejoiced in the prospect of being able to say, on returning to camp, that I had shot a gazelle — just like that. ('How many shots did he take?' 'Oh, one or two.' 'Cor!')

We climbed back into the car and drove on towards Rutba. We had not gone far before we sighted a convoy of vehicles coming towards us. I got out of the car and stopped one of the vehicles and asked the driver if he was going to H.3. He was; and I charged him to deliver the dead gazelle to the Headquarters Officers' Mess. It would (according to Grose) turn bad if we kept it all day in this heat without gutting it first. The driver accepted the duty and we drove on to Rutba.

We found the Warwicks half-way down the main street in a quadrangle of crumbling yellow plaster buildings — dark narrow rooms cleared of the inhabitants and swept out as well as possible, with army blankets hanging under the door openings. There were only four or five officers, and they lunched at a narrow table, asking me to join them. Their Commander was a very bulky man and the Intelligence Officer was cocky. I gave him the maps, information about the enemy, and details of the route. General Clark had brought me a master map on which some features, such as the knolls at Bir Sijeri just beyond the frontier and the tracks to Palmyra and T.3, were marked in red ink. I lent it to the Warwicks and Wilts I.O. for copying. The latter was a surprising youth, ill-equipped, he feared, for his task because he possessed no periscope. This was a new idea to me, and I supposed that he had been reading stories of trench warfare in 1918.

While I lunched in the narrow room, Grose and Williamson were fending for themselves and, on searching the back of the car for provisions, found one of the four-gallon petrol cans leaking. So, after pouring what he could into my tank, Grose gave the rest away to a vehicle of the Warwicks. We drove back soon after lunch.

My gazelle had arrived all right and was roasted for dinner, with a haunch sent over to the Mess waiters and officers' servants, who appreciated it.

After dinner an oil lamp was lit, and Cassano suggested poker. The Brigadier did not want to play, and Peter was reluctant, but agreed to join the table. The rest of us were Dick, Ian, Cassano, Corpo and myself. (Toler and John Hampton were discussing lugubriously, in a bedroom down the corridor, their dreadful insufficiencies of everything.) I forget what stakes we played for, but I do know that Cassano and I were the only winners — Corpo being two pounds five hundred and thirty mils down to me when we went to bed.

There was only another day left; and we spent such time as we had to spare from our jobs in writing last letters to England. We all had a queer sense of foreboding, I think, not easily attributable to the mere fact of going into action again. Indeed, our experiences of that kind tended to give us a false sense of security. I wrote to my wife: 'It all makes one feel rather sad in a way. How small one's possessions and estates have shrunk — the camp bed, the canvas chair, the fat shaving brush, a primus stove, a sheepskin coat, and a suitcase with a few spare clothes and books — but even this goes on a "B" Echelon lorry, to make room for rations and petrol and water in every cranny of the Fighting Group's vehicles . . . . ' An officer of the Pay Corps had arrived to dispense money, and I used my advance pay book. He also undertook to send cables home for us on getting back to Jerusalem.

I had at last wrung enough maps for the whole Brigade from a distracted Edric. His clerks had not even counted correctly those he had allotted to us and he stumped into the Divisional bungalow (next to ours) crying to heaven, "If I hear any more about maps I shall go nuts — absolutely nuts!" (This was not why he was nicknamed 'Nuts'.)* His life was not a happy one. When General Clark had arrived by air from Jersualem, he asked me whether Edric had yet handed over the special map, and, when I said no, sent me to find his harassed Intelligence Officer. Edric was in the sitting-room of another bungalow — broken in soul and body by riding all day in the front of a truck from Habbaniya. (I had driven only as far as Rutba the first day and in a Chevrolet staff car.) Edric's face was as white as a miller's from desert dust, and his hollow

---

*His surname was Nutting.

eyes peered darkly out of it, like an owl blinking in the day. He cursed all Generals and their maps, but found me the missing one. While he searched, I studied a framed photograph, above the bookshelf, of a crusader castle from the air. The great empty oval moat around its massive bastions was shadowed from the sunlight. I wondered if it were the Krak des Chevaliers.

It was Joe's plan that the Brigade should get clear of the wire overnight, and we set out for the desert at about five o'clock. I was engaged at the last moment beside Joe's utility van in fixing the Palmyra map under the talc clipped to his own board. I had learnt something of Joe's ways in over a month, and did not mark it with hieroglyphics, such as some Brigadiers love, showing the enemy's positions. (He knew all that.) But I cut out the scale at the bottom and inset this neatly in the corner, for only the centre of the map would show on the handy board.

"That is the most intelligent thing Intelligence has done yet," he said, and he waited with benign patience for the job to be completed.

Joe stared moodily at the map. "If they had gone into Syria when I wanted them to," he said, "this time last year — after the fall of France, with Tricolour flying from the armoured cars and all the rest of it, we would have been all right. Now I am afraid it is going to be a long and difficult business."

He gave me the cartridges which he had been issued for his service revolver, since he carried an automatic of different calibre. I was glad of these, as I had fired off a good many at the petrol cans.

I went over to my car, and Grose drove it across the wide gravel compound. The other cars of the column were pulling out from the lee of the buildings where they had crouched in order to be inconspicuous to air observation.

We circled to the left outside the gate and, following the eastern wire of the settlement on the outside, came to where the armoured cars were waiting, with a triangular pennant flying from the foremost one. We were to strike due north until we hit the Old Damascus Camel Road, then, turning left, we would soon come to a parting of the ways and must swing right on the Palmyra track.

I waited only for the moment when the head of the column was due to pass the starting point, and then glided forward, waving the armoured cars ahead. The ground dipped, north of H.3, but rose again, and the square wire enclosure, with its comfortable bungalows, its gleaming white square fort, and the high 10,000 gallon water-tower, settled down into the desert landscape behind us.

The Wilts, with Cassano and Glubb, had already gone ahead, but the Warwicks were timed to converge with us along the Old Damascus Road as they came straight up from Rutba. We drove for perhaps an hour, with the rest of the Brigade, moving in a broad band dispersed against the risk of air attack, behind me. I struck the tracks of the Old Damascus Road without difficulty and halted there, as instructed, until Peter came up. He seemed to think we were on the wrong route, for the Warwicks were not in sight. He went off to see what was happening.

We waited about on the desert, and a truckload of Glubb's bedouin came over to me, driven, surprisingly, by an Air Force officer seconded to Glubb for desert experience. He was a cheerful and witty boy with a pert expression on his impish face. He wore a topi and shorts after our own fashion and was not yet gone Arab. His name was Mosley, and he confessed to relationship with the Fascist leader who was now confined to the narrow spaces of Brixton Gaol, while this cousin roamed the wide deserts under bright stars in the company of the nomad bedouin. A Canadian Air Force officer of the armoured cars, called Sector, with a ginger moustache, came over to join in the conversation. Glubb's girls, wearing their buff robes and bright pink headdresses, lounged about on the back of their truck or climbed down to be photographed, displaying the silver-handled knives in their belts and the rifles which they carried proudly. They loved to fire them off and carried, in crossed bandoliers over each shoulder, enough small arms ammunition to last most English troops a whole campaign.

At last we saw the many dotted Warwicks creeping up from the south-east, and they lumbered past us, bumping along the uneven desert tracks. It was more comfortable off the ruts. The whole Brigade began to move again slowly. We came to the signpost, which pointed two ways at a fork in the track; to Damascus and Palmyra. We wound away to the north. Here the desert was softer and there was more scrub about, so that for long stretches it was only possible to keep in the well-worn track. Before long Joe gave the order to halt and disperse for the night. He sent me on to fetch the Warwicks' Major back for orders; and I drove on in the failing light, surprised at how far the advance guard had got. They were, no doubt, making up for their lateness at the rendezvous. I saw them for a considerable distance before I did catch up. The desert seemed to be on fire with their bivouacking. The vehicles were laagered in a square, head to tail, for defence against surprise in the night.

I commented on the number and brightness of the cooking fires for, as Intelligence Officer to the Brigade, camouflage from the air was supposed to be a concern of mine. The Major was not enthusiastic about the display himself, and orders were passed round the square to douse them a bit and get the cooking over hurriedly. I told him that Joe wanted to see him. He asked if I knew what for, but I didn't. I guessed, however, that 'what for' would be what Joe intended to give him. I was not wrong. I got back to camp myself just ahead of him, racing ahead in the dusk, and drove right into Brigade Headquarters by mistake, so that Ian and Peter rushed out in high glee and started pelting my car with stones.

All old feelings of rancour against Peter were blown away on the wind. We were on the warpath again, old comrades, seeking new enemies; and the three of us, Ian, Peter and I sat on Joe's camp bed just out of earshot of the Brigadier, who now had the bulk of the Warwickshire Major, only a shade less massive than himself, face to face with him on the desert and was giving him about as smart a dressing-down as any commander of a unit had ever received from Joe in my experience. The man saluted and went back to his vehicle like a reproved schoolboy who has been up before the beak, and Joe came over to us, feeling much better for releasing such a broadside. Dick drifted into the circle and the Brigade fighting group was complete. Coles had scrounged the mahogany dining-table from our sitting-room at H.3, which drew a mild protest from Joe, but this had so little follow-through that Coles went back to the Mess wagon grinning happily to himself. We ate a good meal and dispersed to the circle of our cars early, for we must start before dawn on the morrow. My safari bed was already laid out on the desert and I was soon asleep.

Grose and Reading slept in their greatcoats on the sand. Williamson was this time travelling in the office truck, which Joe wanted with us as long as possible.

Grose woke me in the dark and had some hot water ready for me to shave. He always packed the small canvas basin in my valise, and had a canvas bucket, which must have come with him from my squadron in the Blues, when I was appointed to the Brigade. It was bitterly cold; we seemed to have risen even higher than H.3, although the ascent was imperceptible. I appeared at breakfast wearing my white sheepskin bedouin shepherd's coat for the first time. Joe stared at it. "Well, well," he said, "whatever is this?" But we all felt too good-natured and excited for reproofs. Dick came in, shivering in his army greatcoat. A thin bush shirt was little protection from the desert cold before sunrise. Most of us had jerseys to go over them. They were fitted with slots for the shoulder tabs and were oddly reminiscent of the Crusader shirts of chain mail. They were in fact a uniform issued to the troops in Palestine.

It was a memorable gathering, that last breakfast on the desert — with Joe sitting like an Old Testament father at the head of the board, with Peter, Ian, Dick and myself, gathered around him. A fighting family. We had been through other trials and other adventures together, and a bond of friendship now sealed us to each other.

We were quickly on the move: the three armoured cars, racing up in formation with the pennant leader in front, cruised majestically past my car, the desert dust clouding out from their huge wheels. I felt a thrill of pride in our adventures. By noon we should have reached our objective. I led the Brigade Headquarters as usual — indeed, I believe that my car out in front, gilded with desert dust, the very tip and point of our broad arrow, had become a familiar talisman. After all it had led the way to Baghdad and had never yet led to disaster.

At first halt I got out and went back to report to Joe with my map as usual. He asked me how far we still had to go before reaching Palmyra, and when I tried with a pair of dividers to calculate the distance, Joe showed me how to spread the dividers on the scale to 20 miles apart, and then proceeded to twirl them merrily along the mapped route, adding the distances easily.

The Syrian frontier, when we reached it, was indicated by two little cairns of stone and a few boulders stretched in a line either side of them.

I drove now at the appointed pace, treading hard on the tails of the armoured cars, sometimes pacing through them, always urging them to go faster. But the Warwicks ahead were slowing down. Now they had stopped: some unidentified armoured cars had been seen on their left. I was cursing their rearmost officer (the I.O.), giving him some hint of what Joe would say to this halting, when Joe himself came up to me in his utility van and asked what in the hell was happening. I told him and he went on to talk harshly to the Major.

We had come in sight of the rising ground each side of Bir Sijeri and near by was a low black camel-hair tent such as the bedouin use. McIlraith, an officer of the Wiltshire Yeomanry now far ahead, came back to me in a greenish staff car with a French prisoner. The man was a Sergeant-Chef of the Desert Camel Corps. He wore a light blue, high-crowned French Army cap with a flat red top; this accorded oddly with his buff calico pantaloons and bare feet in sandals. The man was broadly built and had a small reddish beard. He was quite amiable, but blinked from the loss of his glasses. McIlraith said that the Sergeant-

Chef with a section had been left out at Bir Sijeri as a listening post, and had been overrun by the first truckload of Glubb's bedouin. They had fallen upon the French wireless set with an axe before, we hoped, the startled section had been able to signal what was happening. (What McIlraith may not have known and I would have been very glad to know was only told me, long afterwards, in the convalescent home at Jerusalem by another officer of the Wilts. An aeroplane was seen to take off near the listening post on the arrival of our Column and must certainly have carried warning of our approach.)

McIlraith said that the rest of the captured French section were prisoners with the Wilts, but he had brought back the Sergeant-Chef to me for interrogation. I thanked him, took over the custody of the prisoner and McIlraith raced off to join his regiment again. He tried to make a short cut across the desert south of the Palmyra salt-pan and ran straight into a French armoured car patrol, who took him prisoner, and he was one of those unfortunate officers who were fed from an animal trough in a barn before being flown out of Syria to Vichy France.

I now told Grose to climb into the back of the car with Reading, where the rolls of maps for Palmyra, Homs, Hama, and Alleppo which I had to hand over to the Household Cavalry when they joined us, crowded the back seat. McIlraith had left the Sergeant-Chef's papers with me when he handed the man over. They consisted of a daily record of events at the listening post, signals exchanged with his company in Palmyra, private letters and a French paper-bound translation of *Mein Kampf*. The Sergeant-Chef was embittered about his *lunettes*. He said that the Arabs had smashed up everything including his glasses, while a British officer waited up on a rise for them to get done with it. The bedouin had grabbed anything they wanted, and had smashed the wireless set to pieces in sheer barbarity.

"What is the sense of that?" he asked. "We could not use it ourselves any more."

I gathered that it was an alarming experience to be set upon at breakfast by the wild, black-faced bedouin of our Desert Patrol. He seemed anxious to explain his conduct in surrendering.

"*Que voulez-vous*? A small section and you are suddenly surrounded by a whole army. *Inutile à resister*."

I asked him what signals, if any, had been sent back before the Desert Patrol surprised them. He shrugged his broad shoulders. The usual R.A.S. (*rien a signaller*). If this were all that had passed back from the listening post that morning, it would be splendid. At least we had not yet been visited by enemy aircraft.

I spent the next half-hour looking through the papers. The signals included a special warning, on 9th June, to be on the alert; but since then nothing had occurred out of the normal routine. There was a carbon copy of a long letter from the French signalman asking to be repatriated to France on compassionate grounds. Among the letters was one from the Sergeant-Chef's brother who appeared to be a captain at Mergayoum, where he would now be fighting the British. But in the letter he told his brother how he had 'escaped from the Boche' in France in order to come out to Syria. It was an inverted campaign.

The prisoner saw no point in refusing information about the French troops in Palmyra, because, he said, we must already know everything since Colonel Collet had come over to us with all the detailed knowledge which he possessed of the French defences. There could never, my prisoner said lugubriously, have been such an opportunity for getting first-class intelligence about an enemy. I asked him if there were any German aircraft at Palmyra and he said, "Only the ones you shot down yourselves." Palmyra was not used as a base by the Germans for refuelling their planes on the way to Iraq. "But two of their aircraft were shot down by your Glenn-Martins over the aerodrome and made a forced landing. After that you came and bombed the same two aeroplanes on the ground every day." He would not say if the French had any aircraft there.

We had been going for some hours now and the column was again halted. We were in a defile between high sandstone hills — a feature marked on the maps as Juffa. I walked over to Joe and told him what the prisoner had said. Joe came back to my car. "How many aeroplanes did he say on the aerodrome?" I turned to the prisoner. *"Combien des avions avaient-ils à Palmyre?"* I asked, and Joe interjected grammatically *"Combien d' avions?"* (Joe was right in a general sense, but the correction rankled for I was asking specifically about the number of aircraft about which he had just told me. How many of *the* aircraft '*dont vous venez de parler?*')

I told Joe that the Light Desert Company at Palmyra was the 1st and not the 3rd as we had thought.

"I don't care whether it's the first or the third, so long as there is only one," he replied, and went back to his utility van.

I looked up and saw sharp yellow against the bright blue sky three aircraft flying down the line of our column towards me. They were not too high up for me to distinguish at a glance the blue, white and red circles under the wings and the twin engines, which made me take them for our familiar Blenheims. Even as I watched I saw three bright yellow eggs begin to fall against the blue and my mind, slowly somersaulting to the horrid truth, warned me that there was something wrong with the picture. I threw myself down on the hard ground and the bombs burst seventy-five yards away, blowing the forearm off an officer of the new Australian anti-tank troop. The bombers sped on down the line, dropping further clutches on the immobile columns trapped between the walls of the defile. I got up and looked into the car to ask the Frenchman what kind of bombers they were. He was philosophical.

"I have been bombed by the British," he said, "now I am bombed by the French," and shrugged his shoulders. He said they were certainly Potez 63s.

I went down to the Gin Palace (the big signal truck), which had narrowly escaped. There was a gaping crater beside it, which I judged from my experience in England to have been made by a 75-pound bomb. I sent a signal back to Habforce about this and the rest of the information which now confirmed our own reports.

Joe told me to go ahead and see what was delaying the advance. I arrived among the Warwicks in time to see some more bombs falling where they were spread out on the open plain. This was the reason for their halting. I went back to Joe. Meanwhile signals had come through from the Wilts saying that they had encountered stiff resistance from the French who were waiting for them south of Palmyra. So Joe now decided to take the rest of the Brigade from Juffa up the track which here diverged to T.₃ and try to get inside that. It was garrisoned by a company of the Foreign Legion with Senegalese troops. The column accordingly swung north here from the general north-westerly course we had been pursuing. We had been discovered by the enemy and further surprise was now impossible.

We drove up an incline which led round to the right beyond the sandstone cliffs, and were soon out on the open desert again. Joe began bringing up the battery of 25-pounders; and soon another column of vehicles was seen converging with ours beyond a spur of foothills. It may have been the Household Cavalry coming in from Abu Kemal. The French Sergeant-Chef's eyes began to widen; and he readily believed my exaggeration of the size of the force attacking Palmyra.

"Is that another column coming in?" he asked.

We cannot have been far from T.₃ when the column halted again. Brigade Headquarters were about the middle of the column, so I could not see why we had stopped and there were slight folds in the ground which limited the view. A sharp line of hills bounded our horizon away to the north. Again we found ourselves standing impatiently about on the desert. The three armoured cars which were assigned the role of protecting Brigade Headquarters were dispersed near by, and Arab Legionnaires with a Lewis gun on their truck commanded by a bedu sergeant drove up to ask what was happening. Peter came over and, more to give Reading something to do than anything else, asked me to tell the man not to go away, as we might need him. Reading parleyed with the sergeant, who was loud in his promises of stability, but disappeared in a cloud of dust a few moments later. It was hopeless to try to keep control of these swarthy will o' the wisp warriors. They did not understand or lend themselves to British Army discipline.

Joe now deployed the 25-pounders and set them to shelling T.3. He took the armoured cars and went up to the front in order to find some means, I suppose, of nosing a way into the wired-in enclosure, where the enemy were able to fire at us with machine-guns from the security of concrete pill-boxes across bare and featureless desert. The French were not taking this campaign lying down as we had been led to hope.

One of their armoured cars drove up to the Warwicks, flying a white flag. Our men stood up, hopefully expecting a surrender, only to be met with a treacherous burst of machine-gun fire which scythed away all but eight men in the troop. The men of Vichy were not fighting this war prettily, and indeed they seemed to feel especial spite against the British, and our Free French allies, for surviving when they went down. The French troops in Syria, moreover, including the famous Foreign Legion and other colonial regiments, were determined to show that they could fight, no matter what had happened in the war at home.

I was sitting in the driving seat, looking forlornly at my sun-glasses which had somehow got cracked, and wondering, 'How can I go through the rest of this campaign with a splintered black glass in front of my eye? I shall never be able to get another pair,' when I found Reading standing diffidently by the window. He had an envelope in his hand.

"Excuse me, sir," he said. "Would you take care of this? If anything happens to me, would you see that it is sent to the person addressed on the outside?"

"Something is just as likely to happen to me as to you, Reading," I laughed.

"But I have a copy on me," he persisted, tapping the breast pocket of his shirt.

"Very well then," I reassured him, taking the envelope and pushing it into the dashboard locker, "I will see that it gets sent off if anything happens to you." He smiled dispiritedly and stalked away, eyeing the sky suspiciously.

The vehicles of Brigade Headquarters were still dispersed about the desert at intervals of over two hundred yards, waiting to move forward, when the air became full of hostile aircraft. I took Grose's rifle and potted at a flight of Potez bombers. They sailed down the line of the column dropping bombs, which sent up angry spurts of black explosive edged with a yellow fringe of sand. My shots in no way deterred them, and I handed the rifle to Grose, who wisely made off to a reasonable distance from the car, which Reading had already done, while I got out a camera and photographed the great angry cloud of dust which now clawed the sky from the nearest bomb burst. The Frenchman remained sitting on the front seat to the right of the driving wheel, while I stood by the open driving door of the car on the near side. (It was an American car.) Not far away a Bren was mounted on its anti-aircraft tripod near a lorry, and a man was prancing about with the gun at his shoulder, firing after the bombers, but without effect.

I was standing thus, watching the flowering tulips of war unfold, when my eye was attracted by a swarm of low-wing single-engined De Woitine D.520 fighters, for all the world like British Hurricanes, swooping like wasps upon the firing gunners just over a rise in the ground. I thought, 'Poor devils, they are catching it pretty hot', but the words had scarcely formed themselves in my mind when I saw one of them coming straight on at me. It was a roar and a black shadow and I threw myself flat on the ground which spurted up all round me before the thing had gone over — so low that I felt the draught caused by its rush through the air. I got up, dazed, and thought it time to put on my tin helmet which was lying on the floor of the driving seat, where I had been sitting. I reached for it and asked the Frenchman if he were all right. He was quite unmoved.

I looked round vaguely for Grose's rifle, then remembered that he had taken it. I felt the need to take some action and picked up the camera with the idea of photographing the aeroplane when it came at me again. I should, of course, have seized my prisoner by the arm and shouted, "Come on, mon vieux," and legged it while there was still a second left. But his calm seemed to freeze my own pride and I remained. Besides, vaguely at the back of my mind, was the idea that he could drive off to Palmyra with all the Brigade secrets in my car and the knowledge of everything he had seen. So I turned back, facing the desert, placing the tin helmet on my head with my left hand and holding the stupid camera with the other. There was the black thing roaring at me again, almost on a level with my head. I went down on the desert beside the running board, turning my back to the menace and holding my tin helmet over the side of my head. My ankle felt a crashing blow; the ground throbbed round me, as if it were being beaten with silver rods, and I was stung all over. The violence passed like a storm and I felt a great surprise, 'I have been wounded. This has happened to me. How odd.'

I looked down at my leg. The bright red blood was pumping out in great gulps, pouring down over my khaki stocking into my shoe, filling it up and spilling on to the desert. I thought, 'I shall die, I suppose if that doesn't stop.' My left hand was also bleeding where a bullet had torn across it as I held my helmet. My body seemed all right, except for that single cat o' nine tails lash. I got up on one leg and hopped round the back of the car to the other side. The Frenchman was still in his seat, undamaged, while the windows of the car were starred with holes and part of the windscreen was shot away. There was also a gaping hole in the radiator where a cannon shell had hit it. But I did not know this and it was lucky that the hole was not inside me, for a direct hit from these explosive bullets tears too much away and men die from the bleeding.

The Frenchman said, "*Vous êtes blessé alors?*"

I took a handkerchief out of the pocket in my shorts and asked him if he could fix it tightly around the wound to stop the bleeding. He sat beside me on the running board and made a tight knot. Then I asked if he could drive me to the ambulance. He was not much of a driver, he said (so much for my fears), but would try, and climbed over into the driving seat, while I got in beside him, holding my knee to prevent the foot touching the floor. (The bone was pulped just above the ankle.) I had my revolver still in my holster and could make sure he did not drive away from the battlefield. We went lurching from side to side, possibly because the Frenchman was a bad driver, or shaken by the experience. The steering may have been affected and the tyres were probably in ribbons.

I was not thinking of these things. I saw the white red-crossed circle of the khaki ambulance away to the right and directed him towards it. He pulled alongside and I called for the driver of the ambulance. I gave him an order, "Take charge of this prisoner." The driver was armed with a rifle and accepted the duty, while stretcher-bearers carried me into the ambulance. They were all trembling. A fighter had just machine-gunned the ambulance too — fortunately before anyone was inside it. But the orderly said he had been under the wheels. He wrote down my particulars in a hand so shaky (I don't blame him) that it was laughed at back in base hospitals for the work of a drunkard. "It *would* be the longest day in the year," he said.

I was laid on the upper bunk and soon other casualties were pushed in. Colonel Sparrow appeared, as cheeful as it was possible to be under the circumstances, and said "I am afraid you caught a packet." He attended to the leg first, adjusting the tourniquet. He removed the blood-soaked shoe, cutting through the laces. "You are lucky," he said, "the bullet has gone right between the two bones and come out the other side. There is only just room for a .303 bullet to get through." He seemed astonished, as indeed he might well have been if his surmise had been confirmed by the X-rays later.

"Where else do you feel it?"

I rolled over. "I think there's one in my back."

Fragments of a cannon shell had gone into my shoulder, a glancing shot fortunately, upper left arm and right hip. He slit my shirt away with his scissors and dressed them all. He bound up the ripped and bleeding tear on my left hand, swollen along the edges of the bullet furrow. He counted the wounds — five in all. I thanked him for his kindness and Grose appeared, thrusting his frightened brown face in through the ambulance door. He was not alarmed for his own skin. He smiled a wry smile.

"I hear you're all right," he said. "I mean you aren't going to die." He must have run all the way to the ambulance.

I asked him to get me my greatcoat and a towel. He reappeared with these and also the little green canvas roll of my shaving kit and soap.

"Listen to me," I said, as he bent over the stretcher. "You know my big leather wallet?"

"Yes."

"It has my notebook for this campaign in it — the Enemy Order of Battle, a blueprint of the Persian Army and a road map of Persia and the Caucasus. Hand the whole wallet to Major Grant-Lawson."

"What? With everything that's in it?" he asked incredulously.

"Yes. There's nothing private in it. If he will let you come, you might get a ride in this ambulance in front and hand the car over to Reading. He knows how to drive it. If not, I'm all right. Goodbye. And thanks for all your help." I offered him my right hand and he shook it. He backed out of the confined space, and I never saw him again till after the war.

Reading was even now running as hard as his legs would carry him eastwards, completely unnerved by what had happened. And Grose was needed for other duties.

The wounded man on the upper bunk opposite me was a bombardier, called James, who kept complaining that no one came to dress his hand, which was loosely tied up in a field dressing. I called for the orderly, and asked him to fetch Colonel Sparrow, who came. I whispered to him, "Can anyone look after this chap's hand? I know how busy you are."

But he whispered back, "I'm afraid it's no use. The fingers are half off."

"Well," I said, "perhaps you could do something just to make him feel that he was being attended to."

So Colonel Sparrow fumbled with the man's bandages and told him that he would be better if they were not changed. I asked the Colonel what was going to be done with us. He said that he was having the ambulances driven a few hundred yards away from the rest of the column for the night so that they would be safer. I told him about the reports we had received of bedouin setting upon lonely ambulances and killing the occupants, so I hoped he would put a guard over them. He promised to warn the drivers and orderlies to be on the look-out.

The Colonel then went on with his dressings outside and we were left. The orderly came in from time to time and gave me a drink from his water-bottle. My lips were beginning to feel very parched and to crack painfully. I had forgotten to ask Grose to give me the little jar of cream, on the back window ledge of the car, which I used to prevent this drying of the lips, which afflicted so many of us. So I just lay there running my tongue over my lips, which only made them worse.

My left leg was numb now, and the orderly had put an army blanket folded up under it. I used my greatcoat as a pillow and began talking to my fellow sufferers.

"I expect they will send us back to a dressing station as soon as it is light," I said, to cheer them up, for the prospect of lying in an ambulance all night with wounds was not cheering. The orderly made us swallow white pills to prevent our wounds turning septic.

When dusk was falling outside, the engine of the ambulance started up and we began to move. It was curious, shut up inside with the door shut, not knowing in which direction we were heading. We stopped soon and the door was opened. The orderly said we were parking for the night. I told him to look out for bedouin too, and then I think I went to sleep for I dozed in a sort of delirium. When I woke up in the middle of the night my leg, which had been lying sideways on the blanket pillow, was so stiff I could not move it and I had to sit half up and help it with my hands.

I felt more or less at peace. We would obviously be driven back as soon as it was light and would be well looked after. There would be time to rest. There was one china urinal bottle, and we had to ask the orderly for it when we wanted it.

At first light the driver opened the doors and I could see the bare desert in the ghostly dawn. We seemed to be a long way from any other vehicles. There was a little window of bullet-proof glass beside my face and, as the light grew, I could make out the column of vehicles against a background of purple hills.

"Expect we'll soon be moving now," the driver said cheerfully. He and the orderly made us some tea, which we sipped gratefully. There was nothing to eat without taking something from their rations, but this would not matter if we were going back in an hour or two, and so they gave us a biscuit each, spread with a little sardine from a tin.

Time began to drag by and the men in the ambulance asked me (being an officer) what was happening.

I said, "I expect they are sending an aeroplane up to get us back over the desert quickly, instead of bumping back in this thing. But I wish it would hurry up."

Soon the heat became oppressive and we shifted about restlessly on our stretchers. There was no sign of our moving. I called, "Orderly," but there was no reply. Then I understood why. More aeroplanes were bearing down on us. We could hear the hum grow louder and they were coming straight at us. I quivered as they tore overhead and turned my neck so that I could see through the little window. I saw the aircraft reach the main column and bombs begin to burst along it. There was an answering spurt of flame from one of the 2-pounder anti-tank guns, turned skywards and throwing up white puffs into the blue, but the aeroplanes went on, growing small.

Presently another flight came over. Then another and another. They zoomed down and rushed past to bury their cargo in the immobilised column. And each time it was the same. The orderly and the driver both disappeared into thin air and we were left, wondering whether the planes were after us.

The men became very embittered. "What in the hell is happening? They've fogotten all about us. That's about it."

382

I clung to my aeroplane story, but I did not really believe it.

What had happened?

Next time the orderly returned, looking over his shoulder at the empty sky as he walked, I asked him to fetch one of the doctors. Arundel came. I said, "When are they going to send us back? These chaps are getting browned off."

He said, "We don't know. Colonel Sparrow's orders were to stay here until we hear from him."

"Where is he now?"

"With the Brigade."

"But isn't there an advanced dressing station somewhere?"

"If so, we don't know where it is."

"They are not getting aeroplanes up to evacuate the wounded, then?"

"I'm afraid I don't know more than you do," he said sadly.

He looked tired and hopeless. He had amputated the Australian's arm after the first bombing yesterday — a nasty job for a young doctor in the field. He went away; and we remained where we were.

I learnt afterwards what was happening. Someone at Division had ordered blithely that 'all casualties will be evacuated forward to Palmyra' (which fell thirteen days later). The Military Mind!

It was all part of that silly timetable, which made no provision for a smash-up in front. No one had stopped to wonder what would happen to the wounded if Palmyra did not fall on Day One. Well, it was already Day Two; and still no British aircraft came.

The Vichy forces now saw their opportunity to smash the Brigade while it was halted helpless on the open desert, and every available aircraft was switched to the attack. The Brigade Headquarters, being the vital brain and nerve centre, received especial pounding, but all got it — the Wilts south of Palmyra, the Household Cavalry coming in from the west, the Warwicks, and ourselves.

Bluff John Morrison (later created Lord Morgadale) of the Wilts, who was to join me in Parliament a year later, told me that he had seventeen vehicles under his command on the first morning, and only four left, including the water wagon, next day. The rest were destroyed by air attack. The Australian gunners with them complained bitterly that it was far worse than Crete. The situation improved only in so far as it was possible to dig in.

"We all but carried slit trenches around on our shoulders after the first two days," said John Prideaux, when he visited me in hospital afterwards.

All morning the air was filled with the throb of engines and the roar of bombs. It seemed as if there was no end to them. They swarmed over in relays and cruised round in circles, pitching out bombs on the heads of the helpless troops below. The occasional retort from Bren-guns or Hotchkiss perched on the slender tripods did not even sting them up except one de Woitine, which was sent with a whine and a crash into the sand by the Regimental Corporal-Major's batman in the Household Cavalry's lines. He was given an immediate award of the Military Medal — standing up there on the bare desert, without the cover even of a slit trench, firing back at an aircraft pouring lead and iron past him.

Water must now be conserved if we were to be abandoned in the ambulance for long, and it grew hotter all day. At last the driver's face, still cheerful, popped in at the door. "Orders to move now," he said.

We felt the ambulance vibrate as the engine started and it began to shake along the desert. I lay on my back, my head lolled sideways, looking through the window and I began to think, 'We are going in a queer sort of direction,' for, judging by the sun, we were travelling north — even farther from the Iraq border. I could see the wired-in buildings of T.₃. The water-tower stood up, burnished silver in the sun. The settlement appeared to be some miles away and we were leaving it to the west on our left.

It was two o'clock by the gold wrist-watch my wife had given me before I left England. Already the linen strap (which was essential in such heat) was grimed with sweat and dust. I had lost the spare one before H.₃ and had been obliged to keep washing this one.

Presently the ambulance stopped with a screech of brakes and a jerk.

"Orderly!" I shouted, wanting to ask him if he knew where we were going. But there was no reply; only the deathly silence of the desert upon which was quickly superimposed the drone of aeroplane engines. The sound came swiftly towards us in the stillness. The boy below me, who was lightly wounded, grabbed his tin helmet and hopped out of the back of the ambulance. I saw him hop away. The soldier opposite me, with the torn off fingers, scrambled down off his bunk on to the floor, bending towards the front of the ambulance. The man below him did not move; and I lay rigid holding my tin hat up to my left ear.

The engines roared lower, coming straight at us until the confined space was full of their noise. And above it sounded the crackling overtone of machine-gun fire. I began to repeat a prayer which I had heard often in my childhood; and with a rending crash the box in which we lay was torn apart round us. One bullet passing through the further wall shattered on the bullet-proof glass by my face and I lay there with staring eye watching uncannily a flake of metal whizzing about in the corner of the window until it dashed into my eye socket, where it drew blood under my eyebrow. In the wooden wall just over my body were three bullet-holes which seemed to have come up like snakes out of the

384

ground to gaze at me. The stocking of my right leg was torn across the shin where a bullet had grazed it.

Bombardier James, who had got down off the opposite bunk, was now lying in the one below me.

The aircraft passed on, droning into the silence.

I looked over the side of my stretcher at James. "Are you hit?" I asked.

"Yes," he said quietly, "I'm hit," and I saw the blood streaming out of the side of his leg.

I looked down at the man opposite him. "Are you hit?" I asked. "Yes, I've been hit again." He had a bullet in the foot. I lay back for an instant, and called, "Orderly," (to come and dress their wounds), but there was no response, only the silence of the desert seeming to hold its breath, and the hard unwinking sky. I thought to myself, 'If I lie here no one will blame me, on the other hand I have a towel on the stretcher beside me and if I don't get down somehow to bandage the man below me, my conscience will never leave me in peace.' So I clutched the towel and crawled down over the side of my bunk, letting myself down gingerly on to my good leg. I knew instinctively that the other was broken.

"Here you are," I said and wrapped the towel tightly round the wound so that it stopped the gushing blood. "That's all I can do, I'm afraid."

"Thanks," he said; and I clambered up somehow to my own stretcher and lay there panting.

The lightly-wounded man was the first to come back, still wearing his helmet, which glinted flat and round in the sun, and hopping on his good leg. "I couldn't have stayed in this ambulance if you had crowned me," he explained. Then the orderly and driver reappeared, harassed and began to drag our stretchers out of the ambulance and to lay us about the desert under the blinding sun. I laid my topi, which I still appeared to have with me, over my eyes to shield them.

I tore the end page out of someone's paper-bound 'Penguin' book and wrote a message in pencil for Doc Arundel to send to Peter. 'Can you make some arrangement about getting the ambulances back to a dressing station? There is a massacre going on in them, at the tail of the column.'

The ambulance driver and the orderly had not deserted us. Their orders were to get clear of the vehicle at the approach of aircraft, for without them we should have been even worse off, but their abrupt disappearances were not encouraging.

The ambulance was a total wreck, the tyres all in shreds, the engine holed and bullets through the body. The white circle, with its brilliant red cross, stared reproachfully at the sky. With the vehicle standing still, abandoned by the driver as it had been, the emblem must have been clearly visible at 200 yards, when the pilot fired his burst.

Doc Arundel now came along, and said that he was taking the walking wounded out of their ambulance and giving it to us. The medical equipment lorry had also been destroyed; but he was able to dress the new wounds. My own were mere scratches, but they brought the total score to seven. He now went off up the line and we were pushed into the new ambulance. We had no kit but what we had on our stretchers. The column moved forward a few hundred yards, but soon halted again.

Now began another long wait and I lay there while some sort of peace flowed in again over my nerves, thinking of the poor gazelle I had hounded and shot at; wondering whether this was my retribution: to be chased and machine-gunned again and again until I too died.

It takes a lot to kill a living thing.

Yet around me the sky seemed to grow calm, as if some battle for my soul was over and the menace driven off.

I had succeeded in getting down to help my wounded comrade. Why should I not get down again and see what was happening to the column? If we waited here for salvation we would wait for ever. I saw an iron splint down on the floor of the ambulance and wondered it it would serve as a sort of crutch. I crawled down again telling the others I was going to take a hand myself.

"Thank God for that," they said, and I got out with difficulty, supporting myself by the left and on the round top hoop of the splint. I hopped a yard or two. The line of vehicles stretched away over a rise in the ground. Not far across the desert, in a shallow depression near a little Austin-Seven, crouched two men wearing tin helmets. I recognised one as the junior doctor, Hall. There was a light wind blowing which stirred the occasional shreds of grass which grew here and there among the pebbles on the sand.

"Lieutenant Hall," I called, but my voice drifted away on the breeze.

"Lieutenant Hall," I shouted louder; and again, louder still, "Lieutenant Hall."

He could not or would not hear; so I hobbled nearer, using my ungainly crutch. At last he stirred himself from his hollow and came towards me, dazed, vacant as a tortoise. He was past thinking.

"Where are we going to?" I asked. "The column is going north."

"I don't know." There was despair and indifference in the reply.

"Well, I think some fool is driving in the wrong direction. I know what happens: everybody follows the man in front thinking the chap at the head of a column knows where he is going. I believe we are just wandering aimlessly around the Syrian Desert. You take me in that car of yours up to the front and we can find out."

"I'll get into fearful trouble," he said, "If you get out of your ambulance and I drive you about the desert."

"It's too late to worry about that sort of thing," I assured him. "The only thing is to find out what is happening at the front; or we shall be here for good."

"All right," he agreed. "You wait here and I'll bring the car over." I limped into the off side of the little car, holding my knee as before, and we drove up the scattered column, over rise after rise in the ground, across a track, where we passed under a line of telegraph wires, past the clumsy great supply lorries of the R.A.S.C., and came at last to a low ridge where we identified Doc Arundel's car. We pulled up beside him and I asked what he planned to do.

"I don't know," he said. "We have received no message. The only thing I can think of is to bring the ambulances up here and dig the wounded in for the night."

The idea of anyone having the energy to dig appalled me. The column was now trying to work round into the hills north of Palmyra and the ambulances had merely been tacked on to the tail of it.

"Well, you will have to do something about the walking wounded and the medical stores," I pointed out. "Can I go over to these R.A.S.C. lorries with Hall and see if we can get them to lend us any?"

"You can try by all means," he replied.

So I directed Hall over to a big supply monster. We asked the driver where his officer was and he pointed up a rise in the ground to where a young subaltern was sitting with an N.C.O. beside a rock. I explained the situation to him.

"Have you any lorry you could spare?" I asked. "Otherwise the walking wounded may get left out in the desert."

"We haven't any empty vehicles exactly," he explained, "but we could shift a load I suppose," and gave orders for this to be done.

I waited with Hall in the little Austin-Seven, while the men backed our lorry up to another, and worked with sweating bodies, bared to the waist, at transferring a load of petrol cans and other tackle. At last it was done, and the empty lorry followed us back to the rear of the column, where we had left the ambulances.

We came upon the one to which I and my companions had been transferred. But now it stood abandoned on the desert. Even the wounded had crawled away from it, rather than be caught by another murderous attack while it was not moving. I asked Hall to put me down beside it, while he went on to show the lorry where to pick up the walking wounded and medical stores.

I sat on the ground in the shade of the deserted ambulance, leaning back against the front wheel. I could just see the driver and the others, scattered about over the desert far away. I fumbled with my good hand in the breast pocket of my shirt for my wallet and found a blank airgraph form which I had kept for some such occasion as this. I had a pencil and wrote in bold letters, so that it would be readable if ever it were transmitted. I wrote to my wife telling her that we had been through pretty good hell in the last two days and did not know what was going to happen. If I did not come back she must know that she was the only person I had ever really loved.

I was writing thus, in melancholy strain, when I looked up to see an ambulance scudding across the desert as if it knew where it was going. I waved my left hand, with its white gleam of bandages, and the driver pulled up.

"Where are you coming from?" I asked.

"The Advance Dressing Station," said he.

"What!" I could scarcely believe my ears. "Where is that?"

"Twenty-three miles back."

"Who are you attached to?"

"The Warwicks. I'm going back there for the night. There won't be time to do another trip not by the time I get back to them, there won't."

"Could you find your way back to the Advance Dressing Station?" I asked.

"I should bloody well think I could," was the answer. "I've been doing it all day."

"Well hold on a minute, if you don't mind."

Doc Arundel fortunately came up at this juncture, having supervised the collection of the medical stores and their safe transfer to the borrowed lorry.

"There's a chap here," I told him, "who knows where there is an Advance Dressing Station. There is just an hour of daylight left and he could guide us back there."

"Where is that?" Doc Arundel asked the driver, who said it was at Juffa.

"Captain Somerset is looking after it." That was the other section of the H.₆ Field Ambulance.

"Good enough," said Arundel; and the ambulances were assembled, the wounded called in, packed up and myself thrust firmly on to a stretcher in the ambulance of my rescuer (for such I regarded him).

It was a happy feeling to be heading to care and comfort at last after that terrible day. I did not mind the jolting of the ambulance. For an hour it banged and jumped over stones and ruts, but at length it pulled up and, in the last glimmer of daylight, I saw the flat basin of land in the hills which was Juffa, and there in the middle of it was a great affair of awnings, with slit trenches neatly dug all round.

My stretcher was lifted out and carried over to be laid on the ground beside the dressing station. I looked up to see men who walked about calmly — not harassed from behind into desperate movement. High up on the cliff against the sky, where dusky stars lighted the way for night, men stood silhouetted beside an anti-aircraft gun. It was all wonderfully peacefully and secure.

They made tea for us, and, as I struggled up on one elbow to drink it, the Colonel of the Field Regiment, which provided our gunners, saw me and sat himself down at the head of my stretcher, making me lean back against his broad chest.

"I am not accustomed to this luxury," I observed, trying to joke.

Next to me was laid the man with the torn fingers, Bombardier James, and he told his neighbour how I had got the convoy back. "Thank God for an officer," was his comment.

It was now almost dark, but the A.D.M.S., Colonel Stuart, hearing that I was there, came over and said he had been trying all day to get in touch with the ambulances to tell them where the dressing station was. In the end he had driven up, himself, only to learn with relief that they had started back. "I am very grateful to you," he said.

Michael Lubbock, whom I remembered as a friend of Corpo, and used to come forward to Brigade occasionally, loomed up, lanky in the dark. "Is there anything I can get you?" he asked.

"Yes," I said, "a clean handkerchief and some cream to put on my lips." They had fretted me all day, almost worse than the wounds. "Can you possibly manage that?" I asked.

"Yes, of course. I'll get them at once. I heard that you were wounded. Did you know that Dick Schuster is dead?"

My heart turned over inside me. "No. How did it happen?"

"A bomb this morning." He went off in search of the handkerchief and cream; and I thought about Dick, of all the cheerful times we had spent together. Why should Dick of all people be killed? The kindest, the best of young men?

The Divisional Headquarters was near by, and the G.2 came over, saying that there was a chance of getting me flown back to the hospital in Habbaniya in the morning.

"In that case," I said, "I would sooner shoot myself and have done with it."

I wanted to get back to Palestine. Indeed, this was almost an obsession with me, even if it meant jolting for days over the desert to get there. My vehement dislike of the idea of returning to Habbaniya surprised him, but he went off thoughtfully. The mere idea of the heat and isolation of Habbaniya in my present condition made me despair.

Michael Lubbock returned with two of his handkerchiefs, with thin blue lines on them, and a jar of cream which he insisted on my keeping. It was certainly balm to my blistered face. He stayed talking for a while. The Gunner Colonel was moving about among his own wounded. (Anderson, who had been firing those guns, told me later that he had 25 per cent casualties.)

At last my own turn came to have my wounds dressed, and I was carried round, through the flap of the tent and lifted on to a table. Here I found a short, competent man, with a square sensible head looking down at me. He took the bandages off my leg first and began cleaning it up. Then he redressed the others systematically, cutting my bush shirt away from my arm and shoulder.

When he examined the wound in my back he said, "Half a minute. I think I can see a corner of this fellow. Perhaps I can get it out," but after little probing he thought it wiser to leave the shrapnel where it was until it could be got at in hospital. He had been working thus for hours without pause, but he never tired, and I believe he went on doing it for seventy hours.

Captain Somerset surprised me by saying, "Your interpreter is here."

"What? Wounded?"

"No. Just a bad case of shock."

"I should like to see him."

"He wouldn't recognise you. He is much too far gone."

I persisted in wanting to see him, but the doctor was not helpful, thinking, possibly, that in my own condition I needed rest.

Captain Somerset pronounced my wounds healthy, said they would probably be getting us back in the morning to H.3, where there was another dressing station.

"I hope and pray we are going to Palestine," I told him.

He thought so, and I was lifted out again and laid back in the row of stretchers outside. I think I went to sleep.

I had asked Grose for my camera, determined to get the film developed, and it was on the stretcher beside me. My empty shoe was tied to the chin strap of my pith helmet. I heard the doctor say, as I was lifted off the table, "Careful. There are all sorts of watering cans and things on this stretcher." I accepted it as a reproof for clinging still to the last of my material possessions.

When dawn came we expected any moment to see the first aeroplanes race in from the sky. It took longer than expected to prepare the convoy, but we were to go back to H.3 under guard with an empty supply column. I was put back into the ambulance which had brought us in the night before. I went on to the bottom bunk on the left, facing the door. A red-headed freckled Australian with the left arm off was lifted on the one opposite me. He was in great pain, which the injection of morphia only partially numbed. Above me an Arab Legion driver, stinking dreadfully, and tied up in a frame, was pushed into place. I don't think there was a fourth. I realized how fortunate I was. The doors were shut by my cheerful benefactor, who said, "You'll be in Durban before you know where you are."

Then began a long journey of nearly a hundred and fifty miles, in growing heat, over the rough desert; but it was much worse for the Australian than for me. The Arab Legion driver was too far gone to care much, but kept asking to go back to his family in Amman.

I told the Australian how I had spent four years at school out there and we talked a good deal to keep our spirits up. He spoke very bitterly of a recent public promise by his Prime Minister that Australian troops would not again be sent into action without air support.

We halted once during the day and I wondered if this was due to aircraft again; but it was only a pause for the drivers to brew up, and we were given some tea. We started again soon and were not interfered with; although they had let the officers keep their revolvers in case we were attacked while going over the desert.

We arrived back at H.3, whence we had started three days before. This time I was carried into the fort and laid on a bed in a room with the

Australian, Sandow, and the Arab Legionnaire, whose frame was put on the floor. A doctor came and dressed our wounds, saying that the convoy would push on by stages to H.4, Mafraq and Nazareth, which was a casualty clearing station.

There were some books in the room and I asked for one of these, a bright green bound volume of *The Pickwick Papers*, and began to read it.

I asked if Reading had also been brought back. The doctor was relieved to know who the interpreter was. The medical authorities wanted to know who his next of kin were. I said, "You will find an envelope in his breast pocket. That has the address, but I am sure he would recognise me if you brought him in here."

The doctor shook his head sadly. "No, he wouldn't," and refused to let me see him. I was too weak to argue about it any longer.

In the morning we heard an aeroplane pass overhead and wondered if it were ours or the French. Then the doctor, who was a Major, came in and said that the worst casualties were to be flown back in a plane. The Arab, of course, was going, and so was the Australian. But my red-headed friend surprised us by sitting up and declaring vehemently that he would not go by air. "I have never flown before and I am not going to fly now."

I joined the Major in explaining that he was a fool, that he would otherwise jolt painfully all the way to H.4 one day. Then to Mafraq — another long day. Finally to Nazareth — another day. But he would not hear of it, and, as his nerves were already strung fairly taut by what he had been through, the doctor did not press him and, turning to me, said, "Then you will go instead."

I argued with the Australian after the doctor went out, but it was no use, and presently I was put back on the stretcher and driven with the Arab Legionary and others over to the aerodrome. A dilapidated old Valencia was drawn up there, with the large, red, white and blue rings on her side and a cheeky little gun poking up through the old-fashioned open cockpit in the fuselage. The worst cases were pushed in through the nose of the fuselage, some five in all, while half a dozen more sat on bucket seats against the sides. Bombardier James with the torn fingers, his arm in a sling, sat in the one beside me. He gave me the thumbs up sign with his free hand, and a grin. I remember thinking that the slightest extra weight might deprive somebody else of a passage and took off my revolver and webbing belt which I gave to the doctor, much to the pilot's amusement.

Sitting further up the aeroplane on the opposite side was Remer, a trooper in the Blues, who had been shot through the lip and jaw by a bullet from one of Fawzi's Rifles. The wound had turned septic and he must hold up to his mouth all the time a small enamel basin into which the pus drained. I tried to speak to him, but he could only articulate one word 'Fawzi'. When all were stowed, the old engine revved up and the rickety Valencia went skimming across the landing ground. I looked down, to see the gravel flashing past in a brown band and we were in the air, circling round the little white settlement in its wire enclosure.

Iraq and Transjordan unrolled the brown map of reality beneath me. Within two hours there were trees and ravines below us. My ears were humming. We sailed over the winding grey strip of the Jordan and crossed the rocky hills of Palestine, where olive trees dotted the red soil, and alighted at Lydda. Wrecked aircraft stood about, and others which were ready to take off. A white ambulance was waiting for us, and we were quickly transported to the wooden huts of the hospital inside the encampment of Sarafand. There I was thrust into a ward full of Free Frenchmen, two of whom had been wounded in the recent fighting. An English matron, reading my name, came and peered at me, "You speak English, yes?"

I laughed and replied in her own tongue.

I was only two nights in the hospital at Sarafand, where Colonel Moore, the Colonel of the A.M.P.C. depot in the camp, came down to see me, and another officer from the same Mess (where I had stayed on a driving and mechanics course), who sent home a reassuring cable to my wife. I was finally taken down to Lydda Station in an ambulance, and thrust into a hospital train, which dragged itself, with many halts, for five hours up the winding railway to Jerusalem.

We felt bitterly that they might have driven us that short distance of thirty miles in ambulances. Thus we were far more exhausted on arrival at the station in Jerusalem than we need have been.

There were two hospitals in the Holy City, one on Mount Scopus, and I was carried into an ambulance bound for the other.

We drove through a narrow gateway into a quiet little garden, and a forbidding amazon in starchy white uniform eyed the two other officers who had been sent on the same train, officers of the K.O.R.R. with light head wounds, and told them to get out and walk. She had me carried out, trying to hide the sympathy she felt, and I was lifted into a bed on the ground floor. Another Australian nurse, a rugged but homely dame, bustled in to ask if I were any relation to Sir Dudley de Chair, and I felt almost as if I had come home. I gave them the particulars they asked for, and they found me clutching *The Pickwick Papers* and my other little personal belongings, such as the camera, which, I had persuaded myself, they would snatch from me.

"What are you hiding there?" asked Sister Hobson, and put them briskly away into the drawer of the white metal table beside me. Then, and not till then, did I collapse. I had come a long way from Palmyra.

It was in Jerusalem, when I was convalescing, that I discussed with Lawrence's Armenian friend, Altounyan, the difference between this type of war and the previous one. He had been wounded in eighteen places at Passchendaele, where he won the Military Cross. He was not far away from me when I was wounded before Palmyra, and he surprised me by saying that, if he had to choose which to go back to, he would sooner return to Passchendaele.

"There you had a temendous amount of moral support. You had a great deal of noise on your own side; a great artillery barrage firing over your head. You had the feeling of being in it with others. In this type of desert warfare you are left all alone, far from the nearest vehicle. Your driver is shot to ribbons beside you," (and it was his driver who was tied up in a frame and shared the ambulance with me). "You are then quite alone; and out of a clear sky you are set upon by one of these fighters. It is a purely personal form of persecution. A cone of fire descends on your head, and it goes on attacking you until the ammunition is exhausted."

This had happened to Altounyan, who was miraculously not hit, while he lay with his arm across a wounded patient. For Altounyan was a doctor who did not follow his instructions to 'disperse' and leave the wounded to their fate.

I cannot offer an opinion. I was three years old when the Great War broke out, and the descriptions of that war have always made it seem to me unbelievably horrible. I can only offer a picture of the Second World War; and that in its brightest light. But Altounyan stuck to his point. "There is a limit to the amount of horror that the human mind can take in, and it soon reaches saturation point."

There was a final shock in store for me. Looking up from my bed I could see through the doorway into the dim hall at the foot of the staircase; and there, staring ahead of him with unseeing eyes, was Joe Kingstone, biting the inside of his right forefinger as he had a habit of doing. There he stood bareheaded, in his shirt and the great girth of his shorts, still wearing his brown suede desert boots with the crepe rubber soles. Beside him was Colonel Stuart, the A.D.M.S., who had driven him all the way back from the battlefield. After four days and nights of struggle and heat and strain in the face of an impossible task, and without rest, our gallant Brigadier had collapsed on the desert. At the last he was worrying about the water-supply for the Wilts (which was all right); but in the teeth of a blizzard of bombs, bullets, and cannon shell from the air, the plan imposed on him had gone awry; while back in Jerusalem, behind the stout defences of their mahogany desks, men were saying, "We may have to send some aircraft up to Palmyra after all. Our chaps seem to be having a rough time of it." And as they sipped their drinks in the bar downstairs, they added, "It is worrying about those casualties up there — not being able to get them back. We should have thought of Palymra not falling. It is most annoying."

Thus spake a senior Staff Officer of Force Headquarters, a little turkeycock of a man, when he came at length to see me some months later in the Convalescent Home surrounded by olive trees, at Talbieh near the King David Hotel.

He said, "I meant to go and look you up in hospital one day, but I played squash instead."

He had never been in action, although it must be admitted that no officer in peacetime was ever more belligerent. He arranged the lunch for the Armistice delegates when the fighting was all over and the Convention was signed at Acre. A very good lunch it was, I am told, and he was mentioned in despatches for gallant *or* distinguished services in the Middle East.

How was Palmyra to become the Splendid Affair which Winston Churchill called it? Was it not in the endurance of those who held their ground against odds until the ring around Palmyra was closed; until our 25-pounders could shatter the morale of the garrison inside the fortress, which their aircraft, in spite of its overwhelming local superiority in the air, never succeeded in doing to ours; until finally the men of Kingcol, those who survived, passed through the noble ruins to occupy the desert oasis? With the fall of Palmyra, the whole flank of the Syrian position was exposed and the Household Cavalry, Wilts and Warwicks raced on to Quariatein, Homs, Hama and Aleppo.

But long before they had occupied the historic Citadel which guards the approaches from Turkey and the Cilician Gates, the government of General Dentz had sued for Armistice. Nor were the men of Kingcol to remain long at ease, and were soon streaming back over their familiar hunting grounds to Baghdad, Khanaquin and up the Pai-Taq Pass to

Persia where they flogged their old trucks all the way to Tehran, while the Russians were bearing down from the Caucasus. So Peter had need of my maps after all. And in the Persian capital the booted warriors of the Soviet Union toasted the health of His Majesty's Life Guards and Blues. But in that picturesque ceremony I was to play no part.

On the sixth day some Tomahawks were sent up to Palmyra and shot down six De Woitine fighters over the battlefield, while the British troops below cheered deliriously. Bobo Roxburghe, with binoculars glued to his eyes, shouted the score: "A right and left. Another — and another." After that the enemy flew warily and high.

Of the five of us in the Brigade fighting group only two were left, and Ian told me afterwards that they looked at each other and began to giggle, wondering who would go next. Peter wrote to me in hospital, hoping that I would soon recover and be able to come back, adding, 'Those two days were more terrible than anything I could ever have imagined possible.'

So in the end it was Peter who saw it through; sending for Eric Gooch, the rock-like second-in-command of the Life Guards, to take over command of the Brigade. And I could picture Eric's square, tin-helmeted face ducking cheerfully when the bullets flew over and his great brown moustaches flaring out over the desert as an oriflamme of defiance to the men of Vichy. Andrew Ferguson had been left with malaria and his batman at T.2, where they only escaped Fawzi Kuwuckji's raiding band by twenty minutes, when an Indian Army ambulance raced in to collect them. And, like David Smiley, also convalescing from malaria after the campaign, he found time to visit me twice in hospital during a brief week's leave in Jerusalem.

Fawzi himself created some havoc with our supply lines, until his car was dived at by a Hurricane, blasted with holes, and the guerrilla leader, wounded in fourteen places (so rumour had it), was flown to a hospital in Berlin. Across the deserts of war which separate us I salute him as the best of our enemies: a wounded man.

Grose sent my kit after me and enclosed a letter, saying that he was now driving the new Brigadier (who had arrived to take over from Eric Gooch). They were ambushed by the French after the Armistice and Grose received a flesh wound in the arm during the scuffle, but it was not serious enough to take him away from duty. Whatever might happen to the rest of us, I felt sure that Grose would be in at the kill.

It was a neat turn of fate which sent me at last to the Convalescent Depot at Nathanya, next to the now deserted camp on the

Mediterranean shore from which we had set out on our adventures. Kingcol was no more; for, without Joe Kingstone, the column which he had led to Baghdad and Palmyra became a nameless brigade. Three of the five members of the familiar fighting group were gone. Dick was killed, without a mark on his body, by the concussion of a bomb, and was buried in his slit trench out there on the hard Syrian Desert. I was crippled, possibly for life, because half the nerves and sinews which controlled my left foot were shot away.

I must be counted among the ruins of Palmyra. Indeed, the only ruin I saw at Palmyra was myself; but the others are more worthy of attention — older and more famous.

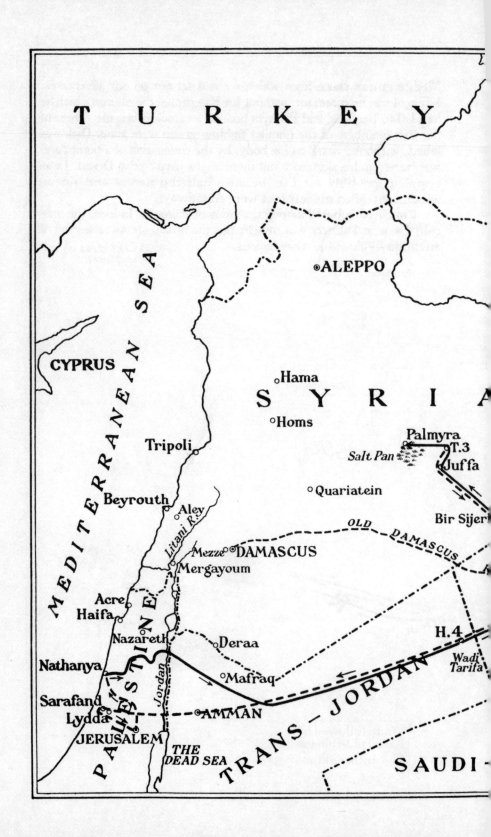

TURKEY

MEDITERRANEAN SEA

CYPRUS

⊙ALEPPO

SYRIA

○Hama

○Homs

Tripoli

Palmyra
Salt Pan ⟶T.3
⊙Juffa

Beyrouth

○Quariatein

Bir Sijeri

Aley
○
Litani R.

Mezze ○⊙ DAMASCUS

OLD DAMASCUS

Mergayoum

Acre ○
Haifa ○

Nazareth ○

○Deraa

H.4

PALESTINE

Nathanya

Jordan

○Mafraq

Wadi
Tarifa

Sarafand

TRANS - JORDAN

Lydda ○ ○AMMAN

JERUSALEM

THE
DEAD SEA

SAUDI-

Tel Hallah • Qasr Kadhim Pasha • Tel Bubash Sham
Tel Askar • Police Post Tel Khitab
Tel Abu Adham Taji R.S. • Tel Ajuz
A'bad as Saiyid • Tel Turabi
Saliha al Khall • Nazal Salman Police Post
Tel Kumar Tel Asfal Gharb • Afandi Qaleh Saiyid
a Quf Lake Ta'aliba Hashim Naqib
looded Ground Saiyid Taha Haur Umm
Palm al Kavir
Qualeh Hasan Grove
as Suhail Nazal Hikmat Bak
Tel Abyadh R.S. Bridge of Boats
ihiyah KADHIMAIN Al Mu'adhdham
Tel Manthar FERRY (RAILWAY) Baghdad North R.S.
AQQA QUF Ancient temple DIFAA BAGHDAD
(100' high) ST. OF SILVERSMITHS Baghdad East R.S.
Tel Khairhabat BRITISH EMBASSY
Tarajif WASH WASH CHANNEL SARGON GATE POS
CULTURAL EXPERIMENTAL BAGHDAD AIRPORT
ARCH FARM Floods ZI HOTEL
TA. FORWARD Baghdad West R.S. CAMP HINAIDI
NG TO AQQA QUF OBSERV'N POST FORWARD IRON BR. CANTONMENT
(WITHDRAWN) OBSERV'N POST PALACE OF ROSES
Tel Jarbyah ANTI-TANK DITCH
NDING GROUND ROYAL R. TIGRIS RASHID
LODGE AERODROME
Tel Shunalfi WIRELESS
III . Tel Nusaifiyat Tel Ramal Salm STA.

Baiji
Suleiman Beg
THE RIVER EUPHRATES Samarra
Abu Kemal RIVER EUPHRATES THE RIVER TIGRIS
Haditha Khan al
Mashahida
A Hit Ramadi R.A.F. Kadhimain
Abu Tibin Falluja BAGHDAD
R Abu Jir Khan Nuqta
Kutbah Wadi Abu Furukh L. Habba... Mujara
3 Musaiyib
I Razaza
Kerbala

Fort Nuqaib
Diwaniya

ABIA Route followed by Kingstone's column from Nathanya to
Baghdad & Palmyra in May & June 1941 marked thus
The Author's Route returning from Palmyra " " - - - -
MILES
0 10 20 30 40 50 100